Origami ^{6}

II. Technology, Art, Education

Origami 6

II. Technology, Art, Education

Proceedings of the Sixth International
Meeting on Origami Science, Mathematics, and Education

Koryo Miura

Toshikazu Kawasaki

Tomohiro Tachi

Ryuhei Uehara

Robert J. Lang

Patsy Wang-Iverson

Editors

AMERICAN MATHEMATICAL SOCIETY

2010 *Mathematics Subject Classification*. Primary 00-XX, 01-XX, 51-XX, 52-XX, 53-XX, 68-XX, 70-XX, 74-XX, 92-XX, 97-XX, 00A99.

Library of Congress Cataloging-in-Publication Data

International Meeting of Origami Science, Mathematics, and Education (6th : 2014 : Tokyo, Japan) Origami^6 / Koryo Miura [and five others], editors.
  volumes cm
  "International Conference on Origami Science and Technology ... Tokyo, Japan ... 2014"—Introduction.
  Includes bibliographical references and index.
  Contents: Part 1. Mathematics of origami—Part 2. Origami in technology, science, art, design, history, and education.
  ISBN 978-1-4704-1875-5 (alk. paper : v. 1)—ISBN 978-1-4704-1876-2 (alk. paper : v. 2)
  1. Origami—Mathematics—Congresses. 2. Origami in education—Congresses.
I. Miura, Koryo, 1930– editor. II. Title.
QA491.I55 2014
736′.982–dc23
                                                                            2015027499

$Origami^6$ is dedicated to the memory of Klaus Peters (1937–2014), founder with Alice Peters of A K Peters, Ltd., publisher of $Origami^3$, $Origami^4$, and $Origami^5$, among many other genre-crossing books. His vision informed and explored the relationships between mathematics and many other fields, not least of which is the mathemagical world of origami.

Contents

III. Mathematics of Origami: Rigid Foldability

IV. Mathematics of Origami: Design Algorithms

Part 2: Origami in Technology, Science, Art, Design, History, and Education

V. Origami in Technology and Science

VI. Origami in Art, Design, and History

VII. Origami in Education

Acknowledgments

There are many people and organizations to thank for making it possible to present you, the reader, with this two-volume set of $Origami^6$. The publication of $Origami^6$ is made possible through their efforts over several years. First came the creation of committees to plan for and raise funds for the 6th International Meeting on Origami Science, Mathematics, and Education (6OSME), which took place August 11–13, 2014, in Tokyo, Japan. The *Organizing Committee* managed the details—from small to large—of making the meeting a reality: Ichiro Hagiwara, Yuko Adachi, Yan Chen, Koshiro Hatori, Takashi Hojyo, Sachiko Ishida, Kaori Kuribayashi-Shigetomi, Hideo Komatsu, Jason Ku, Jun Maekawa, Yuji Matsumoto, Jun Mitani, Seiji Nishikawa, Yoshio Tsuda, and Makoto Yamaguchi. The *Program Committee* members (including the $Origami^6$ editors) helped to shape the vision for the meeting: Roger Alperin, Hideaki Azuma, Erik D. Demaine, Martin L. Demaine, Emma Frigerio, Tomoko Fuse, Koshiro Hatori, Thomas C. Hull, Yves Klett, Kaori Kuribayashi-Shigetomi, Jun Maekawa(who edited the book of program and abstracts), Yoshinobu Miyamoto, Kazuya Saito, Koichi Tateishi, Arnold Tubis, and Zhong You. *Supporting organizations* provided time and financial support to help defray the cost of the meeting and to ensure participants took away memorable and positive experiences from the event: Tokyo-Shiki Co., Origami House, Miura-ori lab, Gabriella & Paul Rosenbaum Foundation, Toyo Corporation, Takeo Co., Kawakami Sangyo Co., Heiwa Paper Co., Maeda Corporation, Noiz Architects, Asahi Press, and Issey Miyake. *Special thanks* go to Gabriella & Paul Rosenbaum Foundation for providing scholarships to students and to Japan Origami Academic Society and Origami House (Makoto Yamaguchi, Eiko Matsuura, and Satoshi Kamiya) for their extraordinary efforts to ensure that the meeting proceeded smoothly.

The executive managers for 6OSME were Seiji Nishikawa and Tomohiro Tachi, who oversaw the event's smooth operation. Robert J. Lang and Patsy Wang-Iverson served as the international driving forces. Kiyoko Yoshizawa and Koji Miyazaki managed the origami exhibitions, old and new. Koshiro Hatori, Jason Ku, and Anne Lavin oversaw hospitality, including planning field trips for meeting participants. Masami Isoda and Masahiko Sakamoto offered participants an opportunity to observe a ninth grade public lesson in mathematics at the Junior High School attached to Tsukuba University in Otsuka, Japan.

Reviewers played a crucial role in ensuring the meeting offered high-quality experiences. They reviewed the abstracts submitted for consideration for presentation, and then they reviewed the manuscripts submitted for publication in $Origami^6$, offering detailed suggestions for improvement and then re-reviewing many manuscripts. A large number of individuals offered their services as reviewers, and we thank them for their time and commitment to the work: Hugo Akitaya,

Roger Alperin, Byoungkwon An, Richard Askey, Martin Barej, Alex Bateman, Alessandro Beber, sarah-marie belcastro, Mark Bolitho, Landen Bowen, Suryansh Chandra, Yan Chen, Herng Yi Cheng, Rostislav Chudoba, Keenan Crane, Erik D. Demaine, Martin L. Demaine, Peter Engel, Evgueni Filipov, Robin Flatland, Haruaki Fukuda, Matthew Gardiner, Ilan Garibi, Robert Geretschläger, Koshiro Hatori, Barry Hayes, Susanne Hoffmann, Takashi Horiyama, Larry Howell, Thomas C. Hull, Ushio Ikegami, Sachiko Ishida, Miyuki Kawamura, Martin Kilian, Yves Klett, Goran Konjevod, Jason Ku, Kaori Kuribayashi-Shigetomi, Anna Lubiw, Jun Maekawa, Spencer Magleby, Rupert Maleczek, Yoshinobu Miyamoto, Koji Miyazaki, Jeannine Mosely, Jun-Hee Na, Chris Palmer, Marian Palumbo, Rachel Philpott, Helmut Pottmann, Katherine Riley, Kazuya Saito, Saadya Sternberg, Cynthia Sung, Motoi Tachibana, Koichi Tateishi, Minoru Taya, Naoya Tsuruta, Emiko Tsutsumi, Arnold Tubis, Naohiko Watanabe, Michael Winckler, and Zhong You.

We thank the American Mathematical Society (AMS) for their unstinting support and publishing of *Origami⁶*, in particular Sergei Gelfand for keeping us focused and on track, Teresa Levy for her beautiful artwork, Peter Sykes and Denise Wood for their marketing prowess, and Michael Haggett for pulling it all together. Lastly, we are indebted to Charlotte Byrnes for agreeing to undertake the chore of improving the books you hold in your hands.

Koryo Miura
Toshikazu Kawasaki
Tomohiro Tachi
Ryuhei Uehara
Robert J. Lang
Patsy Wang-Iverson

Introduction

The apparently disparate fields of origami (the Japanese art of paper-folding), mathematics, science, technology, design, and education have made tenuous connections with each other throughout recorded history, but they became firmly linked in 1989, with the First International Conference on Origami Science and Technology, organized by Humiaki Huzita and held in Ferrara, Italy. The outcome of that meeting was a book [Huzita 91]. That first conference, which brought together practitioners in origami, mathematicians, scientists, technologists, engineers, and educators, set the course for a series of meetings and subsequent proceedings books, in Otsu, Japan in 1994 [Miura 97]; Asilomar, California, USA in 2001 [Hull 02]; Pasadena, California, USA in 2006 [Lang 09]; Singapore in 2010 [Wang-Iverson et al. 11]; and, most recently, in Tokyo, Japan in 2014. Over a hundred papers were presented by speakers from 30 countries at that conference, spanning topics ranging from the mathematical fundamentals of origami to algorithms for origami design, applications in architecture, deployable structures, microfabrication, and the use of folding in teaching and pedagogy. With each year, the breadth, diversity, and depth of work in the field have grown. It has resulted in collaborations between scientists and artists, engineers and teachers, in numerous structures, mechanisms, devices, and artworks, and, most tangibly, in the collection of papers in the book you are holding right now.

Each Origami in Science, Mathematics, and Education (OSME) conference has grown in size and breadth, reflecting the many connections between the world of folding and diverse other fields. Traditionally, the art of origami has been one of great restriction: a single sheet of paper (usually), formed by folding only, with no cuts (again, usually). Yet, this restrictive rule set not only gave rise to vast variety in artistic forms, but the techniques that artists discovered to create their forms have turned out to have applications across technology. In addition, as the power of folding came to the attention of scientists, mathematicians, and technologists, they, in turn, brought powerful tools—abstraction, analysis, optimization, computation—to the world of folding, giving rise not just to new artworks but to new engineering applications that better the human condition. With the combination of geometric precision and physical tangibility that folding provides, it continues to serve as an educational tool, with ripple effects that extend far beyond the narrow province of paper alone.

As with previous volumes in this series, this book presents a cross section of the latest developments in the marriage between origami and scientific and technological fields. Those developments grow and expand, and there is no greater evidence of that growth than the fact that this work is now in two printed volumes.

Part 1 focuses on some of the deepest connections between origami and other fields: the mathematics of origami, whose roots go back well beyond the OSME phenomenon with developments on solving algebraic equations using origami back in the mid-twentieth century, and still older explorations of the mathematical properties of folded surfaces. Modern investigations form a rich and vibrant field; new results presented here include work on constructability, connections to graph theory and coloring, and a host of design algorithms that bring in concepts from two- and three-dimensional geometry. The mathematical underpinnings of folding and their implications remain a source of active exploration, as you will see in the many papers in this work.

Part 2 focuses on the connections between origami and more applied areas of science: engineering, physics, architecture, industrial design, and even other artistic fields that go well beyond the usual folded paper. When origami enters other fields, the medium changes: applications of origami use polymers, metals, textiles, and more as the folding medium, and they call for new developments in algorithms, manufacturing techniques, computational tools, and process development. In addition, the applications of origami are often informed and influenced by the deep roots of historical folding, and you will find history, design, and art among the rich mélange of interdisciplinary work explored in this volume. While origami can call upon highly abstruse mathematical concepts, it also can play a powerful role as a classroom tool at all educational levels, even the elementary grades. A number of papers explore and demonstrate the utility of origami as a pedagogical tool in mathematical education.

As is often the case in the academic milieu, the most exciting and novel developments take place at the edges of existing fields, where disparate and unexpected bodies of knowledge mix and interact—illustrated elegantly here by the interdisciplinary applications of origami.

Origami[6] contains a unique collection of papers accessible to a wide audience, including those interested in art, design, history, and education and researchers interested in the connections between origami and science, technology, engineering, and mathematics. We hope you will enjoy the works in these two volumes, both for their own interest and as harbingers (and perhaps triggers) of more exciting developments to come.

The Editors of *Origami*[6]:

Koryo Miura
Toshikazu Kawasaki
Tomohiro Tachi
Ryuhei Uehara
Robert J. Lang
Patsy Wang-Iverson

Bibliography

[Huzita 91] Humiaki Huzita (editor). *Proceedings of the First International Meeting of Origami Science and Technology*. Padova, Italy: Dipartimento di Fisica dell'Università di Padova, 1991.

[Miura 97] Koryo Miura (editor). *Origami Science and Art: Proceedings of the Second International Meeting of Origami Science and Scientific Origami*. Shiga, Japan: Seian University of Art and Design, 1997.

[Hull 02] Thomas Hull (editor). *Origami^3: Proceedings of the Third International Meeting of Origami Science, Mathematics, and Education*. Natick, MA: A K Peters, 2002. MR1955754 (2003h:00017)

[Lang 09] Robert J. Lang (editor). In *Origami^4: Fourth International Meeting of Origami Science, Mathematics, and Education*. Natick, MA: A K Peters, 2009. MR2590567 (2010h:00025)

[Wang-Iverson et al. 11] Patsy Wang-Iverson, Robert J. Lang, and Mark Yim (editors). *Origami^5: Fifth International Meeting of Origami Science, Mathematics, and Education*. Boca Raton, FL: A K Peters/CRC Press, 2011. MR2866909 (2012h:00044)

V. Origami in Technology and Science

Comparison of Compressive Properties of Periodic Non-flat Tessellations

Yves Klett, Marc Grzeschik, and Peter Middendorf

1. Introduction

Non-flat (or 2.5D) origami tessellations[1] have been the focus of recent research concerned with the development of new core structures for application in sandwich constructions. These tessellation can offer good mechanical performance in combination with other, secondary functionality that has not yet been offered by other, state-of-the-art materials   [Herrmann et al. 05,   Kolax 04,   Kehrle and Kolax 06,   Klett et al. 09], [Klett and Drechsler 11, Klett 13].

To qualify for advanced lightweight construction, new folded cores need to compete with well-known and long-proven core types like foams, woods, and especially honeycomb cores. The incredible diversity of tessellated structures and the large number of possible variations even within one cell-type family not only are a huge advantage in terms of flexibility and potential for optimization, but also widen the field for the systematic exploration of useful structures and their properties enormously.

One way to go about analyzing this possible multitude of configurations is to use finite element (FE) methods. This approach can be implemented quickly for idealized models and produces results for arbitrary amounts of tessellations. However, the comparison between results from such simulations and real-world tests have shown significant deviations: Simulations of ideal geometries usually predict substantially higher strengths and stiffnesses compared to real-world tests [Heimbs et al. 08, Fischer 11].

For realistic predictions of folded core properties, FE models need to include information about manufacturing-related imperfections and augmented material models, which are not yet readily available (especially in the case of paper-like and anisotropic composite materials). Simulations including such a level of detail have been developed, but at the moment these still require a lot expertise and computational effort [Fischer 11, Sturm et al. 14, Fischer 15] and have to be calibrated using results from real-world experiments in any case. Additionally, many of these methods are restricted to very specific unit cell geometries and cannot be reliably applied to arbitrary 2.5D tessellations.

Thus, destructive testing of folded core hardware will be indispensable for the foreseeable future. In the context of screening tessellated cores, the manufacturing process also generates much more data than just a set of numerical values: How easy is the folding, how

---

[1]Tessellations tiling the plane with nonzero extent in the z-direction.

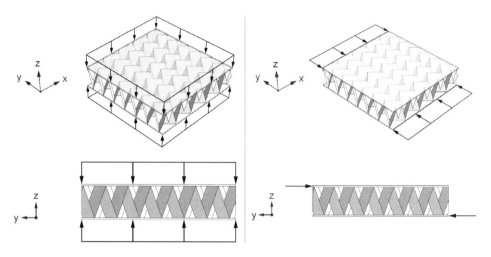

FIGURE 1. Perspective and front views of a sandwich sample consisting of two face sheets and a folded core: compression loading (left) and shear loading in y-direction (right). Forces are distributed evenly by the face sheets.

well does a certain geometry work with a given base material, and what are the optimal manufacturing parameters?

Several studies concerning the mechanical properties of 2.5D tessellations with a strong emphasis on Miura-ori (and derivatives) have been carried out [Miura 75], [Heimbs et al. 08, Miura 09, Schenk and Guest 11, Fischer 11, You and Gattas 13], [Sturm and Fischer 15, Johnson et al. 15], but the large diversity of study goals, virtual and real test setups, geometric scales, manufacturing methods, and materials used very much complicate the comparison of available results.

The goal of this study is twofold: to generate comparable test data for a number of well-known and not-yet-tested tessellations, and to evaluate the usefulness of a simple testing strategy using available sheet material together with newly developed compression testing fixtures to minimize the effort necessary to screen the many varieties of interesting tessellations in a reproducible and timely fashion.

2. Mechanical Performance of Sandwich Core Materials

Flatwise compression, shear strengths, and stiffnesses count among the most important mechanical properties of sandwich core materials. In the case of flatwise shear, stiffnesses and strengths of nonisotropic core materials depend on the shear direction [Zenkert 93, Carlsson and Kardomateas 11]. Figure 1 illustrates the different load orientations for flatwise compression and shear.

Compressive properties are commonly used for preliminary assessment of core performance because compressive testing can be carried out with comparatively low effort compared to shear testing [Hexcel Composites 99, ASTM 11b, DIN 82a].

Two methods exist: unstabilized, or bare, testing, where a core sample is simply put and compressed between two test plates, and stabilized testing, where the core sample is bonded to a set of face sheets before compression. Stabilized testing is necessary for cores that might otherwise show undesired lateral movement and destabilization. For woods, foams, and honeycomb materials, unstabilized testing is often suitable, while a

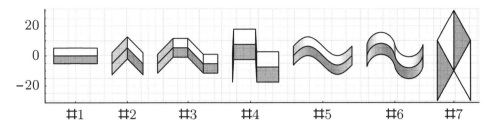

FIGURE 2. Top view of unit cells #1–#7 for size comparison (grid subdivision is 5 mm). All cells feature a height of 20 mm.

majority of prevalent folded cores require stabilization. For standard honeycomb materials, bare testing results in approximately 5–10% lower strengths compared to stabilized testing [Hexcel Composites 99].

For shear testing, bonding to a set of stiff test plates is always necessary, adding a lot of effort for sample preparation, bonding, and subsequent removal [ASTM 11a, DIN 82b]. While shear properties of the core are an essential factor in sandwich design, the considerable overhead for testing can prove prohibitive in the context of a screening program with many possible core configurations or materials that are difficult to bond [Grzeschik 13].

To enable the screening of a potentially *huge* number of tessellated cores, a different stabilization method than the usually permanent bonding is highly desirable. For this purpose, new reusable testing fixtures were developed that enable compressive testing of folded core samples with minimum overhead.

3. Unit Cell Choice and Sample Geometry

For this study, seven sample geometries were chosen. The corresponding unit cells are displayed in Figure 2 on a 5 mm grid. All unit cells have been designed to an identical height of 20 mm and unit density of 200 m^{-1}. The unit density is defined by the quotient of the area of paper within a given unit cell by its effective volume and has a unit of $m^2/m^3 = m^{-1}$. The actual density of a core panel is computed by multiplying the unit density with the grammage of the used base material. For the paper used in this study, this results in a nominal density of 200 $m^{-1} \times 0.126$ kg/$m^2 = 25.2$ kg/m^3.

Geometry #1 is the simplest possible variety of a folded core: a pleat with all straight creases. This variety is trivially easy to manufacture and serves as a baseline for simplicity. Unit cell #2 is a classical Miura-ori type with 90° zig-zag angle between major crease segments. This cell is also the base for geometry #3, which embeds two additional horizontally aligned sets of faces. Type #4 uses the same template but changes the zig-zag angle from $2 \times 45°$ to $2 \times 87°$ for a nearly blocked configuration.

Another quite different-looking, if closely related, tessellation type is represented in geometries #5 and #6. The curved folds are based on a slightly stretched sine function and a biarc (two tangentially joined semicircles), respectively.

For geometry #7, a classic waterbomb pattern was chosen and scaled to meet the particular height and density specifications. One major difference to all preceding geometries is the fact that the upper surface of the structure will consist of discrete peaks, while all other geometries feature line contact on both sides.

The size comparison in Figure 2 shows quite clearly the resulting differences in overall dimensions and face orientations and gives first clues on probably differing mechanical properties. To give an impression of the resulting tessellations used for the compression

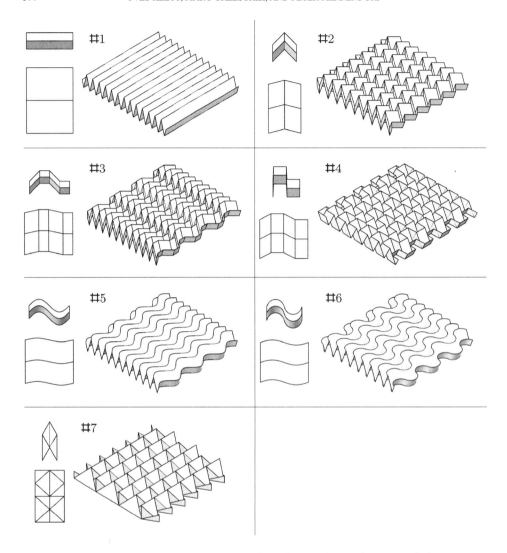

FIGURE 3. Geometries #1 to #7: unit cell seen from above (top left), developed unit cell crease pattern (bottom left), and perspective view of the tested sample geometry (right). All sample geometries feature a unit density of 200 m^{-1}, which for the chosen base material results in a nominal density of 25.2 kg/m^3.

test, each of the unit cells is displayed in Figure 3 together with its developed crease pattern and the actual sample geometry, which is determined by the maximum number of whole unit cells that fit into a 150×150 mm testing fixture. To eliminate potential influences of differently supported edges, additional (non-load-bearing) flaps were added to the front and back major creases (Figure 4).

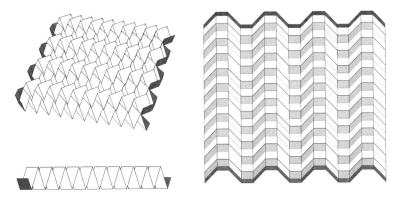

FIGURE 4. Sample for geometry #3: perspective and front views (left) and top view (right). The additional, non-load-bearing flaps added to the front and back major creases are marked in dark gray.

4. Sample Preparation and Test Setup

All samples were prepared by laser-scoring EnDURO ICE130 paper by Sihl [SIHL GmbH 14]. This material consists of a paper-film-paper laminate and offers excellent tear-resistance and foldability in conjunction with the chosen scoring method. The average weight of the paper is (126 ± 2) g/m^2 with an average thickness of (160 ± 10) μm. The material was not chosen for its mechanical performance but to provide a commercially available medium with reproducible properties that is well suited to folding by hand, is nontoxic, and does not require additional curing or relaxing after folding.

The paper features a distinctly visible grain in the rolling (L-) direction, and the developed samples were oriented with the minor creases perpendicular to the grain direction (see Figure 5). Due to an oversight, samples #3-1, #5-5, and #6-1 were produced with a perpendicular paper orientation. The results (see Figure 9) show no obvious influence of the changed grain orientation for these samples.

The sheets were engraved with precomputed crease patterns on a Trotec Speedy 400 flatbed plotter with a 60 W CO$_2$ laser source. The crease lines were scored rather robustly, fusing the inner thermoplastic film to the outer paper layers and creating a well-defined but still sufficiently tough hinge. Identical scoring parameters were used for all samples. All samples were folded by hand. No separate tooling (even if available) was used with the intent to introduce comparable amounts of imperfection into the samples.

To provide samples conforming as close as possible to the designed geometry, a set of acrylic plates was produced for each tessellation type, with grooves conforming to the lower (respectively, upper) contact area of the samples. For the plates, 4 mm extruded acrylic was engraved with a 90° V-groove at 2.5 mm depth. Samples are fitted into the grooves without any additional bonding. The difference between the proposed setup and a bonded test is that the conforming creases retain rotational degrees of freedom in the grooves not available to bonded samples. This may lead to earlier buckling, especially in the case of geometry #1, and thus result in conservative strength estimates.

The fixtures are immediately reusable after testing, and fitting of a new sample takes only a few seconds. This is a major advantage over a standard test setup, wherein folded samples need to be bonded permanently to disposable face sheets, in terms of speed, cost, and waste reduction.

FIGURE 5. Detail of a #2 sample positioned between upper and lower fixtures. The darker, laser-scored creases and the grain direction are visible
on closer inspection.

The test plates fix the folded, otherwise still pliable, sample into the designed geometry
and inhibit lateral movement of the lower/upper contact points during testing, partially
mimicking the function of the usual bonding.

The transparent material allows for easy checking of correct positioning of the folded
sample within the test plates (Figure 5). Especially for the curved tessellations, the fixtures are essential to provide a defined testing geometry, because the samples exhibit lively
spring-back after folding.

A Schenck-Trebel 250 kN universal testing machine was used for compressive testing. Forces were measured with a Class 1 25 kN load cell, and the displacement was
measured with an inductive HBM WA20 displacement transducer. In accordance with
DIN 53291 [DIN 82a], the samples consisting of the folded core within the acrylic fixtures
were placed between two parallel plates and the plates were closed with a constant speed
of 0.5 mm/min. Displacement and force were logged with a frequency of 10 Hz with a
HBM Spider8 data acquisition system. For each geometry with the exception of #7, six
samples were prepared to achieve an acceptable degree of statistical assurance. The measured densities showed slight deviations due to material and production fluctuations, and
ranged 25.0 kg/m^3 to 26.5 kg/m^3, with a median of 25.3 kg/m^3.

5. Analysis and Discussion

The compressive strengths and stiffnesses were computed for each sample by evaluating the maximum stress σ_{max} and a secant modulus as indicated in Figure 8 and shown
in Table 1. All measured stress-strain curves are displayed in Figure 9. All results have

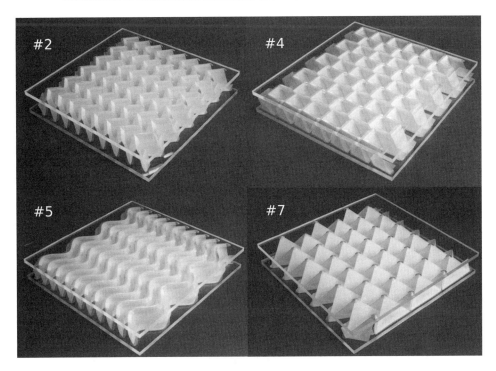

FIGURE 6. Samples of geometries #2, #4, #5, and #7 set between the acrylic testing fixtures. The qualitative difference in the upper surface contact area between #7 and all other samples is clearly visible.

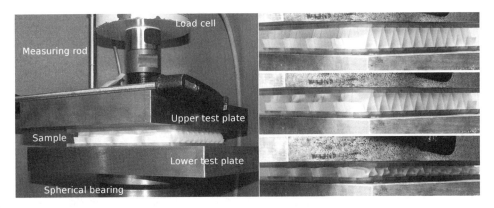

FIGURE 7. Test setup with a #6 sample (left). Successive compression of a #3 sample (right).

been normalized with respect to the nominal density of 25.2 kg/m^3 using the effectively determined densities of each sample. The non-load-bearing flaps were compensated for in the determination of the weights and effective areas.

5.1. General observations. Most samples display a rather long settling phase, which may be caused in part by the comparatively soft material and the setting of the samples into the testing fixtures together with manufacturing imperfections. During testing, the

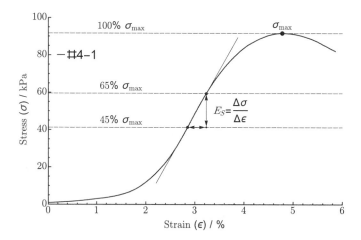

FIGURE 8. Stress-strain diagram of sample #4-1. The maximum stress σ_{max} and a secant modulus E_S between 45% and 65% of σ_{max} are marked.

Geometry	#1	#2	#3	#4	#5	#6	#7
σ_{max} / kPa	9.3	80.19	83.48	86.41	94.53	125.29	36.73
σ_σ / kPa	0.57	2.52	5.47	3.84	7.2	9.12	1.57
c_{V_σ} / %	6.17	3.15	6.56	4.45	7.61	7.28	4.27
E_S / MPa	1.11	6.58	7.41	4.19	10.72	10.76	1.26
σ_E / MPa	0.19	0.91	0.92	0.24	3.15	2.72	0.16
c_{V_E} / %	17.02	13.83	12.48	5.77	29.44	25.31	12.63

TABLE 1. Results of flatwise compression for all geometries. Displayed are mean values for strength (σ_{max}), compressive modulus (E_S) as indicated in Figure 8, and their respective standard deviations (σ) and variational coefficients (c_v). All results have been normalized with regard to the nominal density of 25.2 kg/m^3.

contact areas of all samples stayed firmly within the fixture's grooves. Due to the small number of tested samples, no outliers were removed, which amounts to fairly large standard deviations.

After the initial settling, most samples show a fairly linear behavior between 45% and 65% of σ_{max}, which is the reason for the evaluation of the stiffness by a secant between these two stress levels. A slight exception is geometry #1, where the onset of buckling occurs almost immediately and nonuniformly. Geometry #7 also exhibits rather shaky curves due to immediately on-setting micro-buckling, which nevertheless produces consistent results for strength and stiffness.

Overall, the consistency of the results for strength and stiffness appear to be within acceptable bounds, given the manual folding, the comparatively soft material, and the first application of the new testing fixtures. In the cases of geometries #5 and #6, the diagrams show two rather distinct outliers with higher strength and stiffness together with a shorter settling phase, which may be due to a better-than-average folding result. Visual inspection of these samples did not reveal any obvious differences.

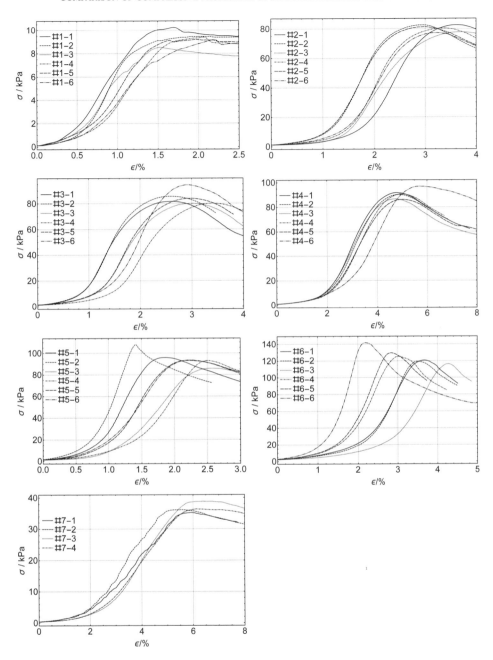

FIGURE 9. Stress-strain diagrams of all tested samples. The strain and stress ranges have been adapted individually to maximize visual content.

In general, the spread for modulus measurements is larger than for strength evaluation. Especially for both curved geometries, the modulus measurement results in a much larger standard deviation compared to all other cell types. This hints at larger manufacturing tolerances for the curved samples, an assumption that is also supported by the (subjectively)

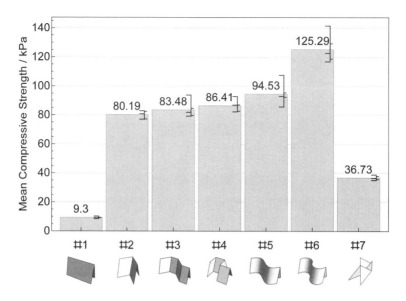

FIGURE 10. Mean compressive strength for all cell types. The brackets indicate the measured minima and maxima and the first, second (median), and third quartiles.

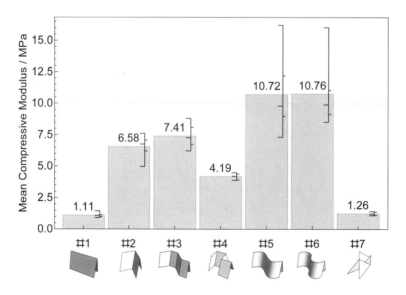

FIGURE 11. Mean compressive modulus for all cell types, with bracketed minima, maxima, and quartiles.

more difficult folding of the samples by hand. These tolerances seem to have a much bigger influence on modulus than on strength.

5.2. Individual comparison. Geometry #1 performs—as expected—rather poorly regarding strength and stiffness. The large straight faces have the lowest buckling strength

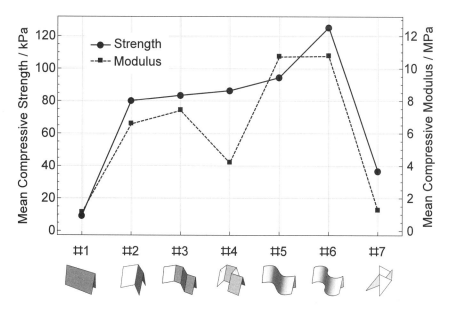

FIGURE 12. Mean compressive strengths and moduli overview.

of all examined geometries. Global buckling sets in almost immediately but is reversible up to high strain levels, so the structure performs almost spring-like.

The Miura-ori derivative series perform on a much higher level, with a slight tendency toward higher strengths from #2–#4. Stiffness-wise, #4 shows significantly lower values that #2 and #3. One reason for this behavior can be found in the different orientations of the unit cell faces toward the z-direction, which induce inhomogeneous strains and stresses. The performance of #4 could be further boosted by bonding of the touching surfaces, an additional production step not considered in this study.

Of great interest are the results for the curved unit cells, especially because no previous results of real-world measurements have been available until now. Both curved geometries #6 and #7 perform equally regarding stiffness and show more than 40% increase compared to the best straight-creased geometry #3. While a better performance due to the higher buckling resistance of the curved surfaces is to be expected in theory, it is gratifying to observe this effect in real-world tests.

There seems to be a correlation between σ_{max} and the strain at which the strength is reached, with lower strengths occurring at larger strains. Both curved geometries have an outlier with higher-than-average strength and stiffness, which hints at the potential for even better performance by elimination of present manufacturing issues. Unfortunately, the samples were not numbered after their production order, so the influence of eventually changing folding skills could not be ascertained.

Another relevant result concerns the difference in compressive strength between #5 and #6. Geometry #5 performs almost on the same strength level as the Miura-ori derivatives, while #6 tops this by more than 30%. The most obvious explanation for this increase lies in the different curvatures of the major creases (see Figure 2): While the sinusoidal curve of #5 shows a nearly straight segment and overall changing curvature gradients, the curvature for #6 is constant for any point on the curve (with exception of the sign change at the joining point), which results in a homogenous buckling strength along the crease direction.

Finally, the waterbomb pattern #7 exhibits intermediate strength and a stiffness that is only marginally higher than that of #1. The failure mode of #7 is quite different from all other candidates: Rather than buckling globally, the structure wrinkles and crushes from the top points downward and shows a long force plateau after reaching σ_{max} compared to a continuous drop as shown by geometries #2–#6. Compared to #1, the deformation beyond σ_{max} is not reversible.

6. Additional Remarks

The presented method has produced interesting and coherent results. To interpret these correctly, it is important to view them in the context of the test setup and its intended scope as a quick, adaptable screening tool:

- *Comparability:* The acrylic fixtures realize something of a hybrid between standard unstabilized and stabilized tests, especially regarding the boundary conditions at the crease–fixture interface. Compared to honeycomb bare testing, we expect the results for folded cores using the presented method to be more conservative. Additional studies to compare the current setup with stabilized methods are ongoing. Finally, potential influences of different fixture-groove shapes need to be investigated.
- *Fabrication influences:* The manual folding of all samples introduces varying amounts of imperfection and is dependent on the difficulty to obtain a given structure. The laser-scoring of the creases was chosen for its ease of use, but it also introduces additional weaknesses the magnitude of which remains to be quantified. This is especially important for a fair comparison with curved tessellations that do not contain vertical (minor) score lines at all. On the other hand, the introduced setup may prove very useful for looking into such production influences, which have not yet been studied in-depth due to prohibitive effort caused by stabilized testing.
- *Limitations:* The fixture setup is only useful for compressive testing and cannot be easily adapted for shear testing. However, a low-effort shear test method is extremely desirable and will be a focus of future research, incorporating experience gathered with this study.

7. Conclusion

We have shown the application of a new, low-effort method for testing the compressive properties of tessellation-based folded cores. Stiffness and strength for seven different core types have been evaluated, and the results of the application of reusable acrylic testing fixtures are encouraging. All samples were laser-scored and folded by hand from a commercially available medium with minimum tooling effort. Together with the new test setup, this allows for quick and uncomplicated screening of different tessellations and materials.

The test results for well-known Miura-ori derivatives are consistent with already existing research. Newly added curved folds show that they perform significantly better than all other tested varieties and that a mostly constant curvature of the load-bearing surfaces seems to be beneficial in terms of compressive strength. An alternative waterbomb pattern shows intermediate performance but interesting crushing behavior.

The proposed testing method seems suitable for screening of yet-untested core structures. Because of the simplicity of the setup and the possible use of standard materials, we hope that other groups might be interested in adopting the presented method. This should result in great opportunities for round-robin testing and for further provisioning of reliable and reproducible data that will help to optimize the test procedure and—most importantly—facilitate the design of future high-performance folded-core structures.

References

[ASTM 11a] American Society for Testing and Materials. *Standard Test Method for Shear Properties of Sandwich Core Materials*. ASTM C273, 2011. (Available at http://www.astm.org/Standards/C273.htm.)

[ASTM 11b] American Society for Testing and Materials. *Standard Test Method for Flatwise Compressive Properties of Sandwich Cores*. Active Standard ASTM C365, 2011. (Available at http://www.astm.org/Standards/C365.htm.)

[Carlsson and Kardomateas 11] L. A. Carlsson and G. A. Kardomateas. *Structural and Failure Mechanics of Sandwich Composites*. New York: Springer, 2011.

[DIN 82a] Deutsches Institut fuer Normung. *Testing of Sandwiches; Compression Test Perpendicular to the Faces*. Technical report DIN 53291, 1982. (Available at http://www.beuth.de/en/standard/din-53291/939476.)

[DIN 82b] Deutsches Institut fuer Normung. *Testing of sandwiches; Shear test in flatwise plane*. Technical report DIN 53294, 1982. (Available at http://www.beuth.de/de/norm/din-53294/939687.)

[Fischer 11] Sebastian Fischer. "Rechnerische Ermittlung der mechanischen Eigenschaften von Faltkernen." PhD dissertation, Universität Stuttgart, 2011.

[Fischer 15] Sebastian Fischer. "Aluminium Foldcores for Sandwich Structure Application: Mechanical Properties and FE-simulation." *Thin-Walled Structures* 90:0 (2015), 31–41. (Available at http://www.sciencedirect.com/science/article/pii/S0263823115000063.)

[Grzeschik 13] M. Grzeschik. "Performance of Foldcores Mechanical Properties and Testing." In *ASME 2013 International Design Engineering Technical Conferences and Computers and Information in Engineering Conference*, No. DETC2013-13324. New York: ASME, 2013.

[Heimbs et al. 08] Sebastian Heimbs, Peter Middendorf, C. Hampf, F. Hähnel, and K. Wolf. "Aircraft Sandwich Structures with Folded Core under Impact Load." In *8th International Conference on Sandwich Structures (ICCS-8)*, edited by A. J. M. Ferreira, pp. 369–380. Porto: FEUP, 2008. (Available at http://www.heimbs-online.de/Heimbs_2008_Aircraft_Sandwich_Structures_with_Folded_Core.pdf.)

[Herrmann et al. 05] Axel S. Herrmann, Pierre C. Zahlen, and Ichwan Zuardy. "Sandwich Structures Technology in Commercial Aviation." In *Sandwich Structures 7: Advancing with Sandwich Structures and Materials*, edited by O. T. Thomsen, E. Bozhevolnaya, and A. Lyckegaard, pp. 13–26. Houten: Springer Netherlands, 2005.

[Hexcel Composites 99] Hexcel Composites. "HexWeb™ Honeycomb Attributes and Properties." Technical report, 1999. (Available at http://www.hexcel.com/Resources/DataSheets/Brochure-Data-Sheets/Honeycomb_Attributes_and_Properties.pdf.)

[Johnson et al. 15] Alastair Johnson, Sebastian Kilcher, and Sebastian Fischer. "Design and Performance of Novel Aircraft Structures with Folded Composite Cores." In *Structural Integrity and Durability of Advanced Composites*, edited by P. W. R. Beaumont, C. Soutis, and A. Hodzic, Chapter 29. Amsterdam: Elsevier, 2015.

[Kehrle and Kolax 06] R. Kehrle and M. Kolax. "Sandwich Structures for Advanced Next Generation Fuselage Concepts." Presented at SAMPE Europe Technical Conference, Toulouse, France, September 13–14, 2006.

[Klett and Drechsler 11] Y. Klett and K. Drechsler. "Designing Technical Tessellations." In *Origami⁵: Fifth International Meeting of Origami Science, Mathematics, and Education*, edited by Patsy Wang-Iverson, Robert J. Lang, and Mark Yim, pp. 305–322. Boca Raton, FL: A K Peters/CRC Press, 2011. MR2866909 (2012h:00044)

[Klett et al. 09] Y. Klett, K. Drechsler, R. Kehrle, and M. Fach. "Cutting Edge Cores: Multifunktionale Faltkernstrukturen." In *4. Landshuter Leichtbau-Colloquium*, edited by O. Huber and M. Bicker, pp. 131–138. Landshut: LC Verlag, 2009.

[Klett 13] Yves Klett. "Auslegung multifunktionaler isometrischer Faltstrukturen für den technischen Einsatz." PhD dissertation, Universität Stuttgart, 2013.

[Kolax 04] Michael Kolax. "Concept and Technology: Advanced Composite Fuselage Structures." *JEC Composites* 6/7 (2004), 31–33.

[Miura 75] Koryo Miura. "New Structural Forms Sandwich Core." *Journal of Aircraft* 12:5 (1975), 437–441.

[Miura 09] Koryo Miura. "The Science of Miura-Ori." In *Origami⁴: Fourth International Meeting of Origami Science, Mathematics, and Education*, edited by Robert J. Lang, pp. 87–99. Wellesley, MA: A K Peters, 2009. MR2590567 (2010h:00025)

YVES KLETT, MARC GRZESCHIK, AND PETER MIDDENDORF

[Schenk and Guest 11] M. Schenk and S. D. Guest. "Origami Folding: A Structural Engineering Approach." In *Origami⁵: Fifth International Meeting of Origami Science, Mathematics, and Education*, edited by Patsy Wang-Iverson, Robert J. Lang, and Mark Yim, pp. 291–303. Boca Raton, FL: A K Peters/CRC Press, 2011. MR2866909 (2012h:00044)

[SIHL GmbH 14] SIHL GmbH. "Technical Data Sheet EnDURO ICE 130." http://www.papierenduro.pl/ktp/6710%20-%20EnDURO%20Ice%20130%20-%20E08350.pdf, 2014.

[Sturm and Fischer 15] Ralf Sturm and S. Fischer. "Virtual Design Method for Controlled Failure in Foldcore Sandwich Panels." *Applied Composite Materials* (February 2015), 1–13.

[Sturm et al. 14] R. Sturm, Y. Klett, Ch. Kindervater, and H. Voggenreiter. "Failure of CFRP Airframe Sandwich Panels under Crash-Relevant Loading Conditions." *Composite Structures* 112:0 (2014), 11–21.

[You and Gattas 13] Z. You and J. Gattas. "Quasi-Static Impact Response of Alternative Origami-Core Sandwich Panels." In *ASME International Design Engineering Technical Conferences*, No. DETC2013-12681. New York: ASME, 2013.

[Zenkert 93] D. Zenkert. *An Introduction to Sandwich Construction*. Stockholm: Department of Lightweight Structures, Royal Institute of Technology, 1993.

INSTITUTE OF AIRCRAFT DESIGN, UNIVERSITY OF STUTTGART, GERMANY
E-mail address: yves.klett@ifb.uni-stuttgart.de

INSTITUTE OF AIRCRAFT DESIGN, UNIVERSITY OF STUTTGART, GERMANY
E-mail address: marc.grzeschik@ifb.uni-stuttgart.de

INSTITUTE OF AIRCRAFT DESIGN, UNIVERSITY OF STUTTGART, GERMANY
E-mail address: peter.middendorf@ifb.uni-stuttgart.de

Numerical Analysis of Origami Structures through Modified Frame Elements

Kazuko Fuchi, Philip R. Buskohl, James J. Joo, Gregory W. Reich, and Richard A. Vaia

1. Introduction

Geometrically reconfigurable engineering designs are fundamental for the broad application areas of packaging, deployment, self-assembly, morphing, and multifunctional devices. Origami design concepts have recently gained interest as a means to program these reconfigurable and shape-changing structures. In fact, some design tools for connecting a three-dimensional shape to the requisite two-dimensional pattern of folds are already available [Tachi 09, Lang 98]. However, in many situations the optimal shape for a given function is unknown, necessitating the inclusion of the relevant physics for the device, be it mechanical, thermal, electromagnetic, etc., into the design process. Thus, analysis and optimization tools are required to enable the evaluation of these application-specific metrics. This chapter introduces a modified frame element formulation to efficiently integrate mechanical metrics such as stiffness, deformation, and energy distribution within the origami structure design.

Among the existing origami analysis methods, the most extensively used is rigid origami. It considers facets and foldlines as rigid components with no thickness and assumes that foldlines act like perfect hinges [Tachi 09, belcastro and Hull 02]. Though this mathematical approach guides problems focused on applications whose performances are closely tied to geometry, other metrics such as mechanical energy cannot be extracted from such a formulation. Other design methods based on shell elements have been developed [Peraza-Hernandez et al. 13], in which realistic folding motions are captured. This approach normally requires a fine mesh to capture details of the deformation both near and away from a crease. When design iterations are anticipated, such accurate analysis becomes unaffordable. A recently introduced modified truss model [Schenk and Guest 11] provides an alternative with a low computational cost that is suited for design problems with small to modest deformations [Fuchi et al. 14]. The frame element approach, proposed herein, enables modeling of facet and foldline compliance with a resolution and computational cost between those of truss-based and shell-based models.

Our model, inspired by the truss-based concept, is based on frame elements, which can capture additional modes of bending and torsion. Folding is modeled using torsion springs against rotational degrees of freedom about the fold axis. This allows for an explicit description of the fold angles and the underlying mechanics. By adjusting the properties of the frame elements and torsion springs, origami structures can be studied in a range of

All authors contributed equally to this work.

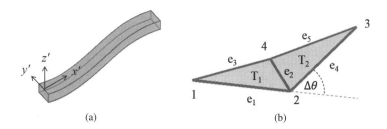

(a)   (b)

FIGURE 1. Polygons within a crease pattern are modeled through frame elements. (a) Frame element in the local coordinate system; (b) Assembly of two triangles.

regimes from rigid origami to locally compliant folding. In the following sections, the model formulation is presented and then followed by (1) a demonstration of its mechanical tunability and (2) its implementation with an optimization algorithm to determine the optimal combination of folding directions.

2. Modified Frame Element Model

Frame elements capture transverse, rotational, and axial deformations, as illustrated in Figure 1(a). The finite element formulation of an origami frame-based structure is similar to that of a conventional frame structure; however, foldlines are modeled through additional torsion springs, which requires a special treatment of the connectivity. To do this, extra degrees of freedom (DOFs) are inserted to duplicate local x'-rotations and are coupled back to the original DOFs through torsion springs. Details of this procedure are explained using a simple system of two triangular facets sharing one foldline, shown in Figure 1(b).

First, element stiffness matrices for three-dimensional frame elements are computed. The element stiffness matrix k'_e for frame element e in the local (primed) coordinates is a 12 × 12 matrix and has dependency on Young's modulus E, shear modulus G, cross sectional area A, moments of inertia I, J, and length l. The components of the element stiffness matrix can be found in a number of finite element textbooks (e.g., pg.255 in [Chandrupatla and Belegundu 02]). The element stiffness matrix can be transformed from the local to the global (unprimed) coordinate as

$$k_e = L^T k'_e L$$

using the transformation matrix

(2.1) $$L = \operatorname{diag}(\beta, \beta, \beta, \beta),$$

where β is a block matrix composed of directional cosines:

$$\beta = \begin{bmatrix} l_1 & m_1 & n_1 \\ l_2 & m_2 & n_2 \\ l_3 & m_3 & n_3 \end{bmatrix}.$$

For an origami structure with a flat initial configuration, all frame elements are assumed to lie along the same plane; without loss of generality, we can define this as the global xy-plane. The global reference frame is necessary for the construction of L. Following the arrangement used in [Chandrupatla and Belegundu 02], the 12 DOFs within a frame

Triangle	Element	Nodes	DOFs
T_1	e_1	$\{1, 2\}$	$\{1, 2, 3, 4, 5, 6, 7, 8, 9, 10, 11, 12\}$
	e_2	$\{2, 4\}$	$\{7, 8, 9, 10, 11, 12, 19, 20, 21, 22, 23, 24\}$
	e_3	$\{4, 1\}$	$\{19, 20, 21, 22, 23, 24, 1, 2, 3, 4, 5, 6\}$
T_2	e_4	$\{2, 3\}$	$\{7, 8, 9, \text{25,26,27}, 13, 14, 15, 16, 17, 18\}$
	e_5	$\{3, 4\}$	$\{13, 14, 15, 16, 17, 18, 19, 20, 21, \text{28,29,30}\}$
	e_2	$\{2, 4\}$	$\{7, 8, 9, \text{25,26,27}, 19, 20, 21, \text{28,29,30}, \}$

TABLE 1. Connectivity table for a two-triangle system.

element connecting nodes i and j are denoted

$$q' = \left[u_i', v_i', w_i', \theta_i', \phi_i', \psi_i', u_j', v_j', w_j', \theta_j', \phi_j', \psi_j' \right]$$

with three translational displacements u', v', w' and three rotational displacements θ', ϕ', ψ' at each node in the element's local coordinates.

To compute the connectivity, frame elements, nodes, and DOFs are numbered in each triangle. In general, node i is associated with DOFs from $6(i-1) + 1$ to $6i$, but extra rotational DOFs are inserted at nodes along foldlines. For instance, after all components associated with triangle T_1 in Figure 1(b) are numbered, nodes 2 and 4 reappear as triangle T_2 is considered. At this time, new numbers (25–27 and 28–30) are assigned to the rotational DOFs, creating co-located rotational DOFs at nodes along the foldline. Numbering of frame elements, nodes, and DOFs for a two-triangle system is summarized in Table 1; co-located DOFs inserted later are highlighted in gray in the table. The original and co-located local x'-rotational DOFs are then coupled together through a torsion spring as

$$(2.2) \qquad \tau_{\theta_i'} = \kappa_i \Delta \theta_i = \kappa_i \left(\theta_{if}' - \theta_i' \right)$$

for node i at a foldline, where $\tau_{\theta_i'}$ is the torque required to create a fold angle $\Delta \theta_i$ and κ_i is the spring constant. The co-located DOF of θ_i' is denoted θ_{if}'. A linear spring is assumed in this work; i.e., the torque required to create a fold is assumed to be directly proportional to the fold angle. The assumption of constant stiffness is justified for small fold angles as there is no external or internal load contributing significantly to affect folding. However, nonlinear, inelastic deformation has been shown to drive fold angle retention behavior [Abbott et al. 14], which is expected to be significant at larger fold angles and near facet closure. This behavior is dependent on the thickness and material properties of each system, and the construction of a more accurate fold stiffness model requires further investigation.

Rewriting Equation (2.2) in a matrix form as

$$\tau_{\theta_i}' = \kappa_\theta' \begin{bmatrix} 1 & -1 \\ -1 & 1 \end{bmatrix} \begin{bmatrix} \theta_i' \\ \theta_{if}' \end{bmatrix},$$

$$\tau_{\phi_i}' = \kappa_\phi' \begin{bmatrix} 1 & -1 \\ -1 & 1 \end{bmatrix} \begin{bmatrix} \phi_i' \\ \phi_{if}' \end{bmatrix},$$

$$\tau_{\psi_i}' = \kappa_\psi' \begin{bmatrix} 1 & -1 \\ -1 & 1 \end{bmatrix} \begin{bmatrix} \psi_i' \\ \psi_{if}' \end{bmatrix}$$

for the x'-, y'- and z'-rotational DOFs, the relations pertinent to torsion springs at foldlines can be organized in a matrix form as $\tau = k_o q_o$ using a 12×12 matrix

$$k_o^{ij'} = \begin{bmatrix} \kappa^{i'} & -\kappa^{i'} & 0 & 0 \\ -\kappa^{i'} & \kappa^{i'} & 0 & 0 \\ 0 & 0 & \kappa^{j'} & -\kappa^{j'} \\ 0 & 0 & -\kappa^{j'} & \kappa^{j'} \end{bmatrix}$$

for a foldline connecting nodes i and j, where $\kappa^{i'} = \mathrm{diag}(\kappa_\theta^{i'}, \kappa_\phi^{i'}, \kappa_\psi^{i'})$. The corresponding arrangement of rotational DOFs is

(2.3) $$q_o^{ij'} = \left[\theta_i', \phi_i', \psi_i', \theta_{if}', \phi_{if}', \psi_{if}', \theta_j', \phi_j', \psi_j', \theta_{jf}', \phi_{jf}', \psi_{jf}' \right].$$

Torsion springs inserted for the y'- and z'-rotations are made significantly larger than those for the x'-rotation as only x'-rotation corresponds to folding. The above expressions can be transformed into the global coordinates, using the transformation matrix L found in Equation (2.1), as

$$k_o^{ij} = L^T k_o^{ij'} L.$$

Positive rotation is defined as a clockwise rotation about the axis from node i to node j. With this convention, the DOFs in Equation (2.3) can be organized such that the sign of fold angle $\Delta \theta_i = \theta_{if}' - \theta_i'$ is consistent with the type of fold throughout the entire structure as follows:

(2.4) $$\begin{cases} \text{mountain fold} & \text{if } \Delta\theta_i > 0, \\ \text{valley fold} & \text{if } \Delta\theta_i < 0, \\ \text{flat} & \text{if } \Delta\theta_i = 0. \end{cases}$$

Assembly of frame element stiffness matrices k_e and fold stiffness matrices k_o^{ij} using the connectivity table in Table 1 yields a global stiffness matrix K for a simple origami structure with two triangles. The system equation for origami structures referring to more-complex crease patterns can also be constructed through an assembly of more triangles. However, multiple foldlines meeting at a node would cause unintended coupling of the torsion springs inserted at the foldlines. In order to decouple the torsion springs, vertices are removed by creating holes. As a result, facets are described as higher-order polygons. This way, the connectivity computation for any crease pattern follows the same procedure as above because each foldline is always shared by two facets.

For origami tessellations, periodic boundary conditions can be used for efficient analysis. To do this, frame element DOFs and foldline DOFs at the original boundary are solved and then applied as the state variables at the matched boundary, as shown in Figure 2.

Adopting the connectivity computation technique described earlier, the numbering of co-located rotational DOFs at foldlines are typically far from the original DOFs associated with node numbers, creating a sparse global stiffness matrix with a large bandwidth. This can be rectified by reordering DOFs to reduce the bandwidth using an algorithm such as the reverse Cuthill-McKee ordering [George and Liu 81] prior to solving. Sparse matrix solving methods improve computational time by efficient storage. However, the key driver of computational cost is the number of DOFs, which increases by roughly an order of magnitude between truss-to-frame and frame-to-shell formulations.

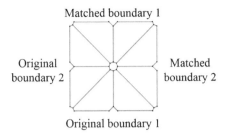

FIGURE 2. Periodicity is enforced by copying DOFs at the original boundary to the matched boundary.

3. Modal Analysis

The mechanics of thin sheets is complex. Rigid origami reduces this complexity to a series of rotations about a pattern of predefined folds, sacrificing information on compliant deformation modes that may be important for certain applications. The modified frame approach includes these compliant modes via the bending, torsion, and stretching of the individual members. By appropriately scaling the stiffness related to these modes, the deformation response of the system can be separated out according to different strain energy levels. The tuning capability of the modified frame method is particularly useful in a design optimization context. Foldlines can be virtually removed with the assignment of a large stiffness value, without the reprogramming of the node connectivity required for fold removal. The ability to identify the folding-only motions of an origami pattern is also important for optimization problems, where the initial direction of folding can affect the convergence of the optimization process.

To demonstrate these advantages, modal analyses of stiffness matrices from simple structures were performed. Eigenvalues found through solving an eigenvalue problem: $K\phi = \lambda\phi$ were plotted to illustrate the effect of varying properties on the structural stability. Modal energy levels of a single fold with varying fold stiffness κ are plotted in Figure 3(a) using characteristic length $l = 1$, Young's modulus $E = 1.0 \times 10^8$, and moment of inertia $I = 8.33 \times 10^{-6}$ in SI (l [m], E [Pa], I [m^4], κ [Nm/rad]) or consistently scaled units. The mode shapes in Figure 3(c) demonstrate the ability to identify folding in both rigid and compliant facet regimes. For instance, an origami structure with compliant, but inextensible, facets can be defined using modest moments of inertia for the frame members while retaining a high axial stiffness. This would correspond to a material with a large Young's modulus, E, but small thickness. Similarly, folding-only deformations may be isolated by assigning the fold stiffness to be much smaller than the stiffness of stretching and bending, as outlined in Figure 4. The mechanical properties of this situation are comparable to a corrugated cardboard box with foldlines of varying degrees of perforation.

The transition from compliant to rigid folding is demonstrated in the eigenvalues versus fold stiffness plot of a single-vertex structure shown in Figure 4(a). The fold stiffness of the dashed lines, κ_v, was varied relative to the constant fold stiffness of the other interior lines, κ, as defined in Equation (2.2). At each stiffness ratio, the eigenvalues of the structure were collected. As seen in both Figures 3 and 4, eigenmodes with stretching and in-plane bending occur at high energy levels (gray lines). Solid black lines indicate a consistent mode shape with varying stiffness, while the dashed lines represent regimes of mode mixing. At small κ_v/κ, the lowest-energy mode shape is folded about the dashed lines (I). The

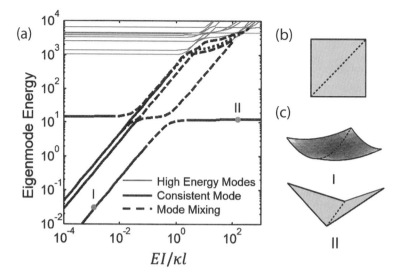

FIGURE 3. Modal analysis for rigid and compliant modes: (a) Eigenmode energy versus the bending-to-fold-stiffness ratio, $EI/\kappa l$; (b) flat state fold pattern; and (c) mode shapes in the rigid fold (I) and compliant (II) modes. Characteristic length $l = 1$, Young's modulus $E = 1.0 \times 10^8$, moment of inertia $I = 8.33 \times 10^{-6}$, and fold stiffness κ is variable.

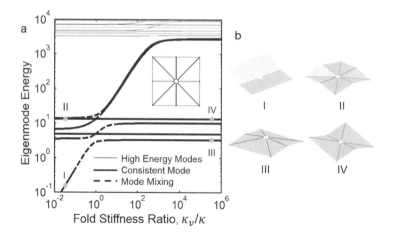

FIGURE 4. Modal analysis for foldable modes: (a) Eigenmode energy versus fold stiffness ratio, κ_v/κ; (b) mode shapes of parts I–IV on the plot. Dashed lines indicate stiffness κ_v and solid lines stiffness κ.

highest fold-only mode shape involves folding about all foldlines (II). As κ_v/κ increases, the number of eigenmodes associated with folding decreases from six to four. The four mode shapes available at high κ_v/κ are equivalent to the folding-only mode shapes of the structure without the dashed lines. The low- and high-energy mode shapes in this regime

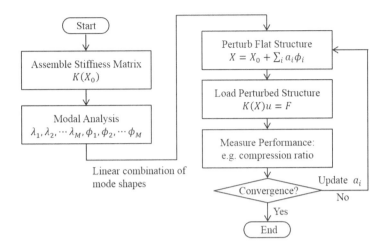

FIGURE 5. A combination of mode shapes is optimized and used to perturb the structure.

are observed at III and IV. These examples not only demonstrate the ability of the model to isolate folding-only deformations, but also highlight the ability to detect how changes in the underlying structure affect the space of foldable motions. These types of insights are relevant for fold stiffness, fold pattern, and fold perturbation optimization problems.

Each structure is constructed using frame elements with all interior lines associated with co-located DOFs that enable folding. Recall that a hole is needed at each internal vertex to decouple fold stiffnesses between foldlines. The effect of the size of holes on the rest of the structure is minor, because co-located rotational DOFs enable relative rotations of adjacent facets without causing any deformation in the short elements created along holes. However, using holes that are too small without caution may lead to inappropriately proportioned (non-slender) elements and can cause unintended low-energy deformations that are difficult to isolate.

4. Fold Perturbation Optimization

Adaptive origami structural design requires not only the determination of optimal crease patterns but also optimal fold sequences. Fold sequence design begins with the initial fold-type (mountain/valley) assignment, which is a particularly important design decision as the number of foldable paths diminishes after the initial perturbation off of the flat state. The initial fold directions can be optimized by combining the folding-only eigenmode analysis with static analysis under a fixed load, as demonstrated with the following example of an in-plane loading of a sheet.

In-plane compression of the thin sheet is an important problem of mechanical instability and has connections to the highly cited Miura-ori fold patterns. The characteristic mountain-valley zig-zag pattern of the Miura-ori has been correlated with the out-of-plane displacement of a bi-axially compressed elastic plate [Tanizawa and Miura 78]. This study evaluates an analogous problem of single axis, in-plane compression, posed in a different manner. What is the optimal combination of fold directions to achieve maximal in-plane compression?

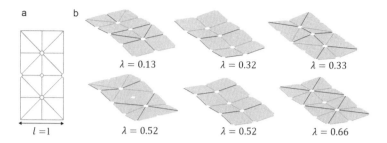

FIGURE 6. Folding modes have eigenvalues in the order of 10^{-1}. Stiffness values are set such that only modes above $\lambda = 10^3$ involve deformations other than folding. (a) Crease pattern in the unit cell. (b) Mode shapes.

The design process starts with the construction of the system stiffness matrix $K(X_0)$ at a flat initial state X_0, followed by a modal analysis. A perturbation of the structure off of a flat state is then decided, described as a linear combination of fold mode shapes. The displacement field u under loading is found through a static analysis by applying an in-plane compression force F on the perturbed structure X and solving the system equation $K(X)u = F$. The design optimization problem is to find the optimal linear combination of folding modes such that the in-plane compression is maximized. The total strain energy associated with the perturbation U is constrained to limit the input energy requirement. The design optimization process is summarized in a flowchart in Figure 5, and the optimization problem is stated as follows:

(4.1)
$$\begin{aligned} \text{Find} \quad & a_1, a_2, \ldots, a_M \text{ that} \\ \text{minimizes} \quad & f = \max\{X_{2,\text{top}}\} \\ \text{subject to} \quad & U \le U_{\max} \\ & X = X_0 + \textstyle\sum_{i=1} a_i \phi_i, \end{aligned}$$

where M is the number of fold modes. The problem is posed as a minimization of the deformed y-coordinates of nodes at the top surface with an in-plane loading from the right boundary. This problem specification ensures that the translation of the horizontal force applied to the vertical in-plane compression is the main focus of the design.

A numerical experiment is conducted using a structure shown in Figure 6(a). Periodic BCs are applied in the modal analysis by matching the DOFs of the original and matched boundaries, as illustrated in Figure 2. Mode shapes within the folding regime are listed with their corresponding eigenvalues in Figure 6(b). As these mode shapes follow periodic BCs, each pattern in the unit cell can be used to tile the xy-plane. A finite number of cells (e.g., 3×3) are repeated to create a tessellation for the in-plane compression test. Mechanical properties used in the example are summarized in Table 2. The optimization problem is solved using MATLAB's optimization toolbox "fmincon." Sequential quadratic programming is selected as the optimization algorithm for its efficiency; the update of the perturbation coefficients continues until the process is terminated when the first order optimality condition is satisfied within a tolerance (1×10^{-6}).

Figure 7(a) shows the optimal perturbation of the unit of periodicity, described as a linear combination of folding eigenmode shapes. The loaded periodic structure in Figure 7(b) shows a pattern similar to the Miura-ori, with some mild folds across what would be facets in the Miura-ori. Although similar crease patterns appear in the upper and lower

E	G	I	κ'_θ	$\kappa'_{\phi,\psi}$	$U_{\max}$
1.0×10^8	1.0×10^8	8.3×10^{-6}	0.1	1.0×10^6	0.01

TABLE 2. Properties used for optimization, in SI units (E [Pa], G [Pa], I [m^4], κ [Nm/rad], U [J]) or equivalent.

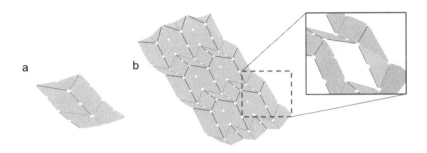

a   b

FIGURE 7. Optimal perturbation for minimum projected area under in-plane compression. (a) Perturbed unit cell. (b) Loaded periodic (3×3) structure.

a   b

FIGURE 8. Optimal perturbation for minimum projected area with higher perturbation energy. (a) Perturbed unit cell. (b) Loaded periodic (3×3) structure.

halves of the perturbed pattern in Figure 7(a), the fold type (mountain/valley) assignments are opposite. This indicates that the obtained solution would not be available using only one of the basic units, i.e., the lower half of Figure 6(a), and the solution has a dependency on the choice of the unit cell. The optimal perturbation pattern obtained here minimizes the vertical length of the tessellation upon application of a horizontal in-plane compression. A relatively tight constraint on the perturbation energy is used here. As higher energy modes are typically associated with mode shapes with more creases, a tight constraint leads to a simpler folding pattern. One of the main challenges in the implementation of adaptive origami structures lies in the development of complex actuation systems, and the perturbation energy is a relevant metric to constrain complex actuations required for initial perturbation.

The problem is solved again with a higher perturbation energy allowed, $U_{\max} = 0.02$. While the new design in Figure 8 requires twice as much energy in perturbation, the performance only improves by less than 1%. This confirms the efficiency of the Miura-ori as a way to initiate an in-plane compression. The performance measure used in this study, however, only considers the initial compression step and does not guarantee an optimal terminal state or sequence of origami folding. Nonlinear mechanical analysis and path-dependent optimization strategies are needed to address these challenges.

5. Conclusions

Adaptive origami structures are a unique platform for engineering problems requiring multiple spatial configurations. The modified frame model and optimization approach presented in this study provide a method to objectively evaluate the mechanical performance of an origami structure throughout the design process. The intermediate level of mechanical detail of the modified frame element, compared with alternative approaches of truss and shell element models, is a balanced tradeoff between accuracy and computing costs. Frame members offer tunable facet compliance not considered in rigid origami simulation, without the high resolution and computational load of full solid or shell finite element modeling. The benefit of computationally inexpensive frame elements is especially advantageous when considered in the present context of design optimization.

The optimization of this study focused on mechanical parameters, such as the compression ratio and mechanical energy of the perturbation. Additional physics could be added for specific applications as necessary. The linear static analysis of the current model is a limitation for evaluating large folding motions. Future work to include nonlinear analysis of the origami geometry and material behavior will extend these results into large folding and more-complex material regimes. In all, this study provides a framework for systematic origami device design for geometrically reconfigurable applications.

Acknowledgments

This research is supported under AFOSR funding, LRIR 13RQ02COR. The authors would like to thank Drs. Joycelyn Harrison and David Stargel for their enthusiasm and support of the project.

References

[Abbott et al. 14] Andrew C. Abbott, Philip R. Buskohl, James J. Joo, Gregory W. Reich, and Richard A. Vaia. "Characterization Techniques of Creases in Polymers for Adaptive Origami Structures." In *ASME 2014 Conference on Smart Materials, Adaptive Structures and Intelligent Systems*, No. No. SMASIS2014-7480. New York: ASME, 2014.

[belcastro and Hull 02] sarah-marie belcastro and Thomas C. Hull. "Modeling the Folding of Paper into Three Dimensions Using Affine Transformations." *Linear Algebra and Its Applications* 348 (2002), 273–282. MR1902132 (2003b:15003)

[Chandrupatla and Belegundu 02] Tirupathi R. Chandrupatla and Ashok D. Belegundu. *Introduction to Finite Elements in Engineering*, Third Edition. Upper Saddle River, NJ: Prentice-Hall, 2002.

[Fuchi et al. 14] Kazuko Fuchi, Philip R. Buskohl, James J. Joo, Gregory W. Reich, and Richard A. Vaia. "Topology Optimization for Design of Origami-Based Active Mechanisms." In *ASME 2014 International Design Engineering Technical Conferences and Computers and Information in Engineering Conference*,No. DETC2014-35153. New York: ASME, 2014.

[George and Liu 81] Alan George and Joseph Liu. *Computer Solution of Large Sparse Positive Definite Systems*. Upper Saddle River, NJ: Prentice-Hall, 1981. MR646786 (84c:65005)

[Lang 98] Robert J. Lang. "Threemaker 4.0: A Program for Origami Design." http://www.langorigami.com/science/computational/treemaker/TreeMkr40.pdf, 1998.

[Peraza-Hernandez et al. 13] Edwin Peraza-Hernandez, Darren Hartl, Edgar Galvan, and Richard Malak. "Design and Optimization of a Shape Memory Alloy-Based Self-Folding Sheet." *Journal of Mechanical Design* 135:11 (2013), 111007.

[Schenk and Guest 11] Mark Schenk and Simon D Guest. "Origami Folding: A Structural Engineering Approach." In *Origami^5: Fifth International Meeting of Origami Science, Mathematics, and Education*, edited by Patsy Wang-Iverson, Robert J. Lang, and Mark Yim, pp. 291–304. Boca Raton, FL: A K Peters/CRC Press, 2011. MR2866909 (2012h:00044)

[Tachi 09] Tomohiro Tachi. "Simulation of Rigid Origami." In *Origami⁴: Fourth International Meeting of Origami Science, Mathematics, and Education*, edited by Robert J. Lang, pp. 175–187. Wellesley, MA: A K Peters, 2009. MR2590567 (2010h:00025)

[Tanizawa and Miura 78] Kazuo Tanizawa and Koryo Miura. "Large Displacement Configurations of Bi-axially Compressed Infinite Plate." *Japan Society for Aeronautical and Space Sciences, Transactions* 20 (1978), 177–187.

WRIGHT STATE RESEARCH INSTITUTE, BEAVERCREEK, OHIO
E-mail address: kazuko.fuchi@wright.edu

AIR FORCE RESEARCH LABORATORY, WRIGHT-PATTERSON AFB, OHIO
E-mail address: philip.buskohl.1@us.af.mil

AIR FORCE RESEARCH LABORATORY, WRIGHT-PATTERSON AFB, OHIO
E-mail address, Corresponding author: james.joo.1@us.af.mil

AIR FORCE RESEARCH LABORATORY, WRIGHT-PATTERSON AFB, OHIO
E-mail address: gregory.reich.1@us.af.mil

AIR FORCE RESEARCH LABORATORY, WRIGHT-PATTERSON AFB, OHIO
E-mail address: richard.vaia@us.af.mil

A Study on Crash Energy Absorption Ability of Lightweight Structures with Truss Core Panel

Yang Yang, Xilu Zhao, Sunao Tokura, and Ichirou Hagiwara

1. Introduction

Lightweight structures have been widely used for aircrafts, trains, and vehicles because they make it possible to reduce materials usage and gas consumption and to improve fuel economy, which is good for the environment, in addition to the structures' performance of stiffness and strength. Developing a lightweight structure that meets performance requirements of strength, stiffness, vibration, and crash energy absorption is becoming a big research challenge [Shibukawa 09, Noor et al. 96, Kaman et al. 10, Qiao and Wang 05, Nilsson and Nilsson 01].

One such form, the *truss core panel*, is a structure invented based on the research of space-filling regular tetrahedrons and octahedrons combined, because neither regular tetrahedra nor regular octahedra can fill space without gaps individually regardless of the simplicity in their shapes [Saito and Nojima 07, Nojima and Hagiwara 12, Nojima 05, Nojima and Saito 05, Nojima 00]. They have desirable aspects in bending stiffness and in shear strength. In prior work, the relationship between the geometrical pattern of truss core panels and their mechanical characteristics was investigated. It was shown that geometrical parameters have obvious effects on the bending stiffness and on the in-plane shear strength [Saito et al. 08]. The formability of truss core panel employing a simple press method of nonlinear analytical simulation and using multipurpose dynamic analysis software LS-DYNA was confirmed [Tokura and Hagiwara 08]. Also, the results of the core shape optimization to improve the impact energy absorption ability of the truss core panel by using LS-DYNA were presented [Tokura and Hagiwara 10]. However, when a truss core panel structure receives an impact load from the lateral direction, the tendency for bending is noticeable, which creates a major obstacle for using structures based on the truss core panel structure as the collision strength member.

In order to solve this problem, we propose a new lightweight structure that consists of a truss core panel (TCP) and a reinforced part (called the *insert member*) with optimized geometric parameters to seek the maximum crash energy absorption under a weight control condition. The geometric parameters of the structure based on a honeycomb panel (HCP) was optimized also to verify the superiority of the proposed structure.

2. Crash Analysis of the Structure Based on TCP

Figure 1 shows the proposed structure based on TCP. Figure 2 shows the crash analysis model, where the clamped boundary conditions were applied at one end of the structure.

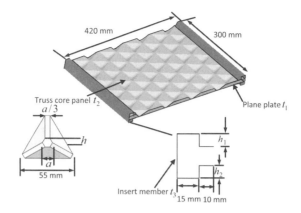

FIGURE 1. The proposed structure based on TCP.

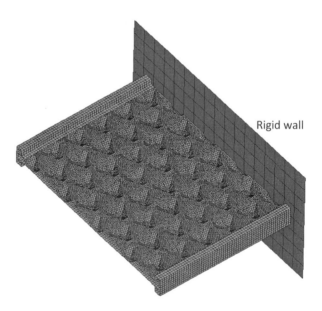

FIGURE 2. Crash analysis model.

A rigid wall impacts the structure with an initial velocity of 55 km/h, and the contact condition between the structure and the rigid wall was defined by the *AUTOMATIC_SURFACE_TO_SURFACE command in LS-DYNA. The model was meshed with quadrilateral elements. All the elements were modeled with a character size between 3 mm and 5 mm. The number of elements is 25,257, and the number of nodes is 25,478.

The cores are connected to the plates and the side members by spot-welding elements to create the contact condition of the nodes in each component. Because spot welding is considered to have a significant influence on the crash energy absorption, and to be closer to the real thing, we set up the spot-welding model using a beam element. Furthermore, because there is a possibility that the spot welding will break in the actual impact, a rupture criterion is set to an equivalent strain of 0.3 according to the reference at

Young's modulus	210 GPa
Poisson's ratio	0.3
Density	7.8×10^{-6} kg/mm^3
Yield stress	270 MPa

TABLE 1. Material properties of the model.

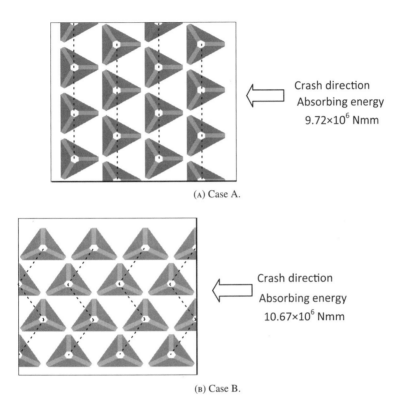

Crash direction
Absorbing energy
9.72×10^6 Nmm

(A) Case A.

Crash direction
Absorbing energy
10.67×10^6 Nmm

(B) Case B.

FIGURE 3. The directions of TCP and absorbing crash energy.

http://www.ncac.gwu.edu/. Steel was used as the material in the simulation. Table 1 presents the material properties.

The strain energy of all the elements is obtained by the following equation for the evaluation of the crash energy absorbing performance of the structure:

$$E_{\text{absorb}} = \sum_{i=1}^{N} \int_V \sigma \eta dV,$$

where N is a number of elements.

Figure 3 shows two cases, A and B. The crash energy absorption of Case A is about 10% different from that of Case B due to the relationship between the triangular cores of TCP and the crash direction, as shown in Figure 3. In Case A, the crash direction is perpendicular to the panel, and the recesses of the cores form equally spaced rows on the TCP. This relationship causes the straight crushing to wrinkle easily. On the other hand, in Case B, the crash direction is perpendicular to the panel, and the recesses of the cores are equally spaced in an S-shape. This relationship makes the crushing wrinkle happen in an S-shape, which makes the buckling resistance bigger. So, Case B absorbed more crash energy, which was confirmed by numerical analysis. In our work, we used Case B in the proposed structure.

3. Study on the Improvement of Crash Energy Absorption

We optimized the geometric parameters design of the proposed structure based on TCP by the optimization method RSM [Zhao 08] for crash analysis.

3.1. Model's settings of optimization. The optimization question considering the proposed structure as the target is expressed as follows:

$$
\begin{array}{lll}
& \text{find} & x = [a, h, h_1, h_2, t_1, t_2, t_3]^T ; \\
(3.1) & \text{target function} & E = f(x); \\
& \text{constraint condition} & W \le 3.2 \text{ kg.}
\end{array}
$$

In Equation (3.1), there are seven design variables $x = [a, h, h_1, h_2, t_1, t_2, t_3]^T$, as shown in Figure 1; a is the edge length on the top of core, h is the height of core, h_1 is the height of insert member on the truss core panel side, h_2 is the height of insert member on the plate side, t_1 is the thickness of plate, t_2 is the thickness of truss core panel, and t_3 is the thickness of insert member. The variation range of each design variable is as follows:

$$10 \text{ mm} \le a \le 30 \text{ mm,} \qquad 8 \text{ mm} \le h \le 12 \text{ mm,}$$

$$0 \text{ mm} \le h_1 \le 12 \text{ mm,} \qquad 0 \text{ mm} \le h_2 \le 12 \text{ mm,}$$

$$0.8 \text{ mm} \le t_1 \le 1.4 \text{ mm,} \qquad 0.8 \text{ mm} \le t_2 \le 1.4 \text{ mm,} \qquad 0.8 \text{ mm} \le t_3 \le 1.4 \text{ mm.}$$

The target function $E = f(x)$ is chosen to find the maximum crash energy absorption when the crushing deformation reaches 70% of the full length of structure. In the constraint condition $W \le 3.2$ kg, W is the weight of the proposed structure based on TCP, and 3.2 kg is the weight of the existing proposed structure.

3.2. Optimized result. Since the analysis time runs quite long and the design space is complex, we decided to use RSM as the optimization technique. For RSM to find a meaningful solution, it is necessary that the objective function be sufficiently smooth. Even though the load-time and deformation-time diagrams have low- and high-frequency waves, the crash energy absorption value calculated by integration is a smooth function. Therefore, RSM is an appropriate method for optimization of energy absorption. When RSM is used to solve the optimization expression in Equation (3.1), the geometry optimization calculation procedure is as follows. First, the L27 orthogonal table is chosen to generate sample data following the design geometric parameters and variation range. Second, these sample data are used to change the structure models respectively for the crash analysis. From the analysis results, we obtain the crash energy and the weight of structures, which are necessary for the optimization calculations. Finally, the one-to-one relationship between the sample data and the characteristic values is organized for RSM. Lastly, the optimized solution is obtained by doing the calculations using the approximate formula. Now, we have to build the proposed TCP structure with the calculated optimized geometric variables and then to confirm the accuracy of the calculations through crash analysis using LS-DYNA.

	Before Optimization	After Optimization
Edge length of upper triangle of core .... (a)	15 mm	30 mm
Height of core .... (h)	10 mm	12 mm
Height of insert member on core side .... (h_1)	8.5 mm	12 mm
Height of insert member on plate side ... (h_2)	8.5 mm	12 mm
Thickness of plate .... (t_1)	1.0 mm	0.8 mm
Thickness of truss core panel .... (t_2)	1.0 mm	1.4 mm
Thickness of insert member .... (t_3)	1.0 mm	1.4 mm
Crash energy absorption	10.67 MNmm	17.37 MNmm

TABLE 2. Comparison of design variables before and after optimization.

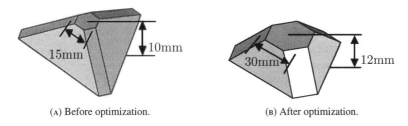

(A) Before optimization.   (B) After optimization.

FIGURE 4. The core shapes based on TCP before and after optimization.

A comparison of results before and after optimization is shown in Table 2. As seen in Table 2 and Figure 4, the thicknesses of the TCP and the insert member after optimization are bigger than those of the initial structure. The crash energy absorption has been increased, up 62.79% from 10.67 MNmm to 17.37 MNmm, by using geometry optimization.

4. Comparison of Results on TCP and HCP Structures

In order to confirm the crash energy absorption effect of the proposed structure based on TCP, a structure based on HCP is used for comparison. Considering the geometry and sizes shown in Figure 1, we built the structure based on HCP as shown in Figure 5, and we performed the crash analysis simulation under the same conditions as the crash analysis of the structure based on TCP. The comparison of energy absorption ability between these optimal structures was investigated. The insert members and plates of the honeycomb panel are connected by spot welding.

In the case of the HCP, the absorbing crash energy of Case A is about 18% different from that of Case B, due to the relationship between the HCP arrangement and the crash direction as shown in Figure 6. We used Case B as the compared object to verify the superiority of the structure based on TCP, because the crash energy absorption of Case B is more than that of Case A.

Here, in order to compare the crash energy absorption performance, the crash energy absorption optimal result of the structure based on HCP is compared to that of the structure based on TCP. The target function and the constraint conditions are the same as with the optimized setting of the structure based on TCP. The variation range of each design variable

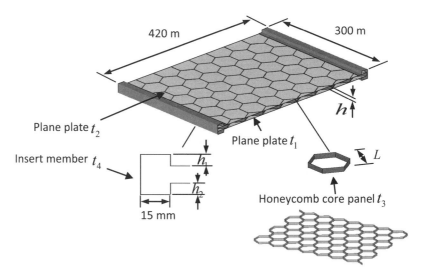

FIGURE 5. The structure based on HCP.

	Absorbing Energy (MNmm)	Mass (kg)	Absorbing Energy per Mass (MNmm/kg)
Optimal structure based on TCP	17.37	3.2	5.43
Optimal structure based on HCP	14.65	3.2	4.58

TABLE 3. Comparison of energy absorption ability of the optimal structures based on TCP and HCP.

was set as follows:

$45 \text{ mm} \leq L \leq 55 \text{ mm}$, $8 \text{ mm} \leq h \leq 12 \text{ mm}$, $0 \text{ mm} \leq h_1 \leq 12 \text{ mm}$,

$0 \text{ mm} \leq h_2 \leq 12 \text{ mm}$, $0.8 \text{ mm} \leq t_1 \leq 1.4 \text{ mm}$, $0.8 \text{ mm} \leq t_2 \leq 1.4 \text{ mm}$,

$0.8 \text{ mm} \leq t_3 \leq 1.4 \text{ mm}$, $0.8 \text{ mm} \leq t_4 \leq 1.4 \text{ mm}$.

Table 3 shows the comparison results of crash energy absorption between optimal structures based on TCP and HCP. From the simulation results, we can see that the crash energy absorption for the structure based on TCP is 18.53% higher than that of the structure based on HCP.

Images of the crash load and the crash energy absorption during the collapse deformation process are shown in Figure 7 and Figure 8, respectively. The collapse shapes during collapse deformation are shown in Figure 9. The left side in Figure 9 shows the collapse shape of the structure based on TCP, and the right side in Figure 9 shows the collapse shape of the structure based on HCP. Each pickup crash time in Figure 9(a)–(d) respectively corresponds to the times marked by A–D in Figures 7 and 8.

Point A in Figures 7 and 8 and Figure 9(a) show the crash load, the energy absorption, and the collapse shape, respectively, when the first buckling of the crash occurred. The initial peak load of the optimal structure based on TCP is clearly lower than that of the optimal structure based on HCP. This means that, compared to the optimal structure based

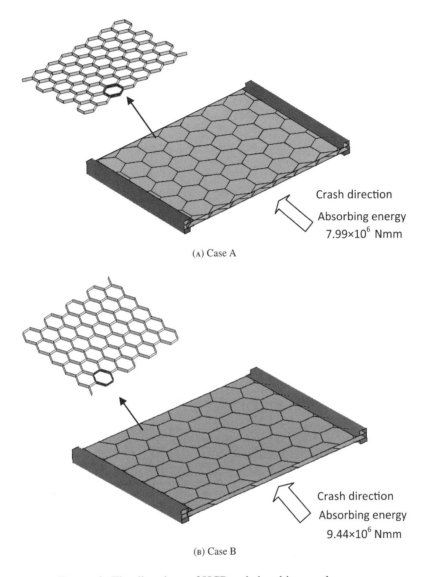

(A) Case A

(B) Case B

FIGURE 6. The directions of HCP and absorbing crash energy.

on HCP, the optimal structure based on TCP is structurally flexible relatively due to the triangular pyramid cores, which are arranged uniformly on the plate.

Point B in Figures 7 and 8 and Figure 9(b) show the crash load, the energy absorption, and the collapse shape, respectively, when the first buckling is fully formed and the next buckling starts to form. From the change in the crash load of the two structures, the crash load increased because the second buckling of two structures was forming. Compared to the optimal structure based on HCP, the buckling of the optimal structure based on TCP was narrow and was mostly concentrated in the first column of triangular pyramid cores, so it did not affect the back end of the structure very much. The crash load of the structure based on TCP has a relatively higher value than the structure based on HCP during the

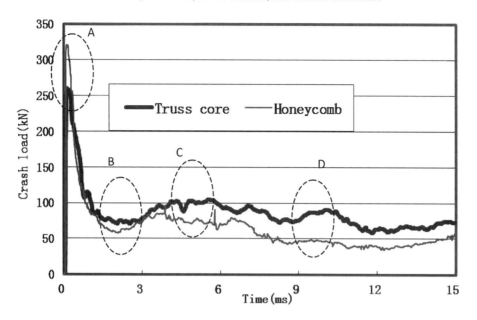

FIGURE 7. Crash load of the optimal structures based on TCP (thick line) and HCP (thin line).

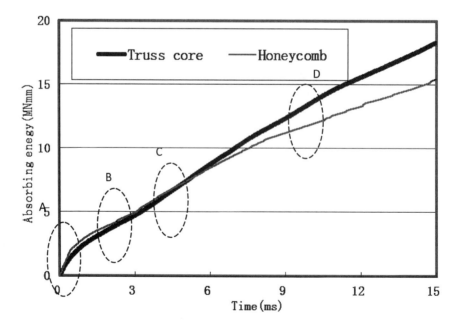

FIGURE 8. Crash energy absorption of the optimal structures based on TCP (thick line) and HCP (thin line).

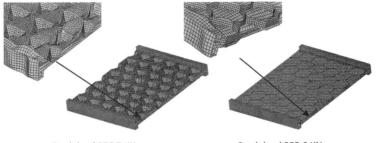

Crash load 256.7 KN
Absorbing energy 0.4 MNmm

Crash load 305.6 KN
Absorbing energy 0.6 MNmm

(A) At crash time 0.1 ms.

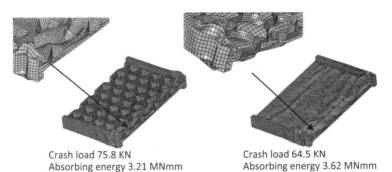

Crash load 75.8 KN
Absorbing energy 3.21 MNmm

Crash load 64.5 KN
Absorbing energy 3.62 MNmm

(B) At crash time 1.6 ms.

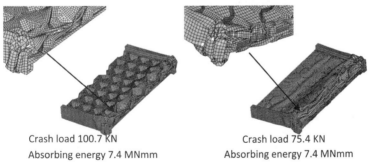

Crash load 100.7 KN
Absorbing energy 7.4 MNmm

Crash load 75.4 KN
Absorbing energy 7.4 MNmm

(c) At crash time 5.0 ms.

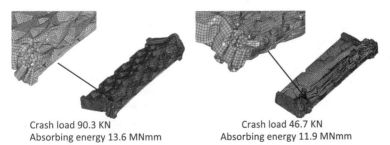

Crash load 90.3 KN
Absorbing energy 13.6 MNmm

Crash load 46.7 KN
Absorbing energy 11.9 MNmm

(D) At crash time 10.0 ms.

FIGURE 9. Collapse shapes of the structures based on TCP (left) and HCP (right) during crash.

collapse deformation process after the first buckling formed, as shown in Figure 7. The crash load and the mechanical work have a higher value in the case when the deformations of each structure are equal, indicating that the crash energy absorption amount is greater.

Point C in Figures 7 and 8 and Figure 9(c) show the crash load, the energy absorption, and the collapse shape, respectively, when the crash energy absorption amounts of the structures based on TCP and HCP are the same. As shown in Figure 8, compared to the structure based on HCP, the crash energy absorption of the structure based on TCP is smaller in the first half of collapse deformation but tends to be higher in the second half. The time of energy absorption reversal happened at point C in Figure 8, where the crash energy absorption of the structure based on TCP begins to exceed that of the structure based on HCP. As shown in Figure 9(c), the stacked buckling is smaller in the forepart of the structure based on TCP. Meanwhile, the pre-crash shape of the back end of the structure based on TCP is preserved. Conversely, collapse deformation occurred in the back end of the structure based HCP along with the forepart.

Point D in Figures 7 and 8 and Figure 9(d) show the crash load, the energy absorption, and the collapse shape, respectively, in the final stage of the collapse deformation. Comparing the final buckling mode, the structure based on HCP fell down in the vertical direction, but the structure based on TCP never failed.

5. Conclusions

(1) The problem of vertical bend when the truss core panel is crashed from the lateral direction has been solved. In order to improve the crash energy absorption as much as possible, the insert members on both sides are included in the proposed structure based on TCP.

(2) RSM is used as the optimization technique.

(3) In order to verify the superiority of the proposed lightweight structure based on TCP, the structure based on HCP is optimized and used for comparison. According to the simulation results, the structure based on TCP is capable of absorbing more energy than the structure based on HCP for structures of the same mass.

References

[Kaman et al. 10] M. Kaman, M. Solmaz, and K. Turan. "Experimental and Numerical Analysis of Critical Buckling Load of Honeycomb Sandwich Panels." *Journal of Composite Materials* 44:24 (2010), 2819–2831.

[Nilsson and Nilsson 01] E. Nilsson and A. C. Nilsson. "Prediction and Measurement of Some Dynamic Properties of Sandwich Structures with Honeycomb and Foam Cores." *Journal of Sound and Vibration* 251:3 (2001), 409–430.

[Nojima 00] T. Nojima. "Origami Model for Folding Method of Plate and Cylinder." *Transactions of the Japan Society of Mechanical Engineers C* 66:643 (2000), 1050–1056.

[Nojima 05] T. Nojima. "Panel and Its Manufacturing Method." Japanese Patent 2005-209031, 2005.

[Nojima and Hagiwara 12] T. Nojima and I. Hagiwara. *Mathematics of Origami and Its Application*. Tokyo: Kyoritsu Shuppan, 2012.

[Nojima and Saito 05] T. Nojima and K. Saito. "Plate and Piece of Plate." Japanese Patent 2005-245045, 2005.

[Noor et al. 96] A. Noor, W. S. Burton, and C. W. Bert. "Computational Models for Sandwich Panels and Shells." *The American Society of Mechanical Engineers, Rev.* 49:3 (1996), 155–199.

[Qiao and Wang 05] P. Qiao and J. Wang. "Mechanics of Composite Sinusoidal Honeycomb Cores." *Journal of Aerospace Engineering* 18:1, (2005), 42–50.

[Saito and Nojima 07] K. Saito and T. Nojima. "Development of Light-Weight Rigid Core Panels." *Journal of Solid Mechanics and Materials Engineering* 1:9 (2007), 1097–1104.

[Saito et al. 08] K. Saito, T. Nojima, and I. Hagiwara. "Relation between Geometrical Patterns and Mechanical Properties in Newly Developed Light-Weight Core Panels." *Transactions of the Japan Society of Mechanical Engineers A* 74:748 (2008), 1580–1586.

[Shibukawa 09] T. Shibukawa. "Weight Reduction and Miniaturization Technology for Green Politics." *Journal of the Japan Society of Mechanical Engineers* 112:1088 (2009), 535–563.

[Tokura and Hagiwara 08] S. Tokura and I. Hagiwara. "Forming Process Simulation of Truss Core Panel." *Transactions of the Japan Society of Mechanical Engineers A* 74:746 (2008), 81–87.

[Tokura and Hagiwara 10] S. Tokura and I. Hagiwara. "Shape Optimization to Improve Impact Energy Absorption Ability of Truss Core Panel." *Transactions of the Japan Society of Mechanical Engineers A* 76:765 (2010), 564–572.

[Zhao 08] X. Zhao. "Development of Simple Optimization System by Using Response Surface Method." *Proceedings of the Conference on Computational Engineering and Science* 13:1 (2008), 101–104.

INSTITUTE FOR ADVANCED STUDY OF MATHEMATICAL SCIENCE, MEIJI UNIVERSITY, JAPAN
E-mail address: tz12014@meiji.ac.jp

SAITAMA INSTITUTE OF TECHNOLOGY, JAPAN
E-mail address: zhaoxilu@sit.jp

TOKURA SIMULATION RESEARCH CORPORATION, JAPAN
E-mail address: tokura.sunao@tokurasimresearch.com

INSTITUTE FOR ADVANCED STUDY OF MATHEMATICAL SCIENCE, MEIJI UNIVERSITY, JAPAN
E-mail address: ihagi@meiji.ac.jp

Toward Optimization of Stiffness and Flexibility of Rigid, Flat-Foldable Origami Structures

Evgueni T. Filipov, Tomohiro Tachi, and Glaucio H. Paulino

1. Introduction

Rigid-foldable origami consists of stiff panel elements connected by flexible fold or hinge elements. The premise of these origami patterns is that they can fold and unfold without deforming the panel elements, which makes these systems especially useful for large-scale structural applications where thickened panels can be connected with more flexible hinge joints [Tachi 09b, Tachi 11]. In reality, rigid origami structures can experience deformations that do not correspond to rigid folding and thus the stiffness behavior of such systems is of great interest [Schenk and Guest 11, Wei et al. 13]. Amongst various origami patterns, the Miura-ori folding pattern has gained substantial interest in the past few years because it allows flat and rigid folding of a sheet [Mahadevan and Rica 05, Miura 09, Schenk and Guest 11, Wei et al. 13, Gattas et al. 13, Schenk and Guest 13]. Recently, Miura-ori–like patterns have also been used to create tubular structures that are also rigid- and flat-foldable [Tachi 09a, Tachi and Miura 12, Miura and Tachi 10].

Optimization for folding systems has also been a topic of interest in recent years. For example, Fuchi and Diaz have shown an optimization algorithm that uses a ground structure approach to find a folding pattern with desired geometric properties and a minimum number of crease lines [Fuchi and Diaz 13]. Other research has optimized bistable compliant mechanisms to design retractable structures that require minimal force for deployment [Ohsaki et al. 13]. Optimization for the stiffness of origami structures, however, has not yet been explored in detail.

In this chapter we discuss ideas for optimizing the stiffness of rigid-foldable structures. Stiffness modeling for optimization problems needs to be thorough or it may lead to inaccurate or misleading solutions [Haftka and Gürdal 92]. Here, we improve upon an established model [Schenk and Guest 11] to create a scalable model that takes into account the elastic properties and thickness of the thin origami sheets. We explore methods for modeling the bending of prescribed origami folds, bending of more stiff origami panels, and shear and tensile stretching of these panels. We study the global stiffness of the Miura-ori–inspired tube structures [Tachi 09a] by investigating the eigenvalues and corresponding eigenmodes of the system. The first six eigenmodes correspond to rigid body motion in

This work was partially funded by the National Science Foundation (NSF) through grants CMMI 1234243 and CMMI 1321661. The first author is grateful for support from the NSF Graduate Research Fellowship and the Japan Society for the Promotion of Science Fellowship. We also acknowledge support from the Donald B. and Elizabeth M. Willett endowment at the University of Illinois at Urbana-Champaign.

three-dimensional space, the next mode corresponds to the rigid folding motion, and subsequent modes represent structural deformation. We use constraints on the pattern to ensure that it remains rigid- and flat-foldable, and we then modify the geometry to show optimal cases for structural stiffness and flexibility. By varying geometric parameters, we can minimize or maximize the seventh and/or subsequent eigenvalues of the structure. Minimizing an eigenvalue makes the structure more flexible and easier to fold, whereas maximizing an eigenvalue makes the structure stiffer. Similarly, eigenvalue band-gap maximization can be used to simultaneously control two eigenmodes. This procedure can be used to minimize the rigid folding eigenmode, making the structure easier to fold and deploy, while at the same time it would maximize the bending modes causing the structure to be stiffer for external loadings.

The chapter is organized as follows: Section 2 discusses the geometric properties of the rigid flat-foldable origami tubes studied in this paper; Section 3 presents numerical methods for simplified scalable modeling of origami systems; the general stiffness properties of the tubes are discussed in Section 4; Section 5 provides optimal cases for the origami tube structures; and Section 6 presents concluding remarks.

2. Rigid- and Flat-Foldable Origami Tubes

In this work we restrict our study to a simple subset of the origami tubes that is available in the literature. Figure 1 shows the definition of a Miura-ori cell in our study. The acute vertex angle α along with the dimensions a and c are sufficient to define the geometry of the Miura-ori cell, and the dihedral angle θ_0 can be used to define the folded configuration of the cell. The Miura-ori cell is then repeated and reflected to create a tube. For example, Figure 1(c) shows a tube that is 10 panels (5 cells) long and is folded in different configurations. The tube is flat-foldable in both directions, and the total extended length of the tube L_{Ext} can be calculated as

$$(2.1) \qquad L_{\text{Ext}}(c, N, \alpha, \theta_0) = cN \frac{\tan(\alpha) \sin(\theta_0/2)}{\sin(\alpha) \sqrt{1 + \tan(\alpha)^2 \sin(\theta_0/2)^2}},$$

where N is the number of panels repeating in the direction of c. The maximum (full) length that the tube can reach can be found by $L_{\text{Full}} = L_{\text{Ext}}(c, N, \alpha, \theta_0 = 180°) = cN$. Figure 1(c) shows how different structures ($\alpha = 85°$, $\alpha = 70°$, and $\alpha = 55°$) expand at different rates when related to the dihedral angle. Thus, it is also useful to consider the percentage of the full extended length when comparing the configuration of different structures, as this quantity gives a physical definition of the deployment of the structure.

3. Modeling of Origami Structures

When performing structural optimization, it is especially important that the mechanics of the analytical models are properly defined. If not, it is common for the optimization procedure to find local minima that are artifacts of the numerical model. In this section we describe the numerical modeling of thin sheets in origami systems. A previously established model [Schenk and Guest 11] is used as a basis, and several improvements are discussed. We incorporate scaling effects for the structure and make the panel stiffness dependent on the thickness (t), the elastic modulus (E), and Poisson's ratio (v) of the material. The formulation for fold modeling is also updated, and a ratio is used to relate the bending stiffness of panels to the bending stiffness of a fold. The model provides an improved basis for origami stiffness simulation, while keeping the formulation simple and modeling the origami components (panels and folds) as individual elements. The simplicity of this

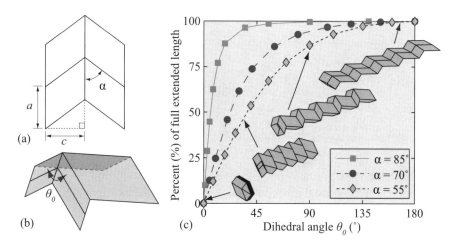

FIGURE 1. Construction of a rigid- and flat-foldable origami tube: (a) geometric definition of a single Miura-ori cell, (b) folding configuration for the Miura-ori cell, and (c) dihedral angle θ_0 versus tube length as a percent (%) of the maximum extension length for tubes with $\alpha = 55°$, $\alpha = 70°$, and $\alpha = 85°$. The tube with $\alpha = 55°$ is shown folded at $\theta_0 = 2°$, $35°$, $90°$, and $170°$.

model makes it a good option for origami optimization, but we also acknowledge that it is not an ideal substitution to a detailed finite element (FE) model composed of nonlinear shell elements. The stiffness matrix ($\mathbf{K}$) for the origami structure incorporates stiffness parameters for (1) panels stretching and shearing ($\mathbf{K}_S$), (2) panels bending ($\mathbf{K}_B$), and (3) bending of prescribed fold lines ($\mathbf{K}_F$). The global stiffness matrix is constructed as follows:

$$(3.1) \qquad \mathbf{K} = \begin{bmatrix} \mathbf{C} \\ \mathbf{J}_B \\ \mathbf{J}_F \end{bmatrix}^T \begin{bmatrix} \mathbf{K}_S & \mathbf{0} & \mathbf{0} \\ \mathbf{0} & \mathbf{K}_B & \mathbf{0} \\ \mathbf{0} & \mathbf{0} & \mathbf{K}_F \end{bmatrix} \begin{bmatrix} \mathbf{C} \\ \mathbf{J}_B \\ \mathbf{J}_F \end{bmatrix},$$

where the compatibility matrix ($\mathbf{C}$) and Jacobian matrices ($\mathbf{J}_B$ and $\mathbf{J}_F$) relate the stiffness of elements to the nodal displacements as discussed in detail in Sections 3.1 to 3.3. Each node has three degrees of freedom (x, y, and z displacement), and the stiffness matrix is of size $n_{\text{dof}} \times n_{\text{dof}}$, where n_{dof} is the total number of degrees of freedom in the system. The mass for each panel is calculated from the panel volume and the material density ρ. A mass matrix $\mathbf{M}$ for the entire structure is constructed by distributing $1/4$ of the panel mass to each of the connecting nodes.

3.1. Panel stretching and shearing (bar modeling). The stiffness of panels for in-plane, axial, and shear loads is simulated using the indeterminate bar frame shown in Figure 2(a). A general formulation for bar elements is used with an equilibrium matrix ($\mathbf{A}$) relating internal bar forces ($\mathbf{t}$) to nodal forces ($\mathbf{f}$) as $\mathbf{At} = \mathbf{f}$; a compatibility matrix ($\mathbf{C}$) relating bar nodal displacements ($\mathbf{d}$) to bar extensions ($\mathbf{e}$) as $\mathbf{Cd} = \mathbf{e}$; and finally a diagonal matrix ($\mathbf{K}_S$) relating the bar extensions to the local forces as $\mathbf{K}_S \mathbf{e} = \mathbf{t}$. As further described in [Schenk and Guest 11], using the static-kinematic duality that $\mathbf{C} = \mathbf{A}^T$, the linear system for stretching and shear of the panels (i.e., the bars) is represented as the first row of Equation (3.1). The crossed bar frame (Figure 2(a)) has six bars connected only at the four corner nodes of the origami panel. This crossed bar geometry was chosen because

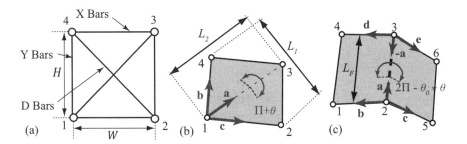

FIGURE 2. Model schematics for (a) bars simulating panel stretching and
shear, (b) a rotational hinge for panel bending, and (c) a rotational hinge
simulating bending along a prescribed fold line.

individual bar properties can be defined, such that the entire frame behaves as an isotropic
panel. The bar stiffness parameters (i.e., components of $\mathbf{K}_S$) are defined for each bar as

$$(3.2) \qquad\qquad K_S = \frac{EA_B}{L_B},$$

where L_B is the bar length and the bar area (A_B) is defined differently for the horizontal (X
Bars), vertical (Y Bars), and diagonal bars (D Bars). The appendix (Section 7) contains a
detailed discussion on how the bar areas are defined to achieve isotropic material behavior
for the entire panel. The model exhibits realistic tensile and shear stiffness behavior when
a Poisson's ratio of $\nu = 1/4$ is used in the formulation.

3.2. Panel bending modeling. The stiffness of the panels in bending is simulated as
an angular constraint between two adjacent facets of the panel. Figure 2(b) shows a model
schematic of a panel bending along the diagonal 1-3. For small deformations, the choice of
the diagonal does not affect the kinematics, however it affects the stiffness of the element
[Schenk and Guest 13]. Similar to previous research, we formulate our model assuming
that bending occurs along the shorter diagonal because the bending energy will be lower
along the shorter path. An angular constraint F is formulated based on the dihedral bending
angle θ. As shown in [Schenk and Guest 11], the angle can be calculated by using cross
and inner products of the vectors $\mathbf{a}$, $\mathbf{b}$, and $\mathbf{c}$ that are based on the nodal coordinates of the
panel $\mathbf{p}$. The constraint can be defined as

$$F = \sin\theta(\mathbf{p}),$$

and a corresponding Jacobian for the panel bending $\mathbf{J}_B$ is calculated as

$$d\theta = \frac{1}{\cos\theta}\sum\frac{\partial F}{\partial p_i}dp_i = \mathbf{J}_B\mathbf{d},$$

where $\mathbf{d}$ are the displacements of the panel nodes. The second row of Equation (3.1)
incorporates the panel bending by using the Jacobian matrix with the diagonal matrix $\mathbf{K}_B$
to incorporate the stiffness corresponding to each panel.

Assuming the in-plane stiffness of the paper is high enough to prevent local buckling, the panel is expected to bend with curvature only in one direction, as discussed
in [Demaine et al. 11]. This phenomenon is especially similar to the bending of thin
sheets with restrained edges that has been studied in some detail [Lobkovsky et al. 95,
Lobkovsky 96, Witten 07]. The bending energy of thin sheets with restrained edges is
somewhat higher, because tensile forces develop over the sheet's surface, and flexural

deformations become restricted to a small area, which is focused at the bending ridge (i.e., the diagonal 1-3 in Figure 2(b)). Thus, the elastic energy of the panel bending scales approximately as $k(L_2/t)^{1/3}$, where k is the bending modulus of the sheet defined as $k = (Et^3)/(12(1 - v^2))$ [Lobkovsky 96]. We choose to calculate the individual panel stiffness as

$$(3.3) \qquad K_B = C_B \frac{Et^3}{12(1 - v^2)} \left(\frac{L_2}{t}\right)^{1/3},$$

because this incorporates the effect of the L_2/t ratio in restricting the bending of a thin sheet. The factor C_B is set to 0.794 based on approximations from numerical results in [Lobkovsky 96]. This methodology has not been validated for origami systems, so the authors believe that future studies can better verify the scaling properties of thin panels in origami and can substantiate the constant C_B. The definition in Equation (3.3) tends to be stiffer than if we were to assume constant curvature bending of the sheet.

3.3. Fold bending modeling. Modeling of the fold component of the origami structure is in many ways similar to the model for bending of panels. Realistic origami behavior does not allow for significant out-of-plane deformations along fold lines as discussed in [Demaine et al. 11], and thus it is sufficient to use a simplified approach to model the origami fold as a rotational spring along a line. Figure 2(c) shows the model for a fold spanning between nodes 2 and 3 that connects two panels (1-2-3-4 and 2-5-6-3). The length of the fold is L_F and the stiffness is expected to scale linearly with this length because curvature and bending energy are expected to exist only on the infinitesimally small width of the fold. The same constraint formulation presented in Section 3.2 is used to formulate two independent fold elements from the two vector sets: (1) **a**, **b**, and **c** and (2) $-$**a**, **d**, and **e**. This approach distributes the stiffness of the fold to all relevant nodes on the two adjacent panel elements.

The actual behavior and stiffness of origami folds is not well understood yet. For now, we assume that only elastic deformations occur, and we assume that the folds are less stiff than the bending of panels. A factor R_{FP} is introduced to relate the stiffness between the bending of a fold with length $L_F = 1$ and the bending of a panel with a diagonal of $L_2 = 1$. For our analyses we use $R_{FP} = 1/10$, however the value of this quantity should be further investigated. For the fold stiffness, we obtain an equation similar to Equation (3.3) that scales linearly with L_F:

$$K_F = R_{FP} \frac{L_F}{2} C_B \frac{Et^3}{12(1 - v^2)} \left(\frac{1}{t}\right)^{1/3}.$$

4. Stiffness Properties of Tube structures

Eigenvalue analyses are used to study the stiffness and flexibility of the origami structures. The linear dynamics system is used to solve the underlying eigenvalue problem formulated as

$$\mathbf{K}\mathbf{v_i} = \lambda_i \mathbf{M}\mathbf{v_i}, \quad i = 1, \ldots, n_{\text{dof}},$$

where λ_i is the ith eigenvalue and $\mathbf{v_i}$ is the corresponding eigenmode of the structure. Here, we use the eigenvalues and eigenmodes to represent the global behavior of the structure in relation to the mass and stiffness of the system. The eigenvalues (λ) have units of $1/s^2$ and could alternatively be converted to frequencies $(\omega^2 = \lambda)$. A base case of the analysis is shown in Figure 3 for a tube where $\alpha = 55°$, $N = 10$, and $a = c = 1$. The thickness of the material is $t = 0.01$, the Young's modulus is $E = 10^6$, the Poisson's ratio is $v = 1/4$, the density is $\rho = 1$, and the factor relating fold to panel stiffness is $R_{FP} = 1/10$. The

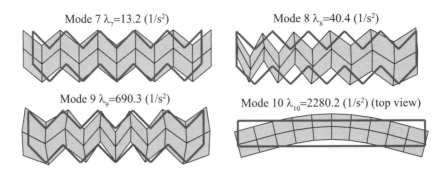

FIGURE 3. Normalized mode shapes #7 to #10 of tube structure with $\alpha = 55°$ and $a = c = 1$ when it is deployed to $\theta_0 = 90°$. The undeformed outlines of the tube are shown as thick lines.

first six eigenmodes correspond to rigid body motion of the structure in three-dimensional space, thus they are omitted in our study. Figure 3 shows the eigen modes corresponding to the seventh to tenth eigenvalues of the structure when deployed to a configuration with $\theta_0 = 90°$. The rigid folding motion corresponds to the seventh mode of the structure where the system can fold and unfold without deforming the panel elements, and thus deformation occurs primarily in the more-flexible fold elements. The eighth mode is a type of "squeezing" mode, where one end of the structure is folded while the other end is unfolded. This mode results in bending of the fold and the panel elements; however, the panels do not stretch or shear, and thus the total energy is only slightly higher than that of the seventh eigenmode. Subsequent modes contain stretching and shearing of the panels, which requires much higher energy than the bending deformations.

Figure 4(a) shows the eigenvalues of the structure in Figure 3 compared to the dihedral angle θ_0. There is substantial mode switching for higher modes and at the extreme ends of the spectrum. The mode switching is a result of the changing geometry of the structure; for example, when the structure reaches a nearly flattened state $\theta_0 \approx 180°$, bending of the structure globally (mode #10 at $\theta_0 = 90°$) becomes easier than folding of the structure. Figure 4(b) shows the effect of reducing the factor R_{FP}, when keeping all other parameters of the analysis the same. The fold elements become much more flexible, and the seventh and eighth eigenvalues drop. Since the seventh mode depends only on the fold elements, its eigenvalue drops more substantially and the gap between λ_7 and λ_8 is effectively enlarged. In practice, this type of behavior can be achieved through making the panels out of thick rigid material, while making the folds from thinner and more flexible material, e.g., cloth. In Figure 4(c) we show the behavior of the structure with the thickness reduced to $t = 0.001$, but all parameters are kept the same as before. Reducing the thickness of the material reduces the axial and shear stiffness linearly, but the bending stiffness of the panels and folds is reduced at a much higher rate ($t^{2\frac{2}{3}}$). Due to this, both the seventh and eighth eigenvalues drop substantially. Note that since the mass and axial/shear stiffness both vary linearly with the thickness, modes #9 and higher are not substantially influenced by this change.

5. Optimization for Tube Structures

For practical applications, architects and engineers may want to improve the stiffness characteristics of origami structures by minimizing or maximizing certain eigenvalues of

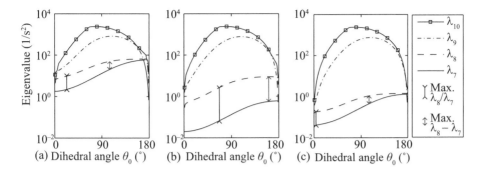

FIGURE 4. (a) Eigenvalue spectrum for the base tube structure ($\alpha = 55°$, $a = c = 1$, $N = 10$, $t = 0.01$, $E = 10^6$, $\nu = 1/4$, $\rho = 1$, and $R_{FP} = 1/10$) through the deployment ($\theta_0 = 0° - 180°$), (b) eigenvalue spectrum for the structure now with $R_{FP} = 1/1000$, and (c) eigenvalue spectrum for the structure now with $t = 0.001$.

the structure. Minimizing an eigenvalue would make the structure more flexible in the corresponding mode, and maximizing it would make the structure stiffer. For example, it would be beneficial to minimize the seventh eigenvalue thus making the structure easier to deploy, but it would also be beneficial to increase the eighth and subsequent modes to make the structure stiffer for other loading scenarios. This can be achieved by performing optimization to maximize the ratio λ_8/λ_7 or the gap $\lambda_8 - \lambda_7$. The ratio λ_8/λ_7 is a good theoretical benchmark where the eighth eigenvalue is the highest in relation to the seventh, while the gap $\lambda_8 - \lambda_7$ is a more practical solution where we obtain the largest physical space between the two eigenvalues. In this study we choose to focus on the gap $\lambda_8 - \lambda_7$, but the ratio could also be used to provide interesting results. To gain a better understanding of the tube stiffness and the influence of the geometric parameters, we perform several optimization cases by using only one variable to modify the structure geometry and one variable to define the configuration. For all of our optimization examples, a generalized objective function and constraints are

$$\max_{(\alpha,t,a,c,N,\theta_0)} \beta = (\lambda_8 - \lambda_7),$$

$$\text{such that } L_{\text{Full}}(c, N) = cN = L_s,$$

$$V(a, c, t, N) = 4actN = V_s,$$

where β is the band-gap, L_{Full} is the full extension length, and V is the solid material volume of a given tube. The maximum length and volume are constrained to be the same as those of the base case analysis in Section 4 (i.e., $V_s = 0.40$ and $L_s = 10$).

5.1. Optimization with respect to the acute vertex angle α. The first optimization case uses the acute vertex angle α as the design variable to define the structure. Using this design variable has no effect on the length or volume of the structure because all other parameters remain the same. Figure 5(a) shows the gap $\lambda_8 - \lambda_7$ with respect to the dihedral angle θ_0 and α. In the early and late phases of the deployment ($\theta_0 < 10°$ and $160° < \theta_0$), there are locations of local minima and maxima, and these can be attributed to the mode switching that occurs in those regions. In the medium range of deployment, there is a smoother variation in magnitude of the gap $\lambda_8 - \lambda_7$, and a line shows the configuration at which the maximum gap can be obtained for each structure (α). Structures with high α

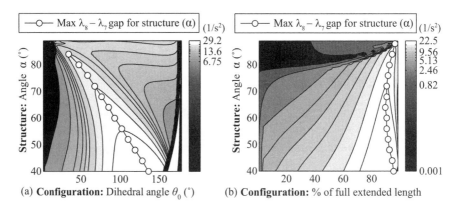

(a) **Configuration:** Dihedral angle θ_0 (°)   (b) **Configuration:** % of full extended length

FIGURE 5. Structure definitions and configurations that maximize the gap $\lambda_8 - \lambda_7$ for tube with $a = c = 1$ and $N = 10$: (a) dihedral angle (θ_0) versus acute vertex angle (α), and (b) percent (%) of full extended length versus acute vertex angle (α). Note that logarithmic scale is used.

perform better (have a higher gap) when θ_0 is lower, and the optimal dihedral angle grows as α decreases. However, Figure 5(a) is somewhat misleading because for each structure, the angle θ_0 corresponds to a different configuration in the expansion sequence as was demonstrated in Figure 1(c).

Alternatively, Figure 5(b) shows the gap instead defining the configuration as a percentage (%) of the full extended length (L_{Full}). When using this measure, it is apparent that the structures (regardless of α) reach their optimal point at about 95% expansion. The gap for structures with $\alpha > 80°$ is especially low in early phases of the deployment, because in those phases, these tubes are susceptible to bending modes and mode switching. Furthermore, tubes with lower α have a higher gap for all configurations with respect to the expansion. This is because panel bending in mode #8 becomes more pronounced for lower α, and thus λ_8 and gap become higher. In other words, mode #8 occurs with little panel bending when α is high, and thus the energy and λ_8 are lower.

5.2. Optimization with respect to panel dimension a. For Figure 6(a), the base structure ($\alpha = 55°$) is used again and dimension a is used as the design variable to study its effect on the gap $\lambda_8 - \lambda_7$. The number of panels and variable c are kept the same, and thus the thickness of the panels is defined as $t = 0.01/a$ to maintain a constant volume for the structure. The results for this analysis, when using the expansion length to define the configuration, are shown in Figure 6(a). Again, all structures reach their optimal point when in a configuration that is close to fully extended (80%–97%). Furthermore, structures where the dimension a is lower and the thickness t is higher have a higher gap ($\lambda_8 - \lambda_7$). This phenomenon can be attributed to two factors: (1) The panel and fold stiffness scale with $t^{2\frac{2}{3}}$ as t increases and λ_8 increases more because it engages both fold and panel elements, and (2) smaller panels are stiffer than larger panels. Note that the rotational hinge stiffness (defined through $\mathbf{J}_B$) varies with respect to L_1^2.

5.3. Optimization with respect to the number of panels N. A final optimization case uses the number of panels (N) as the design variable, c is redefined as $c = 10/N$ to satisfy the constraints V_s and L_s, and all other tube parameters are kept the same. Figure 6(b) shows the results for this analysis. The structures with more panels tend to have only

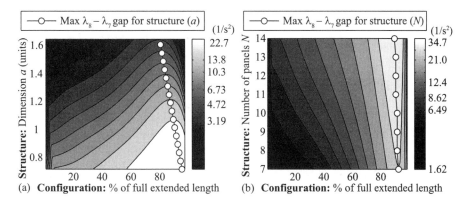

FIGURE 6. Structure definitions and configurations that maximize the gap $\lambda_8 - \lambda_7$ for structure where $\alpha = 55°$ and $N = 10$: (a) percent (%) of full extended length versus dimension a and $c = 10/N$, and (b) percent (%) of full extended length versus the number of panels (N).

a slightly higher band-gap than structures with the same parameters but less panels. With more panels the length L_2 is reduced and the energy of each panel in bending decreases as $L_2^{1/3}$; however, because more panels are added, the total energy for mode #8 and λ_8 increase only slightly.

6. Conclusions

This work first describes a computational method for modeling the stiffness character-istics of origami structures. We introduce simplified scalable measures for the stretching, shear, and bending of thin elastic sheets, as well as the stiffness of more-flexible prescribed fold lines. The computational method is used to perform elastic eigenvalue analyses to study the behavior of rigid- and flat-foldable tube structures that are derived from the Miura-ori pattern. The energies of different eigenmodes are studied, and optimization is performed to maximize the band-gap between the seventh and eighth modes, as this makes the structure more flexible for deployment, yet stiffer for other loading cases. To increase the band-gap, a trivial solution would be to make the folds out of much more flexible mate-rial than the panels, thus making the rigid folding mode very soft. Alternatively, designers may choose to (1) use structures with lower acute vertex angle α, (2) use a smaller tube height a and instead make the material proportionally thicker, or (3) use more panels over the length of the structure. The analysis techniques and optimization methods described here are intended to enable researchers to optimize stiffness in origami systems.

7. Appendix: Bar Element Definitions

The indeterminate bar frame shown in Figure 2(a) can be defined such that it will ex-actly exhibit Poisson effects for tensile loading in both directions (i.e., isotropic behavior).

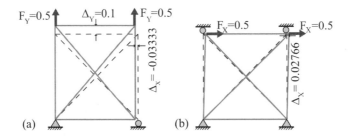

FIGURE 7. Bar model for simulating panel stretching and shear: (a) tensile patch test of model (original configuration shown with dashed lines), and (b) shear patch test of model.

This can be achieved when the bar areas of Equation (3.2) are defined as

$$A_X = t\frac{H^2 - \nu W^2}{2H(1 - \nu^2)},$$

$$A_Y = t\frac{W^2 - \nu H^2}{2W(1 - \nu^2)},$$

(7.1)
$$A_D = t\frac{\nu(H^2 + W^2)^{3/2}}{2HW(1 - \nu^2)},$$

for the horizontal (X Bars), vertical (Y Bars), and diagonal (D Bars) bars, respectively. The variable H is the height and W the width of the panel. Figure 7(a) shows the frame model defined with $W = H = 1$, $t = 0.01$, $E = 1000$, and $\nu = 1/3$ and subjected to a tensile patch test. Figure 7(b) shows the same frame model subjected to a shear patch test. In shear loading, the model behavior is highly dependent on the chosen Poisson's ratio. As can be observed from Equation (7.1), when a low ν is used, the diagonal bars have a low area and this results in the frame having a low shear stiffness. The converse is also true, and this relation is opposite to the realistic shear behavior of isotropic materials. However, when ν is set to $1/3$, the frame model behaves exactly the same in shear as a homogeneous, isotropic block of material. Each of the diagonal bars carries a force of $F/2$ in the x-direction, and a lateral displacement occurs based on the bar stiffness definition (i.e., Equations (3.2) and (7.1)). When $\nu = 1/3$, the bar frame displacement exactly matches the lateral displacement of a solid block with dimensions $W \times H \times t$ loaded in pure shear, analytically defined as

(7.2)
$$\Delta_x = \frac{FH}{GWt},$$

where F is the total shear force and G is the shear modulus defined as $G = E/(2(1 + \nu))$ for a homogeneous, isotropic, linear elastic material. With $\nu = 1/3$, the frame is scale independent for shear loadings, and furthermore if the problem in Figure 7(b) is re-meshed, then the frame model converges to the same solution as any generic FE approach. However, because only a single six-bar frame is used to model each panel, the shear stiffness of the panel is overestimated by this model (similar to FE approaches). In reality, the shear patch test converges to a higher displacement than the exact solution from Equation (7.2) because, in addition to the shear deformations, tensile deformations also occur over the width and height of the patch. Using a lower Poisson's ratio, we can artificially reduce the shear stiffness of the frame, so we choose to instead use $\nu = 1/4$ because at this ratio a single bar frame exhibits approximately the same shear deformation as the patch test performed on a mesh of 2500 finite elements.

References

[Demaine et al. 11] Erik D. Demaine, Martin L. Demaine, Vi Hart, Gregory N. Price, and Tomohiro Tachi. "(Non)existence of Pleated Folds: How Paper Folds between Creases." *Graphs and Combinatorics* 27:3 (2011), 377–397. MR2787424 (2012i:52030)

[Fuchi and Diaz 13] Kazuko Fuchi and Alejandro R. Diaz. "Origami Design by Topology Optimization." *Journal of Mechanical Design* 135:11 (2013), 111003.

[Gattas et al. 13] Joseph M. Gattas, Weina Wu, and Zhong You. "Miura-Base Rigid Origami: Parameterizations of First-Level Derivative and Piecewise Geometries." *Journal of Mechanical Design* 135:11 (2013), 111011.

[Haftka and Gürdal 92] Raphael T. Haftka and Zafer Gürdal. *Elements of Structural Optimization.* New York: Springer Science & Business Media, 1992.

[Lobkovsky et al. 95] Alexander Lobkovsky, Sharon Gentges, Hao Li, David Morse, and Thomas A. Witten. "Scaling Properties of Stretching Ridges in a Crumpled Elastic Sheet." *Science* 270:5241 (1995), 1482–1485.

[Lobkovsky 96] Alexander Lobkovsky. "Boundary Layer Analysis of the Ridge Singularity in a Thin Plate." *Physical Review E* 53:4 (1996), 3750–3759. MR1388237 (97b:73052)

[Mahadevan and Rica 05] Lakshminarayanan Mahadevan and Sergio Rica. "Self-Organized Origami." *Science* 307:5716 (2005), 1740.

[Miura and Tachi 10] Koryo Miura and Tomohiro Tachi. "Synthesis of Rigid-Foldable Cylindrical Polyhedra." *Journal of the International Society for the Interdisciplinary Study of Symmetry* 9 (2010), 204–213.

[Miura 09] Koryo Miura. "The Science of Miura-Ori: A Review." In *Origami^4: Fourth International Meeting of Origami Science, Mathematics, and Education*, edited by Robert J. Lang, pp. 87–99. Wellesley, MA: A K Peters, 2009. MR2590567 (2010h:00025)

[Ohsaki et al. 13] Makoto Ohsaki, Seita Tsuda, and Hidekazu Watanabe. "Optimization of Retractable Structures Utilizing Bistable Compliant Mechanism." *Engineering Structures* 56 (2013), 910–918.

[Schenk and Guest 11] Mark Schenk and Simon D. Guest. "Origami Folding: A Structural Engineering Approach." In *Origami^5: Fifth International Meeting of Origami Science, Mathematics, and Education*, edited by Patsy Wang-Iverson, Robert J. Lang, and Mark Yim, pp. 293–305. Boca Raton, FL: A K Peters/CRC Press, 2011. MR2866909 (2012h:00044)

[Schenk and Guest 13] Mark Schenk and Simon D. Guest. "Geometry of Miura-Folded Metamaterials." *Proceedings of the National Academy of Sciences* 110:9 (2013), 3276–81.

[Tachi and Miura 12] Tomohiro Tachi and Koryo Miura. "Rigid-Foldable Cylinders and Cells." *Journal of the International Association for Shell and Spatial Structures* 53:4 (2012), 217–226.

[Tachi 09a] Tomohiro Tachi. "One-DOF Cylindrical Deployable Structures with Rigid Quadrilateral Panels." In *Proceedings of the IASS Symposium*, pp. 2295–2305. València, Italy: Editorial Universitat Politècnica de València, 2009.

[Tachi 09b] Tomohiro Tachi. "Simulation of Rigid Origami." In *Origami^4: Fourth International Meeting of Origami Science, Mathematics, and Education*, edited by Robert J. Lang, pp. 175–187. Wellesley, MA: A K Peters, 2009.

[Tachi 11] Tomohiro Tachi. "Rigid-Foldable Thick Origami." In *Origami^5: Fifth International Meeting of Origami Science, Mathematics, and Education*, edited by Patsy Wang-Iverson, Robert J. Lang, and Mark Yim, pp. 253–264. Boca Raton, FL: A K Peters/CRC Press, 2011. MR2866909 (2012h:00044)

[Wei et al. 13] Zhiyan Y. Wei, Zengcai V. Guo, Levi Dudte, Haiyi Y. Liang, and Lakshminarayanan Mahadevan. "Geometric Mechanics of Periodic Pleated Origami." *Physical Review Letters* 110:21 (2013), 215501.

[Witten 07] Thomas Witten. "Stress Focusing in Elastic Sheets." *Reviews of Modern Physics* 79:2 (2007), 643–675. MR2326936 (2008e:74052)

UNIVERSITY OF ILLINOIS AT URBANA-CHAMPAIGN, URBANA, ILLINOIS
E-mail address: filipov1@illinois.edu

DEPARTMENT OF GENERAL SYSTEMS STUDIES, THE UNIVERSITY OF TOKYO, JAPAN
E-mail address: tachi@idea.c.u-tokyo.ac.jp

GEORGIA INSTITUTE OF TECHNOLOGY, ATLANTA, GEORGIA
E-mail address: paulino@gatech.edu

Structural Engineering Applications of Morphing Sandwich Structures

Joseph M. Gattas and Zhong You

1. Introduction

1.1. Foldcores and folded sandwich structures. The exploration and application of folded plate geometries at structural and architectural scales has often been with single-layered folded skins [De Temmerman et al. 07, Gioia et al. 12, Weinand 09]. This requires folded plates to resist combined bending, shear, and axial loading. Thus, plate-thickening methods have been developed to ensure adequate strength and stiffness [Tachi 11]. A more efficient load transfer for thin-walled structures is achieved when applied loads are transmitted through in-plane membrane stress with suppressed local buckling behaviours. For example, a typical truss transmits bending and shear loads via axial loading of top, bottom, and central chords, which can therefore be designed as thin-walled hollow sections.

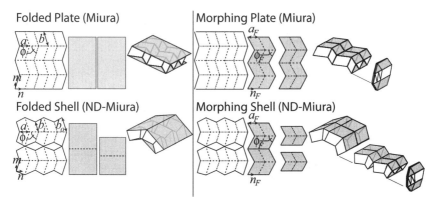

FIGURE 1. Crease patterns and assembled folded (left) and morphing (right) sandwich structures.

This load-carrying mechanism, where bending loads are transmitted as in-plane face stresses and shear loads as in-plane core stresses, has been achieved in origami-core sandwich panels termed *foldcores* [Miura 72, Heimbs 13]. They typically consist of a planar

The authors are grateful to University of Queensland undergraduate students Hayden Warren, Tamsin Cash, Nicola White, Steven Ettema, Samuel Rech, and Acacia Stevenson for their assistance in construction of the prototypes discussed in this work.

Miura core pattern with attached flat top and bottom skins, however curved shells have also been proposed [Nojima and Saito 06, Alekseev 11, Künstler and Trautz 11]. In attaching faces to curved foldcores, a problem is encountered in that continuously curved face sheets do not continuously contact the core. At small scales, adhesive is sufficient to bridge the gap [Gattas and You 14b], but at large scales faceted faces are required to ensure that a continuous core-face bond is created [Gattas and You 14a]. Such faces are also easier to construct, requiring creasing, rather than continuous bending, of face sheets. The folded core and face assemblies are broadly termed *folded sandwich structures* (FSSs) and can be planar plate structures or curved shell structures, with examples of both shown in Figure 1 (left). Folded plates are created as per typical origami-core sandwiches, with flat top and bottom skins attached to a folded core pattern. The shown example uses a Miura core pattern, defined with nomenclature described in [Gattas et al. 13]: A Miura pattern is uniquely defined by side lengths a and b, sector angle ϕ, longitudinal and lateral crease counts m and n, and any folded variable parameter, for example, a dihedral or edge angle. A folded shell is similarly created by attaching faceted face sheets to a curved Miura-derivative pattern, for example, a non-developable (ND) Miura pattern uniquely defined with the parameters described above but with outer and inner side length parameters, b_o and b_i, respectively, replacing b.

1.2. Morphing sandwich structures. An efficient load-carrying mechanism is achieved in FSSs, however the attached faces suppress the deployment mechanism of the folded core. This flaw was demonstrated on the Plate House, an 18 m^2 cardboard transitional shelter that required seven hours for assembly [Gattas 13b]. Deployablility is often a proviso for employing origami-based structural forms [Tachi 10] so this kinematic suppression is problematic. Recent research has proposed layered assemblies of rigid sheets for tubular applications [Miura and Tachi 10, Yasuda et al. 13] and planar morphing foldcore meta-materials [Schenk and Guest 13, Gattas 13a]. These have been combined with FSS arrangements to generate a new class of plate-based mechanisms termed *morphing sandwich structures* (MSSs).

An MSS consists of an FSS in which faceted face sheets are embedded with a sub-pattern, typically a Miura-derivative, which has a kinematic mechanism that preserves the core range of motion between the nearly flat-folded and deployed forms. Morphing plate and shell examples are shown in Figure 1 (right). Core patterns are defined as for FSSs. Face patterns consist of a Miura pattern that spans the partially folded core sheet. The fully unfolded face sheet constrains the core sheet in a deployed configuration but otherwise maintains a compatible mechanism from the deployed to nearly flat-folded forms (see Figure 2). Face parameters can be calculated as dependant parameters from the common side length and edge angle and are designated by the subscript F. Compared with previous types of layered morphing plates where a single face unit was designed to span a single core unit [Schenk and Guest 13], the double span of the morphing sandwich structure allows the central face hinge to be braced against the central core ridge when deployed. In folded shell configurations, the faceting provides additional suppression of the rigid folding mechanism. Thus, a stable deployed morphing structure is achievable.

This chapter presents three early applications of morphing sandwich structures, shown in Figure 2, to highlight the key features of potential use in structural engineering. For each, an explanation of geometric design, fabrication, and deployment is presented. Section 2 discusses the Drop Beam, a modular component of a steel floor system that can deploy and lock under self-weight impact loads. Section 3 discusses the Rhino Shell, a cardboard transitional shelter that forms a rapidly deployed, non-rectilinear structural envelope with

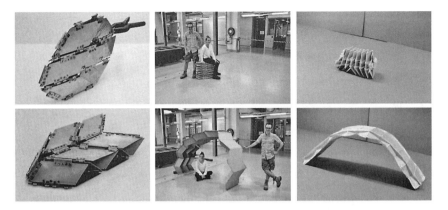

FIGURE 2. Steel Drop Beam (left), cardboard Rhino Shell (middle), and glass-fiber Crease Bridge (right): packaged configurations (top) and deployed configurations (bottom).

few constituent plate sizes. Finally, Section 4 discusses the Crease Bridge, a morphing shell bridge that can function both as a temporary structure and as reinforcement and formwork for a permanent concrete structure.

2. The Drop Beam

2.1. Geometric design. Typical lightweight steel floor systems require multiple components: floor decking, joists, bearers, and various connecting components to attach them all together. The Drop Beam was developed as an example of an alternate morphing sandwich floor system. It possesses multiple beneficial attributes compared to a traditional floor: It can be pre-assembled off-site from a minimum number of components, packaged for transport, and deployed and installed on-site with minimal additional construction effort.

The Drop Beam, shown in Figure 3, was designed as the smallest repeated module of a morphing plate structure and so consists of the components described in Section 1.1. The core sheet is defined by $a = 100$ mm, $b = 200$ mm, $\phi = \pi/3$, $m = 3$, $n = 6$, and lateral edge angle $\eta_Z = \pi/2$ in its final deployed state. A compatible face sheet has the same m, b, and η_Z parameters when completely unfolded, plus $a_F = 141$ mm, $\phi_F = \pi/4$, and $n_F = 3$. It was constructed to investigate three aspects of the morphing sandwich application: whether deployment under out-of-plane self-weight loading was possible, whether hinged modular plates could be built from off-the-shelf components, and whether a self-locking mechanism could be built with the same.

2.2. Fabrication and deployment. The shown prototype was fabricated from mild steel with plate thickness of $t_p = 1$ mm. Eight identical face plates and ten identical core plates were cut to the above plate dimensions. Off-the-shelf steel hinges were then spot-welded to the plates in a staggered arrangement, with crease polarity dictating whether hinges were welded above or below a given plate surface as shown in Figure 3(b, 4). No plate thickness considerations were made because the small maximum plate slenderness ratio of $t_p/a = 1/100$ and the slight centerline eccentricity introduced by hinge locations allowed the prototype to successfully rigidly fold to a nearly flat-folded state as shown in Figure 2 and Figure 3(b, 1). The precise extent to which plate thickness and centerline offset limited the flat-foldability has not yet been investigated. Similarly, the effect that

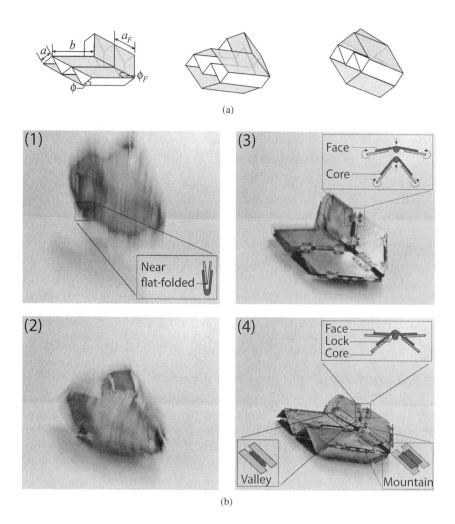

FIGURE 3. Steel Drop Beam. (a) Morphing plate in deployed, partially folded, and nearly flat-folded configurations. (b) Drop deployment, one second time scale.

the eccentricity has on beam strength has not yet been considered. However, the present prototype was sufficient to show that morphing sandwich structures can be fabricated with reasonable ease from off-the-shelf building materials.

Following fabrication, two methods of deployment were tested to simulate on-site beam deployment. First, the prototype was placed on a smooth base sheet in a folded configuration and released to deploy under its own self-weight. Second, the prototype was dropped from a height of 1 m to deploy on impact with the ground, shown in Figure 3(b). In both cases, an out-of-plane loading was applied to face ridges, which generated a coupled in-plane expansion and thus deployed the beam in a manner close to the ideal simulated rigid-mechanism deployment. In the second case, self-locking was achieved with a slightly overlapped face and core hinge: When dropped, the face hinge is forced underneath the core hinge and is secured by the overlap, shown in Figure 3(b). The forces required to

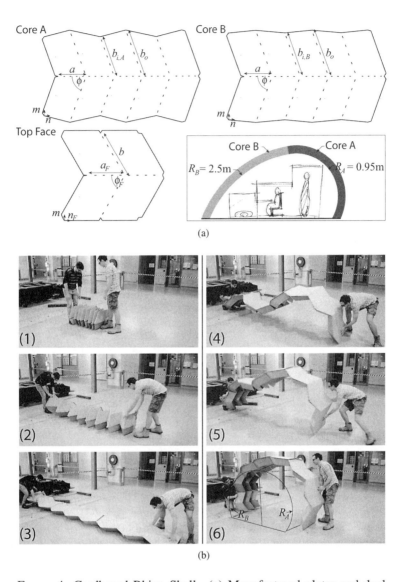

FIGURE 4. Cardboard Rhino Shell. (a) Manufactured plates and dual-curvature section. (b) Stage 1 (in-plane) deployment (left) and Stage 2 (faceting) deployment (right).

deploy, unlock, or lock morphing sandwich structures have not yet been investigated; however, the present prototype was successful in proving the feasibility of on-site deployment and self-locking of steel morphing sandwich structures.

3. The Rhino Shell

3.1. Geometric design. The Rhino Shell [Cash et al. 14] is a cardboard shelter designed to demonstrate MSS capabilities suitable for transitional shelters, i.e., shelters that

generate a rapid and convenient housing solution. Two specific capabilities were of interest: Morphing sandwich shells can form complex structural profiles with few unique
parts, and morphing sandwich shells can be preassembled and rapidly deployed on-site,
as discussed above for the Drop Beam. Neither capability is easily achievable with traditional clad-frame structures. To show the first capability, the Rhino Shell was designed
with a dual-curvature profile consisting of tangential arcs of different radii. Such a profile
forms an efficient habitation envelope in elevation as shown in Figure 4(a, bottom right).
A full-scale shelter with width of 3.5 m and dual-curvature profile with tangential arc radii
of 1.9 m and 5.0 m generates a structural form that meets Shelter Centre transitional shelter design guidelines [Shelter Centre 10] for floor area greater than 18 m^2 and head height
greater than 1.8 m for 65% of the floor area.

Fabrication of a complete full-scale shelter, discussed further below, proved not to be
feasible for the present project, so a half-scale, unit-width shelter was constructed. The
above dual-curvature profile was scaled to tangential arc radii 0.95 m and 2.5 m. This
profile could be matched by a piecewise assembly of two ND-Miura core patterns with
a continuous faceted outside Miura face pattern. Dimensions for each were chosen so
that just three repeated pieces were required for manufacturing: a single face piece that is
constant over the entire profile, plus a core pattern for each of the curvature regions. The
face pattern had parameters of a_F = 275mm, b = 350 mm, ϕ_F = $\pi/3$, m = 3, n_F = 3, and
η_Z = $2\pi/3$ when deployed. The first core pattern, designated Core A with radius 0.95 m,
had parameters of a = 205 mm, $b_{i,A}$ = 300 mm, b_o = 350 mm, ϕ = 70°, m = 3, and n = 6.
The second core pattern, designated Core B with radius 2.5 m, had identical parameters
except with $b_{i,B}$ = 330 mm replacing $b_{i,A}$. Core A, Core B, and the face parts are shown
in Figure 4(a). Eight face plates, four Core A plates, and four Core B plates are required
to assemble the complete Rhino Shell. The use of a uniform face pattern constraint across
the dual-curvature effectively decouples the two core patterns so the boundary between the
two is discrete. For future prototypes, a constraint could instead be applied such that core
patterns are continuous across the boundary. This is possible with the Miura-derivative
piecewise assembly process described in [Gattas and You 15].

3.2. Fabrication and deployment. Rhino Shell plates were cut on a 1.2 m × 2.4 m
CNC router from 6 mm thick cardboard. Following manufacture, core and face plates were
stitched together along a row of matched holes embedded along the plate ridges. For the
present prototype, this stitching was simply done by hand with string. Once stitched, the
Rhino Shell could be packaged in a compact nearly flat-folded package, shown in Figure
4(b, 1). CNC fabrication took approximately 2 hours and subsequent stitching took two
people approximately 3 hours, so total assembly and packaging took approximately five
hours.

A deployment of the Rhino Shell prototype is shown in Figure 4(b). For morphing
shells of this type, deployment happens in two stages. Stage 1 consists of an in-plane
expansion with a single-DOF mechanism controlled by the continuous Miura face sheet.
Stage 2 consists of kinking the face facets until the discontinuous core segments bear on
each other, with the kinking suppressing the mechanism and generating a stable structure. Deployment time was approximately 15 seconds for two people, and a similar time
is required for packaging. The prototype thus successfully demonstrated the morphing
shell's most useful features for transitional shelter application: tool-less and rapid on-site
deployment, space-efficient packaged configuration, and a layered plate form that provides
insulation, structural redundancy, and security. Ongoing research is investigating morphing
shell strength, stiffness, and alternative construction methods and materials.

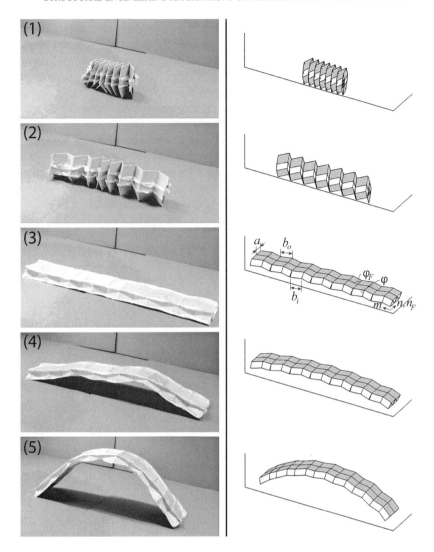

FIGURE 5. GFRP Crease Bridge. Prototype folding motion (left) and simulated folding motion (right).

4. The Crease Bridge

4.1. Geometric design. The use of origami patterns for concrete formwork has been proposed previously [Smith et al. 13] as a cheap means to encase complex geometric forms. The continuous internal channels of morphing sandwich structures mean that they can similarly be used as a type of origami formwork. As they also possess a structural capacity and stability in their standard (non-concrete filled) form, additional functional attributes beyond simple encasement are possible. First, morphing shells could function as a lower load bearing structure prior to concrete in-fill. Second, morphing shells could partially or fully self-prop during concrete curing. Finally, if top and bottom face ridges are suitably fixed to core ridges, morphing shells could function as structural reinforcement and confinement for the encased concrete, similar to concrete confined by fiber-reinforced polymers.

Successful harnessing of these attributes would address problems with emergency infrastructure used following natural disasters, specifically the need to provide temporary infrastructure for a rapid return to normal community operation, without discouraging communities from upgrading or rebuilding their own permanent infrastructure. An in-depth structural feasibility study of such a formwork is beyond the scope of the present investigation; however, a small-scale prototype was constructed to demonstrate the feasibility of deployment, propping, and in-filling of such a system. Termed the Crease Bridge [Ettema et al. 14], the prototype is a concept application whereby a morphing shell structure forms a portable bridge that can be instantly deployed in flooded regions for emergency pedestrian and light vehicle thoroughfare (access/evacuation) and following emergency use, can be used to encase and reinforce a permanent concrete bridge. A ND-Miura morphing shell geometry was used with components as discussed in Section 1.2. This was sufficient to fit a uniformly curved arch profile while providing a continuous faceted top surface to function as a bridge deck. The initial prototype was constructed at a small scale with a 1200 mm span and 200 mm rise. The corresponding morphing shell core pattern had parameters $a = 53$ mm, $b_i = 91$ mm, $b_o = 95$ mm, $\phi = 80°$, $m = 15$, $n = 6$, and lateral dihedral angle $\theta_A = 157°$ when fully deployed. Continuous face patterns then had parameters $a_F = 71$ mm, $\phi_F = 75°$, and $n_F = 3$. The outside face additionally had $b_F = b_o = 95$ mm, and the inside face had $b_F = b_i = 91$ mm, shown in Figure 5.

4.2. Fabrication and deployment. Each layer of the Crease Bridge was composed of a continuous glass-fiber reinforced plastic sheet (GFRP). In a full-scale application, face GFRP can act to resist bending loads, front and back side GFRP can resist lateral loads, and all GFRP acts as confinement and protection for the concrete. Minimal additional steel would therefore be required to create durable and efficient GFRP-reinforced concrete structures. Each layer of the present Crease Bridge was manufactured with selective resin impregnation similar to that described in [Saito et al. 14]. A mask was applied to keep hinge regions free of resin, such that they remained soft and foldable relative to the stiff, resin-impregnated panel regions. Face and core layers were then joined together with a simple hand-stitching method to create the morphing assembly. Similar to the Rhino Shell, initial deployment was in two stages: in-plane expansion and subsequent facet-forming lifting, shown in Figure 5. The Crease Bridge had an additional stage whereby in-fill was pumped into the top channel (between core and top face) and allowed to cure to form a final, permanent configuration. In a full-scale application this would be a concrete, however the present prototype simply used expanding foam. The prototype was seen to be stable after lifting and propping and after in-filling.

Figure 5 also shows a comparison between the prototype (left) and idealized, rigid folding motion (right). It can be seen that the prototype reaches a far steeper curvature than designed. A similar phenomenon was observed in the Rhino Shell. This was attributed to semi-rigid plates, semi-flexible hinges, and construction tolerances. Investigations into the resolution of these real-world considerations with existing rigid origami solutions has begun [Schenk and Guest 11], but it is an ongoing research problem that is of crucial importance for full-scale origami-based structures. Other research questions also remain pertaining to the structural capacity of the morphing shell as concrete reinforcement and the use of alternate folded formwork geometries.

5. Conclusion

This paper has presented a brief overview of the geometric design, fabrication, and deployment of a set of prototypes developed to demonstrate particular capabilities of morphing sandwich structures. The primary focus has been capabilities suitable for structural engineering applications. The Drop Beam is a component of a lightweight steel floor system capable of self-deployment and self-locking from drop impact. The Rhino Shell is a cardboard shelter with an extremely rapid deployment time, plus a complex dual-curvature sectional profile that is difficult to economically construct as a traditional clad-frame structure. Finally, the Crease Bridge is a concept GFRP arch that can be used in a temporary capacity or in-filled with concrete to create a structurally efficient and durable structure.

References

[Alekseev 11] K. A. Alekseev. "Geometrical Simulation of Regular and Irregular Folded Structures." *Russian Aeronautics (Iz VUZ)* 54:1 (2011), 84–88.

[Cash et al. 14] T. Cash, H. Warren, N. White, and J. M. Gattas. "Rhino Shell: A Flat-Pack and Rapidly-Deployed Morphing Shell Transitional Shelter." http://www.jamesdysonaward.org/projects/rhino-shell, 2014.

[De Temmerman et al. 07] N. De Temmerman, M. Mollaert, T. Van Mele, and L. De Laet. "Design and Analysis of a Foldable Mobile Shelter System." *International Journal of Space Structures* 22:3 (2007), 161–168.

[Ettema et al. 14] S. Ettema, S. Rech, A. Stevenson, and J. M. Gattas. "Crease Bridge: Temporary Folding Infrastructure that Converts to Permanent Structural Concrete Formwork." http://www.jamesdysonaward.org/projects/crease-bridge, 2014.

[Gattas and You 15] J. M. Gattas and Z. You. "Geometric assembly of rigid-foldable morphing sandwich structures." *Engineering Structures* 94 (2015), 149–159.

[Gattas and You 14a] J. M. Gattas and Z. You. "Folded Shell Structures." World Patent Application WO2014170650. http://worldwide.espacenet.com/publicationDetails/biblio?FT=D&CC=WO&NR=2014170650A2. 2014.

[Gattas and You 14b] J. M. Gattas and Z. You. "Quasi-static Impact Response of Single-Curved Foldcore Sandwich Shells." In *ASME 2014 International Design Engineering Technical Conferences and Computers and Information in Engineering Conference*, pp. V05BT08A044–V05BT08A044. New York: American Society of Mechanical Engineers, 2014.

[Gattas et al. 13] J. M. Gattas, W. Wu, and Z. You. "Miura-Base Rigid Origami: Parametrisations of First-level Derivative and Piecewise Geometries." *Journal of Mechanical Design* 135:11 (2013), 111011.

[Gattas 13a] J. M. Gattas. "Morphing Origami Panels: Geometry and Construction." In *Proceedings of the 15th Young Researchers' Conference, 15th March 2013*, pp. 40–41. London: The Institution of Structural Engineers, 2013.

[Gattas 13b] J. M. Gattas. "Plate House: A Fast, Flexible, Flatpack Shelter." YouTube video, https://www.youtube.com/watch?v=JwUXHOYXQ1M, 2013.

[Gioia et al. 12] F. Gioia, D. Dureisseix, R. Motro, and B. Maurin. "Design and Analysis of a Foldable/Unfoldable Corrugated Architectural Curved Envelop." *Journal of Mechanical Design*, 134:3 (2012), 031003.

[Heimbs 13] S. Heimbs. "Foldcore Sandwich Structures and Their Impact Behaviour: An Overview." In *Dynamic Failure of Composite and Sandwich Structures SE 11*, Solid Mechanics and Its Applications 192, pp. 491–544. Houten: Springer Netherlands, 2013.

[Künstler and Trautz 11] A. Künstler and M. Trautz. "Deployable Folding Patterns Using Stiff Plate Elements." *Bautechnik* 88:2 (2011), 86–93.

[Miura and Tachi 10] K. Miura and T. Tachi. "Synthesis of Rigid-Foldable Cylindrical Polyhedra." *Journal of the International Society for the Interdisciplinary Study of Symmetry* 9 (2010), 204–213.

[Miura 72] K. Miura. "Zeta-Core Sandwich: Its Concept and Realization." *Inst. of Space and Aeronautical Science, University of Tokyo, Report* 480 (1972), 137–164.

[Nojima and Saito 06] T. Nojima and K. Saito. "Development of Newly Designed Ultra-light Core Structures." *JSME International Journal, Series A: Solid Mechanics and Material Engineering* 49:1 (2006), 38–42.

[Saito et al. 14] K. Saito, S. Pellegrino, and T. Nojima. "Manufacture of Arbitrary Cross-Section Composite Honeycomb Cores Based on Origami Techniques." *Journal of Mechanical Design* 136:5 (2014), 051011.

[Schenk and Guest 11] M. Schenk and S. D. Guest. "Origami Folding: A Structural Engineering Approach." In *Origami⁵: Fifth International Meeting of Origami Science, Mathematics, and Education*, edited by Patsy

Wang-Iverson, Robert J. Lang, and Mark Yim, pp. 293–305. Boca Raton, FL: A K Peters/CRC Press, 2011. MR2866909 (2012h:00044)

[Schenk and Guest 13] M. Schenk and S. D. Guest. "Geometry of Miura-Folded Metamaterials." *Proceedings of the National Academy of Sciences* 110:9 (2013), 3276–3281.

[Shelter Centre 10] Shelter Centre. *Transitional Shelter Standards 10b*. Geneva: Shelter Centre, 2010.

[Smith et al. 13] A. Smith, O. O'leary, and M. Kaczynski. "Crease, Fold, Pour: Advancing Flexible Formwork with Digital Fabrication and Origami Folding." http://vimeo.com/61861393, 2013.

[Tachi 10] T. Tachi. "Geometric Considerations for the Design of Rigid Origami Structures." In *Proceedings of the International Association for Shell and Spatial Structures (IASS) Symposium 2010, Shanghai, China*, pp. 771–782. Madrid: IASS, 2010.

[Tachi 11] T. Tachi. "Rigid-Foldable Thick Origami." In *Origami^5: Fifth International Meeting of Origami Science, Mathematics, and Education*, edited by Patsy Wang-Iverson, Robert J. Lang, and Mark Yim, pp. 253–264. Boca Raton, FL: A K Peters/CRC Press, 2011. MR2866909 (2012h:00044)

[Weinand 09] Y. Weinand. "Innovative Timber Constructions." *Journal of the International Association for Shell and Spatial Structures* 50:2 (2009), 111–120.

[Yasuda et al. 13] A. Yasuda, T. Yein, T. Tachi, K. Miura, and M. Taya. "Folding Behaviour of Tachi-Miura Polyhedron Bellows." *Proceedings of the Royal Society A: Mathematical, Physical and Engineering Science* 469:2159 (2013), 20130351.

SCHOOL OF CIVIL ENGINEERING, UNIVERSITY OF QUEENSLAND, AUSTRALIA
E-mail address: j.gattas@uq.edu.au

DEPARTMENT OF ENGINEERING SCIENCE, UNIVERSITY OF OXFORD, UNITED KINGDOM

Toward Optimization of Stiffness and Flexibility of Rigid,
Flat-Foldable Origami Structures,
Evgueni T. Filipov. Tomohiro Tachi, and Glaucio H. Paulino

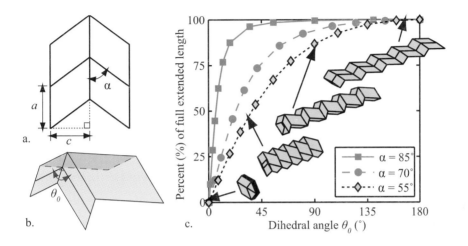

FIGURE 1. Construction of a rigid- and flat-foldable origami tube: (a) geometric definition of a single Miura-ori cell, (b) folding configuration for the Miura-ori cell, and (c) dihedral angle θ_0 versus tube length as a percent (%) of the maximum extension length for tubes with $\alpha = 55°$, $\alpha = 70°$, and $\alpha = 85°$. The tube with $\alpha = 55°$ is shown folded at $\theta_0 = 2°$, 35°, 90°, and 170°. (Page 411)

Structural Engineering Applications of Morphing Sandwich Structures,
Joseph M. Gattas and Zhong You

FIGURE 2. Steel Drop Beam (left), cardboard Rhino Shell (middle), and glass-fiber Crease Bridge (right): packaged configurations (top) and deployed configurations (bottom). (Page 423)

Thin-Walled Deployable Grid Structures,
Jonathan Ho and Zhong You

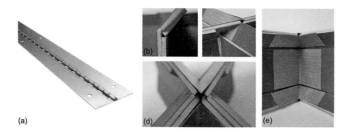

FIGURE 11. Hinge construction: (a) a steel piano hinge, and (b, c, d, e) paper hinges in the joints of a folding thick-walled grid structure. (Page 444)

Magnetic Self-Assembly of Three-Dimensional Microstructures,
Eiji Iwase and Isao Shimoyama

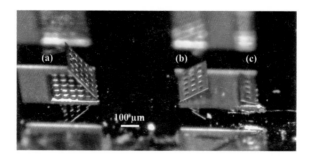

FIGURE 3. Fold-up angles of different-shaped structures in an external magnetic field of 5.0 kA/m. The length of each microplate structure is (a) 300 μm, (b) 200 μm, and (c) 100 μm. (Page 474)

Planning Motions for Shape-Memory Alloy Sheets,
M. Ghosh, D. Tomkins, J. Denny, S. Rodriguez, M. Morales, and N. M. Amato

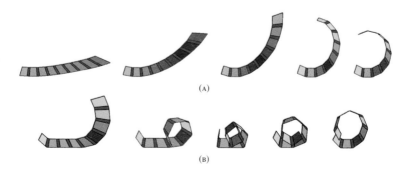

FIGURE 7. Intermediate folding configurations of Tube SMA robot in Figure 6(a) (a) without gravity and (b) with gravity. (Page 509)

*oricreate: Modeling Framework for Design and Manufacturing
of Folded Plate Structures*,
Rostislav Chudoba, Jan van der Woerd, and Josef Hegger

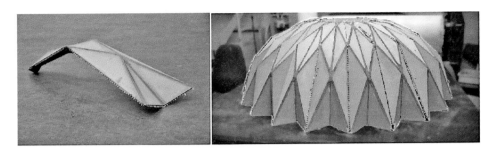

FIGURE 10. Oridome realized using 16 folded segments. (Page 534)

Rotational Erection System (RES): Origami Extended with Cuts,
Yoshinobu Miyamoto

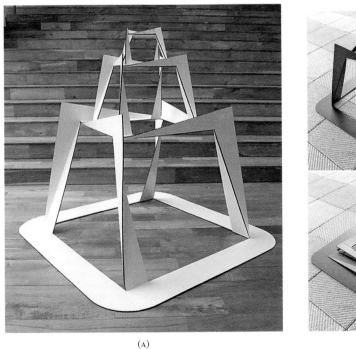

(A)

(B)

FIGURE 9. Meter scale samples: (a) $120 \times 120 \times 120$, $t = 0.5$ cm, and (b)
$57 \times 57 \times 37$, $t = 0.5$ cm. (Page 544)

Folding Perspectives: Joys and Uses of 3D Anamorphic Origami,
Yves Klett

FIGURE 4. Orbit of a real-world anam-ori with alternatingly colored rows. The images were taken with a focal length of 44 mm (35 mm equivalent) at 45° inclination. (Page 585)

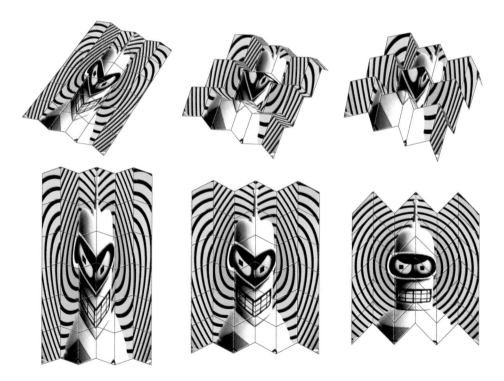

FIGURE 11. Folding of one of our favorite robots on a Miura grid: perspective view (top), and top view as intended for the undistorted final image (bottom). See also [Klett 13b]. (Page 590)

Master Peace: An Evolution of Monumental Origami, Kevin Box and Robert J. Lang

(a)

Figure 5: (a) *White Bison* in 12-inch and 20-inch lengths. (Page 605)

(b)

Figure 7: (b) *Flight of Folds*, full size. (Page 607)

(A)

(B)

FIGURE 12. (a) Final assembly on site. (b) The finished *Hero's Horse*. (Page 610)

FIGURE 12. Three bracelets. Inside-out: copper, gold-plated silver, and silver. (Page 619)

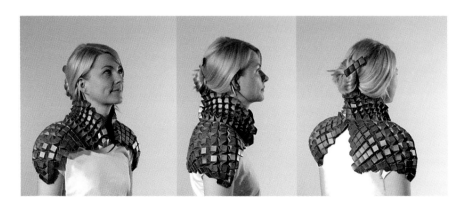

FIGURE 22. Shoulder cape. (Page 623)

FIGURE 3. Union Station. (Page 627)

FIGURE 4. Level-three Snowflake Sponge. (Page 628)

The Kindergarten Origametria Programme,
Miri Golan and John Oberman

FIGURE 9. Collage of six examples of the same folded shape, perceived as different subjects by different children. (Page 675)

Using Origami to Enrich Mathematical Understanding of Self Similarity and Fractals,
Ali Bahmani, Kiumars Sharif, and Andrew Hudson

FIGURE 4. Fourth iteration of SierpinsQube fractal pyramid. (Image courtesy of Ali Bahmani.) (Page 728)

Sound-Insulating Performance of Origami-Based Sandwich Trusscore Panels

Sachiko Ishida, Hiroaki Morimura, and Ichiro Hagiwara

1. Introduction

The objective of this study is to evaluate the sound-insulating performance of trusscore panels using a vibro-acoustic finite element method. Also, a theoretical representation of the transmission loss (TL) of trusscore panels is analyzed.

Lightweight but highly rigid panels are essential materials for the construction of industrial products such as space structures and vehicles, including airplanes, cars, and trains. Honeycomb panels are the most versatile materials for this purpose and have fulfilled these requirements for decades because of their high stiffness-to-weight ratios. However, because honeycomb panels must be manufactured by gluing separate panels, there are fatal drawbacks such as peeling off due to unexpected heavy loads, which can lead to catastrophic damage to the products constructed with the panels. In addition, such glued structures are generally weak under heat. To overcome these shortcomings, various types of origami-based core panels have been developed [Miura 71, Saito and Nojima 07, Fischer et al. 09, Schenk and Guest 09, Klett and Drechsler 11, Schenk and Guest 13]. For example, Saito and Nojima developed trusscore panels that are based on a spatial tessellation technique that fills space with polyhedrons [Saito and Nojima 07] and are manufactured by pressing metallic flat plates and welding the pressed plates [Saito et al. 09a]. Trusscore panels require welding rather than gluing and are therefore expected to be resistant to heat, while maintaining sufficiently less weight and high rigidity [Saito et al. 09b].

Highly rigid panels could also potentially serve as partitions to separate rooms, because the stiffness of a partition improves its sound insulation performance. Methods to measure sound insulation performance have been standardized by both International Standards (ISO) [ISO 14] and Japanese Industrial Standards (JIS) [JIS 00a, JIS 00b] for years, and arbitrarily designed panels can be used as partitions. Ng and Hui measured the sound insulation of honeycomb panels according to ISO standards and compared their measured and theoretical TLs [Ng and Hui 08]. However, numerical methods are still under development. Recent papers have demonstrated the computed TLs of various partitions, such as double-leaf partitions and sandwich panels, including honeycomb panels, using vibro-acoustic finite element analysis [Franco et al. 07, Guerich and Assaf 13, Qian et al. 13, Xin et al. 13]. Qian et al. compared the computed TL of sandwich panels with the measured and theoretical TLs and concluded that the agreement was reasonable [Qian et al. 13]. However, the effect of the mass has been the only focus of theory, and the relationship between panel stiffness and sound insulation has not been discussed.

In this paper, the TL is computed using MSC Nastran, a versatile software for finite element analysis, to evaluate the sound insulation performance of sandwich panels. In particular, the effect of the panel stiffness on sound insulation is focused on in order to evaluate the potential of highly rigid panels as partitions. Next, the characteristics of the computed TL are analyzed and compared with the theoretical TL for single-leaf and double-leaf partitions. Finally, it is concluded that the sound-insulating performance is strongly influenced by the panel stiffness in the low-frequency region and that even geometrically complex sandwich panels follow the theoretical formulation of TL for a simple single-leaf panel with mass and stiffness equivalent to those of the complex panels.

2. Theory of Sound Insulation

2.1. Definition of sound transmission loss. The sound transmission through a partition between adjacent chambers is considered. Let us denote the total sound power incident on the partition and the power transmitted to the other chamber through the partition as I_i and I_t, respectively. Then, the TL is given by

$$(2.1) \qquad \mathrm{TL} = 10 \log_{10} \frac{I_i}{I_t}.$$

The incident power can be expressed by

$$(2.2) \qquad I_i = \frac{c}{4} S E_1,$$

where S is the area of the partition, E_1 is the energy density in the incident chamber, and c is the sound velocity. The transmitted power is also expressed by

$$(2.3) \qquad I_t = \frac{c}{4} A_2 E_2,$$

where A_2 is the equivalent absorption area of the receiving chamber and E_2 is the energy density in the receiving chamber. Substituting Equations (2.2) and (2.3) into Equation (2.1) yields

$$(2.4) \qquad \mathrm{TL} = 10 \log_{10} \frac{E_1}{E_2} - 10 \log_{10} \frac{A_2}{S}.$$

The energy densities E_1 and E_2 are obtained by

$$(2.5) \qquad E_i = \frac{\dfrac{1}{2}\rho \displaystyle\sum_{j=1}^{N_i} \dfrac{p_j^2}{\rho^2 c^2} V_j}{\displaystyle\sum_{j=1}^{N_i} V_j} \qquad (i = 1, 2),$$

where ρ is the density of the medium, p_j is the sound pressure at node j, V_j is the volume around node j, and N_i ($i = 1, 2$) is the number of nodes in the incident and receiving chambers, respectively.

2.2. Theoretical normal incidence transmission loss for single-leaf and double-leaf partitions. Kusuda and Inoue reported that the TL for a single-leaf partition is formulated as

$$(2.6) \qquad \mathrm{TL} = 10 \log_{10} \left[1 + \left(\frac{\pi m f}{\rho c} \right)^2 \left\{ 1 - \left(\frac{f_r}{f} \right)^2 \right\}^2 \right],$$

where f is the frequency and m is the mass of the partition per unit area [Kusuda and Inoue 05], and f_r is the resonant frequency of the partition given by

$$f_r = \frac{1}{2\pi} \sqrt{\frac{k}{m}}.$$

In this study, Equation (2.6) is considered to be the theoretical TL for a single-leaf partition. For the relatively high-frequency region where $f \gg f_r$, with $\rho = 1.29$ kg/m^3 and $c = 340$ m/s in air, Equation (2.6) reduces to

(2.7) $$TL = 20 \log_{10} mf - 42.5.$$

Equation (2.7) shows that the TL depends on the mass, excluding the effect of the stiffness of the partition. It is the so-called *normal incidence mass law* [Fahy 01]. On the other hand, for the relatively low-frequency region where $f \ll f_r$, Equation (2.6) can be approximately expressed as

(2.8) $$TL = 20 \log_{10} mf - 42.5 + 10 \log_{10} \left[1 - \left(\frac{f_r}{f}\right)^2 \right]^2.$$

Equation (2.8) implies that the stiffness of the partition $k\ (= m(2\pi f_r)^2)$ is also an important factor to determine the TL. Hence, Equation (2.8) can be considered a *stiffness law*.

For double-leaf partitions, the TL is formulated as

(2.9) $$TL = 10 \log_{10} \left[1 + 4\left(\frac{\omega m}{2\rho c}\right)^2 \left\{ \cos\frac{\omega d}{c} - \left(\frac{\omega m}{2\rho c}\right) \sin\frac{\omega d}{c} \right\}^2 \right],$$

where d is the distance between the parallel double-leaf partitions and $\omega\ (= 2\pi f)$ is the angular frequency [Ohta 90, pp. 183–188, 191–194]. Equation (2.9) shows the mass law for double-leaf partitions. To consider the effect of the partition stiffness on sound transmission, we add the last term of Equation (2.8) to Equation (2.9) and define the TL for the double-leaf partitions as follows:

(2.10) $$TL = 10 \log_{10} \left[1 + 4\left(\frac{\omega m}{2\rho c}\right)^2 \left\{ \cos\frac{\omega d}{c} - \left(\frac{\omega m}{2\rho c}\right) \sin\frac{\omega d}{c} \right\}^2 \right] + 10 \log_{10} \left[1 - \left(\frac{f_r}{f}\right)^2 \right]^2.$$

If $\cos(\omega d/c) = (\omega m/(2\rho c)) \sin(\omega d/c)$ is satisfied, the first term of Equation (2.10) approaches zero, and therefore, the TL significantly decreases. This condition can also be represented by the following form:

(2.11) $$f_{rm} = \frac{1}{2\pi} \sqrt{\frac{2\rho c^2}{md}}.$$

The frequency f_{rm} is called the *mass-air-mass resonance frequency*.

As shown above, the theoretical TLs for geometrically simple partitions, such as single-leaf and double-leaf partitions, can be formulated and have been reported in textbooks and papers. However, the theoretical TLs for complex partitions, including sandwich panels, have not been formulated in a rigorous manner.

3. Origami-Based Sandwich Trusscore Panels

Saito and Nojima developed trusscore panels, which are designed based on a spatial tessellation technique that fills space with polyhedrons and are manufactured by pressing metallic flat plates and welding two pressed plates (or one pressed plate and a flat plate) to each other to make a sandwich [Saito and Nojima 07, Saito et al. 09a]. Saito et al. reported that trusscore panels are characterized by high stiffness [Saito et al. 09b]. Figure 1 shows

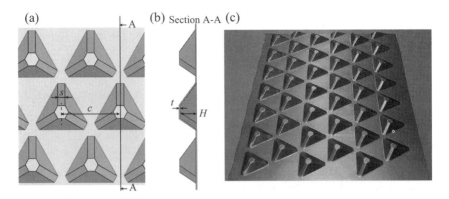

FIGURE 1. Geometry of the trusscore panel and prototypes: (a) Top view, where c = pitch length (65 mm) and s = fillet width (8 mm). (b) Cross-sectional view at Section A-A, where H = height of the panel (18 mm) and t = thickness of the plate (0.514 mm). (c) A pressed panel made of steel. Figure 1(c) was extracted from [Saito et al. 09b]

Material	Young's modulus (N/m^2)	Density (kg/m^3)	Poisson ratio
Steel	2.0×10^{11}	7.9×10^3	0.3

TABLE 1. Specifications of panel material.

the geometry of the panels and a prototype made of steel. The pitch length, the fillet width, the height, and the thickness of the panel are 65 mm, 8 mm, 18 mm, and 0.514 mm, respectively. In this study, the sound insulation performance of trusscore panels will be numerically investigated and compared with theoretical values.

4. Numerical Computation and Discussion

4.1. Numerical model. For numerical simulation, the trusscore panel mentioned in Section 3 was modeled as shown in Figure 2(a). The panel was 210 mm × 210 mm, and the structure consisted of a pressed panel firmly jointed with a flat panel to make a sandwich. The trusscore panel was set up between two adjacent chambers, each 0.9 m in length, as a partition (Figure 2(b)). The trusscore panel was simply supported at all the edges, and the sounds from the sound source installed at the left wall of the left chamber or the incident chamber were incident normally to the panel. The panel and air domains (i.e., two chambers and hollows in the panel) were meshed, and nodes at the same coordinates in the panel and air were coupled. Thus, vibro-acoustic computation was performed to consider the interaction between the vibration of the plate and the sound transmission in air. Then, the computed sound pressures p_j at every node in the chambers were summed up to acquire the energy density by Equation (2.5). The acquired energy density was substituted into Equation (2.4). However, the second term of Equation (2.4) was unknown. To acquire the TL, the second term was considered as a correction term, and its value was adjusted based on the theoretical TL. The material of the panel was steel, whose specifications are shown in Table 1.

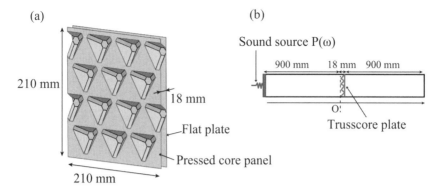

FIGURE 2. Dimensions and setup of the trusscore panel.

4.2. Numerical results and discussion. Figure 3 shows the numerically acquired TL of the trusscore panel with the solid line. The theoretical TL shown by the dashed line is that of a single-leaf plate, as given by Equation (2.8), whose mass and stiffness are essentially equivalent to those of the trusscore panel (i.e., the material was not steel). The TL of the trusscore panel dramatically decreases around 530 Hz, corresponding to the first natural frequency of the trusscore panel as shown in the theoretical TL. For comparison, the dotted line in Figure 3 shows the theoretical TL for double-leaf plates with essentially the same mass and stiffness as those of the trusscore panel. The theoretical TL for the virtual double-leaf plates has two dips: One is around 530 Hz, the first natural frequency, because the virtual plates have a stiffness equivalent to that of the trusscore panel, and the other is around 325 Hz, which corresponds to the mass-air-mass resonance frequency given by Equation (2.11). This result demonstrates that the computed TL of the trusscore panel exactly corresponds to the theoretical one for the equivalent single-leaf plate. Even if the trusscore panel had hollows between the plates, the TL does not follow the theoretical one for the corresponding double-leaf plates, as can be seen in the appearance of the mass-air-mass resonance frequency. We conclude that the hollows do not affect the sound insulation because the plates are firmly jointed, and therefore, the acoustic energy cannot be damped by air in the hollows.

Figure 3 also demonstrates that the trusscore panel can insulate sound effectively in the low-frequency region, which was below 400 Hz in this example. Note that the region depends on the first natural frequency of the panel. The effectiveness results from the mechanical properties of the panel; in the low-frequency region, the high stiffness, which is the third term in Equation (2.8), is more dominant than the first term. Thus, for effective sound insulation in the low-frequency region, designing stiff partitions is one likely solution, because this characteristic makes the first natural frequency higher and the stiffness-dependent region wider. The trusscore panel shown in Figure 2 will be considered as a reference hereafter. The experimental trusscore panel had several design parameters, as shown in Figure 1(a,b), and it was possible to optimize them to obtain the stiffest possible panel while still having a mass equivalent to that of the reference trusscore panel. Figure 4 shows that optimizing the trusscore panel can increase the first natural frequency to 1730 Hz and improve the sound-insulating performance below 1200 Hz compared to that of the reference trusscore panel. In addition, Figure 4 shows the computational and theoretical TLs for a honeycomb panel, which is a well-known, versatile sandwich panel.

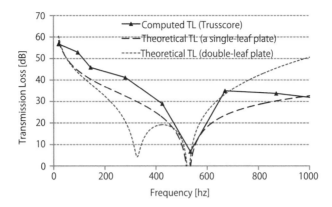

FIGURE 3. Transmission loss of the trusscore panel; the theoretical TLs for the corresponding single-leaf and double-leaf plates are also given, assuming that they have mass and stiffness equivalent to those of the trusscore panel.

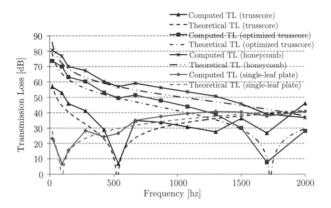

FIGURE 4. Transmission loss of the trusscore panels, honeycomb panel, and single-leaf plate; the theoretical TLs for the corresponding single-leaf plates are also given, assuming that they have mass and stiffness equivalent to those of the panels.

In this study, a honeycomb panel with mass and panel height equivalent to those of the reference trusscore panel was modeled as an example. As a result, the honeycomb panel was much stiffer than even the optimized trusscore panel, and therefore, its TL was higher than that of the trusscore panel. The theoretical TL is given by Equation (2.8) for a single-leaf plate as well as for the trusscore panel because each component of a honeycomb panel is also firmly jointed, even if the honeycomb panel has hollows. In the case of a single-leaf plate with a mass equivalent to that of the reference trusscore panel, the TL was much lower in the low-frequency region because the plate was not sufficiently stiff. As conventional sound-proofing techniques, such as the usage of sound absorbing materials, are not effective in the low-frequency region, trusscore and honeycomb panels could both be valid solutions.

In this study, the correction term of Equation (2.4) was uniformly -6 dB because the corrected TL agreed well with the theoretical TL for a single-leaf plate. However, the analytical meaning of -6 dB has not yet been interpreted. This challenge is a topic for future work.

5. Conclusion

In this paper, the sound-insulating performance of trusscore panels, which are origami-based sandwich panels, was numerically evaluated using a vibro-acoustic finite element method. The following is a summary of the results:

(1) The TL of trusscore panels follows the theoretical TL of the corresponding single-leaf plate even if the panels have inner hollows because the panels are firmly jointed. Therefore, the acoustic energy cannot be damped by air in the hollows. This discussion can be also applied to honeycomb panels.

(2) Trusscore panels can insulate low-frequency sounds effectively because of their high rigidity. As conventional sound-proofing techniques, such as the use of sound absorbing materials, are not effective in the low-frequency region, trusscore and honeycomb panels could both be valid solutions.

References

[Fahy 01] Frank Fahy. *Foundations of Engineering Acoustics*. Burlington, MA: Elsevier Academic Press, 2001.

[Fischer et al. 09] Sebastian Fischer, Klaus Drechsler, Sebastian Kilchert, and Alastair Johnson. "Mechanical Tests for Foldcore Base Material Properties." *Composites: Part A*, 40 (2009), 1941–1952.

[Franco et al. 07] Francesco Franco, Kenneth A. Cunefare, and Massimo Ruzzene. "Structural-Acoustic Optimization of Sandwich Panels." *Transactions of the ASME, Journal of Vibration and Acoustics*, 129 (2007), 330–140.

[Guerich and Assaf 13] Mohamed Guerich and Samir Assaf. "Optimization of Noise Transmission through Sandwich Structures." *Journal of Vibration and Acoustics* 135 (2013), 051010.

[ISO 14] ISO. "ISO 16283-1:2014: Acoustics—Field Measurement of Sound Insulation in Buildings and of Building Elements—Part 1: Airborne Sound Insulation." *ISO Standards Catalogue*, http://www.iso.org/iso/home/store/catalogue_tc/catalogue_detail.htm?csnumber=55997, February 15, 2014.

[JIS 00a] Japanese Industrial Standards Committee. "JIS A1416: Acoustics-Method for Laboratory Measurement of Airborne Sound Insulation of Building Elements." http://www.jisc.go.jp/app/pager?id=340798, Janaury 7, 2000. (In Japanese.)

[JIS 00b] Japanese Industrial Standards Committee. "JIS A1417: Acoustics-Field Measurement of Airborne Sound Insulation of Buildings." http://www.jisc.go.jp/app/pager?id=340803, Janaury 7, 2000. (In Japanese.)

[Klett and Drechsler 11] Yves Klett and Klaus Drechsler. "Designing Technical Tessellations." In *Origami⁵: Fifth International Meeting of Origami Science, Mathematics, and Education*, edited by Patsy Wang-Iverson, Robert J. Lang, and Mark Yim, 305–322. Boca Raton, FL: A K Peters/CRC Press, 2011. MR2866909 (2012h:00044)

[Kusuda and Inoue 05] Shinya Kusuda and Yasuo Inoue. "Sound Transmission Loss of Stiffness Law for Low Frequency Noise." In *Proceedings of the 15th Symposium on Environmental Engineering*, 39–42. Tokyo: Japan Soceity of Mechanical Engineers, 2005. (In Japanese.)

[Miura 71] Koryo Miura. "Structural Form and Geometry." *Journal of the Japan Society of Mechanical Engineers* 19:211 (1971), 36–47. (In Japanese.)

[Ng and Hui 08] C. F. Ng and C. K. Hui. "Low Frequency Sound Insulation Using Stiffness Control with Honeycomb Panels." *Applied Acoustics* 69 (2008), 293–301.

[Ohta 90] Mitsuo Ohta. *Kiso Butsuri Onkyo Kogaku*. Tokyo: Asakura Publishing Co., Ltd., 1990. (In Japanese.)

[Qian et al. 13] Zhongchang Qian, Daoqing Chang, Bilong Liu, and Ke Liu. "Prediction of Sound Transmission Loss for Finite Sandwich Panels Based on a Test Procedure on Beam Elements." *Journal of Vibration and Acoustics* 135 (2013), 061005.

[Saito and Nojima 07] Kazuya Saito and Taketoshi Nojima. "Development of Light-Weight Rigid Core Panels." *Journal of Solid Mechanics and Materials Engineering* 1:9 (2007), 1097–1104.

[Saito et al. 09a] Kazuya Saito, Kota Takeda, Sunao Tokura, and Ichiro Hagiwara. "Relation between Geometrical Patterns and Press Formabilities in Newly Developed Light-Weight Core Panels." *Transactions of the
Japan Society of Mechanical Engineers, Series A* 75:751 (2009), 381–387. (In Japanese.)

[Saito et al. 09b] Kazuya Saito, Taketoshi Nojima, Hiroaki Morimura, and Ichiro Hagiwara. "Evaluation of
Bending Rigidity in Newly Developed Light-Weight Core Panels." *Transactions of the Japan Society of
Mechanical Engineers, Series A* 75:750 (2009), 259–265. (In Japanese.)

[Schenk and Guest 09] M. Schenk and S. D. Guest. "Folded Textured Sheets." In *Proceedings of the International Association for Shell and Spatial Structures (IASS) Symposium 2009*, edited by Alberto Domingo and
Carlos Lazaro, pp. 2328–2336. Valencia, Spain: Universidad Politecnica de Valencia, 2009.

[Schenk and Guest 13] Mark Schenk and Simon D. Guest. "Geometry of Miura-Folded Metamaterials." In *Proceedings of the National Academy of Sciences* 110:9 (2013), 3276–3281.

[Xin et al. 13] F. X. Xin, T. J. Lu, and C. Q. Chen. "Sound Transmission through Simply Supported Finite
Double-Panel Partitions with Enclosed Air Cavity." *Journal of Vibration and Acoustics* 132 (2013), 011008.

DEPARTMENT OF MECHANICAL ENGINEERING, MEIJI UNIVERSITY, JAPAN
E-mail address: sishida@meiji.ac.jp

DEPARTMENT OF MECHANICAL AND AEROSPACE ENGINEERING, TOKYO INSTITUTE OF TECHNOLOGY, JAPAN

MEIJI INSTITUTE FOR ADVANCED STUDY OF MATHEMATICAL SCIENCES, MEIJI UNIVERSITY, JAPAN

Thin-Walled Deployable Grid Structures

Jonathan Ho and Zhong You

1. Introduction

The only known deployable grid structure is the square grid. These have already been used in packaging for separating individual products within packing boxes, or as a means of filling excess volume. A typical cardboard square grid, shown in Figure 1, is formed by sliding together cardboard strips, each of which have precut slots about half the height of the strip, and these slots meet with a slot on an intersecting strip. This type of grid lacks rigidity and structural stability, meaning only small loads can be applied to the grids. All the slots in a strip are cut on the same side so there is no restraint for the continuous part of the strip, resulting in the strip collapsing sideways under any significant load. Attempting to use alternating slots can significantly complicate the assembly process and requires the strips to be flexible to allow them to be interlaced.

In this work, we present a new concept using a known flat-foldable origami pattern known as the *Tachi–Miura polyhedron* [Miura and Tachi 10]. This rigid-foldable origami that forms a flat quadrilateral grid was combined with a raised web structure in the middle,

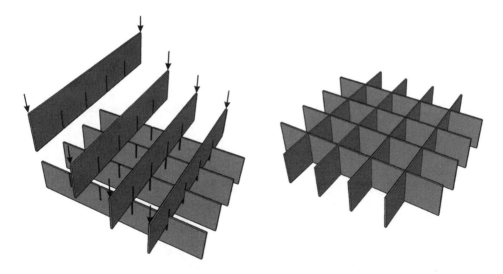

FIGURE 1. Conventional assembly process for a square packaging grid.

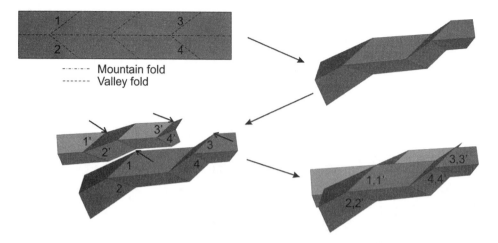

FIGURE 2. The Miura-ori pattern, mirrored to give two strips that are joined at coincident fold lines.

forming a grid structure. The raised web structure is compatible with the original folding concept, and the new grid structure remains rigid-foldable. Moreover, the new grid structure can be expanded by repetition, leading to the creation of large deployable grid structure. The concept can be readily extended to other geometries, including multiple-layer grid structures, curved webs, and structures with a hexagonal grid. The concept is valid for material with nonzero thickness. With a suitable selection of materials, these structures can be used as roofs, partition walls, and impact-resistant packaging materials.

2. The Tachi–Miura Polyhedron Derived Grid Mechanism

The design of a new flat-foldable mechanism takes an approach similar to one based on the Miura-ori pattern [Miura 89], but without rotating the mirrored pattern. Figure 2 shows a Miura-ori pattern, which will also be referred to as a *strip* because the mechanism will be made of several strips joined together. A strip is mirrored, and then the two strips are joined along the diagonal valley folds, marked 1–4 and $1'$–$4'$. Note that, in the terminology of rigid origami, a mountain fold (dash-dot line) is folded so that the crease becomes a ridge pointing out of the page, and a valley fold (dashed line) is folded with a trough going into the page.

This new mechanism, known as the *Tachi–Miura polyhedron derived grid system*, can fold completely flat to form a quadrilateral grid in the flattened condition, as shown in Figure 3. It has only one degree of freedom, which means that the mechanism can be folded by applying forces to only two opposing points. It can be transformed from its fully folded configuration to partially deployed configurations and finally to the fully deployed configuration.

The grid mechanism can be repeated periodically in three dimensions by using multiplication factors N_x, N_y, or N_z, where N_x is the number of strips used, N_y is the number of repetitions of a single valley or mountain fold of the Miura-ori pattern along the strip, and N_z is the number of individual rigid sheets in the vertical direction. In Figure 4(a), $N_x = 6$ and $N_y = 8$, and in Figure 4(b), $N_y = 8$ and $N_z = 6$.

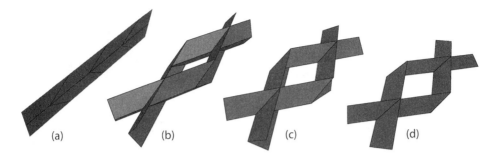

FIGURE 3. Folding sequence of a Tachi–Miura polyhedron derived grid mechanism: (a) fully folded, (b, c) partially deployed, and (d) fully deployed configurations.

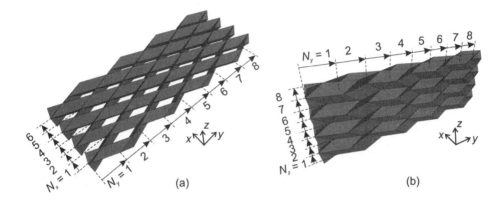

FIGURE 4. Repetition of the grid mechanism in (a) the x- and y-directions and (b) the y- and z-directions.

This particular assembly, however, cannot be used as a load-bearing grid structure simply because of its flat-foldability. It does not have the depth required in a grid structure to provide sufficient stiffness.

3. Foldable Grid Structure with Vertical Webs

To form an orthogonal three-dimensional raised grid with load-bearing capability, the flat-foldable grid mechanism analysed in Section 2 is used. The two halves of the mechanism on either side of the centerline are separated (Figure 5(a)–(b)), and vertical panels with alternating mountain and valley folds are inserted between them (Figure 5(c)). When attached to adjacent panels and deployed, the new vertical sheets form a grid that is constrained to the final geometry of the mechanism, so that when fully deployed it forms a grid with orthogonal vertical web structures, as shown in Figure 5(d)–(g).

The fold pattern generated from this particular grid shape is shown in Figure 6, where d denotes the vertical separation of the two halves of the flat-foldable mechanism, which is also the height of the web h_d, or the unit height of the deployed structure, and c is the width of the top and bottom flanges. The folding angle is $\alpha = 45°$.

The grid can be repeated in the x, y-plane by repetition of the pattern of alternating mountain and valley folds in the y-direction (Figure 7(a)) or by use of multiple mirrored

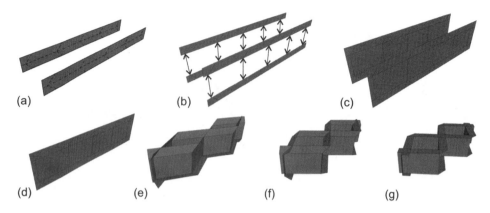

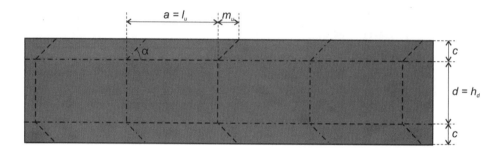

FIGURE 5. Formation of a raised orthogonal grid from an orthogonal flat-foldable mechanism.

FIGURE 6. Fold pattern for a three-dimensional square grid.

fold patterns attached together sequentially in the x-direction (Figure 7(b)). However, these forms of repetition result in a flat-foldable mechanism with grid lines running diagonally (Figure 7(c)) rather than parallel to the sides of the grid.

As can be seen in Figure 7, the halves of the flat-foldable mechanism on either side of the grid form flanges above and below the structural web of the vertical panels, similar to a cold-rolled parallel flange channel found in steel structures. The grid intersections consist of two layers of material joined together along the hinge, resulting in greater joint rigidity than the conventional method of forming a grid by cutting slits out of strips of cardboard and interlacing the strips.

4. Tall Foldable Grid Structures

As for the flat-foldable mechanism, the three-dimensional grid mechanism can be repeated in the z-direction by mirroring in the x, y-plane to produce tall grids (Figure 8). It can be seen that by mirroring the pattern for the grid (which consists of a Miura-ori pattern divided by a vertical web), a whole, reversed, flat-foldable mechanism is created in between successive web strips. If, rather than a whole mechanism (of height $2c$), only a half mechanism is used, then the three-dimensional grid can still be formed. However, as can be seen in Figure 9, this causes the successive webs to be offset from one another by

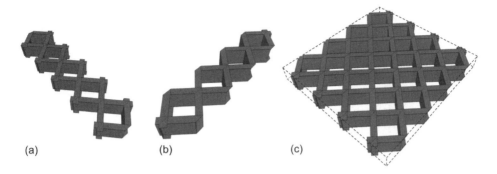

FIGURE 7. Repetition in (a) the x-direction, (b) the y-direction, and (c) the x- and y-directions.

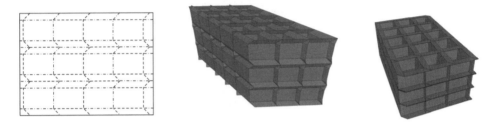

FIGURE 8. Repetition of the three-dimensional grid in the z-direction.

FIGURE 9. Half of the flat-foldable mechanism is used between each of the layers of vertical webs, causing the load-bearing elements of the grid to become offset.

distance c in both the x- and y-directions. If the grid was to be used for load-bearing applications, the load path of a vertical force applied to the top layer would be offset as well, resulting in a lower load-bearing capacity than if the load path followed a straight line.

5. Foldable Grid Structure with Curved Webs

If the concept of vertical webs is now extended so that there are many layers of webs, each using a different angle $\alpha_1, \alpha_2, \ldots, \alpha_4$, as shown in Figure 10, then the result is a grid with a multi-faceted join line that is equivalent to joining together several flat-foldable grid mechanisms from Section 3, each with a different value of folding angle α. This could lead to a foldable grid structure with a curved web.

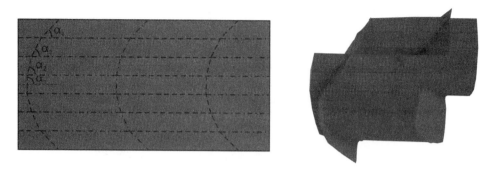

FIGURE 10. Fold pattern and model of a grid with a multi-faceted curved web.

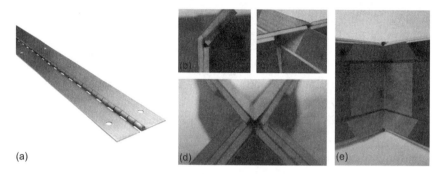

FIGURE 11. Hinge construction: (a) a steel piano hinge, and (b, c, d, e) paper hinges in the joints of a folding thick-walled grid structure.

The concept of curved webs enables a designer to geometrically tailor a grid structure to obtain desirable structural properties under impact. For instance, a web with greater curvature will be less stiff than a structure with a more vertical web. As a result, the structure will become softer under out-of-plane impact.

6. Thickness

So far, the grid structures are generated from a sheet of negligible thickness. However, when considering the grids for practical uses such as those mentioned in Section 1, the likely materials of construction would be cardboard, wood, or other sheet materials of finite thickness. The thickness of the flat plates, therefore, needs to be considered, because a non-negligible thickness has an effect on the construction of joints.

Steel piano hinges (Figure 11(a)) would provide a suitable method of construction for the rotating hinges of the folding grid structure. Other methods, e.g., plastic-molded joints, may also be possible. These designs must be analyzed according to the load-bearing requirement of a particular application. Thick sheets cannot be of uniform thickness because during deployment they overlap each other. Where such hinges are used, sections of thick sheets must be cut away; this has been considered using the card model shown in Figure 11(b)–(e). All the required joints for a folding grid structure can be formed using this system of hinges and cutaways.

FIGURE 12. Deployment of a single intersection of a thick-walled fold-able rigid grid structure.

Once the variable thickness of the sheets and the hinge placement has been carefully considered, construction of a foldable rigid grid structure (Figure 12) is the same as described in Sections 3 and 4, except that sheet material of any thickness can now be used.

7. Conclusion and Future Work

The work detailed here shows that it is possible to manipulate a Miura-ori fold pattern to give a mechanism in the shape of a quadrilateral grid that can fold into two flat states. It is subsequently possible to combine this with a grid of vertical webs to generate a foldable grid structure that can fold into one flat state—the other flat state being replaced by a deployed three-dimensional grid that is constrained by the mechanism. This has greater stability than an unconstrained grid, as well as being quicker and easier to deploy.

Following this, a study of the sheet thickness of folding quadrilateral grid structures was carried out to give a viable construction method of thick, rigid sheets using piano hinges. Some practical applications for the grid structure have been suggested, and it is hoped that the principles described here can potentially be used in engineering applications.

Future work could be carried out to investigate the strength and stiffness properties of a folding grid constructed using the principles of thickness and hinged joints. Additionally, work could be carried out to assess the energy absorption properties of the grid structure with a curved web.

References

[Miura 89] K. Miura. "Map Fold a La Miura Style, Its Physical Characteristics and Application to the Space Science." In *Research of Pattern Formation*, edited by R. Takaki, pp. 77–90. Tokyo: KTK Scientific Publishers, 1989.

[Miura and Tachi 10] K. Miura and T. Tachi. "Synthesis of Rigid-Foldable Cylindrical Polyhedral." *Journal of the International Society for the Interdisciplinary Study of Symmetry, Special Issues for the Festival Congress, Gmuend, Austria* 9 (2010), 204–213.

UNIVERSITY OF OXFORD, OXFORD, UNITED KINGDOM

UNIVERSITY OF OXFORD, OXFORD, UNITED KINGDOM
E-mail address: zhong.you@eng.ox.ac.uk

Deployable Linear Folded Stripe Structures

Rupert Maleczek

1. Introduction

This chapter presents research on deployable structures consisting of linear folded stripes. Based on the investigation that an equal-sided flat hexagonal network from linear folded stripes represents a mobile mechanism, the aim of this research is to develop strategies to transform this flat mechanism into a three-dimensional one.

Linear folded stripes represent a folding system consisting of rectangular stripes in unrolled condition, which are assembled in folded state into reticular three-dimensional structures. The stripes are glued together during the fabrication process. The stripes can be fabricated from long rolls of constant-width sheet material. Similar to honeycomb cores of classical sandwich panels [Kalweit et al. 06], the structure occupies in its flat state a very small amount of space, as the linear stripes are aligned up completely (Figure 1). Therefore, this method is potentially useful for large-scale deployable structures.

The estimation that rotational bodies from linear folded stripes are deployable structures, as formulated in earlier publications [Maleczek and Genevaux 12], will be partly proved here. Another issue in this work will be an answer to the question of if and how other surfaces as rotational bodies can be approximated with deployable stripe systems.

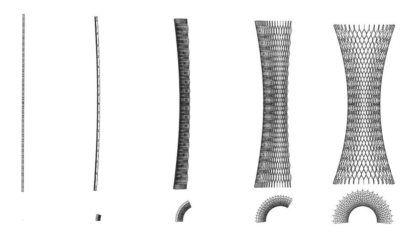

FIGURE 1. A deployable, rotational structure, top views (top) and side views (bottom).

Figure 2. A convertible assembly in folded (left), intermediate (center), and flat packed state (right).

In order to be able to discuss these issues, regular and irregular deployable hexagonal cells and their constraints, as well as their ability to form deployable structures, will be discussed. The ability to perform rigid or non-rigid folding will be investigated.

A reticular system of linear folded stripes consists of several stripes, wherein a minimum of two stripes is necessary to form one or more hexagonal cells. Each stripe is a rigid-foldable mechanism. Until now, most structures were generated with the aim to assemble a three-dimensional stable structure from a single rigid-foldable stripe.

For this particular research, the deployability of an entire assembled stripe system will be investigated. One aim is to discuss the first results on the geometric constraints to form reticular structures assembled from linear folded stripes that can be folded into a flat rectangular package (Figure 2).

This work will show that even if linear stripe segments are rigid in both their unrolled and final three-dimensional assembled state, the motion they exhibit to transform from one spatial configuration to another will utilize rigid or non-rigid folding transformations, depending on their geometric constraints.

At the actual state of research, this seems to be acceptable, because the motion of an entire stripe system is very complex and not yet completely solved by the author. But, it must be considered that one important issue for future investigation is the generation of rigid-foldable systems [Hull 13, Tachi 10]. The focus in this particular chapter is the generation of structures with equal-sided hexagonal cells and a first analysis of these structures for their ability to form deployable systems.

2. Hexagonal Cells from Linear Folded Stripes

A linear folded stripe describes a folding system consisting of a planar rectangle with one or more folding edges in unrolled condition [Maleczek and Genevaux 11]. In this study, folds are defined by straight edges only, are not intersected by other folds, and therefore form segments with four corners. A linear folded stripe has no torsion in its segments.

As shown in Figure 3, two stripes A and B, with four folds each, have to be assembled in order to create a hexagonal cell [Hensel et al. 08]. For one single hexagonal cell, five stripe-segments divided by four folds, from two stripes, are necessary. These two stripes are assembled at the first and the last segment of each stripe. The two assembled segments, named *contact segments*, are aligned in a common plane that is defined by a common main direction and main orientation. The segments located between two contact segments are

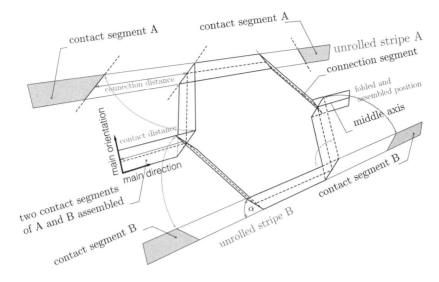

FIGURE 3. Two stripes assembled to a hexagonal cell.

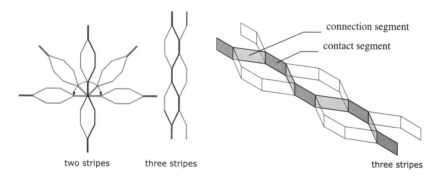

FIGURE 4. Constraints between the number of the stripes in a hexagonal structure.

named *connection segments*. The connection and the contact distances are measured along the middle axis of the stripes.

As two stripes will generate only two consecutive hexagons, the generation of a continuous hexagonal structure requires a minimum of three stripes (Figure 4, left).

In this reticular structure, every stripe except for the two stripes on the borders consists of alternating contact and connection segments. In other words, in an assembled stripe structure, every single stripe forms cells with the two neighboring stripes (Figure 4, right). Every second contact segment of each stripe is therefore connected to every second contact segment of the neighboring stripe on each side. This particular configuration, named *open linear folded stripes* [Maleczek and Genevaux 11], is the topic of this particular investigation.

3. Deployable Hexagonal Cells

The previous study investigated two preliminary types of hexagonal cells consisting of a pair of stripes. One is generated from "linear folded parallel stripes" [Maleczek 11]

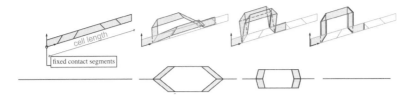

FIGURE 5. A deployable hexagonal cell from linear folded parallel stripes.

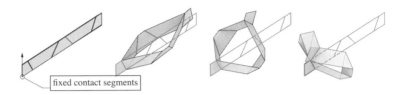

FIGURE 6. A deployable hexagonal cell from predefined linear folded stripes.

while the other is generated from "predefined open stripes" [Maleczek and Genevaux 11]. The deployable cells generated from linear folded parallel stripes require equal segment lengths and a mirrored foldable axis to build a rigid-foldable mechanism that can be folded to a flat package.

The second type made from predefined stripes [Maleczek and Genevaux 12] also creates a deployable mechanism, but in contrast to the parallel cell, the potential contact segments in the middle are not located in parallel planes. This configuration leads to self-intersection.

As shown in Figures 5 and 6, two contact segments are fixed, and the other two contact segments are translated along the mirroring axis (Figure 5) or rotated in the mirroring plane (Figure 6) to deploy the cell. A similar mechanism is described by Tomohiro Tachi and Koryo Miura to generate rigid-foldable cylinders [Tachi and Miura 12].

As the structures described here consist of rectangular stripes with alternating fold-lines, which are not intersecting, instead of a crease pattern, the degree of freedom may be different than that of the described one-degree-of-freedom structure by Tachi and Miura.

4. Deployable Rotational Bodies

Rotational bodies from linear folded stripes [Maleczek and Genevaux 12] consist of rectangular stripes that are generated between two planes that form a *boundary condition* (Figure 7). The name *boundary condition* is based on the affect that their relationship has on the entire stripe structure. The two planes alternatingly contain the contact segments. The intersection of these planes defines the rotational axis of the entire structure. If the angle between the planes is a division of π by an even number, the structure can be folded to a closed rotational body. Each structure consists of identical stripes that are mirrored along these planes.

The geometric constraints of a series of cells that consist of mirrored elements in the rotational direction, from which each cell is a rigid-foldable system, encourages the assumption that such an assembly must be rigid-foldable.

A series of paper models indicated that structures from predefined stripes are foldable, but most configurations must be considered non–rigid-foldable, meaning that they have

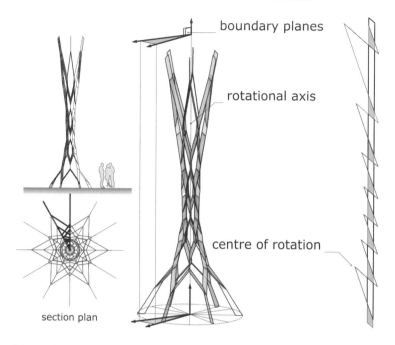

boundary planes

rotational axis

centre of rotation

section plan

FIGURE 7. A rotational structure with a mirrored folding axis (left and center) and the unrolled stripe with its centers of rotations (right).

torsion in some segments during the folding procedure. The problem is the exact orientation of the contact segments during motion. As each stripe represents a rigid-foldable system on its own, every second contact segment must be aligned in the same plane that acts as the mirroring plane for the neighboring stripe.

The analysis of the exhibited motion shows that the contact segments of tested structures during a motion are in parallel but not in identical planes. To allow the contact segments to be aligned in identical planes, the connection segments need to be torsionally deformed during motion. The distance between these parallel planes is linked to the number of stripes, the distance of the cells to the middle axis, and the lengths of the cell's segments. The only cells that exhibit a rigid folded motion are those cells that have one contact segment with the main direction parallel to the rotational axis of the structure. Therefore, most rotational bodies from predefined structures are non–rigid-foldable.

As shown in Figure 8, the simplest rotational body is one ring of single cells. One ring of cells always builds a rigid-foldable structure. As soon as the structure consists of two rings of cells, the structure is only rigid-foldable if the adjacent cells have a common center. Therefore, exceptions are rotational bodies, with foldlines that have one common center.

A common rotational center for all foldlines allows for a rigid-foldable structure, with the connected contact segments in the same plane during motion, without any torsion in the connection segments.

During the motion of the stripe structure, all contact segments exhibit a motion in the mirroring planes. Their motion in this moving plane is a rotation. This rotation depends

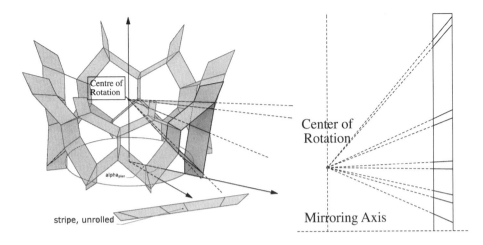

FIGURE 8. A rigid-foldable system, where all extended foldlines intersect in one point.

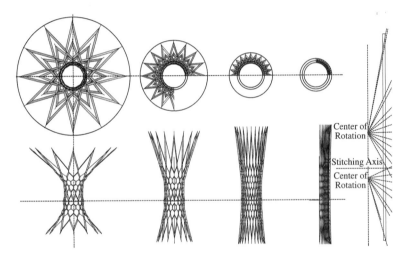

FIGURE 9. A rigid-foldable rotational structure with two centers of rotation.

on the distance to the rotational axis and the angle between the main direction and the rotational axis. The only segment of one stripe that is not rotated during motion is a segment that has a main direction parallel to the rotational axis in the three-dimensional state.

To generate structures with more than one rotational center, two rotational bodies can be stitched at this particular contact segment. A very simple solution for a structure with two rotational centers is a structure that is mirrored at this particular segment normal to the rotational axis (Figure 9). The author could not yet arrive at a reasonable conclusion for the question of whether deployable structures with more than the two described centers exist.

The number of possible predefined open stripe configurations did not yet allow a complete investigation on all rotational bodies, and therefore the author could not yet identify other rigid-foldable structures from predefined open linear folded stripes.

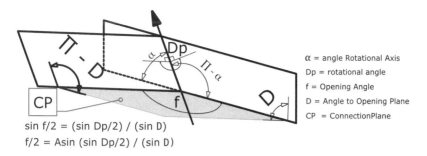

α = angle Rotational Axis
Dp = rotational angle
f = Opening Angle
D = Angle to Opening Plane
CP = ConnectionPlane

sin f/2 = (sin Dp/2) / (sin D)
f/2 = Asin (sin Dp/2) / (sin D)

FIGURE 10. Dependency of the foldlines and the middle axis of a stripe after Berthomier.[1]

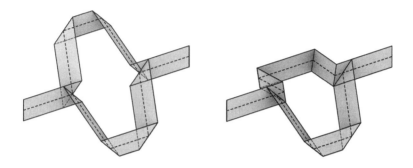

FIGURE 11. A regular (left) and an irregular (right) hexagonal cell.

5. Surface Approximations with Parallel Stripes

The second system that is investigated for its ability to form deployable structures with equal segment length is named *linear folded parallel stripes* [Maleczek 11]. In a parallel stripe system, all contact segments of the entire structure lie in a parallel plane. As this type of stripes is a so-called post-defined system, given surfaces can be approximated. For this particular purpose, two different methods were developed to form a rigid-foldable structure in three-dimensional state and in flat packed state.

The first strategy is based on a geometric method that intersects the connection segments with the given surface in a *sequential* method, and the second method uses a construction method for ellipses based on a given diagonal grid. The two methods generate different types of cells. A differentiation between regular and irregular cells can be made by the position of folds in relation to the folds of the neighboring stripe at each contact segment.

As shown in Figure 10, each stripe has an "axis" that forms in the folded state, which is a polyline from which each segment is identical with the stripe segment's main direction. As this polyline can be used to define the foldlines depending on the main orientation of the segments, it must be generated during a surface approximation process in relation to the given surface. This polyline is not only sufficient to define the stripes geometry with the help of the main orientation, but is also necessary to differentiate between regular and irregular cells.

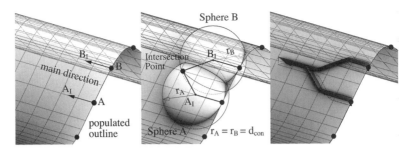

FIGURE 12. Generation of a regular deployable cell, with equal cell lengths.

If the two polylines that define the axis of one cell have vertices with identical positions, we name these cells *regular* cells. Otherwise, we name the cells *irregular* cells (Figure 11).

5.1. Sequential method. The sequential method is a very simple strategy to generate hexagonal cells with equal cell lengths of the adjacent members.

In the first step, an outline that is populated with a series of points is defined from which the cells will be generated in the main direction. Each point represents the starting point from two contact segments' axis of two stripes. The first segment of the above-described polyline is generated in the main direction with the desired contact segment length. As the consecutive segments axis must end in a common point on the surface, the intersection circle of two spheres with the connection distance as radius is intersected with the surface. This intersection point defines the starting point of the next contact segment (Figure 12). From these new points, the procedure is repeated to form a hexagonal polyline network that represents the axis of the stripe assembly. This approach generates regular cells only.

5.2. Diagrid method. The second strategy generates the hexagonal polylines with the help of a surface-based *diagrid*. Each vertex of this grid represents the midpoint of the middle axis from a contact segment. To generate a hexagonal cell from these midpoints, we define these points (A, B) as reference for a new ellipse, and we define the desired length (L_{cell}) of the cell as the major axis length. The given main direction allows generation of the polyline with the help of the polar coordinates relative to the focus of an ellipse, as shown in Figure 13.

As an ellipse is described by the relation between the foci and the lengths of the major axis with a triangle, this triangle has to be transformed into a Z-shaped polyline that describes a quarter of a hexagonal cell.

To calculate the distance c of the contact segment measured from the midpoint, we define the entire cell length L_{cell}. The major axis of the ellipse is defined by the foci A and B. The angle ϕ is defined through the main axis of the ellipse and the main direction of the stripe system. The relation within the ellipse allows the calculation of the distance r. In order to generate the Z-shaped polyline, the point A must be translated in the main direction by the distance c, and the point B must be translated in reverse to the main direction by the distance c. As the lengths of c can differ enormously within one single cell, the author proposes to move points A and B in and to reverse the main direction so the contact segments will have enough common surface for its assemblies. Cells generated with this particular method can be irregular and regular ones.

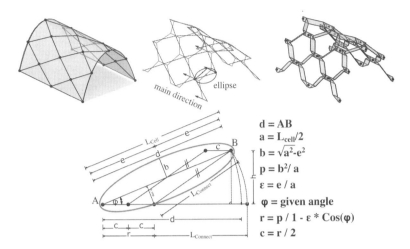

$$d = AB$$
$$a = L_{cell}/2$$
$$b = \sqrt{a^2 - e^2}$$
$$p = b^2 / a$$
$$\varepsilon = e / a$$
$$\varphi = \text{given angle}$$
$$r = p / 1 - \varepsilon * \cos(\varphi)$$
$$c = r / 2$$

FIGURE 13. The diagrid method on an extruded surface including the point relations.

FIGURE 14. A deployable structure generated from a planar spatial curve.

6. Deployable Structures from Parallel Stripes

Both types of reticular structures are in their conception rigid-foldable structures in assembled state and in flat packed state. With the actual configurations, most structures tend to have torsion in the segments during their motion from one state to another. As this is the starting point for a more detailed investigation, at the actual state of investigation only one type of structure can be identified as rigid-foldable.

6.1. Rigid-foldable structures. This study gave geometric analysis for the rigid-foldability of surfaces generated by extrusion based on a curve approximated with linear folded parallel stripes (Figure 14).

The surfaces need to be extruded in the main direction of the parallel stripe system from planar curves. Here, the cells consist of two mirrored segments from two adjacent stripes normal to the main direction. Other rigid-foldable types are for future study.

6.2. Non–rigid-foldable structures. The standard case of surfaces approximated with parallel stripes that consist of cells with equal cell length can be assumed to be non–rigid-foldable structures. Torsion is necessary to adjust the position in space from the "rigid-foldable" position of the contact segments to the geometrical necessary position. Therefore, the author interprets torsion as a phenomenon that is linked to a distance. The larger the distance is, the more torsion must be in the segment. Depending on the density of the hexagonal grid, the torsion during movement differs enormously. Different

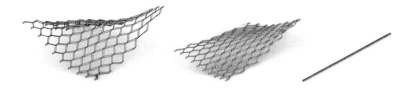

FIGURE 15. A deployable structure from linear folded stripe that is non–rigid-foldable.

structures have different maximum distances, from their rigid folded positions to their necessary assembled positions, during their movement. The author is looking for a relation between cell length and maximum distance during motion, to classify structures as deployable within a certain tolerance during their motion. The structure in Figure 15 is generated on a hyperbolic paraboloid created from straight lines. The distance of the necessary points of the touching contact segments during motion is in its maximum at eight percent of the cell length. The structure is foldable as a paper model but, as explained above, only with torsion in the segments.

As each cell affects its neighbors during the movement, the understanding of the entire movement of such a structure is one of the main issues for further investigation.

7. Conclusion

The author discussed a method for deployable structures consisting of linear folded stripes. The actual state of research on pre- and post-defined open linear folded stripes were discussed. First results and estimations on rigid- and non–rigid-foldable structures consisting of predefined stripes as well as from post-defined open stripes were presented. The author explained that rotational structures sharing one center or a pair of centers and parallel stripes with single extrusion direction are rigidly foldable configurations, and he underlined his estimation that all other configurations are non–rigid-foldable.

8. Outlook

As this paper represents a starting point for comprehensive research on deployable stripes, there are more open than answered questions. The focus of the research is the understanding and further development of deployable stripe structures with a focus on the development of rigid-foldable structures.

This development requires a deeper investigation on the relation of the folds within one single cell, as well as in an entire structure. It will also be part of the investigation if additional folds, described as *free stripes*, will allow more freedom during the motion of a structure (Figure 16).

Simultaneously, the implementation of actuators based on the degrees of freedom will be investigated. Therefore, cooperation with engineering and geometry specialists should be established. Future research will explore building large-scale prototypes and investigate methods for adding overall rigidity to the entire structure in a fixed position.

Acknowledgments

This first study is supported by the Tiroler Wisenschaftsfonds (TWF-GZ-UNI-0404-900).

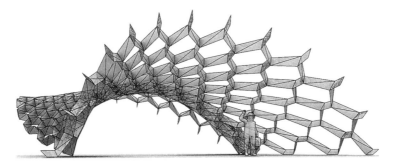

FIGURE 16. A structure from linear folded free stripes.

References

[Hensel et al. 08] M. Hensel, A. Menges, M. Weinstock, and A. Kudless. "Honigwabenstrukturen." *Form Follows Performance* 188 (2008), 56–59.

[Hull 13] Thomas Hull. *Project Origami: Activities for Exploring Mathematics*, Second Edition. Boca Raton, FL: A K Peters/CRC Press, 2013. MR2987362

[Kalweit et al. 06] A. Kalweit, C. Paul, S. Peters, and R. Wallbaum, *Handbuch für Technisches Produktdesign*. Berlin: Springer-Verlag, 2006.

[Maleczek 11] Rupert Maleczek. "Linear Folded (Parallel) Stripe(s)." In *Computational Design Modeling*, edited by Christoph Gengnagel, Axel Kilian, Norbert Palz, and Fabian Scheurer, pp. 153–160. Berlin: Springer-Verlag, 2011.

[Maleczek and Genevaux 11] R. Maleczek and C. Geneveaux. "Open and Closed Linear Folded Stripes." In *Taller, Longer, Lighter: Proceedings of the IABSE-IASS Symposium 2011*, CD-ROM. London: IABSE/IASS, 2011.

[Maleczek and Genevaux 12] Rupert Maleczek and Chloe Genevaux. "Pre-defined Open Linear Folded Stripes." In *Advances in Architectural Geometry 2012*, edited by Lars Hesselgren, Shrikant Sharma, Johannes Wallner, Nicolo Baldassini, Phillipe Bompas, and Jaques Rayaud, pp. 175–184. Paris: Springer, 2012.

[Tachi 10] Tomohiro Tachi. "Geometric Considerations for the Design of Rigid Origami Structures." In *Proceedings of the International Association for Shell and Spatial Structures (IASS) Symposium 2010, Shanghai, China*, pp. 771–782. Madrid: IASS, 2010.

[Tachi and Miura 12] Tomohiro Tachi and Koryo Miura. "Rigid-Foldable Cylinders and Cells." *Journal of the International Association for Shell and Spatial Structures* 53:4 (2012), 217–226.

INSTITUTE OF DESIGN, UNIT KOGE, FACULTY OF ARCHITECTURE, UNIVERSITY OF INNSBRUCK, AUSTRIA
E-mail address: rupert.maleczek@uibk.ac.at

Gravity and Friction-Driven Self-Organized Folding

Günther H. Filz, Georg Grasser, Johannes Ladinig, and Rupert Maleczek

1. Introduction

This chapter presents ongoing research related to the self-organized folding of fiber cement and textile concrete sheet elements, with gravity and friction as guiding concept. Textile concrete is mostly produced in textile-like sheets that present the potential to create three-dimensional (3D) objects from developable surfaces. This type of manufacturing is consistent with the process of paper folding widely known and described as origami. Most folding techniques and the resulting objects are related to origami patterns and processes [Demaine and O'Rourke 07]. One technique, *force-induced folding*, is still rather unexplored, and only a few examples of research on this topic have been published so far. One example, the diamond-shaped pattern known as the *Yoshimura pattern* [Tarnai 97], appears when a cylinder is deformed under compression. Another well-known example is crumpled paper that can be described as a radical example of origami [Tachi 14]. The mechanical behavior of paper and that of textile concrete exhibit many similarities including a small ability to stretch, which can be neglected for this particular investigation. In contrast to most origami-inspired approaches where 3D objects result from predefined fold patterns that are governed by a specific folding logic, the 3D objects presented here result from a self-organized processes with gravity (self-weight) and friction as the principal forming parameters.

In this context, the genesis of self-organized folds is not random but caused by set boundary conditions and follows precise physical principles. Through defined boundary conditions, we can indirectly control the 3D result while producing predetermined shapes or emergent shapes created by stopping the process at any point in time while the material is still malleable. Finally, the desired shape is "frozen" though drying and curing, thus allowing the creation of 3D objects without using conventional formwork. As the concrete textile material exhibits a phase change during curing, the folding process allows the construction of theoretically developable surfaces. After the material has hardened, the resulting shape can be described as a *developable folded shell structure* [Preisinger 06].

Here, the authors present a general approach of self-organized folding, the associated fabrication process, and the initial results of a numerical simulation protocol based on physical models and related material properties. The resulting numerical simulation protocol produces predictions of folding behavior in industrially produced sheets that are 93% accurate and sufficient to be used in an architectural design process. The simulated behavior has been verified by physical prototyping including the "Wien Products" table. Ongoing research is developing refined numeric simulation of the material properties based

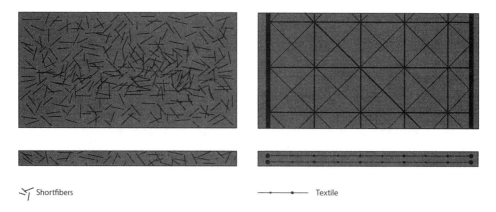

FIGURE 1. Reinforcement principle of fiber cement and textile concrete.

FIGURE 2. Fiber cement and textile concrete, produced as soft and wet sheets (left), with thickness from 8 to 12 mm, compared to concrete filled into a rigid formwork or textile mold (right), which lead to fundamentally different results.

on physical prototypes as well as preparing an overview of basic and complex forms where folds affect one or more sheets for eventual application in architecture.

2. Forming Fiber Cement and Textile Concrete without Formwork

In the last decades, prefabricated reinforced-textile concrete has been used in a wide range of applications in architecture and design. Recent improvements in fabrication and reinforcement techniques allow the construction of thin-walled, relatively lightweight elements, which have a high flexural strength and are suitable for façade applications. Enhanced structural performance can be achieved through the inclusion of short fibers, fiber bundles, or textile fabrics into a cement matrix. The specification of density, direction, and location of reinforcement affects not only material and structural performance but also anisotropic properties in general, which have an essential impact on deformation properties during the soft state of the material. In this example, prefabricated sheet material is used, so the orientation of fibers or textiles (Figure 1) is consistent and plays only a minor role; but, it will be examined as a potential form-influencing or guiding parameter in later investigations.

Fiber cement and textile concrete are produced as soft and wet sheets up to 3500×1250 mm with thickness ranging from 8 to 12 millimeters (Figure 2, left). These sheets harden within a few hours and become fully cured in 28 days. Once cured, the weight of the sheet is between 15 and 30 kg/m^2 depending on the material composition.

The fabrication and forming processes associated with fiber cement and textile concrete have to account for the significant self-weight of concrete while also addressing the flexibility of the material before it is cured. Despite these difficulties, the ability for the material to be formed in "soft" state presents interesting opportunities for architectural application and opens the possibility for creating new shapes in a variety of ways. In industrial production scenarios, flat sheets are produced for façade paneling or other cladding purposes. In these contexts, the flexibility of the material prior to curing is perceived as a limitation that complicates the production process and makes the "wet" sheet very difficult to handle consistently.

Previous approaches to forming objects from textile concrete involve molds that force the sheet into a specific geometry—similar to slump molding or casting (Figure 2, right), projects by Mark West, Remo Pedreschi, and others [Orr et al. 12]. In this case, the authors are interested in a process that provides large variety of formal potential through a minimum of inputs with the least effort possible. The investigation is therefore based on foldable structures generated in the soft state rather than molded and formed geometries.

3. Self-Organization and Boundary Conditions

The process of transforming sketches and drawings into a materialized, built reality uses geometry as a precise tool for communicating and predicting shape. In this context shape is meant to be the geometrical part of a material object, which can be perceived with our visual sense. As soon as the material itself and the process of production or fabrication are taken into consideration the desired, precisely predicted shape can usually be obtained by composing the object from prefabricated, mostly planar elements and in cases of fluent shapes by enormous efforts in terms of formwork.

Another way to generate shapes is by self-organization [Filz et al. 14]. In order to fabricate 3D objects from textile concrete, which comes in planar sheets, self-organized folding driven by constraints and boundary conditions offers the opportunity to create a great variety of 3D forms. Folds, caused by material displacement due to its shear stiffness determined by the transformation of planar surfaces into 3D shapes, are in general an undesirable effect in architecture and structural analysis. On the other hand, this way of generating folds can be seen as a self-organizing process and the final result as a self-organizing form that exhibits new design potential.

In this context, *self-organizing* should be understood as a controlled forming process of sheet material dictated by a prescribed boundary condition [Ma and You 11]. Reading the direction and magnitude of these folds as a unity of self-weight and flow of forces, we can assume structural advantages when using these forms simultaneously as architectural geometry and structural element; we follow the rules of form-finding rather than force a geometry into being—a process that happens on a consciously controllable level. Here, the object is generated in a process where folding represents the "passive" result of given boundary conditions. Because objects generated in self-organized processes are governed by physical parameters like gravity, friction, and self-weight, additional performance properties are realized that can influence the structural performance of the object. For this particular research, the authors developed a process logic that makes 3D deformations based on given boundary conditions predictable, resulting in a simplification of the simulation process that is necessary to constrain the boundary conditions. While this process produces a potentially desirable structural benefit, the research predominately concentrates on the interrelation of shape and material properties.

4. Methods and Investigation

The actual investigations are based on prototypical experiments with the material in soft state. These experiments provide feedback for the development of the digital approaches that offer a precise simulation and prediction of the resulting object at freely set

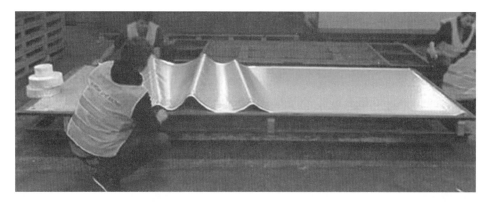

FIGURE 3. Fiber cement experiments at the University of Innsbruck, 2012.

 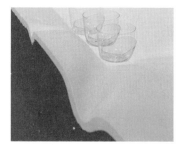

FIGURE 4. Table for "Wien Products" trade fair Paris 2012 (left) and a detailed view (right).

boundary conditions. In this context, the challenge in the physical experiment is the handling of the material without making the handling itself an erratic factor, and in the simulation the challenge is the complex interplay of material properties, boundary conditions, and physical parameters such as gravity and friction of the material on the equipment.

4.1. Physical fabrication. The first physical experiments—in trial-and-error loops—were mainly design-driven but revealed the enormous potential of material, technology, and technique. The authors were also involved in manual fabrication processes in factories, working with various fabrication methods and material consistencies. In preliminary tests (Figure 3), the "wet" material was formed with the help of simple objects that were moved in space to deform the material in a controlled way. Even if the output was sufficient for design purposes like the tables for "Wien Products" (Figure 4), the presented results can be seen either as random or as a combination of expert knowledge and hands-on experience. The results were neither precisely predicted nor exactly reproducible.

In a series of physical tests, three different methods for the fabrication process were developed. These methods are characterized in terms of cost, time consumption, and precision. They can be summarized into the two groups: *Boundary First* (Manual Draping Method and Automated Draping Method) and *Material First*.

4.1.1. *Manual Draping Method.* The Manual Draping Method (Figure 5) is a Boundary First Method, which means that the material is draped onto set boundary conditions. It is a cost-efficient method to position soft sheets on horizontally distributed objects to initiate folding. Manual draping of soft concrete sheets implies the risk of material damage as

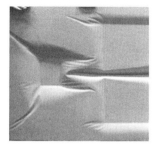

FIGURE 5. Manual Draping Method principle (left) and a physical object made by this method (right).

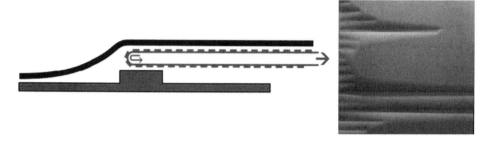

FIGURE 6. Automated Draping Method principle (left) and a physical object made by this method (right).

well as unwanted deformation during the draping process and imprecision in the process of placing the sheet.

4.1.2. *Automated Draping Method.* The Automated Draping Method (Figure 6) is another Boundary First Method, but here the process by which the sheets are placed on a horizontal surface is automated. Therefore, it is a fast and efficient fabrication process. On the other hand, deformation heights were limited to a maximum of 100 mm by machinery accessible to the authors, thus limiting the variety of forms.

4.1.3. *Material First Method.* The Material First Method is a method developed by the authors where the material is precisely placed in a plane. All boundary conditions, which initiate self-organized folding, are prescribed in a second step. While inherently flexible, the Material First Method fabrication process is highly precise. In this process, the only prescribed parameter are the bounding condition, thus providing much freedom in design. Simultaneously counteracting parameters in the self-organized form-finding process are limited to gravity, friction, and material properties like stretch or bending resistance.

4.2. Initial investigations. The authors choose the Material First Method for the development of a numerical simulation method because in this method the constraints are focused on simple repeatable boundary conditions. This fabrication method allows a simulation of the deformation of the sheet, based on the fact that an effector is only moved in one single direction.

In order to gain deeper insight into the genesis and patterns of self-organized folds independent of a certain material, basic investigations by means of simple boundary conditions were made.

FIGURE 7. Material First Method principle (left) and a physical object made by this method (right).

A first set of models were made from 700×700 mm sheets, deformed through different effector geometries in various positions of the effector on the x- and y-axes. To guarantee a comparability of results in terms of folding processes and forms (and later of structural behavior), a series of 700×700 mm sheets were examined. These sheet elements were treated by different effectors, such as squarish or cylindrical effector in various heights, proportions, and positions. A series of physical models revealed several parameters including general folding patterns, radii of surface curvature in dependence of material properties, and the interdependence of sheet dimensions and effector-proportions, which are essential in developing the later analysis and simulation values.

4.3. Numerical simulation. The development of a numerical simulation platform allows for fast and precise prediction of physical objects in any scale and in large numbers. Compared to modeling software packages like 3D Studio-Max Reactor, Cinema 4D, or Rhino Grasshopper Kangaroo, Maya N-Cloth based on the "Nucleus Engine" delivered the most accurate results in replicating the material performance and self-organized folding behavior that were observed in physical tests. This virtual environment is commonly used in architectural design and allows for embedding physical constraints like forces (gravity, friction, etc.) as well as general processing of data according to material properties [Stam 09]. The key concept of the simulation framework is the interaction of all elements as a system of particles that collide and exert forces on each other. The complex behavior of dynamic elements like textiles emerges from a network characterized by the distance between particles and the angles of cross links. During simulation, the positions of particles are found according to set constraints such as stretch, bending, and collisions in an iterative process. For numerical simulation, the setup of boundary conditions in terms of geometry and (force) directions emerges from previously described physical fabrication experiments, is shown in Figure 8, and is defined as follows:

- A planar square mesh has fixed dimensions of 700×700 units.
- A range of variable two-directional (UV) subdivision parameters enables the mesh to react on different material densities and allows the property of being directional dependent (anisotropic).
- Because numerical simulation needs a planar collision surface—the numerical equivalent to a platform in physical tests—the mesh is placed with negligible distance to a planar surface and is attracted by Earth's gravity. Its lateral position is stabilized by a friction value that is dependent on the material to be simulated (e.g., Eternit has friction value 10; see Section 5).

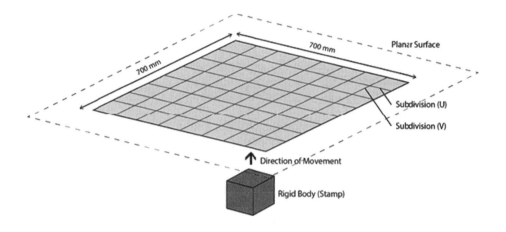

FIGURE 8. Setup for digital simulation.

- An effector as rigid body in primitive form is moved in reverse direction to gravity from below, deforming the mesh.

While the physical fabrication variables are based on physical and mathematical laws and units, the utilized simulation framework has an internal logic to interpret the necessary physical constraints driven by abstract values and ranges. Even if the parameters are given to the simulation engine as abstract values in the form of numbers or percentages, the engine generates valid results. In our research, the approximation of simulated geometry to the geometry of the 3D-scanned objects from physical tests can be seen as an indicator of appropriate simulation values. The transfer of physical properties into numerical simulation is based on iterative loops of matching/deviating geometries. The numerical result is approximated to physical tests by a calibration of simulation values (inverse analysis) seeking for the best geometrical fit. In this sense, real physical values like forces or stresses are assigned to abstract sets of values and ranges of software instead of physical units.

First attempts resulted in a numerical reduction of parameters and focused on those that influence the emerging geometry and self-organized folding the most. Besides the general pattern formation, the most important factors that to date fed back the simulation loop are material properties like mass and friction as well as stretch, compression, and bend resistance. Additional complexity by phase transition from wet to dry states, material handling, time, etc. affect the fabrication process and are indirectly considered in the numerical simulation. Therefore, the parameters of the nucleus engine are interpreted for this particular investigation as follows:

- *Mass* determines the density or weight of a simulated textile when its simulation framework gravity is greater than 0.0.
- *Friction* and *stickiness* determine how much an object resists relative motion on collision with itself and other objects. As friction represents an adhesion force in the tangent direction, stickiness acts in the normal direction.
- *Stretch resistance* is defined as in-plane stiffness and specifies the resistance force under tension. A low value results in stretchy material behavior like spandex, while high-resistance material behaves similar to burlap.

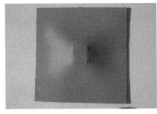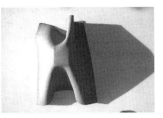

FIGURE 9. Folded fiber cement sheets from a 100×100 mm effector with variable height based on a 700×700 mm developed sheet.

- *Compression resistance* is applied to links/springs when their lengths are less than their rest lengths. One with low resistance tends to crumple.
- *Bend resistance* specifies the resistance across edges when under strain. A high value results in stiffness while a low bend resistance leads to softness and hanging.
- *Thickness* specifies nonvisible surface offset of self-collisions or passive object collisions and determines how thick the simulated object appears.

5. Evaluation of Results

The evaluation criteria are based on the geometrical comparison in terms of match/deviation of physically fabricated and numerically simulated objects as described above. The main parameter to find reliable values for the nucleus engine was the distance between defined points on the simulated 3D mesh and the scanned physical object. For the analysis, a genetic algorithm was developed [Shiffmann 12, pp. 390–443]. Such algorithms are used for search problems and mimic natural evolution via methods like selection, crossover, and mutation. Evolutionary algorithms use a population of members—each equipped with a set of genes that defines its properties—in order to evolve toward fitter solutions. Each member in the population represents a different sheet that derives its material properties from its values. For a fitness category, the displacement of each member to scanned objects is calculated via closest point evaluations—the lower the displacement, the better the material properties of its member. In order to avoid the optimization of parameters for a single object, we choose to simulate the form-finding process in three different stages of deformation related to three different heights of the effector. At present, results from physical models can be properly simulated to a geometrical precision of more than 93% match with a 3D scan and therefore also predicted with similar precision in the digital space without having a physical object in advance.

The computing executed as long as significant improvements of the model could be achieved. The calculated calibration values finally were defined as average values used for simulating fiber cement material from the company Eternit:

Mass	1	Friction	10
Stretch resistance	60	Compression resistance	1
Bend resistance	0.1	Thickness	0.495
Mesh subdivision	1.33		

As the results from physical experiments generate complex surface-geometries (Figure 9), 3D scanning (Figure 10) was the most efficient approach to analyze and compare geometries to numerical simulation (Figure 11) in terms of surfaces, section lines, and radii of curvature (Figures 9–13).

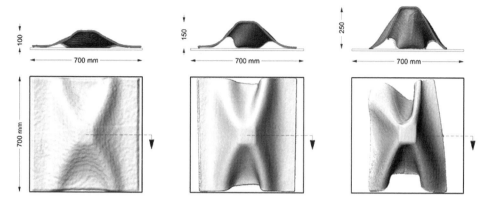

FIGURE 10. A 3D scanned geometry of folded fiber cement from a $100 \times$ 100 mm effector with variable height based on a 700×700 mm developed sheet.

FIGURE 11. Numerical simulation of physical objects from Figures 9 and 10.

FIGURE 12. Folded fiber cement sheets from a cylindrical effector with variable height based on a 700×700 mm developed sheet (center) and simulation (right).

6. Closing the Feedback-Loop: Case Study "Wien Products" Table

As proof of concept and to verify predictability, the table that was form-found by a combination of expert knowledge and hands-on experience for the "Wien Products" Exhibition in 2012 was numerically simulated with material properties adapted to numerical simulation with the same effector. Figure 12 shows the comparison of a "random" physical object and a digitally simulated ("predicted") result, which documents a highly precise match (Figure 13).

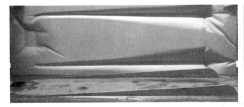

FIGURE 13. Comparison of a physical table form-found by a combination of expert knowledge and hands-on experience for the "Wien Products" Exhibition in 2012 (left) and a numerically simulated table in 2014 with material properties adapted to numerical simulation with the same effector (right).

7. Conclusion

Our research has some basic approaches in common with origami. Probably the greatest differences are the process of self-organized, instead of predefined folding, and the possibility of stopping this process in any state during the "wet" phase of fiber cement or textile concrete.

This work discussed different fabrication techniques for physical prototyping of textile concrete and fiber cement. The Material First Method was evaluated as the most efficient for delivering highly precise results. Using this method, a series of basic investigations with standardized sheets and simple effectors at variable heights were executed, 3D-scanned, evaluated, and compared with numerical simulations. The magnitude of material parameters was reduced to a minimum, gravity and friction being the most important ones. Simultaneously, the numerical simulation process generated geometries that range in ca. 93% precision compared to the geometry of physical experiments. In addition, this realization guarantees a high grade of predictability of digitally designed objects, which was proved by the case study of the "Wien Products" table.

The ongoing research seeks to enhance the precision of the simulation through iterative digital-material prototypes while fine-tuning the definitions of material properties and their numerical simulation. In addition, a taxonomy of forms has been generated to provide an overview of basic and complex forms where folds affect one or more sheets that are possible to produce for purposes in architecture. Preliminary results can be seen in Figure 14.

References

[Filz et al. 14] Günther H. Filz, Rupert Maleczek, and Christian Scheiber. *FORM – RULE | RULE – FORM 2013.* Innsbruck, Austria: Innsbruck University Press, 2014.

[Demaine and O'Rourke 07] Eric D. Demaine and Joseph O'Rourke. *Geometric Folding Algorithms: Linkages, Origami, Polyhedra.* Cambridge, UK: Cambridge University Press, 2007. MR2354878 (2008g:52001)

[Ma and You 11] Jiayo Ma and Zhong You. "The Origami Crash Box." In *Origami^5: Fifth International Meeting of Origami Science, Mathematics, and Education,* edited by Patsy Wang-Iverson, Robert J. Lang, and Mark Yim, pp. 277–290. Boca Raton, FL: A K Peters/CRC Press, 2011. MR2866909 (2012h:00044)

[Orr et al. 12] John Orr, M. Evernden, A. Darby, and T. Ibell (editors). *Proceedings of the Second International Conference on Flexible Formwork.* Bath, UK: University of Bath, 2012.

[Preisinger 06] Clemens F. Preisinger. "Numerical and Experimental Investigations Regarding the Transformation of Flat Slabs to Double Curved Shells." PhD dissertation, Technische Universität Wien, Vienna, Austria, 2006.

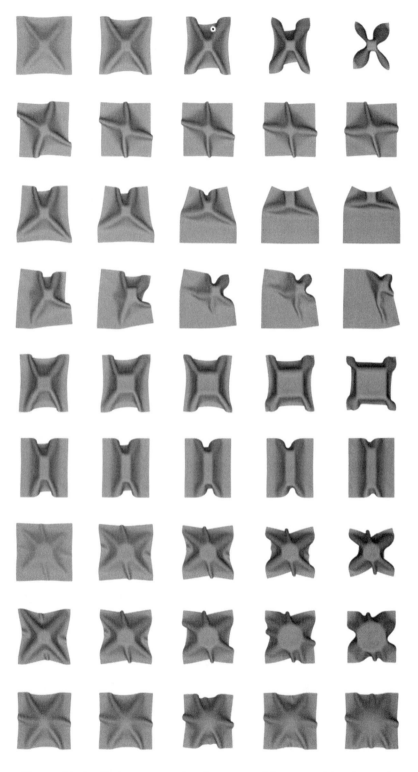

FIGURE 14. Preliminary example of a canon of forms resulting from effectors in different proportions (top views).

[Shiffmann 12] Daniel Shiffman. *The Nature of Code: Simulating Natural Systems with Processing*. Self-published, 2012.

[Stam 09] Jos Stam. "Nucleus: Towards a Unified Dynamics Solver for Computer Graphics." In *Proceedings of the IEEE International Conference on Computer-Aided Design and Computer Graphics*, pp. 1–11. Los Alamitos, CA: IEEE Press, 2009.

[Tachi 14] Tomohiro Tachi. "Geometric Design of Rigid Origami and Curved Origami." Plenary talk at 16th International Conference on Geometry and Graphics (ICGG 2014), Innsbruck, Austria, August 4–8, 2014.

[Tarnai 97] Tibor Tarnai. "Folding of Uniform Plane Tesselation." In *Origami Science and Art: Proceedings of the Second International Meeting of Origami Science and Scientific Origami*, edited by K. Miura, pp. 83–91. Shiga, Japan: Seian University of Art and Design, 1997.

UNIVERSITY OF INNSBRUCK, FACULTY OF ARCHITECTURE, INSTITUTE OF DESIGN, UNIT.KOGE STRUCTURE AND DESIGN, AUSTRIA
E-mail address: guenther.filz@uibk.ac.at

UNIVERSITY OF INNSBRUCK, FACULTY OF ARCHITECTURE, INSTITUTE FOR EXPERIMENTAL ARCHITECTURE, AUSTRIA
E-mail address: georg.grasser@uibk.ac.at

UNIVERSITY OF INNSBRUCK, FACULTY OF ARCHITECTURE, INSTITUTE FOR EXPERIMENTAL ARCHITECTURE, AUSTRIA
E-mail address: johannes.ladinig@uibk.ac.at

UNIVERSITY OF INNSBRUCK, FACULTY OF ARCHITECTURE, INSTITUTE OF DESIGN, UNIT.KOGE STRUCTURE AND DESIGN, AUSTRIA
E-mail address: rupert.maleczek@uibk.ac.at

Magnetic Self-Assembly of Three-Dimensional Microstructures

Eiji Iwase and Isao Shimoyama

1. Introduction

In this work, we describe a technique for using a magnetic field to fold two-dimensional (2D) microplates into three-dimensional (3D) microstructures less than 1 mm in size.

Micromachining is well suited to fabricating microstructures on 2D surfaces. Complex 3D microstructures, however, are not as easy to fabricate by micromachining. Therefore, we have used a technique for fabricating crease patterns in 2D microplates using micromachining and then folding the 2D microplates into 3D structures. It is well known that tiny iron filings stand upright when placed on a permanent magnet. The reason for this behavior is shape magnetic anisotropy. Using the same principle, a thin magnetic microplate can be made to stand upright by applying a magnetic field perpendicular to the substrate.

In Section 2, we explain the theory of torque acting on magnetic microplates. In Section 3, we discuss examples and applications of 3D structures produced using shape magnetic anisotropic torque.

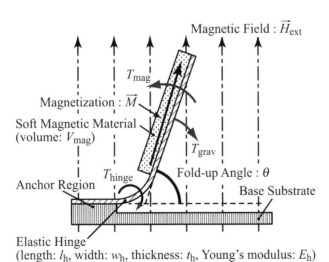

FIGURE 1. Schematic diagram showing a magnetic microplate structure using an elastic hinge and torques acting on a magnetic microplate in the magnetic field.

2. Principle and Theoretical Analysis

To analyze the behavior of a magnetic microplate in a magnetic field theoretically, we first considered a basic structure consisting of a cantilever plate and an elastic hinge, which is anchored on a base substrate, as shown in Figure 1. We used a permalloy and nickel as the plate and elastic hinge materials, respectively. Because the microplate structure is very thin and tiny, the microplate structure is anchored and supported by a silicon base substrate. For theoretical analysis, we assume that the hinge region deforms in the elastic range. Furthermore, we consider the plate region to be a rigid structure because it is thickly coated with a soft magnetic material. In the schematic diagram shown in Figure 1 of torque acting on a magnetic microplate in a magnetic field, T_{mag} is the magnetic anisotropic torque due to an external magnetic field on the microplate, T_{hinge} is the torque generated by elastic deformation of the hinge region, and T_{grav} is the gravitational torque due to the mass of the microplate. The following equation describes how the microplate is lifted up:

(2.1) $T_{\text{mag}} = T_{\text{hinge}} + T_{\text{grav}}.$

We can calculate T_{mag}, T_{hinge}, and T_{grav} as follows. In a uniform magnetic field, the magnetic anisotropic torque T_{mag} is given by the following equation:

(2.2) $T_{\text{mag}} = V_{\text{mag}} \left| \overrightarrow{M} \times \overrightarrow{H_{\text{ext}}} \right|,$

where V_{mag}, M, and H_{ext} represent the volume of the magnetic microplate, the magnetization of the magnetic material, and the strength of the external magnetic field, respectively. Because of its thin shape, a magnetic microplate is more difficult to magnetize in the thickness direction and is easier to magnetize in the length direction. This is called *shape magnetic anisotropy*. Therefore, in the case of an extremely thin plate, we can assume that the plate is magnetized in the length direction due to shape magnetic anisotropy (although, strictly speaking, the magnetization direction is slightly misaligned from the length direction). Furthermore, when we use a material with high magnetic susceptibility, the magnetization M can also be assumed to be the saturation magnetization M_s. Applying these assumptions, Equation (2.2) can be modified as follows:

(2.3) $T_{\text{mag}} = V_{\text{mag}} M_s H_{\text{ext}} \cos \theta,$

where θ represents the angle between the substrate and the microplate, or the fold-up angle.

The elastic torque of the hinge region, T_{hinge}, and the gravitational torque of the magnetic microplate, T_{grav}, can be calculated from the following equations:

(2.4) $T_{\text{hinge}} = E_h \dfrac{w_h \cdot t_h^3}{12 l_h} \theta,$

(2.5) $T_{\text{grav}} = V_{\text{mag}} \dfrac{\rho_{\text{mag}} g}{2} l_{\text{mag}} \cos \theta,$

where E_h, l_h, w_h, and t_h represent the Young's modulus, length, width, and thickness of the hinge, respectively. The density and length of the magnetic microplate are represented respectively by ρ_{mag} and l_{mag}, and g represents the gravitational acceleration (9.8 m/s^2).

When we rearrange Equation (2.1) into the form

(2.6) $T_{\text{mag}} - T_{\text{grav}} = T_{\text{hinge}}$

and substitute Equations (2.3), (2.4), and (2.5) into Equation (2.6), we obtain the following equation:

(2.7) $V_{\text{mag}} \left(M_s H_{\text{ext}} - \dfrac{\rho_{\text{mag}} g}{2} l_{\text{mag}} \right) \cos \theta = E_h \dfrac{w_h \cdot t_h^3}{12 l_h} \theta.$

If we use a permanent magnet, the strength of the magnetic field H_{ext} decreases rapidly with increasing distance from the surface of the magnet. Therefore, when the length of the magnetic microplate l_{mag} is on the order of hundreds of millimeters, the left side of Equation (2.7) is negative. This indicates that a plate of this size is not lifted up, regardless of the hinge design. Therefore, when we use a commercially available permanent magnet for magnetic self-assembly, the microplates that can be used are limited in size to tens of millimeters. In contrast, when the length of the microplate l_{mag} is less than 1 mm, the gravitational torque is much smaller than the magnetic anisotropic torque and thus is negligible.

When permalloy, which is an alloy of nickel and iron, is used, M_s is 1.0 T and ρ_{mag} is 8.6×10^3 kg/m^3. For example, for a 1-mm microplate in a magnetic field of 40 kA/m, which is feasible using a permanent magnet,

$$M_s H_{ext} = 1.0[\text{T}] \times 40 \times 10^3 [\text{A/m}] = 4.0 \times 10^4 [\text{N/m}^2]$$

and

$$\frac{\rho_{mag} g}{2} l_{mag} = \frac{8.6 \times 10^3 [\text{kg/m}^3] \times 9.8 [\text{m/s}^2]}{2} \times 1 \times 10^{-3} [\text{m}] = 4.2 \times 10^1 [\text{N/m}^2].$$

As these example calculations show, the term from the magnetic torque equation ($M_s H_{ext}$) is 10^3 times larger than the term from the gravitational torque equation (($\rho_{mag} g/2) l_{mag}$).

When the length of the microplate l_{mag} is less than 1 mm, the gravitational torque is negligible, and Equation (2.7) can be rearranged as follows:

(2.8)
$$\frac{\theta}{\cos\theta} = \frac{12 M_s}{E_h} \frac{V_{mag} \cdot l_h}{w_h \cdot t_h^3} H_{ext},$$

where $\theta/\cos\theta$ is a monotonically increasing function of θ. The size of the fold-up angle can thus be determined from the right side of Equation (2.8). If the coefficient of H_{ext} on the right side of Equation (2.8) is large, the value of θ increases even in a weak magnetic field. Therefore, the hinged structure becomes more sensitive to the magnetic field. The term $12 M_s/E_h$ is dependent only on the material, but the term $(V_{mag} \cdot l_h)/(w_h \cdot t_h^3)$ is dependent on the shape of the hinge and the shape of the microplate. Therefore, we call the term $(V_{mag} \cdot l_h)/(w_h \cdot t_h^3)$ the *sensitivity factor*, denoted by S, and we use this factor to control the sensitivity to the magnetic field. Using this dimensionless factor S, it is possible to create structures of varying sensitivity on the same substrate.

3. Fabrication of Three-Dimensional Microstructures

Figure 2 shows the process we used to fabricate a microplate structure. First, a 0.28-μm-thick silicon dioxide (SiO$_2$) film was produced by thermal oxidation of a silicon (Si) substrate. An adhesion layer of chromium (Cr) was formed on top of this film, and a 0.2-μm-thick layer of nickel (Ni) layer was sputtered onto that layer (Figure 2(a)). Next, a crease pattern was formed in the Cr and Ni layers. The hinge region and plate region have etching holes (Figure 2(b)) to permit release later. The uncoated areas, such as the hinge region, were covered with photoresist, and the Ni layer was used as a seed layer to electroplate the permalloy layer (Ni 80%, Fe 20%) to a thickness of 4.5 μm (Figure 2(c)–(d)). Finally, the SiO$_2$ layer was removed using hydrogen fluoride (HF), and the Si substrate was etched by reactive ion etching using tetrafluoromethane (CF$_4$) and oxide (O$_2$) (Figure 2(e)). The Si etching is isotropic, so only the areas that have etching holes, i.e., the plate and hinge regions, were released. Therefore, if this fabrication process is used, the plate region needs etching holes as shown in Figures 3–7. If plates without etching holes

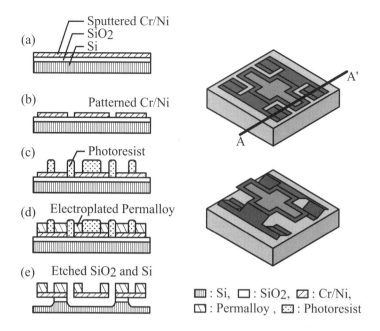

FIGURE 2. The fabrication process for 3D microstructures.

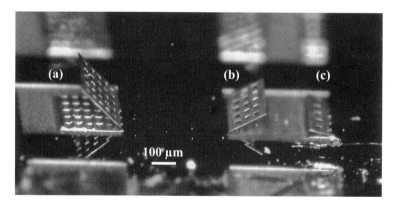

FIGURE 3. Fold-up angles of different-shaped structures in an external magnetic field of 5.0 kA/m. The length of each microplate structure is (a) 300 μm, (b) 200 μm, and (c) 100 μm.

are required, we should choose a different releasing method. Despite the variation in the etching rate between Si and SiO_2, the SiO_2 layer was also removed by the reactive ion etching, so the SiO_2 layer under the plate and hinge regions was also removed. We used nickel, which has a Young's modulus of 210 GPa, to fabricate the hinge. Permalloy was used to fabricate the plate region because of its high magnetic susceptibility and high saturation magnetization of 1.0 T. Thus, even in a weak magnetic field, a large torque can be produced.

Figure 3 shows the different fold-up angle properties of microplate structures with different sensitivity factors. We can change the property by changing the sensitivity factor

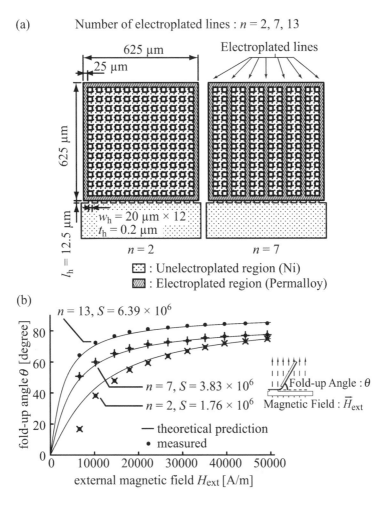

FIGURE 4. (a) Dimensions of the microplate structures, which are only different in the electroplated region. (b) The theoretical curves and measurement results of the fold-up angle under an external magnetic field.

$S = (V_{mag} \cdot l_h)/(w_h \cdot t_h^3)$. In the case of Figure 3, the length of each microplate structure is different. The structures are lifted to stable positions in less than one second by an external magnetic field. Therefore, we should design a multi-step sequential assembly using the sensitivity factor. If the sensitivity factor is different, we can achieve a multi-step sequential assembly by only putting on a permanent magnet. Furthermore, we can also change the sensitivity factor under keeping the shape of the structure as shown in Figure 4. The structures in Figure 4 are different in the electroplating region only. By changing the area of the electroplating region, V_{mag} and S can be designed (Figure 4(b)). In Figure 4(b), the maximum fold-up angle θ is larger than 84.5 degrees (= 0.47π rad) and the length of the hinges l_h is 12.5 μm. Therefore, radius of curvature r (= l_h/θ) is reached at 8.5 μm. Because a thin hinge layer of 0.2 μm is used, very sharp edges can be achieved.

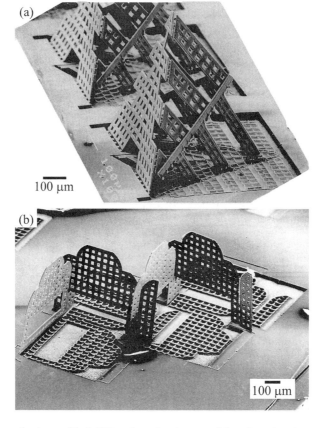

FIGURE 5. Assembled 3D microstructures: (a) microstructures with closed linkages and (b) four-step sequential assembly of four microplate structures.

Using our magnetic self-assembly technique, we have been able to produce complex 3D microstructures, sensors, and actuators. We have assembled complex 3D microstructures with closed linkages and a four-step sequential assembly of four microplate structures as shown in Figure 5 [Iwase and Shimoyama 05, Iwase and Shimoyama 06]. Though we can change the sensitivity factor, the directions of the magnetic torque are the same (i.e., upward direction to the substrate). This is one of design constraints on our method. We can, however, partially solve the constraint by using closed linkages. In addition, recently, many self-folding researchers are focused on a reversible folding [Felton et al. 14, Na et al. 15]. Our method can also achieve the reversible folding. When the external magnetic field is removed, the assembled structures are basically unfolded. On the contrary, if we want to keep the 3D structure without external magnetic field, we can use a Parylene coating or mechanical locking method [Iwase and Shimoyama 03]. The structures of Figure 5(a) are coated with 1-μm-thick Parylene to keep the tetrahedron shape. Though the Parylene is coated in a vacuum chamber, we can set a chip with the structures placed on a permanent magnet into the vacuum chamber. On the other hand, the structure of Figure 5(b) uses a mechanical locking method. The four microplate structures are supporting each other by fiction between the plate structures.

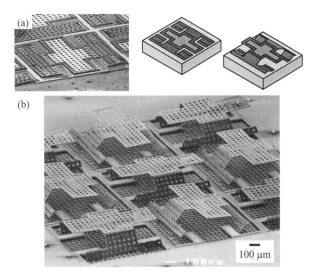

FIGURE 6. 3D microstructures as magnetic actuators (a) before and (b) after assembly.

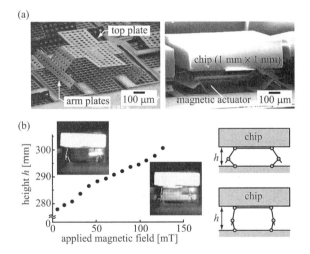

FIGURE 7. (a) Scanning electron microscope (SEM) images and (b) the relationship between the applied magnetic field and the height of the magnetic actuator. A 1-mm-square and 0.2-mm-thick silicon chip is placed on the actuator.

We have also fabricated a tactile sensor with 3D microstructures as sensing units [Noda et al. 12]. Figure 6 shows assembled push-up linkage structures, such as magnetic actuators. The top plates can move up and down depending on the strength of the magnetic field, as shown in Figure 7.

4. Conclusion

Using shape magnetic anisotropy, we succeeded in folding 2D crease patterns, in the manner of origami, to assemble microscopic 3D structures. This technique is suitable for pieces smaller than 1 mm in size and can be used to assemble many microscopic 3D structures simultaneously by placing microfabricated 2D structures on a permanent magnet. Furthermore, using theoretical analysis, we were able to show that the sensitivity to the magnetic field can be represented by a dimensionless number we call the sensitivity factor, S. The value of S can be altered by changing the volume of the magnetic body and the rigidity of the hinge region. Changing the value of S also makes it possible to change the ease of the fold-up angle to magnetic fields within the same substrate. This also permits control of the order of folding. We have successfully applied our magnetic self-assembly technique to the assembly of complex 3D microstructures, sensors, and actuators.

References

[Felton et al. 14] S. Felton, M. Tolley, E. Demaine, D. Rus, and R. Wood. "A Method for Building Self-Folding Machines." *Science* 345:6197 (August 8, 2014), 644–646.

[Iwase and Shimoyama 03] Eiji Iwase and Isao Shimoyama. "Sequential Batch Assembly of 3-D Microstructures by Using a Magnetic Anisotropy and a Magnetic Field." *IEEJ Transactions on Sensors and Micromachines* 123:7 (2003), 224–230. (In Japanese.)

[Iwase and Shimoyama 05] Eiji Iwase and Isao Shimoyama. "Multi-step Sequential Batch Assembly of Three-Dimensional Ferromagnetic Microstructures with Elastic Hinges." *Journal of Microelectromechanical Systems* 14:6 (December 2005), 1265–1271.

[Iwase and Shimoyama 06] Eiji Iwase and Isao Shimoyama. "A Design Method for Out-of-Plane Structures by Multi-step Magnetic Self-Assembly." *Sensors and Actuators A-Physical* 127:2 (March 2006), 310–315.

[Na et al. 15] Jun-Hee Na, Arthur A. Evans, Jinhye Bae, Maria C. Chiappelli, Christian D. Santangelo, Robert J. Lang, Thomas C. Hull, and Ryan C. Hayward. "Programming Reversibly Self-Folding Origami with Micropatterned Photo-Crosslinkable Polymer Trilayers." *Advanced Materials* 27 (2015), 79–85.

[Noda et al. 12] Kentaro Noda, Hiroaki Onoe, Eiji Iwase, Kiyoshi Matsumoto, and Isao Shimoyama. "Flexible Tactile Sensor for Shear Stress Measurement Using Transferred Sub-μm-thick Si Piezoresistive Cantilevers." *Journal of Micromechanics and Microengineering* 22:11 (October 8, 2012), 115025 (7 pages).

WASEDA UNIVERSITY, JAPAN
E-mail address: iwase@waseda.jp

GRADUATE SCHOOL OF INFORMATION SCIENCE AND TECHNOLOGY, UNIVERSITY OF TOKYO, JAPAN
E-mail address: isao@leopard.t.u-tokyo.ac.jp

Folding Augmented: A Design Method to Integrate Structural Folding in Architecture

Pierluigi D'Acunto and Juan José Castellón González

1. Introduction

Origami, the art of folding paper, intuitively shows how folding could be employed to generate complex geometries that have also the potential to perform structurally. As effectively described by Lisa Iwamoto, "Folding turns a flat surface into a three-dimensional one. It is a powerful technique not only for making form but also for creating structure with geometry" [Iwamoto 09]. At the scale of architecture, this is translated into the possibility of using folding as a design operation to generate efficient structures with the capacity of resisting the external loading by form; at the same time, folding can be employed to produce continuous but differentiated forms that are able to address diverse spatial and programmatic requirements. In this regard, as highlighted by Greg Lynn, "If there is a single effect produced in architecture by folding, it will be the ability to integrate unrelated elements within a new continuous mixture" [Lynn 04].

Thanks to its inherent properties, folding has been widely used in architectural education as a source for proto-architectural design, mostly relying on design methods that involve the construction and manipulation of physical models working according to origami techniques [Jackson 11] or more general sheet-material folding [Vyzoviti 03]. It is usually the case, however, that in these design explorations the interplay between space and structure is not made explicit and therefore cannot be entirely investigated by the designer, who addresses it in an intuitive way only. Structural questions, in particular, are often addressed only a posteriori, once the architectural design has been already developed. As a result, during the initial phase of the design process, it is not possible to effectively take advantage of the direct relationship between the structural and spatial potentials of folding.

In general terms, one can identify three main applications of folding to the field of architecture: folding as developable surfaces, folding as transformable mechanisms, and folded-plate structures. A folded geometry is a developable surface when it is possible to map it to a plane by means of isometric transformations only. A folded geometry works as a transformable mechanism if it is deployable and it can be freely folded and unfolded from a compact to an expanded configuration. A folded-plate structure consists of rigid plates that are combined together to form a folded geometry, overall working as a kinematically stable three-dimensional structural system that resists the external applied loads by form. An integration of these different applications of folding to architecture can be also achieved within the same system; this is shown, for example, in the work of Tomohiro Tachi based on computational origami [Tachi 10], in which folding is used to generate developable surfaces that also perform as transformable mechanisms.

The present research is primarily focused on the investigation of architectural folding in the form of folded-plate structures. From an engineering perspective, one of the first and more consistent explorations on the structural properties of folded-plate structures is attributable to Sergio Musmeci, who employed this system at the end of the 1950s for the design of a series of roof structures in reinforced concrete [Musmeci 79]. From an architectural point of view, a reference in this field can be found in the work of Sancho-Madridejos and particularly in the *Capilla en Valleaceron* (1997–2000), which represents the most remarkable project where the architects investigated the spatial opportunities of folding as a method for making space [Sancho and Madridejos 01].

The goal of the research is to introduce a novel design method to consistently integrate structural folding in architecture. The proposed method is aimed at supporting the design process starting from the early conceptual stages. It allows the designer to interactively generate an architectural space based on a free-form folded geometry; it provides, at the same time, the possibility to evaluate the structural properties of the folded system (i.e., its global stability and the magnitude of the internal forces) and to use them as active parameters of the design process. While giving the designer full control on the spatial and structural opportunities of folding, the relationship between the form and the flow of forces inside the folded system is made evident, thus enhancing the effectiveness of folding as a design operation. In this framework, folding is regarded as a way to combine architectural and engineering thinking toward a holistic approach to design.

2. Formalization of the Design Method

The proposed design method to integrate structural folding in architecture is based on a three-dimensional design process that is grounded on the application of simple geometrical operations.[1] Unlike other approaches to architectural folding based on computational origami [Tachi 10], here a surface is virtually folded within a predesigned tetrahedral grid, thus generating the envelope of an enclosed architectural space that, due to its inherent properties, also performs structurally. Being based on geometrical operations only, the proposed design method is, in general, material and scale independent; this allows for the same strategy to be applied to various design scenarios. Nevertheless, restrictions related to specific material properties, fabrication, or scale-dependent constraints can also be addressed and introduced into the design process as geometrical inputs.

The design method includes four main operations. They are not necessarily intended to be implemented following a predefined linear order; in fact, after a complete first iteration of the process, it is possible to re-execute them in a nonsequential way, while keeping intact the overall consistency of the method. Moreover, the same operations can be repeated multiple times during the process, according to the specific design requirements. The operations are as follows:

(A) *Grid generation:* Operation A consists of the generation of a space-filling non-regular tetrahedral grid with edges e and vertices V, which works as a spatial reference for the entire design process (Figure 1(A)). The organization of the tetrahedra within the grid regulates the spatial distribution of the architectural

---

[1]It is important to highlight that folding is here regarded as a virtual design operation and not as an actual physical operation.

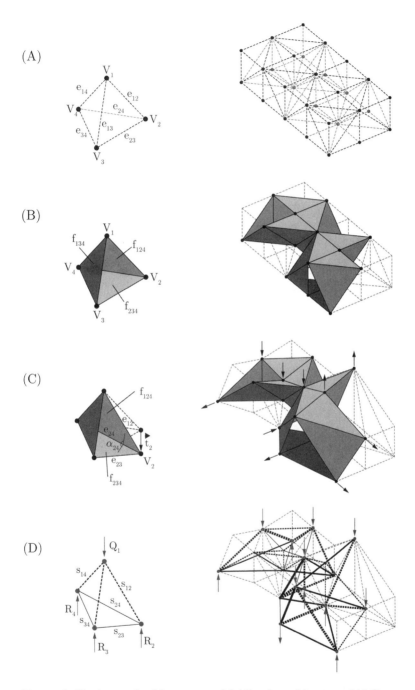

FIGURE 1. Design method for structural folding in architecture: (A) Generation of the tetrahedral grid. (B) Creation of the folded surface and generation of the architectural space. (C) Manipulation of the geometry by moving the vertices of the grid. (D) Evaluation of the internal force flow according to the Plasticity Theory, by means of graphic statics (thick dashed line = compression, thick solid line = tension).

space that will be generated with the following operation. Hence, through Operation A the overall topology of the architectural space is delineated by specifically choosing how many tetrahedra are included in the grid and how they are connected to each other. As such, the definition of the grid can follow explicit programmatic architectural requirements as design inputs. In case a finer resolution is requested for certain parts of the grid, individual tetrahedra could be subdivided into smaller ones. From a structural point of view, the employment of a tetrahedral grid is crucial to attain the global kinematic stability of the folded surface that will be created with the following operation (i.e., the structure does not behave as a mechanism).[2]

(B) *Virtual folding:* Through Operation B, a continuous free-form surface is virtually folded within the previously defined grid (Figure 1(B)); that is, by connecting adjacent faces *f* of the tetrahedral grid, a folded surface is created in the form of an open triangulated mesh.[3] The folded geometry represents the envelope that encloses the requested architectural space. In fact, while producing the folded surface, the actual space is also generated at once. From an architectural perspective, this design approach allows for the conventional tectonic distinction between walls, floor, and ceiling to disappear and to be substituted by the deployment of the folded geometry that performs as a continuous and coherent architectural element and space generator [Carpo 04]. It is through Operation B that the main characteristics of the architectural space can be defined, such as the interior circulation and the number and position of openings to the outside.

(C) *Geometry manipulation:* With Operation C, the geometry of the folded surface can be manipulated by moving the vertices of the tetrahedral grid (Figure 1(C)) using translation vectors **t**. This operation gives the designer the possibility to explore diverse design solutions that share the same topological configuration, as defined with the previous operations; in this way, Operation C provides the opportunity for introducing differentiation and variation into the design process. In particular, the shape and the dimension of the folded geometry can be adjusted in order to meet programmatic and structural requirements or to adapt to certain external boundary constraints, such as environmental or urban questions. With this operation, it is therefore possible to take advantage of the architectural potential of folding to integrate diverse elements and spatial conditions into the same continuous variation of the form [Carpo 04]. Moreover, geometrical restraints can be introduced, with regard to the area $|A_f|$ of the faces of the folded surface, the length $|e|$ of its edges, and the angle α between adjacent faces, to reflect specific design requirements such as material properties, fabrication, or scale-dependent constraints.

(D) *Structural evaluation:* Operation D allows for the structural logic of the previously created folded geometry to be revealed and, with it, the relationship between the internal flow of forces and its overall form (Figure 1(D)). With Operation D the integration between structure and architecture is therefore attained. From an engineering perspective, one of the most peculiar properties of folded structures is their ability to resist the external applied load through their

---

[2]A structural lattice based on a tetrahedral grid has in three dimensions an analogous property of kinematic stability that a triangular grid would have in two dimensions [Wester 11].

[3]In case the faces of the tetrahedral grid lie on the same plane, the correspondent face of the folded surface consists in a triangulated polygon. In general, two or more faces are allowed to meet in the same edge; specific constraints can be introduced in this regard according to the design requirements.

form. In particular, in these structural systems the main internal forces tend to travel along the folded edges, where a local accumulation of high stresses can be observed [Schenk 11]. Because the folded surface is created according to a tetrahedral grid, it is possible to activate within it a load-bearing system that is equivalent to a pin-jointed three-dimensional truss where the folded edges represent the bars of the truss,[4] loaded either in tension or compression [Kotnik and D'Acunto 13], and the vertices correspond to the hinged nodes. A system like this is in general statically indeterminate and the degree of static indeterminacy $\langle n \rangle$ is given by $\langle n \rangle = \langle e \rangle - 3\langle V \rangle + \langle s \rangle$ (where $\langle e \rangle$ is the number of edges, $\langle V \rangle$ the number of vertices, and $\langle s \rangle$ the number of support force variables of the system) [Marti 13, Musmeci 79]. Regarding the truss structure as a rigid-perfectly plastic system, its load-bearing capacity can be assessed according to the *lower-bound theorem*[5] of Plasticity Theory [Muttoni et al. 96]. Following the lower bound-theorem, it is possible to decouple equilibrium, kinematics, and constitutive laws and search for equilibrium solutions only. That is, given an external loading Q, by imposing equilibrium conditions to each node of the structure, the reactions R at the supports and the internal forces s can be evaluated. This process can be performed and visualized by means of *graphic statics*,[6] which makes it is possible to explicitly show the relationship between form and force flow within the structure [Lachauer and Kotnik 10], thereby working as an *operative structural diagram* [Kotnik and D'Acunto 13]. As a result, through Operation D the designer is able to directly address specific structural questions by modifying the geometry of the folded surface.

3. Parametric Digital Tool

A parametric digital tool is under development to facilitate the application of the proposed design method to actual architectural design problems. The parametric tool operates in a three-dimensional software package such as McNeel Rhinoceros 3D or Grasshopper and permits the execution of the design operations, as formalized in the previous section, in a synthetic and intuitive way. In particular, other than supporting the creation of the folded surface based on the tetrahedral grid, the tool allows for the interactive manipulation of the geometry according to a set of parameters. As a result, the designer is able to easily explore different design solutions[7] and is provided at once with real-time direct feedback on the force flow inside the structure [Kotnik and D'Acunto 13]. (Figure 2.)

---

[4] According to this structural model, the faces of the folded surface work as plates rigid in their plane [Tachi 09] and their common edges are regarded as hinge-jointed elements [Wester 11], corresponding to the bars of the truss. Thanks to the presence of the plates, the bars of the truss are restrained along their length against buckling. Moreover, loads perpendicular to the plates are considered as redistributed to the vertices by local bending action in the plane of the plates [Wester 93].

[5] Based on the lower-bound theorem, in a rigid-perfectly plastic system, every loading for which it is possible to specify a statically admissible stress state that does not infringe the yield condition is not greater than the limit load [Marti 13]. The latter can be searched for by exploring the fixed non-plastic domain of the structural system from inside by means of the static method of limit analysis, which is grounded in the lower-bound theorem.

[6] Graphic statics is a synthetic graphical tool by means of which it is possible to search for equilibrium solutions within a loaded structure. The tool is based on the reciprocal relationship between a *form diagram*, representing the configuration of the internal and external forces in relation to the geometry of the structure, and a *force diagram*, representing the equilibrium of the forces [Cremona 90]. Graphic statics can be applied to two- or three-dimensional problems [Schrems and Kotnik 13].

[7] A similar interactive approach can be found in the digital tools for the simulation of rigid origami [Tachi 09], for the freeform design of tensegrity systems [Tachi 12], and for structural design [Lachauer et al. 11].

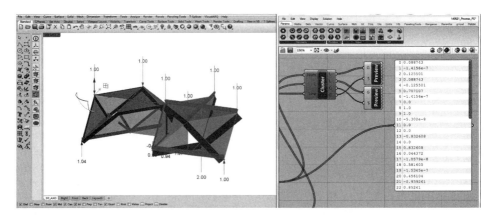

FIGURE 2. Parametric digital tool for structural folding in architecture.

4. Design Implementation

The theoretical formalization of the proposed design method for structural folding in architecture has been informed by the development of a series of architectural design experiments. In order to test the flexibility of the design method and its applicability to diverse design scenarios, the chosen case studies vary in terms of scale and architectural program. Specifically, these case studies have been used to evaluate the effectiveness of the design method with respect to the structural performance and the architectural potentials, and they have provided feedback for the theoretical advances. The parametric digital tool introduced in the previous section has been used as the main operative tool for the design.

The first case study consists in the conceptual design of a pavilion intended as a public entertainment hub as well as a stand for the showcase of consumer electronics products. From an architectural point of view, the main feature of the pavilion is represented by a continuous folded surface that, by wrapping itself in, produces a porous semi-open architectural space (Figure 3). The pavilion is organized on two main levels; the one on the ground floor accommodates an interactive sitting area for children, while the one on top houses a small dark room for projections. In this way, folding has been used to address diverse architectural programs while connecting them together in a coherent way (Figure 4). Access to the top level is allowed by the presence of a ramp that, being part of the folded surface, also doubles as the roof of the sitting area on the lower level. The base of the pavilion is reduced to the minimum in order to limit the footprint of the building on the ground. Thanks to the inherent structural properties of the folded surface, the small dark room for projections completely cantilevers out of the base of the pavilion. In this sense, the project shows a seamless integration between the structural solution and the architectural intention. Although the form of the pavilion presents a high level of complexity, the folded surface has been completely designed by the iterative execution of simple geometrical operations like the ones introduced in the proposed design method (Figure 5).

The second case study is represented by a compact public art gallery, which is entirely contained within a cube with a side length of nine meters (Figure 6). The building is characterized by the presence of a spiraling ramp that directly connects the ground level to the rooftop; the ramp is intended as an architectural promenade that runs through the building and generates a continuous gallery acting as the main exhibition space. A small auditorium is housed beneath the ramp, on the ground floor, and has independent access from the

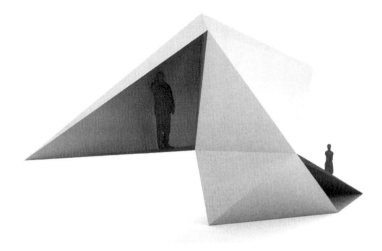

FIGURE 3. Folded pavilion generated using the proposed design method.

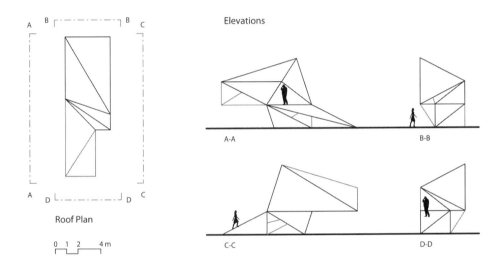

FIGURE 4. Roof plan and elevations for the folded pavilion.

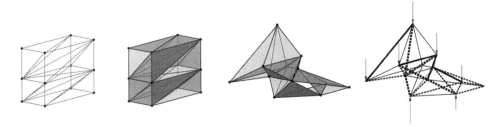

FIGURE 5. Application of the design method (Operations A to D) to the development of a folded pavilion.

FIGURE 6. Folded art gallery generated using the proposed design method.

outside. From a design point of view, the architectural opportunities of folding have been here exploited to produce a continuous surface that unfolded itself while rising up in the shape of the spiraling ramp and then folds back into itself to generate the external envelope of the building (Figure 7). Hence, folding has been used in the building in the form of a porous warped surface that adapts itself into space to accommodate the circulation pattern of the art gallery.

During the design process (Figure 8), specific geometrical constraints have been introduced to limit the angles between adjacent faces of the folded ramp, to avoid undesired steep slopes. In addition, particular attention has been put toward defining the number and the position of the openings of the folded surface to the outside, in order to achieve the requested lighting conditions along the spiraling gallery. The possibility of creating openings in the folded surface is guaranteed by the intrinsic structural capacity of the system based on a tetrahedral grid, which is able to withstand diverse vertical and horizontal loadings by activating a suitable load-bearing configuration.

5. Conclusion and Future Work

The present research has introduced a novel design method to facilitate the integration of structural folding in architecture. Special importance has been put into the formalization of the operations around which the design method is built, in order to reduce the complexity of the design process to the iterative execution of simple geometrical operations. In particular, thanks to the inclusion into the design method of a structural model for folding based on the Plasticity Theory and working with graphic statics, the designer is given the opportunity to explore the spatial possibilities of folding while controlling its structural

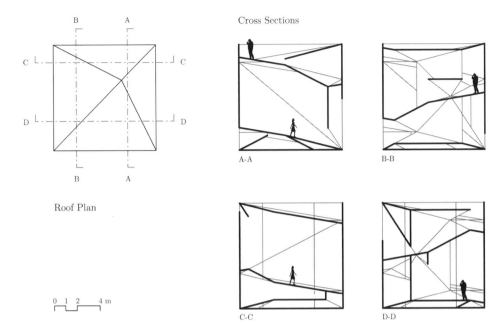

FIGURE 7. Roof plan and cross sections of the folded art gallery.

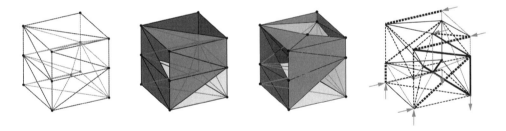

FIGURE 8. Application of the design method (Operations A to D) to the development of a folded art gallery.

potentials in a synthetic and intuitive way. As shown by the case studies analyzed in Section 4, the proposed method allows the designer to effectively combine architectural and engineering thinking starting from the conceptual phase of the design process.

As the next step in the research, the application of the proposed method to the development of additional architectural designs based on folding is expected with the goal to further investigate its applicability to actual design problems. As such, specific context, programmatic, and structural constraints will be taken into account within the design process. In addition, the production of physical full-scale prototypes will also be investigated in the future, to test the design method against material and fabrication issues.

References

[Carpo 04] Mario Carpo. "Ten Years of Folding." In *Folding in Architecture*, Revised Edition, Architectural Design Series, edited by Greg Lynn, pp. 14–18. West Sussex, UK: John Wiley & Sons, Ltd., 2004.

[Cremona 90] Luigi Cremona. "Polygon of Forces and Funicular Polygon as Reciprocal Figures." In *Graphical Statics* (English Translation), pp. 131–142. Oxford, UK: Oxford University Press, 1890.

[Iwamoto 09] Lisa Iwamoto. *Digital Fabrications: Architectural and Material Techniques*, p.62. New York: Princeton Architectural Press, 2009.

[Jackson 11] Paul Jackson. *Folding Techniques for Designers: From Sheet to Form*. London: Laurence King Publishing, 2011.

[Kotnik and D'Acunto 13] Toni Kotnik and Pierluigi D'Acunto. "Operative Diagramatology: Structural Folding for Architectural Design." In *Rethinking Prototyping: Proceedings of Design Modelling Symposium Berlin 2013*, edited by Christoph Gengnagel, Axel Kilian, Julien Nembrini, and Fabian Scheurer, pp. 193–203. Berlin: Universität der Künste Berlin, 2013.

[Lachauer and Kotnik 10] Lorenz Lachauer and Toni Kotnik. "Geometry of Structural Form." In *Advances in Architectural Geometry 2010*, edited by Cristiano Ceccato, Lars Hasselgren, Mark Pauly, Helmut Pottmann, and Johannes Wallner, pp. 193–203. Vienna: Springer, 2010.

[Lachauer et al. 11] Lorenz Lachauer, Hauke Jungjohann, and Toni Kotnik. "Interactive Parametric Tools for Structural Design." In *Taller, Longer, Lighter: Proceedings of the IABSE-IASS Symposium 2011*, CD-ROM. London: IABSE/IASS, 2011.

[Lynn 04] Greg Lynn. "Architectural Curvilinearity: The Folded, the Pliant and the Supple." In *Folding in Architecture*, Revised Edition, Architectural Design Series, edited by Greg Lynn, p. 24. West Sussex, UK: John Wiley & Sons Ltd., 2004.

[Marti 13] Peter Marti. *Theory of Structures: Fundamentals, Framed Structures, Plates and Shells*. Berlin: Wiley-VCH Verlag GmbH & Co. KGaA, 2013. MR3221664

[Musmeci 79] Sergio Musmeci. "La Genesi della Forma nelle Strutture Spaziali." In *Sergio Musmeci o delle Tensioni Incognite*, Parametro 80, edited by Giorgio Trebbi, pp. 13–32. Faenza, Italy: Faenza Editrice S.p.A., 1979.

[Muttoni et al. 96] Aurelio Muttoni, Joseph Schwartz, and Bruno Thürlimann. *Design of Concrete Structures with Stress Fields*. Basel: Birkhäuser, 1996.

[Sancho and Madridejos 01] Juan Carlos Sancho and Sol Madridejos. *Suite en 3 Movimientos*. Madrid: Editorial Rueda S. L., 2001.

[Schenk 11] Mark Schenk. "Folded Shell Structures." PhD dissertation, University of Cambridge, Cambridge, UK, 2011.

[Schrems and Kotnik 13] Maximilian Schrems and Toni Kotnik. "On the Extension of Graphical Statics into the 3rd Dimension." In *Structures and Architecture: New Concepts, Applications and Challenges*, edited by Paulo J. Cruz, pp. 1735–1742. Boca Raton, FL: CRC Press, 2013.

[Tachi 09] Tomohiro Tachi. "Simulation of Rigid Origami." In *Origami^4: Fourth International Meeting of Origami Science, Mathematics, and Education*, edited by Robert J. Lang, pp. 175–216. Wellesley, MA: A K Peters, 2009. MR2590567 (2010h:00025)

[Tachi 10] Tomohiro Tachi. "Architectural Origami: Architectural Form Design Systems Based on Computational Origami." Lecture Notes for MIT Course 6.849, Cambridge, MA, Fall 2010.

[Tachi 12] Tomohiro Tachi. "Interactive Freeform Design of Tensegrity." In *Advances in Architectural Geometry 2012*, pp. 259–268. Vienna: Springer, 2012.

[Vyzoviti 03] Sophia Vyzoviti. *Folding Architecture: Spatial, Structural and Organizational Diagrams*. Amsterdam: Bis Publishers, 2003.

[Wester 93] Ture Wester. "Efficient Faceted Surface Structures." In *Space Structures 4: Proceedings of the 4th International Conference on Space Structures*, edited by G. A. R. Parke and C. M. Howard, pp. 1231–1239. London: Thomas Telford Services, 1993.

[Wester 11] Ture Wester. "3D Form and Force Language: Proposal for a Structural Basis." *International Journal of Space Structures* 26:3 (2011), 229–239.

CHAIR OF STRUCTURAL DESIGN, DARCH, ETH ZÜRICH, SWITZERLAND
E-mail address: dacunto@arch.ethz.ch

CHAIR OF STRUCTURAL DESIGN, DARCH, ETH ZÜRICH, SWITZERLAND
E-mail address: castellon@arch.ethz.ch

Demands on an Adapted Design Process for Foldable Structures

Susanne Hoffmann, Martin Barej, Benedikt Günther,
Martin Trautz, Burkhard Corves, and Jörg Feldhusen

1. Introduction

The construction principle of folding provides an alternative to established concepts when those do not provide satisfactory results for a given task. Applying folds to plates allows one to create strengthened structures that are also deployable. Due to a number of advantageous properties—strengthening, deployability, and spatial partition—origami-based structures are promising for architectural and other engineering applications, as shown in Figure 1.

Since origami, the art of folding paper, represents a wide-ranging art form, there are numerous origami categories, with only some of them eligible for technical applications. Tessellation origami consisting of repeating patterns is one of the most suitable categories. However, besides tessellation origami there are structures allocated to other origami categories such as modular origami or curved origami that also offer potential for engineering tasks. Unfortunately, origami-based deployable plate structures are rarely seen in technical and architectural applications. The few realized structures—for example, the Hörn Bridge in Kiel [GMP 15]—are usually based on an array of longitudinal folds. Furthermore, these structures require supporting mechanisms and thus the principle of origami-based folding

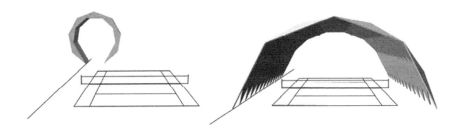

FIGURE 1. Deployable roof structure based on a tessellation origami pattern (Yoshimura [Miura 69]), student project "Origami Modular—Foldable Structure", by C. Bormann.

is not implemented. Besides technical challenges, there is another central reason for the absence of deployable folds in architectural and other engineering applications: Due to its interdisciplinary nature, existing design processes do not work in the development of origami-based deployable structures. Therefore, an adapted design process must be sought out.

The central tasks, issues arising during designing foldable structures, and the adequate methods to be used are not listed, categorized, and compiled in one interdisciplinary document. Publications are rare, or nonexistent, in which anticipated problems, the methods to be used, and a reasonable order of necessary process steps are concretized. An interdisciplinary adapted design process is indispensable in order to build the promising origami-based deployable structures consisting of plate material usable for technical applications, beginning with architectural tasks.

2. Common Design Processes in Architecture and Mechanical Engineering

For the design of transformable structures for architectural applications, architects and mechanical engineers have to cooperate in a multi-disciplinary working group. These two disciplines typically use different design processes, and it is a challenge to combine them.

There is one obligatory design process for all architects and civil engineers who operate in Germany, the fee schedule HOAI [Werner and Pastor 13]. Besides the fee, the HOAI regulates the required project outcomes, the deliverables, and their order. As shown in Figure 2 (left), the design process of the HOAI consists of nine phases. Phases 1–5 broach the issue of design, and phases 6–9 focus on realization concerns. The process depicted in the HOAI is formulated generally for all kinds of building tasks. For this reason, it does not broach any of the special issues arising during the design of deployable folds.

In mechanical engineering, the design process according to the guideline VDI 2221 [VDI 93] is a common approach. It consists of seven steps and ends with the documentation of the finalized design, as shown in Figure 2 (right). Because VDI 2221 is a design process guideline, more methods are drafted compared to the HOAI. For example, a decomposition of the problem into several subproblems is proposed. Comparable to the HOAI, the VDI 2221 guideline is formulated in a general manner and thereby is eligible to develop deployable folds as well. However, specific information is missing about the design of foldable structures, e.g. recommended methods.

In principal, both processes form an adequate basis for an adapted design process to develop deployable folds. As the process steps in VDI 2221 and HOAI correlate with each other, interdisciplinary cooperation is possible.

As both processes do not concern the topic of designing deployable folds, the basic principles have to be compiled empirically. The first step is the identification of recurring typical problems and the categorization of basic functionalities. To get a multiplicity of possible functionalities and typical problems, a variety of different realized projects has to be analyzed. As they do not exist, a first step is the analysis and the evaluation of student design projects.

3. Design Task and Educational Concept of Student Projects

Over the past few years, the authors have performed many interdisciplinary projects, with both architecture and mechanical engineering students. The scope of the work of the mechanical engineering students is rather theoretical, whereas the architecture students' topics are mostly design tasks. As the identification of possible functionalities and the

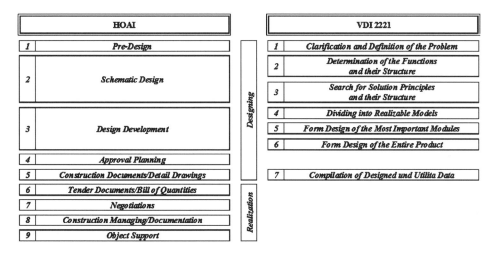

FIGURE 2. Typical processes in architecture (left: according to HOAI (translation based on [BDA 11], partially modified)) and mechanical engineering (right: according to VDI 2221).

compilation of typical problems are more evident on the basis of design projects, the architecture students' projects are the ones presented in this paper. The selected ones are three small design projects, called ad hoc design projects, and a more extensive design project, which represents the main semester task for a master student. In compliance with the examination regulations [RWTH 12], the ad hoc design projects are short-term educational projects with a scope of 1.5 credit points. The task has to be formulated in a free manner and has to contain artistic and philosophical issues. Projects dealing with the art of folding paper fit perfectly into these basically formulated tasks.

3.1. Ad hoc design project "Origami-Installation". The project "Origami-Installation" took place in the 2012–2013 winter term. The two-week task was to design a suspended sculpture for the entrance area of an office. This art object had to deal with origami principles and supporting structures. The space in which the installation was to take place has the dimensions 3.30 m × 2.90 m and a maximum height of 2.00 m. The students were free to decide if this structure is a folded or a foldable origami-based structure. One part of the task was to realize the structure in original dimensions and build it in a final presentation, which made it suitable for work in teams. To motivate the students not to use paper (because of its negligible thickness) but to use plate material instead, corrugated cardboard was provided. Besides the task where only basic information was given for the final presentation, only one intermediate review took place. This first educational project was not interdisciplinary. During the design process, numerous questions about kinematic concerns arose, so it was decided the next ad hoc design project would include an interdisciplinary teaching team consisting of architects and mechanical engineers.

3.2. Ad hoc design project "Miura-Ori". The first interdisciplinary ad hoc design project "Miura-Ori" took place in the 2013 summer term. The task, for a period of three weeks, was the development of a functional, deployable, folded plate structure. This structure was to consist of plates with a thickness of at least cardboard dimensions (paper was not sufficient!), and it was to be made of at least one Miura-ori basic unit. The construction had to fulfill a self-defined function and had to be designed for a place chosen by the

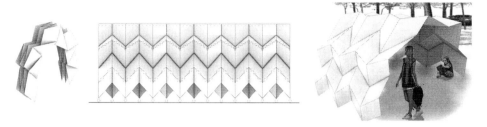

FIGURE 3. Sample result of the project "Miura-Ori", by H. Luh and C. Schmidt.

students. In the introductory presentation, more information was given to the participating students compared to the prior ad hoc project "Origami-Installation". The specific characteristics of the Miura-Ori with its variety of possible arrangements, reaching from radially to alternating to freeform arrays, were broached as an issue. Furthermore, international research activities in the field of technical origami and possible tools were briefly outlined, e.g., the software Freeform Origami [Tachi 15]. Comparable to the previous project, two reviews and presentations took place, but this time a mechanical engineer with expertise in the field of kinematics completed the teaching team. Interesting results (e.g., shown in Figure 3), but above all an awareness for folding-specific challenges, were created during this short period. As this course only generated a few credit points, no further follow-up of these projects took place.

3.3. Ad hoc design project "Origami Modular—Foldable Structure". The comparison of the two previous projects' results showed that with more information and with some interdisciplinary assistance—as it took place in the "Miura-Ori" design project—the specific challenges of folded plate structures are worked out more intensively. In order to optimize the teaching concept and with the aim to achieve even better results, it was decided to integrate one more specialist, a mechanical engineer with expertise in the field of engineering design. This time the task was to develop a functional, deployable folded plate structure that consisted of plates with non-negligible thickness. The structure had to be based on modular origami or tessellation origami. It had to fulfill a self-defined function at an arbitrary place. Besides the presentation about origami and the specific challenges of designing foldable structures, information about mechanisms was given, e.g., [DMG-Lib 15]. As the reviews were conducted by architects and mechanical engineers, the discussions comprised a wide range of architectural, kinematical, and engineering-design concerns. The students gladly accepted these offers and generated a multitude of diverse results based on different origami categories. Basically, it can be confirmed that the generated results improved from project to project as the students were able to identify their specific problems in earlier design stages.

3.4. Design project "Rheinhafen-Bridge". The interdisciplinary teaching concept of the design project "Rheinhafen-Bridge" and selected project results are presented in [Barej et al. 14] and [Hoffmann et al. 13], and therefore it is not discussed here. But, the analysis results are applied in the following sections. Figure 4 shows one representative result of this design project.

FIGURE 4. Project "Rheinhafen-Bridge", by M. Schwab.

4. Development and Results

The development processes as well as the results among the four projects differed considerably for the following reasons: (1) the students spent different amounts of time on their tasks, (2) they worked alone or in groups, and (3) the offered (interdisciplinary) assistance varied.

As the development process of the project "Rheinhafen-Bridge" is already presented in other publications and since the project "Miura-Ori" is neither the initial nor the optimized ad hoc project, representative analyses of the two projects "Origami-Installation" and "Origami Modular—Foldable Structure" are presented here. However, the subsequent generalization is based on the analysis of all projects.

To the review of "Origami-Installation", the students brought a selection of origami patterns and paper models (see Figure 5(a)). They identified the selections independently and intuitively as promising structures. First design approaches and spatial arrangements were examined. This bottom-up approach is often used for ad hoc design projects, as these are formulated very generally and therefore allow a high amount of artistic freedom. Nevertheless, tangible solutions had to be generated during the second week, as corrugated cardboard had to be used. The concept was to first divide the chosen waterbomb structure into square and triangle elements and to reassemble them afterward. In consideration of the plate thickness and in order to allow the desired motion, the elements were positioned on adhesive tape with distances of 0.5–2.0 cm from each other, as shown in Figure 5(b). For design reasons, the adhesive tape was fixed only on the far side. Ropes, to enable transportation and hanging from the ceiling, were fixed at each tip of the four creases (see Figure 5(c)). This joining concept failed as the adhesive tape delaminated. Further, it was impossible to transport the model to the requested place. Therefore, the presentation was held at the students' workplace, to prevent the model from bursting at the inadequate joints. During the transformation of the origami-based structure, some cardboard plates loosened, as shown in Figure 5(d). Despite this apparent failure, this project was extremely helpful for future work as it made the weak points visible.

An example from "Origami Modular—Foldable Structure" is a deployable temporary roof structure. Comparable to the former project, the students initially dealt with folding paper. They first tried objects from the category modular origami, and during their inquiry they found the origami pattern "Little Turtle" [Fuse 90, p. 56]. They modified and simplified this origami pattern, which originally allows the construction of spatial geometric objects. Finally, they developed a new module consisting of plate material connected by hinges. One module consists of three hexagons and twelve triangles. Even this basic module is transformable. Detailed development of the hinges and their connections was not performed within the project, but a conceptual model was built. The plates were connected

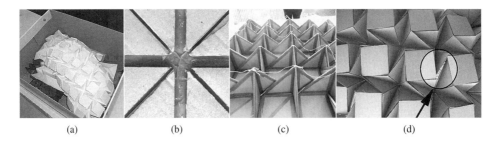

(a)   (b)   (c)   (d)

FIGURE 5. Development process of "Origami-Installation," by L. Heßling, M. Schwab, S. Pascale, and S. Wenquian: (a) Paper model (pre-design/schematic design) and (b)–(d) cardboard model including tape joints and actuator rope (design development).

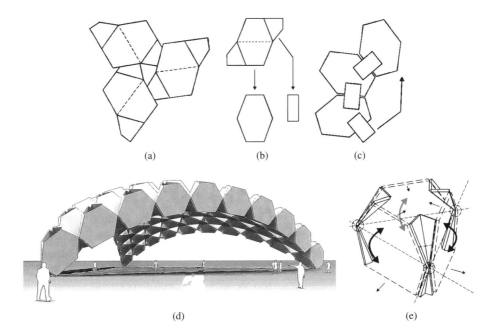

FIGURE 6. Development process of "Origami Modular—Foldable Structure," by F. Francken and H. Elfezazi: (a) Origami pattern (pre-design), (b)–(c) decomposition and composition (schematic design), (d) spatial impression (design development), and (e) construction principle (detail drawing).

with fabric adhesive tape, which allowed a good load transmission. The tape was applied only on the inner side. Although the structure consisted of a great number of modules, it did not rip during the transformation process. To move the entire structure, towing ropes were required at the support points on the base. Figure 6 shows intermediate steps of the design process and the result.

		"Origami-Installation"	"Miura-Ori"	"Origami Modular—Foldable Structure"	"Rheinhafen-Bridge"
1	Pre-design	+	(+)	(+)	+
2	Schematic design	+	+	+	+
3	Design development	+	+	+	+
4	Approval planning	–	–	–	(+)
5	Construction documents/ detail drawings	+	(+)	(+)	+

FIGURE 7. Comparison of process steps, where + means students deal with this phase, (+) means students deal with this phase partially, and – means students do not deal with this phase.

5. Analysis Outcomes Based on Student Design Projects

As student projects are normally not fully realized, they do not cover all phases of the HOAI. The process phases of realization—except for constructing a significant model—are not provided. During the design process, not all phases are dealt with, e.g., the approval planning is excluded. Figure 7 shows which phases were principally dealt with.

Even though the student design projects do not deliver the complete image of a typical design (and realization) process, the results generate a number of application concepts and constructive ideas.

5.1. Functional purposes of origami-based foldable structures. Both the architect and the mechanical engineer normally get a task to fulfill a certain functionality and have to find a suitable solution. Typically, the construction principle is not given in order to allow the best solution.

It is often asserted that origami patterns offer potential for technical purposes, but no precise applications are named. On this account, the construction principle is part of the definition of the student design projects with the aim to generate a number of possible tasks for origami-based structures. Thereby, plenty of interesting ideas for using origami patterns are generated. Some of those are compiled and assigned to their functionalities in Figure 8.

Normally every foldable structure fulfills more than one purpose—for example, every presented project idea is deployable and works as a load-bearing structure—but some of them have other important characteristics. This compilation is not meant as a complete diagram but as a proposal for a scheme that is continuously growing.

It can be noted that the most ideas are generated for the most well-known origami patterns: the Miura-ori folding pattern followed by combined (other) patterns and the Yoshimura folding pattern. This observation leads to the conclusion that the simplest folding patterns from the origami category tessellation origami are the most appropriate ones for architectural tasks, which have to be tested and evaluated in further research activities.

5.2. Typical challenges arising during the design process. Within the four design projects, some folding-specific problems arose again and again. These problems can be assigned to the topics transfer, kinematic challenges, and functionality, as shown in Figure 9.

Transfer problems often appear when the paper model suggests simplicity, which vanishes when the pattern is applied to plate material. As paper has an ideal thickness of zero, many stacked layers depict no problem. However, even a cardboard model shows that the maximum compacted state still has a significant volume, and real flat-foldability is not

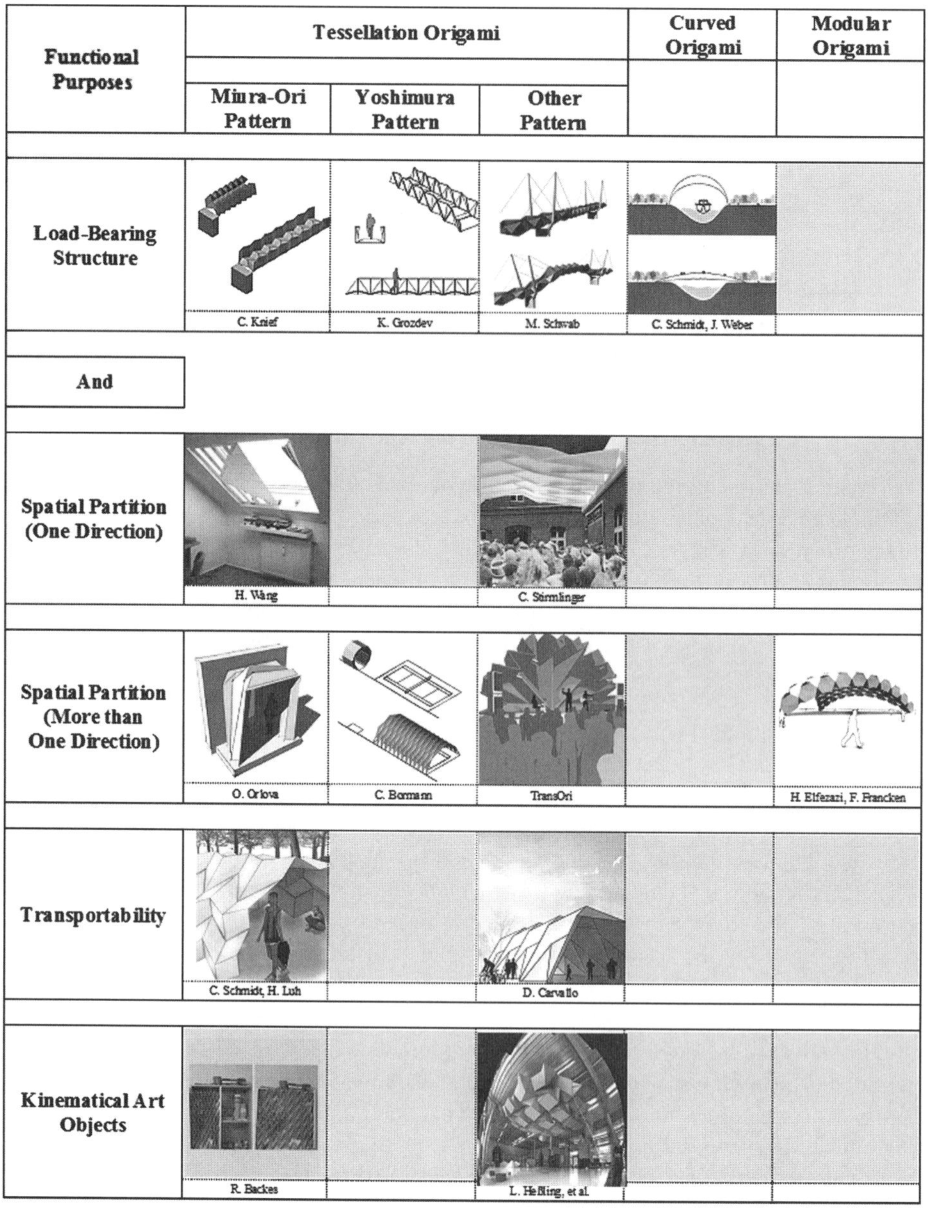

Functional Purposes	Tessellation Origami			Curved Origami	Modular Origami
	Miura-Ori Pattern	Yoshimura Pattern	Other Pattern		
Load-Bearing Structure	C. Knief	K. Grozdev	M. Schwab	C. Schmidt, J. Weber	
And					
Spatial Partition (One Direction)	H. Wang		C. Stirmlinger		
Spatial Partition (More than One Direction)	O. Orlova	C. Bormann	TransOri		H. Elfezazi, F. Francken
Transportability	C. Schmidt, H. Luh		D. Carvallo		
Kinematical Art Objects	R. Backes		L. Heßling, et al.		

FIGURE 8. Functional purposes for origami-based foldable structures.

achievable. The next transfer step during the design process is the one from a functioning cardboard model to a three-dimensional model constructed with CAD software, and it is as challenging as the formerly described one. While the cardboard model performs the desired motion, the plates of the three-dimensional model do not move. This difference may be attributed to too generous tolerances in the connections or infinitesimal deformations of the cardboard plates.

Kinematic challenges of the complete structure arise when motion is not transmitted as expected but the energy dissipates, e.g., in deformation of the plate material. Then,

(a) Transfer.

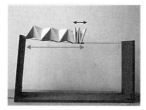
(b) Kinematic challenges.

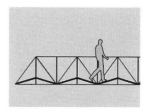
(c) Functionality.

FIGURE 9. Examples of typical problems arising during the design process of foldable structures: (a) "Origami-Installation," by L. Hesssing, M. Schwab, S. Pascale, and S. Wenquian, and (b)–(c) "Origami Modular—Foldable Structure," by K. Grozdev.

supporting structures are required, and thus the principle of folding subsequently cannot be implemented. Further manufacturing tolerances and backlash can lead to restraints and inhibition of motion. The design of joints also forms a kinematic challenge as translational motions can appear and/or the plates have to be beveled. These topics are discussed in [Künstler and Trautz 11], [Tachi 11], and [Buffart and Trautz 13], but many of the mostly intuitively developed student projects lead to these specific problems also.

Challenges of *functionality* arise in the formation of the complete structure and in detail problems. As deployable folded plate constructions consist of angularly connected plates, the pure load-bearing structure often does not deliver functional solutions, and additional layers are necessary, e.g., as shown in Figure 9(c) for a flat walkway. Furthermore, the architectonic details are of high demand especially concerning water conduction and impermeability.

Additionally organizational topics can lead to folding-specific problems, such as the absence of an adequate CAD software and the selection of inappropriate model material.

The biggest challenge at this time might be the already mentioned low degree of popularity of the construction principle of "folding."

6. Conclusion and Outlook

Based on the presented analysis of student projects, possible functionalities and challenges for the construction of deployable folds are presented here. It is also shown that the process steps used by the student designers can be assigned to steps of existing processes.

In both architecture and mechanical engineering, a real project task is normally not formulated as "design a deployable folded plate structure." The task is to "find a structural solution within given functional requirements for a given place" or, formulated more generally, to "find a solution for a given problem."

Thus, the critical planner has to ask the following questions:

- Is a foldable structure a suitable solution for a given task?
- Is a foldable structure competitive to alternative solutions?
- Will a foldable structure (at least in Germany) pass Phase 4 (approval planning), although it is not state of the art and general technical approvals do not exist?

Most of these questions can be answered only under specific conditions.

There are more research and planning activities necessary to make foldable structures a competitive principle for technical applications. Besides further identification of functionalities and the compilation of specific problems for every project phase, one important topic is the development of efficient tools and methods.

In the context of student projects, more information about the design process has to be generated. This goal can be reached if not just the final results are delivered but also the rejected alternatives, including the reasons for rejecting them, are documented. The utilized methods and tools, e.g., software, have to be recorded, and ideally the original files are submitted. To generate basic information for an interdisciplinary-developed valid design process, not just the educational staff but also the student teams should be interdisciplinary. To generate more detailed information, longer working periods and courses with higher relevance within the curriculum are desirable.

In addition to educational activities, superior research projects are necessary. As already shown in Figure 7, student design projects normally do not treat the realization of a structure. According to the authors' experience, many problems arise during these project phases, so realizing an origami-based foldable structure is inevitable. In an ongoing research project, the interdisciplinary design (and its further realization) of a demonstrator is tested and evaluated.

Further planned and realized projects have to be identified and analyzed. The superior target must be the evaluation of the design (and realization) process of real foldable load-bearing structures. After that, an adapted design process can be developed.

There is still a long way to the completion of a valid interdisciplinary design process for developing foldable structures in architectural and technical applications, but the first steps have been taken.

Acknowledgments

The authors want to thank all students who participated in the presented design projects to allow the critical presentation of their results and the Exploratory Research Space at RWTH Aachen for supporting and financing interdisciplinary research activities.

References

[Barej et al. 14] Martin Barej, Susanne Hoffmann, Giovanni Della Puppa, Mathias Hüsing, Burkhard Corves, and Martin Trautz. "Mechanism Theory in Architecture Education." In *New Trends in Educational Activity in the Field of Mechanism and Machine Theory*, Mechanisms and Machine Science 19, edited by Juan Carlos Garcia-Prada and Cristina Castejón, pp. 277–284. Cham: Springer International Publishing, 2014.

[BDA 11] Bund Deutscher Architekten (BDA). "Architects in Germany." http://www.bda-bund.de/fileadmin/ mediaFiles/Bundesverband/pdfs/CoFA_Flyer.pdf, 2011. (Retrieved February 9, 2015.)

[Buffart and Trautz 13] Henri C. Buffart and Martin Trautz. "Construction Approach for Deployable Folded Plate Structures without Transversal Joint Displacement." In *Proceedings of the First Conference Transformables 2013*, edited by Felix Escrig and Jose Sanchez, pp. 331–336. Sevilla: Starbooks, 2013.

[DMG-Lib 15] DMG-Lib. "Digital Mechanism and Gear Library." www.dmg-lib.org/dmglib/main/portal.jsp, retrieved February 9, 2015.

[Fuse 90] Tomoko Fuse. *Unit Origami: Multidimensional Transformations*. Tokyo: Japan Publications, 1990.

[GMP 15] GMP. "Bridge across the River Hoern." www.gmp-architekten.com/projects/ bridge-across-the-river-hoern.html, retrieved February 9, 2015.

[Hoffmann et al. 13] Susanne Hoffmann, Martin Barej, Giovanni Della Puppa, Mathias Hüsing, Martin Trautz, and Burkhard Corves. "Interdisciplinary Design of Movable Structures in Architecture Education." In *Proceedings of the First Conference Transformables 2013*, edited by Felix Escrig and Jose Sanchez, pp. 411–416. Sevilla: Starbooks, 2013.

[Künstler and Trautz 11] Arne Künstler and Martin Trautz. "Wandelbare Faltungen aus biegesteifen Faltelementen" ("Deployable Folding Patterns Using Stiff Plate Elements"). *Bautechnik* 88 (2011), 86–93.

[Miura 69] Koryo Miura. "Proposition of Pseudo-cylindrical Concave Polyhedral Shells." Technical Report No. 442, Institute of Space and Aeronautical Science, University of Tokyo, Tokyo, Japan, 1969.

[RWTH 12] Rheinisch-Westfälische Technische Hochschule Aachen (RWTH). "Prüfungsordnung für den Master-Studiengang Architektur der Rheinisch-WestfÃd'lischen Technischen Hochschule Aachen" ("Examination Regulations for the Master's Degree Program in Architecture at the Rheinisch-Westfälische Technische Hochschule Aachen"). http://arch.rwth-aachen.de/global/show_document.asp?id=aaaaaaaaaacvfta, March 22, 2012.

[Tachi 11] Tomohiro Tachi. "Rigid-Foldable Thick Origami." In *Origami^5: Fifth International Meeting of Origami Science, Mathematics, and Education*, edited by Patsy Wang-Iverson, Robert J. Lang, and Mark Yim, pp. 253–263. Boca Raton, FL: A K Peters/CRC Press, 2011. MR2866909 (2012h:00044)

[Tachi 15] Tomohiro Tachi. "Freeform Origami Software." http://www.tsg.ne.jp/TT/software/, retrieved June 18, 2015.

[VDI 93] VDI-Fachbereich Produktentwicklung und Mechatronik. *Methodik zum Entwickeln und Konstruieren technischer Systeme und Produkte (Systematic Approach to the Development and Design of Technical Systems and Products)*, VDI-Richtlinie: VDI 2221. Berlin: Beuth, 1993.

[Werner and Pastor 13] Ulrich Werner and Walter Pastor. *Vergabe- und Vertragsordnung für Bauleistungen: Honorarordnung für Architekten und Ingenieure (German Construction Contract Procedures: Official Scale of Fees for Services by Architects and Engineers)*. München: Deutscher Taschenbuch Verlag, 2013.

CHAIR OF STRUCTURES AND STRUCTURAL DESIGN, RWTH AACHEN UNIVERSITY, GERMANY
E-mail address: hoffmann@trako.arch.rwth-aachen.de

DEPARTMENT OF MECHANISM THEORY AND DYNAMICS OF MACHINES, RWTH AACHEN UNIVERSITY, GERMANY
E-mail address: barej@igm.rwth-aachen.de

INSTITUTE FOR ENGINEERING DESIGN, RWTH AACHEN UNIVERSITY, GERMANY
E-mail address: guenther@ikt.rwth-aachen.de

CHAIR OF STRUCTURES AND STRUCTURAL DESIGN, RWTH AACHEN UNIVERSITY, GERMANY
E-mail address: trautz@trako.arch.rwth-aachen.de

DEPARTMENT OF MECHANISM THEORY AND DYNAMICS OF MACHINES, RWTH AACHEN UNIVERSITY, GERMANY
E-mail address: corves@igm.rwth-aachen.de

INSTITUTE FOR ENGINEERING DESIGN, RWTH AACHEN UNIVERSITY, GERMANY
E-mail address: feldhusen@ikt.rwth-aachen.de

Planning Motions for Shape-Memory Alloy Sheets

Mukulika Ghosh, Daniel Tomkins, Jory Denny, Samuel Rodriguez,
Marco Morales, and Nancy M. Amato

1. Introduction

In many settings, such as space or deep-sea exploration, the number and types of resources that a mission can accommodate are limited and simply inadequate to dynamically
repurpose a component. This can be overcome using reconfigurable smart materials such
as *shape memory alloys* (SMAs). SMAs remember their original shape such that a deformed SMA can return to a trained shape upon changes in temperature [Jani et al. 14].
Components built from SMAs can adopt many shapes, allowing the same component to be
used for a number of tasks, including new tasks that were not considered before deployment. For example, SMAs can be used to build shape-shifting structures that morph based
on environmental factors such as temperature or light exposure.

A major challenge in planning motions for an SMA robot is that the sheet can bend at
an infinite set of points. Planning motions for SMA robots is important because it not only
allows us to explore the solution space of a particular SMA robot, but it also simulates the
folding path helpful in determining the parameters required to achieve foldings for physical
SMA robots, e.g., how much and where to heat to achieve a desired fold. For example, in
Figure 1 a sheet folds through an intermediate state into a cylinder.

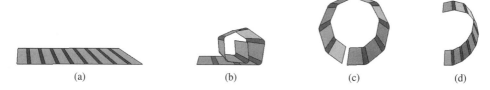

(a)   (b)   (c)   (d)

FIGURE 1. Folding an SMA sheet from (a) its unfolded flat state passing
through a series of feasible (non-colliding and gravitationally stable) intermediate states, like (b), to (c) a folded shape; (d) is an infeasible state,
since it is not gravitationally stable.

This research supported in part by NSF awards CNS-0551685, CCF-0833199, CCF-0830753, IIS-0916053, IIS-
0917266, EFRI-1240483, RI-1217991, by NIH NCI R25 CA090301-11, by Chevron, IBM, Intel, Oracle/Sun,
by Award KUS-C1-016-04, made by King Abdullah University of Science and Technology (KAUST) and by
Asociación Mexicana de Cultura AC. J. Denny supported in part by an NSF Graduate Research Fellowship.

This work describes how an SMA folding problem is modeled so that it can be solved using a state-of-the-art sampling-based motion-planning algorithm. We model the sheets similar to rigid origami [Tachi 11] as groups of inflexible regions connected by flexible regions, which we call *joints*, and restrict the motion of the sheet along the flexible joints. This reduces the bends the sheet can attain to a single dimension. Unlike rigid origami, however, we cannot allow sharp folds of these SMA sheets. Hence, we model the SMA joints to have uniform curvature along the joint length. In addition to modeling the system, we consider the problem of finding not only collision free but also gravitationally stable motions (Figure 1(b)). These are motions that keep the center of mass positioned over some panel of the structure on the ground plane so that it does not topple over. We show how we can apply the *Rapidly-exploring Random Tree* (RRT) [LaValle and Kuffner 01], a common sampling-based planner, to this problem. We augment the original RRT algorithm with a new distance function specific to our SMA robots and a rigidity analysis to see which components can be moved without causing instability (as in Figure 1(d)).

Our specific contributions are as follows:

- a geometric representation of SMA robots useful for sampling-based motion planning;
- a novel definition of motion feasibility that includes collision, curvature, and stability constraints suitable for SMA robots;
- an adaptation of RRTs designed specifically for folding SMA sheets into three-dimensional shapes.

Our results validate our model and motion-planning algorithm for these types of robots by folding a single SMA sheet into multiple interesting three-dimensional shapes. These results show significant flexibility in modeling various planning problems and include physical constraints at a comparable time to not using stability constraints.

2. Preliminaries and Related Work

A robot is a movable object whose state can be described by d parameters, or *degrees of freedom* (DOFs), each corresponding to an object component (e.g., object positions, orientations, and/or link angles). In SMA sheets, the DOFs are the angles of their flexible regions. Hence, a robot's state, or configuration, can be uniquely represented by a point $\langle x_1, x_2, \ldots, x_d \rangle$ in a d-dimensional space (where x_i is the ith DOF), called the *configuration space* (C_{space}) [Lozano-Pérez and Wesley 79]. The subset of all feasible configurations is the *free space* (C_{free}), while the subset of the infeasible configurations is the *obstacle space* (C_{obst}). Thus, the motion-planning problem becomes that of finding a continuous trajectory in C_{free} from a given start configuration to a goal configuration. In general, it is infeasible to compute explicit C_{obst} boundaries [Reif 79], but we can often determine whether a configuration is feasible or not quite efficiently by performing a validity test, e.g., a collision detection test in the *workspace*, the robot's natural space.

Sampling-based methods [Kavraki et al. 96, LaValle and Kuffner 01] are quite successful at solving motion-planning problems. One method, *Rapidly-exploring Random Tree* (RRT) [LaValle and Kuffner 01], explores C_{free} locally by iteratively expanding nodes of the tree toward random configurations until a goal configuration or region has been reached. Many variants have been proposed to address various weaknesses of RRTs [Kuffner and LaValle 00, Karaman and Frazzoli 11]. Sampling-based planners have been applied for planning motions for deformable robots in deformable environments [Rodriguez et al. 06], a related but distinct problem from SMA sheet folding where robots are self-deformable and maintain their total surface area. One of the earlier approaches, f-PRM [Holleman et al. 98, Kavraki et al. 98, Guibas et al. 99], samples the control points of a Bézier surface that models a flexible patch. Configuration validation accounts for collisions and for energy feasibility. Despite their success, however, these approaches do not maintain certain parts as rigid and do not account for contact constraints with a surface, such as gravitational stability.

Folding in robotics has been well studied. Sampling-based techniques have been applied to paper-folding planning [Song and Amato 01], and Balkcom and Mason designed a robotic system to fold paper [Balkcom and Mason 08]. Specialized robotic systems using SMA joints and actuators have been designed for origami folding [An and Rus 12]. Printable, self-folding robots using SMA sheets have also been designed in [Felton et al. 13].

There has been some work analyzing the properties of robots like ours. For instance, a preliminary paper introduced an algorithm to find flat unfoldings of complex geometric shapes [Hernandez et al. 13]. The unfoldings were then fed into complex analysis systems to model them as self-actuating SMA sheets. However, planning collision-free and gravitationally stable motions of these structures is an unexplored problem.

3. An SMA Planner

We propose to apply an RRT planner to SMAs that accounts for gravity as a constraint and that biases the extension of the RRT toward narrow passages produced by the tight constraints in folding. In this section, we describe the algorithm used for planning motions for SMAs. First, we describe how we model SMA robotic systems to define configurations. Then, we describe the distance function, validity test, and rigidity extender used in the planner.

3.1. An SMA RRT planner. We plan the motions of SMA robotic systems using an RRT algorithm, as shown in Algorithm 1. RRT starts from the initial configuration of the robot, q_{root}, and builds a tree that randomly explores the C_{space}. The nodes of this tree are valid configurations for the SMA robot, and its edges are valid paths between the nodes that they connect. Thus, the planning problem consists of generating a tree that has one node close enough to the goal SMA robot configuration. This tree is built by repeatedly randomly selecting a configuration q_{rand}; finding q_{near}, the configuration in the tree that is closest to q_{rand}; and expanding from q_{near} to q_{rand} until either becoming invalid or attaining some maximum distance Δq.

Input: Number of expansion attempts n, root configuration q_{root}, maximum
        expansion length Δq
Output: Tree T
  1: $T.\texttt{AddNode}(q_{\text{root}})$
  2: **for** $1 \ldots n$ **do**
  3:     $q_{\text{rand}} \leftarrow \texttt{RandomCfg}()$ // generate random SMA configuration
  4:     $q_{\text{near}} \leftarrow \texttt{NearestNeighbor}(T, q_{\text{rand}})$ // find closest existing configuration to q_{rand}
  5:     $q_{\text{new}} \leftarrow \texttt{RigidityExtend}(q_{\text{near}}, q_{\text{rand}}, \Delta q)$ // move from q_{near} to q_{rand}
  6:     $\texttt{Update}(T, q_{\text{near}}, q_{\text{new}})$ // add new SMA configuration to tree
  7: **return** T

Algorithm 1: RRT.

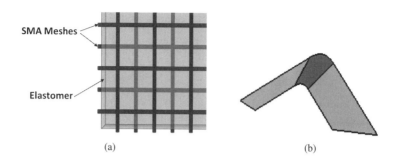

SMA Meshes

Elastomer

(a)   (b)

FIGURE 2. (a) An SMA sheet is a thin, flexible elastomer layer between two grids of prestrained SMA wires, which are used to actuate the sheet. (b) An SMA robot modeled as a thin joint connecting two inflexible regions.

3.1.1. *Generation of random SMA configuration.* (Line 3) The generation of random SMA configurations is performed by obtaining a random joint angle for each of its DOFs using a uniform distribution. As explained in Section 3.2, each of these DOFs are the angles of the flexible regions in the SMA robot.

3.1.2. *Finding the closest existing SMA configuration.* (Line 4) In order to find the closest existing SMA configuration to q_{rand}, we apply the distance function described in Section 3.3 to try to identify the configuration already in the tree that is the "easiest" to transform into q_{rand}.

3.1.3. *Expanding the tree.* (Line 5) The tree is expanded by moving from q_{near} toward q_{rand}. This is done by following a straight path in the C_{space} in small increments, each of which is tested for validity as explained in Section 3.4. If a maximum distance Δq is reached without encountering any invalid configurations, the last configuration found is returned as q_{new}. Otherwise, the last valid configuration is returned as q_{new}. In this expansion, we use a *rigidity extender*, a modification (explained in Section 3.5) introduced in this paper to better deal with complex physical constraints.

3.1.4. *Updating the tree.* (Line 6) The final step of the algorithm is to add the configuration q_{new} to the tree and an edge from q_{near} to q_{new} weighted by the distance between these two configurations.

3.2. Modeling an SMA robotic system. An SMA sheet is composed of a thin, compliant elastomer layer sandwiched between two grids of SMA wires, as shown in Figure 2(a). This composition allows for both strength and stability as stated in [Peraza-Hernandez et al. 13] and allows selective application of heat to achieve a particular folding path. The physical and geometric properties of these sheets are explored in depth in [Peraza-Hernandez et al. 13, Hernandez et al. 13].

To plan the motions of this robot, we need to be able to model each of its potential configurations, i.e., define a mapping from the robot's workspace to its C_{space}. However, an SMA surface can bend at any subset of its infinite points and therefore has infinite degrees of freedom. Because this is computationally infeasible, we introduce a restricted model of an SMA sheet that still preserves many usable configurations.

In this paper, we model SMA sheets as being composed of inflexible SMA regions and flexible SMA joints, similar to rigid origami [Tachi 11]. We can then assume a uniform

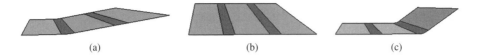

(a)   (b)   (c)

FIGURE 3. Balance distance considers both difference in joint angles and difference in center of gravity. The configurations in (a) and (b) are closely related to each other with respect to joint angles, whereas the configurations in (b) and (c) are closely related to each other with respect to position of the center of mass.

curvature along each joint, perpendicular to the surface of the inflexible regions and parameterized by one DOF. In other words, each joint will attain a uniform curvature throughout its length. In a physical implementation, heat is applied to actuate a region of the SMA; thus, our representation assumes an even application of heat to the joint region, causing this uniform curvature. It should also be noted that, because SMA sheets cannot have sharp folds like rigid origami [Tachi 11], it is important to model smooth curves.

Therefore, a single degree of freedom representing an SMA joint i is just an angle $\theta_i \in [-\pi, \pi]$, which is the total angle of curvature through the joint subject to some physical constraints required by the material's physical properties.

As an example, consider the robot shown in Figure 2(b). This robot is a 21 cm × 10 cm SMA sheet that is modeled by two inflexible 10 cm × 10 cm squares connected by a single 1 cm × 10 cm joint. This robot has one degree of freedom, which is the angle of the SMA joint; in the figure, this joint is actuated to $\frac{\pi}{2}$ radians.

3.3. Balance distance. The distance between two configurations is a numerical representation of the difference between them; i.e., two configurations should have a low distance if one can be easily transitioned into another.

Consider two configurations $\langle \theta_1, \theta_2, \ldots, \theta_n \rangle$ and $\langle \theta'_1, \theta'_2, \ldots, \theta'_n \rangle$ (where n is the DOFs of the robot). Typically, sampling-based algorithms will use the Euclidean distance in C_{space}, $\sqrt{\sum_{i=1}^{n} (\theta_i - \theta'_i)^2}$. However, two configurations that have low difference in joint angles may have very different centers of mass (Figure 3(a,b)); for the sake of gravitational stability, we do not want to consider these configurations to have an easy transition between them because the intermediate configurations might not be gravitationally stable. Additionally, configurations that have a noticeable difference in joint angles can have close (or even identical) centers of mass (Figure 3(b,c)), so it is not sufficient to only look at the difference between the centers of mass of two configurations.

As a compromise, we use a weighted distance metric called *balance distance*. With this metric, the weight w_i of joint i is proportional to the fraction of the sheet's mass actuated by that joint. (For instance, the joint in Figure 2(b) has weight $\frac{1}{2}$, since it divides the sheet in half.) Thus, the weight w_i encodes the contribution of the joint i to the center of mass of the robot. We then evaluate the total distance between two configurations as the sum of the weighted differences, $\sum_{i=1}^{n} w_i \cdot |\theta_i - \theta'_i|$.

This metric ties the two ideas, difference in angles and difference in center of mass, together, since joints that actuate more mass will contribute more to changes in the position of the center of mass.

3.4. Validity. A validity checker is a method for classifying configurations as belonging to either C_{free} or C_{obst}, a basic unit of work for most sampling-based planners. Our validity checker is composed of three parts. First, because the SMA material is relatively stiff and cannot obtain a large radius of curvature, our planning algorithm limits the fold angle based on the length of the joints. Second, we do not allow the robot to collide with itself. To quickly detect collisions, we arrange the inflexible regions into a configuration based on the angles through each joint. Finally, we require the folds of the sheet to be gravitationally stable; that is, the center of mass must be suspended over some panel on the ground plane.

3.4.1. *Radius of curvature.* The SMA sheets considered are relatively stiff; they are not able to obtain a small radius of curvature [Peraza-Hernandez et al. 13]. Obtaining sharp angles is not possible unless the joint has a large length. Therefore, we limit the angle θ in each joint to the range $[-\frac{l}{r}, \frac{l}{r}]$, where r is the radius of curvature of the material. For our simulations, we use r to be $\frac{l_{\max}}{\pi}$ where $l_{\max}$ is the maximum of the joint lengths of the SMA robot. This constraint is imposed implicitly in the sampling phase of our configurations.

3.4.2. *Collision detection.* Since collision detection is much faster for polygons than for curved surfaces, we approximate each curved joint as a series of very thin panels along its length. The approximation error is negligible compared to the improvement in performance obtained due to approximation. After configuring the robot in the workspace, we use a standard collision-detection library [Gottschalk et al. 96] to check its validity.

3.4.3. *Gravitational stability.* The stability of a configuration is checked against the gravitational force. For folding, we do not consider other forces, like friction, nor external actuators to hold the structure. Also, we assume that the structure is always in contact with the ground in such a way that it does not fall down. In many cases this means that at least one full panel is resting on the ground. A body is considered to be in stable equilibrium under gravity if its weight, acting from the center of mass, intersects with the base of the body. Therefore, to determine the stability of an SMA robot at a particular configuration, we compute the center of mass and the base of the robot at that configuration.

The center of mass is approximated as the geometric mean of the configuration, assuming uniform density throughout the SMA joints and inflexible regions. The global position of one of the panels, known as the *base panel*, is fixed (not necessarily fixed to the ground) as input to our system. In future, we will relax this constraint to achieve a more broad set of motions. The global position of the SMA robot at a configuration is then computed using the joint angles and the position of the base panel. As mentioned before, we assume that the structure is always in contact with the ground, so we find all the points where the SMA robot touches the ground plane. The convex hull of those points defines the stable base region for the configuration. If a ray generated from the center of mass, in the direction of the force of gravity, intersects the base region, the configuration is considered to be stable (Figure 4(a)); that is, it is valid in gravity. Otherwise the configuration is deemed unstable or invalid in gravity (Figure 4(b)). This introduces narrow passages in C_{free} as many self-collision–free configurations, such as in Figure 4(b), are considered gravitationally unstable.

3.5. Rigidity extender. In the tree expansion step of the planner (Line 5 of Algorithm 1), we use a *rigidity extender* to better deal with complex physical constraints like gravitational stability that create narrow passages in C_{free}. In many cases, moving a single joint can cause the robot to collide or become gravitationally unstable. However, most other joints can move freely, and must do so in order to attain a new configuration. Rigidity

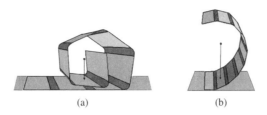

FIGURE 4. (a) Stable and (b) unstable configurations for a particular SMA robot.

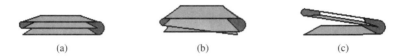

FIGURE 5. Testing the rigidity of joints in the transition from q_{near} toward q_{rand}. (a) q_{near}. (b) Slightly perturbing the left joint in the direction of q_{rand} leads to an invalid configuration, so the left joint is treated as rigid. (c) Perturbing the right joint produces a valid configuration, so this joint is not treated as rigid.

analysis [Thomas et al. 07] allows us to lock joints that cause problems while attempting to adjust the other joints.

Before extending q_{near} toward q_{rand} to produce q_{new}, the rigidity extender tests for rigidity of all joints, as shown in Figure 5, by slightly perturbing each individual joint in q_{near} in the direction of q_{rand}. If that perturbation produces an invalid configuration, that joint is identified as rigid. Once the rigid joints have been identified, the extension from q_{near} toward q_{rand} to produce q_{new} is tried by keeping the rigid joints locked.

4. Experiments

The planning approach in this chapter has been implemented in a C++ motion-planning library developed in the Parasol Lab at Texas A&M University. We demonstrate the effectiveness of our approach in a variety of models shown in Figure 6 and described below:

- *Tube:* (Figure 6(a)) The left flap is longer than the right flap, making this not only an ordering problem (right then left) but also an interesting stability problem.
- *Latin Cross:* (Figure 6(b)) In this problem, we model a reconfigurable Latin cross which begins as a cube and must be reconfigured into a different shape, an octahedron. This example shows how a single cutout can be used to fold into multiple shapes.
- *Bird and Trap:* (Figure 6(c,d)) Cutouts that are folded into interesting shapes (bird and trap).
- *4-Flap:* (Figure 6(e)) Each flap must be folded in a particular order, a difficult task for the planner.

The experiments were run on a Rocks Cluster running CentOS 5.1 with Intel XEON CPU 2.4 GHz processors with the GNU gcc compiler version 4.1. The video results of the folding of the above models can be found at [Parasol Lab 15]. Our video result also contains another example where a single cutout can be used for multiple shapes. As the start

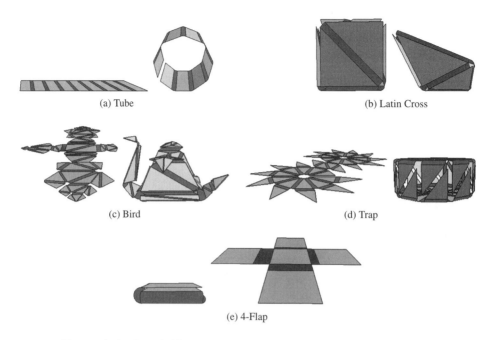

(a) Tube   (b) Latin Cross

(c) Bird   (d) Trap

(e) 4-Flap

FIGURE 6. Various folding problems for SMA sheets. The planner must plan from the start positions, shown on the left, to the goal positions, shown on the right.

TABLE 1. Planning time for the various folding problems.

Environment	DOFs	Without Gravity		Without Rigidity Extender		With All Extensions	
		# of samples	Time (s)	# of samples	Time (s)	# of samples	Time (s)
Tube	8	13	0.052	–	> 600	211	0.422
Latin Cross	11	18	0.075	45	0.451	261	0.476
Bird	63	3	0.591	3	0.643	3	0.633
Trap	39	90	4.700	–	> 600	112	5.714
4-Flap	4	580	0.604	112	0.205	580	0.628

configuration of the additional example is not gravitationally feasible, we do not include its result here.

We present the total planning time for each model, averaged over ten trials, in Table 1. The number of samples and the total planning time for planning without gravity constraint and with rigidity extender are stated in columns 3–4 (labeled "Without Gravity"). The same for planning with gravity but without rigidity extender is given in columns 5–6 (labeled "Without Rigidity Extender"), and the same for planning with both gravity and rigidity extender is given in columns 7–8 (labeled "With all Extensions"). As shown in Table 1, our method can plan for a wide variety of models with complex constraints within reasonable time (which is less than 10 seconds). Thus, the simulation results can be readily used to determine physical properties like the amount of heat to be applied to each joint to fold a physical SMA robot. Without the gravity constraint, many of the intermediate configurations in the folding path are invalid under gravity (See Figure 7). These

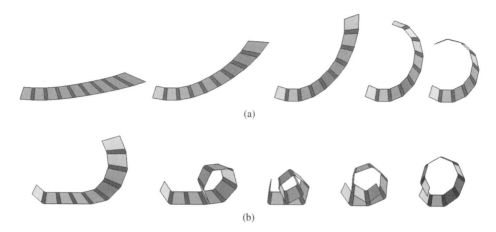

FIGURE 7. Intermediate folding configurations of Tube SMA robot in Figure 6(a) (a) without gravity and (b) with gravity

infeasible intermediate configurations create narrow passages in C_{free}, contributing to the total planning time (as in the Tube and Latin Cross models).

Although planning with gravitational stability takes more time than without, we observe that the gravitational stability check does not heavily contribute to the total time. The 4-Flap and Bird models, which are very stable in all configurations, have the same number of samples and very similar times without gravity.

Unmodified RRT [LaValle and Kuffner 01] could not plan the motions for most of our robots. Table 1 demonstrates that the rigidity extender is required for folding certain SMA robots under gravity. For example, even after 10 minutes the planner was not able to fold the Tube and Vertical Trap models to their goal configurations.

Planning time depends on both the number of flexible SMA joints and the number of samples required to find a path (which is, in turn, dependent on the difficulty of the specific planning problem). For example, Bird has many DOFs, but its time is comparable to 4-Flap, which is a more difficult planning problem.

We do not compare our approach with any other approach because no other planning method is general enough to handle these complex robotic systems, to the best of the authors' knowledge as detailed in Section 2.

Our results show that our model not only is general enough to handle a broad spectrum of robot systems but also can plan for these models in reasonable time.

5. Conclusion

In this work, we show how an existing motion-planning algorithm can be adapted to fold SMA sheets from a flat state to a three-dimensional shape with constraints such as collision-free motion and gravitational stability. We model the SMA sheet as a set of flexible joints connecting inflexible panels to allow selective heating of parts of the sheet to obtain a particular folding. We introduced a new distance function for SMA robots that allows us to better capture the movement from one configuration to another while accounting for gravitational stability, an important constraint in physical systems. We also introduced a rigidity analysis that allows us to lock joints whose motion might lower the probability of finding feasible motions between configurations. Our results show that our model can fold a variety of SMA sheets with the constraints in reasonable time. Thus, the generation of folding paths for a variety of shapes can be used further in the generation of physical parameters, like heat applied to each joint for a physical SMA sheet to fold into a desired shape, and also to evaluate how difference in heat applied would reconfigure the sheet into a different shape.

References

[An and Rus 12] Byoungkwon An and D. Rus. "Programming and Controlling Self-Folding Robots." In *Proceedings of the IEEE International Conference on Robotics and Automation*, pp. 3299–3306. Washington, DC: IEEE, 2012.

[Balkcom and Mason 08] Devin J. Balkcom and Matthew T. Mason. "Robotic Origami Folding." *Int. J. Robot. Res.* 27:5 (2008), 613–627.

[Felton et al. 13] S. M. Felton, M. T. Tolley, C. D. Onal, D. Rus, and R. J. Wood. "Robot Self-Assembly by Folding: A Printable Inchworm Robot." In *Proceedings of the 2013 IEEE International Conference on Robotics and Automation*, pp. 277–282. Washington, DC: IEEE, 2013.

[Gottschalk et al. 96] S. Gottschalk, M. C. Lin, and D. Manocha. "OBB-Tree: A Hierarchical Structure for Rapid Interference Detection." In *Proceedings of the 23rd Annual Conference on Computer Graphics and Interactive Techniques SIGGRAPH '96*, pp. 171–180. New York: ACM, 1996.

[Guibas et al. 99] L. J. Guibas, C. Holleman, and L. E. Kavraki. "A Probabilistic Roadmap Planner for Flexible Objects with a Workspace Medial-Axis-Based Sampling Approach." In *Proceedings of the 1999 IEEE/RSJ International Conference on Intelligent Robots and Systems*, Vol. 1, pp. 254–259. Washington, DC: IEEE, 1999.

[Hernandez et al. 13] Edwin Alexander Peraza Hernandez, Shiyu Hu, Han Wei Kung, Darren Hartl, and Ergun Akleman. "Towards Building Smart Self-Folding Structures." *Computers & Graphics* 37:6 (2013), 730–742.

[Holleman et al. 98] C. Holleman, L. Kavraki, and J. Warren. "Planning Paths for a Flexible Surface Patch." In *Proceedings of the 1998 IEEE International Conference on Robotics and Automation*, Vol. 1, pp. 21–26. Washington, DC: IEEE, 1998.

[Jani et al. 14] Jaronie Mohd Jani, Martin Leary, Aleksandar Subic, and Mark A. Gibson. "A Review of Shape Memory Alloy Research, Applications and Opportunities." *Materials & Design* 56:0 (2014), 1078–1113.

[Karaman and Frazzoli 11] Sertac Karaman and Emilio Frazzoli. "Sampling-Based Algorithms for Optimal Motion Planning." *International Journal of Robotics Research (IJRR)* 30 (2011), 846–894.

[Kavraki et al. 96] L. E. Kavraki, P. Švestka, J. C. Latombe, and M. H. Overmars. "Probabilistic Roadmaps for Path Planning in High-Dimensional Configuration Spaces." *IEEE Trans. Robot. Automat.* 12:4 (1996), 566–580.

[Kavraki et al. 98] Lydia E. Kavraki, Florent Lamiraux, and Christopher Holleman. "Towards Planning for Elastic Objects." In *Robotics: The Algorithmic Perspective*, pp. 313–325. Natick, MA: A K Peters, 1998. MR1694296 (99m:68012)

[Kuffner and LaValle 00] J. J. Kuffner and S. M. LaValle. "RRT-Connect: An Efficient Approach to Single-Query Path Planning." In *Proceedings of the IEEE International Conference on Robotics and Automation*, Vol. 2, pp. 995–1001. Washington, DC: IEEE, 2000.

[LaValle and Kuffner 01] S. M. LaValle and J. J. Kuffner. "Randomized Kinodynamic Planning." *Int. J. Robot. Res.* 20:5 (2001), 378–400.

[Lozano-Pérez and Wesley 79] T. Lozano-Pérez and M. A. Wesley. "An Algorithm for Planning Collision-Free Paths Among Polyhedral Obstacles." *Communications of the ACM* 22:10 (1979), 560–570.

[Parasol Lab 15] "Algorithms and Applications Group: Planning Motion for Shape Memory Alloy Sheets." http://parasol.tamu.edu/sma/, 2015.

[Peraza-Hernandez et al. 13] Edwin A Peraza-Hernandez, Darren J Hartl, and Richard J Malak Jr. "Design and Numerical Analysis of an SMA Mesh-Based Self-Folding Sheet." *Smart Materials and Structures* 22:9 (2013), 094008.

[Reif 79] J. H. Reif. "Complexity of the Mover's Problem and Generalizations." In *Proceedings of the 20th Annual Symposium on Foundations of Computer Science (FOCS)*, pp. 421–427. Los Alamitos, CA: IEEE, 1979.

[Rodriguez et al. 06] Samuel Rodriguez, Jyh-Ming Lien, and Nancy M. Amato. "Planning Motion in Completely Deformable Environments." In *Proceedings of the 2006 IEEE International Conference on Robotics and Automation*, pp. 2466–2471. Los Alamitos, CA: IEEE, 2006.

[Song and Amato 01] G. Song and N. M. Amato. "A Motion Planning Approach to Folding: From Paper Craft to Protein Folding." In *Proceedings of the 2006 IEEE International Conference on Robotics and Automation*, pp. 948–953. Los Alamitos, CA: IEEE, 2001.

[Tachi 11] Tomohiro Tachi. "Rigid-Foldable Thick Origami." In *Origami⁵: Fifth International Meeting of Origami Science, Mathematics, and Education*, edited by Patsy Wang-Iverson, Robert J. Lang, and Mark Yim, pp. 253–264. Boca Raton, FL: A K Peters/CRC Press, 2011. MR2866909 (2012h:00044)

[Thomas et al. 07] Shawna Thomas, Xinyu Tang, Lydia Tapia, and Nancy M. Amato. "Simulating Protein Motions with Rigidity Analysis." *J. Comput. Biol.: Special Issue of Int. Conf. Comput. Molecular Biology (RECOMB) 2006* 14:6 (2007), 839–855. .

PARASOL LAB, DEPARTMENT OF COMPUTER SCIENCE AND ENGINEERING, TEXAS A&M UNIVERSITY, COLLEGE STATION, TEXAS
E-mail address: mghosh@cse.tamu.edu

PARASOL LAB, DEPARTMENT OF COMPUTER SCIENCE AND ENGINEERING, TEXAS A&M UNIVERSITY, COLLEGE STATION, TEXAS
E-mail address: kittsil@cse.tamu.edu

PARASOL LAB, DEPARTMENT OF COMPUTER SCIENCE AND ENGINEERING, TEXAS A&M UNIVERSITY, COLLEGE STATION, TEXAS
E-mail address: jdenny@cse.tamu.edu

PARASOL LAB, DEPARTMENT OF COMPUTER SCIENCE AND ENGINEERING, TEXAS A&M UNIVERSITY, COLLEGE STATION, TEXAS
E-mail address: sor8786@cse.tamu.edu

INSTITUTO TECNOLÓGICO AUTÓNOMO DE MÉXICO, CIUDAD DE MEXICO, MEXICO
E-mail address: marco.morales@itam.mx

PARASOL LAB, DEPARTMENT OF COMPUTER SCIENCE AND ENGINEERING, TEXAS A&M UNIVERSITY, COLLEGE STATION, TEXAS
E-mail address: amato@cse.tamu.edu

Simple Flat Origami Exploration System with Random Folds

Naoya Tsuruta, Jun Mitani, Yoshihiro Kanamori, and Yukio Fukui

1. Introduction

Recent origami design techniques have made possible the design of realistic models. A modern realistic model with complex folds can represent the features of an object in detail. The circle/river method [Lang 96, Meguro 94] is a powerful tool for designing such complex origami models. This algorithm calculates the crease pattern to fold a tree structure that represents the skeleton of the target object. Another algorithm proposed by Tachi [Tachi 09] gives the crease pattern to fold an arbitrary three-dimensional shape of a topological disk. However, there are no practical design tools suitable for simple origami models, which are made with a small number of folds. Existing design algorithms usually result in a complicated crease pattern. It seems that simple origami models are designed by a heuristic approach.

We proposed an enumeration-based approach for exploring simple origami models [Tsuruta et al. 12]. By limiting the folding operations and the number of folds, 136,284 different folded shapes were obtained with up to four folds. In order to find, from a set of obtained pieces, the pieces that look like the shape of something, the pieces that are similar to an input polygon can be extracted by comparing the contour of the folded pieces and the input polygon. Although this enumeration-based approach can discover computer-generated origami models, the folding operations and the number of folds are strictly limited due to combinatorial explosion.

To address this problem, we have proposed an interactive system for exploring simple origami models by random generation of folded pieces [Tsuruta et al. 13]. The key idea is to assist the "action of labeling" (*mitate* in Japanese). The action of labeling in origami is to recognize a folded shape as another object (such as an animal, insect, or flower) because of its color and physical appearance. The system generates origami pieces with several folds automatically, and displays them, so that the user can focus on the labeling action. Every time the user requests another set of pieces, different shapes appear, because the generation process includes randomness. We could discover several origami models. However, the generation algorithm in this prototype system cannot accommodate particular types of folds that have one degree of freedom (DOF) and there was no discussion about discovered models.

This work proposes an improved generation method. The previous system used folds both with and without landmark points. A fold with landmark points refers to a fold such as the corner-to-corner fold. A fold without landmark points refers to a fold placed on a meaningless location. We add the fold that has one DOF, such as a corner-to-edge fold.

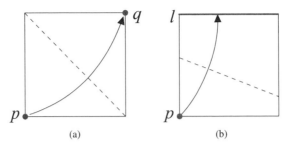

FIGURE 1. Examples of folds without and with DOF, respectively: (a) a fold placing a corner to another corner and (b) a fold placing a corner onto an edge.

A corner-to-edge fold uses landmarks, but the location has one DOF. This new generation method gives various folded pieces that do not appear in the previous system. We also provide another generation method that considers symmetry. The resultant folded shapes differ greatly and look similar to human-designed models. Finally, we discuss the models discovered by our system. We introduce three characteristic groups that are easily recongnized.

2. Random Generation of Simple Folded Pieces

To generate a folded piece automatically, we randomly determine a fold, calculate the folded shape, and repeat this process a given number of times. A fold is composed of three parameters: the location of the fold, the folding direction (mountain or valley), and the number of layers to be folded. The problem is how to determine these parameters. Determining them completely at random will not generate commonly used folds, such as the corner-to-corner fold. Thus, we limit these parameters to generate meaningful folded pieces as if made by a human.

2.1. Location of fold. The location of a fold is described by a combination of points and lines. Initially, an unfolded origami paper has four corner points and four edges. We randomly choose a required number of landmarks. For example, we pick two points at random in the case of the fold that places a point onto another point.

Our previous system [Tsuruta et al. 13] used the sixth Huzita–Justin axiom [Huzita 91, Justin 91] and the random sliding of a fold. All the creases were obtained by the sixth axiom, which places point p_1 onto line l_1 and point p_2 onto line l_2. The obtained fold was slid in a random direction in the last n steps. This random sliding simulates a *judgement fold* (*gurai-ori* in Japanese), which is a folding operation that does not use any references. This folding often appears in later folding steps in an artist's model. Although we could find new origami models (shown in Section 5), this method cannot deal with a fold that has one DOF, such as the corner-to-edge fold. Figure 1 shows examples of a fold with no DOF and a fold with one DOF.

Instead of randomly sliding the folds, we add the following three operations that have one DOF, as shown in Figure 2:

S_1: Fold a line x that passes through a given point A.
S_2: Fold a line x that is perpendicular to a given line l.
S_3: Fold a line x that places a given point A onto a given line l.

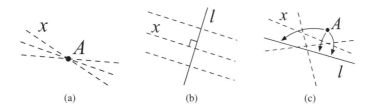

FIGURE 2. Folds with one DOF: (a) a fold that passes through a point, (b) a fold that is perpendicular to a line, and (c) a fold that places a point onto a line.

These operations are three of the five one-fold *alignments* of points and lines described by Alperin and Lang [Alperin and Lang 09]. Although any line in the plane has three degrees of freedom to be specified, these use only one DOF. Hence, we randomly determine the remaining parameter when we use these operations. The remaining parameter is an angle in the case of S_1 and a location on an edge in the cases of S_2 and S_3. Note that several Huzita–Justin axioms may have two or more solutions, but we assume that the folds have no DOF because the solutions are discrete.

2.2. Folding direction and the number of layers to be folded. The folding techniques used in our system are simple valley folds and mountain folds. We randomly choose one of them.

After a location of a fold and its folding direction have been determined, we determine the number of layers to be folded. First, we choose a number k from 1 to m at random, where m is the total number of layers at the current state. Then, we try to fold k layers from the top in the case of valley folds. There are cases where we cannot fold k layers together when the fold intersects with existing creases, because faces adjacent to the existing creases must be folded at the same time. In such cases, we fold the layers together with the next layer and repeat this until we obtain a valid shape. Whether the fold is valid or not can be checked by testing the flat-foldability for the inner vertices. The resultant folded shape is globally flat-foldable as long as we fold the paper from the topmost layer. We perform the same process from the bottommost layer in the case of a mountain fold.

3. Random Generation of Symmetric Pieces

Here, we describe another generation method that considers symmetry. This generation method is an extension of the simple folded piece generation we described in the previous section. We add another parameter, that is, the type of the symmetry axis. The symmetry axis has two types: book and diagonal (Figure 3). We randomly choose one of these at the very beginning of the generation process.

We use multiple folds or the squash fold to make symmetric shapes in one folding step. Both folding operations are calculated based on a single fold. The determination of which folding operation to use depends on a positional relationship between a fold and symmetry axis. This relation can be categorized according to whether they intersect. Figure 4 shows a case where they do not intersect. The figure shows the right half of the square paper. If the flaps folded by an obtained fold intersect the symmetry axis, the flaps are folded again by the axis. Thus, the entire folding operation has at most two simple folds.

Figure 5 shows a case of intersection. The flaps folded by an obtained fold intersect the symmetry axis, except for the case of the fold that is perpendicular to the axis. The

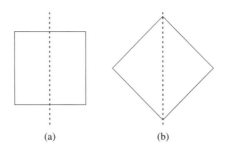

FIGURE 3. Two types of symmetry: (a) book and (b) diagonal.

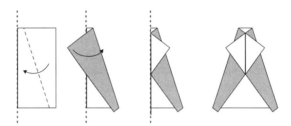

FIGURE 4. An entire folding operation that has two simple folds. The folds do not intersect the symmetry axis.

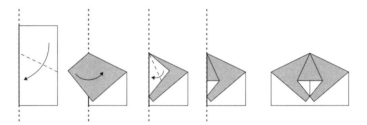

FIGURE 5. An entire folding operation becomes a squash fold when the fold intersects the symmetry axis.

folded part is folded back by the axis and, then, folded back again by the bisector of the angle between the axis and its edge so that the edge lies on the axis. The entire folding operation becomes a squash fold. If the fold is perpendicular to the axis, the entire folding becomes a simple horizontal fold.

The folded shape keeps symmetry as long as we use the above two folding operations. Note that these are not the only ways to maintain the folded shapes' symmetry.

4. Our Proposed System

Our system generates dozens of folded pieces and displays them simultaneously. Figure 6 shows the interface of the system. The user chooses one of the displayed pieces if it looks like a desirable shape such as an animal. The system generates different shapes every time the user requests another set of pieces. The user can perform the following operations:

- Change the number of folds.

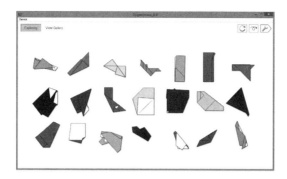

FIGURE 6. Interface of our system.

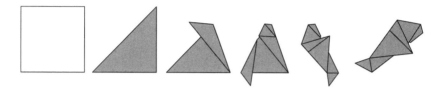

FIGURE 7. Auto-generated diagram of a manatee.

- Request another set of pieces.
- Rotate, turn over, or change the color of the paper.
- Label the selected piece and see its diagram.
- Register the labeled piece to an online database.
- Set the initial state of the generation process.

The last user operation changes the initial state of the generation process. The user can choose the initial state from the diagram. In other words, the first n steps can be fixed by the user.

5. Results

We implemented our system as a Flash application with Action Script. The online origami model database is implemented by MySQL and PHP. Our experiment revealed that a folded piece to be labeled appears after between 10 and 20 retrials on average. The computation time increases exponentially with the number of folds because the number of layers is approximately doubled by a single mountain fold or valley fold. Our system runs in real time on a PC with Intel Core i7 2.6 GHz CPU with the settings of six folds and twenty pieces. Figure 7 shows an example model that we found using the system.

We have also tried to find pieces that resemble existing origami models designed by origami artists. Figure 8 shows a well-known simple origami model, "2 Fold Santa" designed by Paula Versnick [Versnick 10], an origami piece generated by our new generation method that includes folds with one DOF, and an origami piece generated by a previous method using random sliding. The first fold of Paula's Santa is made by placing a corner onto nearly the middle point of an edge. This fold has one DOF. The folds with one DOF make the folded shape neatly and easier to fold in comparison with those that have two DOF. Our new generation method generates more attractive origami pieces.

Figure 9 shows models stored in the online database. These models were generated by the previous generation method we briefly discussed in Section 2.1. We found that

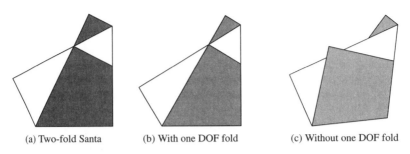

(a) Two-fold Santa   (b) With one DOF fold   (c) Without one DOF fold

FIGURE 8. Comparison of (a) Paula Versnick's two-fold Santa [Versnick 10] and generated pieces (b) with and (c) without a one-DOF fold.

there were similar models and have extracted three interesting groups. The first row in Figure 9 shows three bird models. The paper is folded in half into a triangle in the first step, and the corner becomes the beak of a bird. The second group is hooded persons and four models are included, as seen in the second row. The inside-out representation is used in these models. Inside-out is a technique that uses both sides of the origami paper and is often used for penguins, pandas, and the stripes of zebras. This technique is useful for both simple and complex origami. In simple origami, the inside-out technique enables a wide range of expression with a smaller number of folds. The third group contains two boats and a yacht. Boats and yachts are very typical objects in simple origami. We often see these kinds of models in origami books for children. The inside-out representation is also used in the yacht model. We could not find any characteristics for the models in the fourth or later lines. In other words, these models are rare and hard to discover.

We held a workshop for four small children aged from five to seven years. After 10 minutes of instruction, each child could find about seven models in 40 minutes. Figure 10 shows four of the discovered models. Our exploring system was enjoyable for the small children. However, several steps in the auto-generated diagram are difficult to understand due to the lack of annotation and of distortions that indicate the relationships between the layers.

Figure 11 shows four examples of symmetric models generated by the method we mentioned in Section 3. These models were obtained by two times symmetric folding. Note that a single symmetric folding may contain multiple folds. These models seem as if they could have been designed by humans. Considering symmetry is effective for generating well-arranged folded pieces. Adding other rules will be an interesting challenge; for example, considering rotational symmetry may generate a lot of flowers.

6. Conclusion

We have proposed an interactive exploration system for simple flat origami. Our system generates folded pieces with a specified number of folds and displays them. The user can discover new computer-generated origami models by labeling them, without folding a physical sheet of paper. Folding techniques used in our system are limited to the simple valley fold and mountain fold and the squash fold. Adding other folding techniques such as reverse folds would increase the variety of folded shapes.

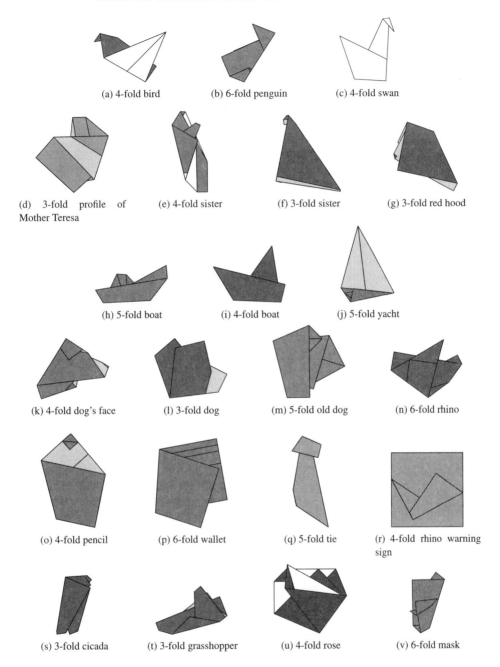

(a) 4-fold bird   (b) 6-fold penguin   (c) 4-fold swan

(d) 3-fold profile of Mother Teresa   (e) 4-fold sister   (f) 3-fold sister   (g) 3-fold red hood

(h) 5-fold boat   (i) 4-fold boat   (j) 5-fold yacht

(k) 4-fold dog's face   (l) 3-fold dog   (m) 5-fold old dog   (n) 6-fold rhino

(o) 4-fold pencil   (p) 6-fold wallet   (q) 5-fold tie   (r) 4-fold rhino warning sign

(s) 3-fold cicada   (t) 3-fold grasshopper   (u) 4-fold rose   (v) 6-fold mask

FIGURE 9. Example models stored in the online database.

Folds that have one DOF have now been added. These folds enable neater shapes than the previous system. Note that it is necessary to perform a quantitative evaluation to determine which method generates more meaningful and recognizable pieces.

The action of labeling in origami may be an interesting research topic. Our results showed that there are characteristic shapes that are easy to recognize. Avoiding the folds

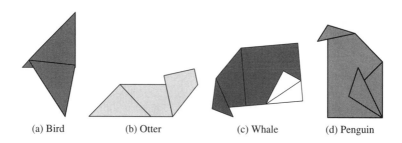

(a) Bird   (b) Otter   (c) Whale   (d) Penguin

FIGURE 10. Example models discovered by small children.

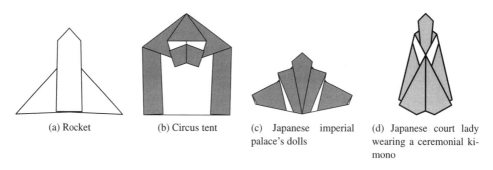

(a) Rocket   (b) Circus tent   (c) Japanese imperial palace's dolls   (d) Japanese court lady wearing a ceremonial kimono

FIGURE 11. Examples models obtained by the generation of pieces with symmetry.

used to generate those shapes will lead to the discovery of different models. In our system, the labeling depends on a person. If we obtain a large number of labeled origami pieces, automatic labeling of simple origami may be possible by artificial intelligence.

References

[Alperin and Lang 09] Roger C. Alperin and Robert J. Lang. "One-, Two-, and Multi-Fold Origami Axioms." In *Origami⁴: Fourth International Meeting of Origami Science, Mathematics, and Education*, edited by Robert J. Lang, pp. 371–393. Wellesley, MA: A K Peters, 2009. MR2590565 (2011b:51030)

[Huzita 91] Humiaki Huzita. "Axiomatic Development of Origami Geometry." In *Proceedings of the First International Meeting of Origami Science and Technology*, edited by H. Huzita, pp. 143–159. Padova, Italy: Dipartimento di Fisica dell'Università di Padova, 1991.

[Justin 91] Jacques Justin. "Resolution par le pliage de l'equation du troisieme degre et applications geometriques." In *Proceedings of the First International Meeting of Origami Science and Technology*, edited by H. Huzita, pp. 251–261. Padova, Italy: Dipartimento di Fisica dell'Università di Padova, 1991.

[Lang 96] Robert J. Lang. "A Computational Algorithm for Origami Design." In *Proceedings of the Twelfth Annual Symposium on Computational Geometry*, pp. 98–105. New York: ACM Press, 1996.

[Meguro 94] Toshiyuki Meguro. "Tobu Kuwagatamushi-to Ryoikienbunshiho (Flying Stag Beetle and the Circular Area Molecule Method)." *Oru* 5 (1994), 92–95.

[Tachi 09] Tomohiro Tachi. "3D Origami Design Based on Tucking Molecules." In *Origami⁴: Fourth International Meeting of Origami Science, Mathematics, and Education*, edited by Robert J. Lang, pp. 259–272. Wellesley, MA: A K Peters, 2009. MR2590567 (2010h:00025)

[Tsuruta et al. 12] Naoya Tsuruta, Jun Mitani, Yoshihiro Kanamori, and Yukio Fukui. "A Computer Aided Design System for Simple Origami Pieces Based on the Enumeration of Folded Shapes (in Japanese)." *Science of Origami* 2:1 (2012), 33–44.

[Tsuruta et al. 13] Naoya Tsuruta, Jun Mitani, Yoshihiro Kanamori, and Yukio Fukui. "An Exploring Tool for Simple Flat Origami Based on Random Foldings." Paper presented at the International Conference on Simulation Technology (JSST2013), Tokyo, Japan, September 11–13, 2013.

[Versnick 10] Paula Versnick. "2 Fold Santa." *Paula's Orihouse*, http://www.orihouse.com/until2012/myroom_kerstman.html, 2010.

TOKYO UNIVERSITY OF TECHNOLOGY, JAPAN
E-mail address: tsurutany@stf.teu.ac.jp

UNIVERSITY OF TSUKUBA, JAPAN
E-mail address: mitani@cs.tsukuba.ac.jp

UNIVERSITY OF TSUKUBA, JAPAN
E-mail address: kanamori@cs.tsukuba.ac.jp

UNIVERSITY OF TSUKUBA, JAPAN
E-mail address: fukui@cs.tsukuba.ac.jp

oricreate: Modeling Framework for Design and Manufacturing of Folded Plate Structures

Rostislav Chudoba, Jan van der Woerd, and Josef Hegger

1. Introduction

The present work on the general modeling support for the development of folded-plate structures (oricreate) was originally motivated by the intention to exploit the principles of folding in the production of free-form thin-walled concrete shells (oricrete). The possibility to achieve different geometrical forms by slight modification of the crease pattern appeared particularly attractive in view of the envisioned production process with mass customization of produced shapes [Tarnai 01]. Prototypes demonstrating the feasibility of the concept were made of textile-reinforced concrete (TRC) plates combining fine-grained concrete matrix with flexible, high-performance textile fabrics. This composite material exhibits high strength and ductility [Konrad and Chudoba 09], [Hegger and Bruckermann 06]. Due to the non-corrosiveness of the carbon or glass fibers, no extra cover is required for its protection [Hegger and Voss 08]. As a consequence, its properties can be highly utilized in thin-walled spatial and shell structures [Scholzen et al. 10, Scholzen et al. 14a, Scholzen et al. 14b, Tysmans et al. 09].

The envisioned production process of folded TRC plates includes the following steps: Factory-produced preforms of the foldable segments are transported to the construction site in a planar form. Preforms with built-in crease patterns are folded to their final shape, and the crease lines are grouted. After the hardening of the grouts, the crease angles are fixed and the oricrete segments are installed at their destination. Possible approaches to the manufacturing process were described for several combinations of fabric reinforcement by the authors in [van der Woerd et al. 13]. Simple demonstration of the oricrete technology is shown on a folded vault shell in Figure 1. The Yoshimura crease pattern was introduced in the formwork before casting using linear spacers below and above the alkali-resistant glass fabric placed in the middle of the 8 mm thin cross section. After casting and hardening, the spacers were removed and the plate was folded into the vault shape with the help of a kinematic crane adapter. In the folded form, the vault was temporarily supported and the crease lines were filled with grout mortar.

The variability of forms is not the only motivation for the development of this technology. Closely related is the issue of high utilization of the applied material in a given shape delivering a high performance in terms of stiffness, ductility, and ultimate strength. Development of design and manufacturing methods for folded-plate elements can serve the basis for further structural concepts such as modularization, lamination, and sandwiching.

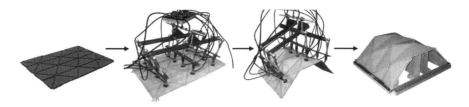

FIGURE 1. Folding of the concrete plate with prefabricated Yoshimura crease pattern to a vault.

The complexity of such a design process calls for a consistent modeling framework with seamless transitions of the product models from one design stage to the other.

The proposed simulation framework supports various types of design/shaping tasks that can be chained to reflect the iterative step-by-step development of an oricrete structure. Components of the framework focused on the kinematic control of the folding process reducing the number of degrees of freedom inherent to the crease pattern were described by the authors in [Chudoba et al. 14]. In the present work we describe the generalized formulation and implementation of the framework giving the possibility to include further goal functions and constraints as plug-ins. The described extensions allow us to include the force flow in the optimization criteria and constraints that will be exemplified by examples including the combined effect of kinematics and gravity.

The kinematic part of the model has been formulated in the context of the development of modeling approaches to rigid origami that appeared during the recent two decades [belcastro and Hull 02, Lang 09, Tachi 10b, Gray et al. 11]. Modeling strategy representing the folding process as a tree structure of folds has been proposed in [Lang 03]. In the approach proposed by Tachi, the dihedral angles between facets are used to introduce the kinematic constraints to be satisfied around a vertex of a crease pattern [Tachi 09, Tachi 10a]. Approaches to the design of cellular structures satisfying specific properties, such as density and mechanical performance, have been presented in [Klett and Drechsler 11].

2. Simulation Framework

The software design of the oricreate simulation framework is guided by the need to reflect the iterative nature of the design process as a pipeline of optimization and simulation steps with seamless transitions between several types of mathematical optimization problems. In each step, adaptations and extensions of the evolving crease pattern model and its intermediate configurations need to be performed. As a starting point for the classification of the software components, let us distinguish four iterative design phases with growing size and complexity of the considered design space (see Figure 2):

A: Starting from an initial crease pattern, modifications of a crease pattern prescribed by the geometrically based goal functions (target shape) and constraints (foldability, compatibility) represent the innermost optimization loop.

B: A challenging task is to include goal functions and constraints involving functionals capturing the relationship between stress resultants and an imposed loading of a folded crease pattern. Closed-form formulations of optimization problems are possible in connection with simplified linear-elastic structural model.

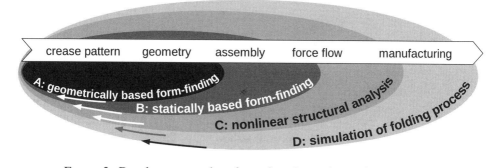

FIGURE 2. Development cycles of growing size and complexity running around an evolving product model, indicating the types of criteria and constraints employed during the distinguished design phases.

C: In order to take into account the geometrical and physical nonlinearity of the load-bearing behavior, nonlinear simulations need to be included to assess the performance of the product. For this purpose, characteristics of the crease lines need to be determined experimentally.

D: Once the final crease pattern and the target configurations are available, the simulation of the folding process delivers the data for the setup and control of a folding machine.

Simulation tasks involved in these design phases are represented by use-case classes of the oricreate package. A use-case class translates the formulation of an underlying optimization problem into an executable form. The instances of use-case classes represent a configured solver for an optimization problem consisting of the crease pattern, optimality criteria, equality constraints, and algorithmic parameters.

Expressed mathematically, each use-case class formulates a constrained optimization problem of the form

$$(2.1) \qquad \min_{\mathbf{u}} f(\mathbf{u}, t) \quad \text{subject to} \quad \mathbf{G}(\mathbf{U}, t) = 0,$$

with $f(\mathbf{u}, t)$ and $\mathbf{G}(\mathbf{u}, t)$ representing the optimality criterion and the equality constraints, respectively. The folding (or optimization) process is controlled by the time parameter t. The crease pattern configuration is described by an array of nodal displacements:

$$\mathbf{u} = u_{im}, \quad i = 1 \ldots N, \quad m = 1, 2, 3,$$

where i represents the node number, m the spatial dimension, and N the number of crease nodes. The task common to all implemented use-case classes is to identify the evolution of the crease node displacements $\mathbf{u}$ for a particular configuration of the constrained optimization problem in Equation (2.1). Possible compositions of a particular optimization problem using the currently implemented and yet-to-be-implemented plug-ins for the listed goal functions (f.1–f.4) and equality constraints (G.1–G.4) are depicted in Figure 3. The implemented plug-ins provide the calculations of both the values and the derivatives of the respective goal function or of the constraint with respect to the nodal displacements $\mathbf{u}$.

The oricreate package has been implemented using the high-level scripting language Python together with the environment for scientific computing bundled in the Enthought Tool Suite [Enthought 13] provided as open-source code. This environment offers a rich set of packages for numerical and symbolical computation and visualization tools (numpy, scipy, sympy, mayavi). For the solution of examples presented in this work, the sequential

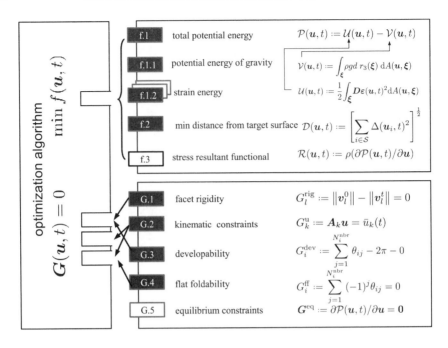

FIGURE 3. Implemented (black) and planned (white) plug-in modules for goal functions $f(\mathbf{u}, t)$ and constraints $G(\mathbf{u}, t)$ that can be dynamically inserted into the open slots of the oricreate simulation framework.

least squares programming (SLSQP) optimization algorithm provided in the scipy package was used [Kraft 88]. Selected plug-ins will be described in the followings section, and their application will be documented on examples of simulation tasks.

3. Intermediate Configuration of Folding

A crease pattern is defined by specifying the nodal positions in the xy plane,

$$\mathbf{x}_i^0 = \left\{ \begin{array}{ccc} x_{i1}^0 & x_{i2}^0 & 0 \end{array} \right\}^T, \quad i = 1 \dots N,$$

and the connectivity between nodes constituting the crease lines and facets,

$$\mathcal{L} := \{ l \to (i, j), \ l = 1 \dots L \wedge \ i, j \in 1 \dots N \wedge i \neq j \}.$$

Furthermore, the mountain and valley assignment of crease lines is included. During the iterative simulation, an intermediate position of a node i at time t is represented by a displacement vector $\mathbf{u}$ as

$$\mathbf{x}_i(t) = \mathbf{x}_i^0 + \mathbf{u}_i(t).$$

In order to support a simple implementation of constraint equations and of goal functions, methods evaluating derived state variables of the crease pattern are provided as core functionality of the package. An example of a derived state variable is an array of vectors along crease lines $l \to (i, j)$ either in the initial configuration

(3.1) $$\mathbf{v}_l^0 = \mathbf{x}_j^0 - \mathbf{x}_i^0$$

or in an intermediate state of folding t

(3.2) $$\mathbf{v}_l(t) = \mathbf{x}_j(t) - \mathbf{x}_i(t).$$

Another example is a list of arrays containing sector angles around each interior node:

$$(3.3) \qquad \theta_{ij} = \arccos{(\gamma_{ij})}, \text{ with } \gamma_{ij} = \mathbf{v}_{\mathrm{nbr}(i,j)} \cdot \mathbf{v}_{\mathrm{nbr}(i,j+1)} / \left\| \mathbf{v}_{\mathrm{nbr}(i,j)} \right\| \left\| \mathbf{v}_{\mathrm{nbr}(i,j+1)} \right\|,$$

where the mapping nbr(i, j) delivers the crease line connecting the ith node with its jth neighboring node whereas the neighbors are enumerated in counterclockwise order. Further implemented derived quantities are the mappings between facets and nodes, facets and lines, the array of normals to each facet, and the array of the current dihedral angles between each of the two facets. These values are provided as dynamically evaluated property attributes of a crease pattern. Consider, for example, the following code using the scripting interface of the package in the form:

```
from oricreate.api import YoshimuraCPFactory                              1
cp_factory = YoshimuraCPFactory(L_x=4, L_y=1, n_x=2, n_y=2)              2
cp = cp_factory.formed_object                                            3
```

A crease pattern is constructed at line 2 using a factory class that generates the coordinates $\mathbf{x}^0$, lines $\mathcal{L}$, and facets $\mathcal{F}$ based on the specified number of tessellation cells n_x and n_y in x- and y-direction, respectively. The result of the generation can be visualized using the `matplotlib` package:

```
import matplotlib.pyplot as plt                                          4
fig, ax = plt.subplots()                                                 5
cp.plot_mpl(ax, facets=True, lines=False, linewidth=2, fontsize=30)      6
```

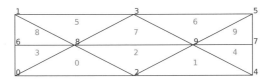

The produced crease pattern object offers a range of attributes calculated on demand, which characterize the intermediate state of folding. For example, the print statements

```
print 'list of sector angle arrays around interior nodes\n', cp.iN_theta                    7
print 'facet areas', cp.F_area                                                               8
print 'total potential energy', cp.V                                                         9
print 'gradient of potential energy with respect to node displacements u\n', cp.V_du        10
```

deliver the list of arrays of sector angles around the interior nodes given in Equation (3.3), the facet area, the total potential energy in Equation (5.1), and its derivatives with respect to node displacement in the initial planar configuration as

```
list of sector angle arrays                                                                 11
[array([ 2.21429744,  0.46364761,  0.46364761,  2.21429744,  0.46364761, 0.46364761]),      12
 array([ 2.21429744,  0.46364761,  0.46364761,  2.21429744,  0.46364761, 0.46364761])]      13
facet area [ 0.5    0.5    0.5    0.25  0.25  0.5    0.5    0.5    0.25  0.25]                14
potential energy 0.0                                                                        15
gradient of potential energy with respect to node displacements u                          16
[ 0.         0.          0.25000001  0.         0.          0.24999999                       17
  0.         0.          0.50000001  0.         0.          0.49999999                       18
  0.         0.          0.25        0.         0.          0.25000001                       19
  0.         0.          0.16666666  0.         0.          0.16666666                       20
  0.         0.          0.83333333  0.         0.          0.83333334]                      21
```

Classes implementing the plug-ins for the constraints and goal functions listed in Figure 3 refer all to the crease pattern object and use the exemplified property attributes in an iterative solution of the underlying optimization problem. Using property attributes that are calculated on demand upon a change of the crease pattern configuration, implementation redundancy of use case implementations can be widely avoided.

4. Equality Constraints

4.1. Constraint G.1: Rigidity. Regarding the crease pattern as a pin-jointed framework of the crease lines, the folding process can be modeled using kinematic equations preserving zero deformation of the crease lines at any stage of folding. The zero-extension condition has been used to study the stiffness properties of the folded sheets [Schenk and Guest 11]. In the present model, we introduce the constant-length constraint of a crease line at an intermediate state of folding and obtain a geometrically nonlinear model reflecting the kinematics as a system of quadratic equations that can be included as equality constraints in the optimization problem in Equation (2.1).[1] In the initial configuration, the length of a crease line l is evaluated as the norm of the vector introduced in Equation (3.1):

$$(4.1) \qquad \ell_l^0 := \left\| \mathbf{v}_l^0 \right\|.$$

Correspondingly, the length of a crease line l in an intermediate configuration t is expressed using the norm of the instantaneous vector in Equation (3.2) as

$$(4.2) \qquad \ell_l(t) := \|\mathbf{v}_l(t)\| = \left\| \mathbf{v}_l^0 + \mathbf{u}_j(t) - \mathbf{u}_i(t) \right\|.$$

The length of all crease lines must remain constant during the folding process, so we require that

$$(4.3) \qquad \ell_l^0 = \ell_l(t).$$

Using Equations (4.1) and (4.2) with the t parameter omitted, the constant-length constraint in Equation (4.3) for a single crease line l can be written as

$$(4.4) \qquad G_l^{(\ell)} := 2\mathbf{v}_l^{0T}\mathbf{u}_j - 2\mathbf{v}_l^{0T}\mathbf{u}_i + \mathbf{u}_j^T\mathbf{u}_j - 2\mathbf{u}_j^T\mathbf{u}_i + \mathbf{u}_i^T\mathbf{u}_i = 0.$$

By applying the constant-length constraint to all crease lines and boundary edges of the crease pattern, a system of L quadratic equations with unknown $3N$ nodal displacements assembled in the vector $\mathbf{u}$ is obtained in the following form:

$$\mathbf{G}^{(\ell)}(\mathbf{u}) = 0.$$

In order to support gradient-based optimization strategies, each criterion implementation includes both the value and its derivatives with respect to the displacement vector $\mathbf{u}$. The derivatives of Equation (4.4) are obtained as

$$\partial G_l^{(\ell)}/\partial \mathbf{u}_i = -2\mathbf{v}_l^{0T} - 2\mathbf{u}_j^T + 2\mathbf{u}_i^T, \qquad \partial G_l^{(\ell)}/\partial \mathbf{u}_j = 2\mathbf{v}_l^{0T} - 2\mathbf{u}_i^T + 2\mathbf{u}_j^T.$$

These terms are assembled in an algorithmic system matrix required for the calculation of the predictor step.

---

[1]For crease patterns with triangular facets, this assumption provides the necessary and sufficient condition for a rigid-foldable crease pattern. For quadrilateral facets, additional constraint equations preserving the planarity of facets must be included.

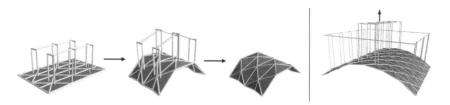

FIGURE 4. Simulation of the kinematically controlled folding process shown for two different versions of a vault shells with tailored crane adapters to condense out the free degrees of freedom to a single one.

4.2. Constraint G.2: Kinematic links. Besides the L rigidity constraints, additional $K < 3N - L$ kinematic equations can be introduced to narrow the domain of the optimization problem. Time-dependent kinematic constraints and linkages enable the simulation of the manufacturing process. The simplest type of kinematic control can be introduced using the constraint equation linking several degrees of freedom:

$$G_k^u := \sum_{i=1}^{N} \sum_{m=1}^{3} A_{kim} u_{im} + \bar{u}_k(t) = 0, \quad k = 1 \ldots K,$$

where A_{ki} are the coefficients and $\bar{u}_k(t)$ the prescribed displacements. Kinematic constraints are assembled in the vector $\mathbf{G}^u(\mathbf{u}, t)$, and the corresponding derivatives of these constraints are assembled in the matrix $\mathbf{B}_{(K \times 3N)}^u$ consisting of the coefficients A_{kim}.

EXAMPLE 4.1 (Folding Device Exploiting Kinematic Condensation). The combination of facet rigidity and explicitly prescribed displacement of individual nodes can be used for the design of simple solutions to the folding process as shown in Figure 4. In the case of the considered Yoshimura crease pattern, multiple free degrees of freedom need to be simultaneously controlled in order to enter the right folding branch of the kinematic space of the structure. By constructing a kinematic adapter consisting of a frame and trusses, the free degrees of freedom inherent to the crease pattern $3N - L$ can be condensed into a single degree of freedom so that the folding process can be controlled using a simple crane. An application example was provided by the authors in [van der Woerd et al. 13]. This type of simulation represents a special case of the fully constrained optimization problem that reduces to a geometrically nonlinear analysis of the system of kinematic equation and is directly solvable using the Newton–Raphson method.

4.3. Constraint G.3: Developability. The criterion of developability is used in the form-finding procedures to ensure that the identified folded configuration can be developed into a planar sheet. This is the case if the sum of the angles θ_j between the crease lines around each interior node i is 2π:

$$G_i^{dev} := \sum_{j=1}^{N_i^{nbr}} \theta_{ij} - 2\pi = 0.$$

With regard to the argument γ_{ij} given in Equation (3.3), the derivatives required for the gradient-based solver of the optimization framework can be expressed as

(4.5) $$\frac{\partial G_i^{dev}}{\partial \mathbf{u}} := \sum_{j=1}^{N_i^{nbr}} \frac{\partial \theta_{ij}}{\partial \mathbf{u}} = \sum_{j=1}^{N_i^{nbr}} \frac{\partial \theta_{ij}}{\partial \gamma_{ij}} \frac{\partial \gamma_{ij}}{\partial \mathbf{u}},$$

where for each pair of consecutive crease lines j and $j + 1$ around a node i,

$$\frac{\partial \gamma_{ij}}{\partial \mathbf{u}} = \frac{(-1)(1 - \gamma_{ij}^2)}{\left\|\mathbf{v}_{\text{nbr}(i,j)}\right\| \left\|\mathbf{v}_{\text{nbr}(i,j+1)}\right\|} \left[\frac{\partial \mathbf{v}_{\text{nbr}(i,j)}}{\partial \mathbf{u}} \cdot \mathbf{v}_{\text{nbr}(i,j)} + \mathbf{v}_{\text{nbr}(i,j)} \cdot \frac{\partial \mathbf{v}_{\text{nbr}(i,j)}}{\partial \mathbf{u}} \right].$$

4.4. Constraint G.4: Flat-foldability. If the crease pattern should be foldable into a flat form, the sum of the alternating angles θ_{ij} between the crease lines around each interior node i is zero [Kawasaki 91]:

$$G_i^{\text{ff}} := \sum_{j=1}^{N_i^{\text{nbr}}} (-1)^j \theta_{ij} = 0.$$

The derivatives of the flat-foldability constraint are obtained in analogy to Equation (4.5). The constraints G.3 and G.4 can be applied in combination with goal functions specifying the desired form of the target shape as will be shown in Example 5.2.

5. Goal Functions

5.1. Goal function f.1: Potential energy. The implementation of plug-ins including the surface integrals over an intermediate configuration of the crease pattern opens up the possibility to characterize the force flow through the spatial structure and to include it in the optimization in a closed form. At present, the implementation is limited to the evaluation of the potential energy of gravity (f.1.1) of a crease pattern in an intermediate configuration $\mathbf{x}(t)$ obtained as an integral:

$$(5.1) \qquad\qquad \mathcal{V} = \int_{A_f} \rho g d \, r_3(\mathbf{s}) \, dA(\mathbf{s}),$$

where ρ, g, and d denote the material density, gravity, and thickness, respectively. The surface coordinate vector $\mathbf{s}$ has two components (s_1, s_2), and an infinitesimal surface area is defined as $dA(\mathbf{s}) = ds_1 ds_2$. The vertical distance of a material point $\mathbf{s}$ to a base level is expressed by the vertical component of the positional vector $\mathbf{r}$ as a scalar function $r_3(\mathbf{s})$.

For a triangular facet, the shape functions $\mathbf{N}$ correspond to the barycentric coordinates $\eta_1, \eta_2 \in (0, 1) \wedge \eta_1 + \eta_2 = 1$ of the form

$$\mathbf{r}(\eta) = \eta_1 \mathbf{x}_1 + \eta_2 \mathbf{x}_2 + (1 - \eta_1 - \eta_2)\mathbf{x}_3.$$

Potential energy of gravity for a facet I is then expressed as

$$\mathcal{V}_I = \int_0^1 \int_0^{1-\eta_2} \rho g d \, r_3(\eta, \mathbf{x}) \, a(\eta, \mathbf{x}) \, d\eta_1 d\eta_2.$$

Based on this formulation, analytical derivatives $\partial \mathcal{V}_I / \partial \mathbf{u}$ can be readily obtained using the chain rule. Both $\mathcal{V}_I$ and $\partial \mathcal{V}_I / \partial \mathbf{u}$ are evaluated using numerical quadrature. Their detailed specification of these expressions, however, would go beyond the scope of this work. The implementation of the potential energy of gravity represents the first step toward the implementation of stored elastic energy (f.1.2) needed to reflect the force flow through the crease pattern:

$$\mathcal{U} = \int_{A_f} \mathbf{D}\varepsilon(\mathbf{s}, t)^2 \, dA(\mathbf{s}).$$

A particularly interesting case for statically based optimization of oricrete folded plate structures appears if we assume the facet rigidity and allow for deformation only along

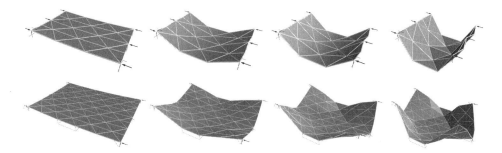

FIGURE 5. Simulation combining the goal function for minimum potential energy of gravity with the constraint on facet rigidity to produce a vault using a Yoshimura crease pattern: Uniform displacement prescribed along the left and right sides (top), and control of corner node displacements (bottom).

the crease lines in the target design configuration, i.e., filled with grout. Then, the stored energy potential reduces to

$$\mathcal{U} = \sum_{l \in \mathcal{L}} \kappa \varphi(t)^2 \ell_l,$$

where κ represents the rotational stiffness of a crease line and φ the change of the dihedral angle between two facets connected with the crease line l.

EXAMPLE 5.1 (Hanging Crease Pattern). In order to exemplify the usage of the energy potential for a particular use case, let us examine the concept of a hanging cloth as an alternative device for the control of the folding process. This type of simulation can also be used for simple statically based shape optimization corresponding to the form-finding concept called *hanging cloth reversed*, which was introduced by Swiss architect Heinz Isler [Isler 61, Chilton 10]. By combining the described criterion on the minimum of potential energy of gravity forces (f.1.1) with the facet rigidity constraint, the Yoshimura vault can be produced by controlling the horizontal displacements as demonstrated on two examples in Figure 5. An example in Figure 6 shows the effect of gravity forces on the waterbomb crease pattern. The combination of kinematic control and gravity forces seems to provide enough means for an inexpensive technique for folding of larger structural shell elements.

5.2. Goal function f.2: Distance to target surfaces. The goal function $f(\mathbf{u})$ for specifying the global form of the structure in the folded state can be introduced as a minimum distance between selected nodes of the crease pattern $\mathcal{S} \subset \mathcal{N}$ and a specified target surface. General global measure of the lack-of-fit between the crease pattern and the target surface is evaluated as the norm of the vector of distances between the crease nodes or points to be attracted by the target surface:

$$(5.2) \qquad f(\mathbf{u}, t) := \|\mathcal{D}(\mathbf{u}, t)\| = \left[\sum_{i \in \mathcal{S}} \mathcal{D}(\mathbf{u}_i, t)^2 \right]^{\frac{1}{2}}.$$

The distance function $\mathcal{D}(\mathbf{u}, t)$ has been introduced as a minimum distance from the target surface $\mathbf{s}(\xi, t)$ with parametric coordinates $\xi = \{r, s\}$. The evaluation of the minimum distance between a node i with position $\mathbf{x}_i(t)$ and surface $\mathbf{s}(\xi, t)$ includes the identification

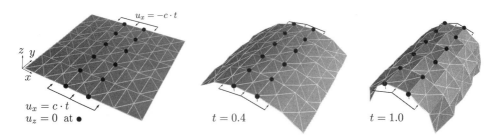

FIGURE 6. Waterbomb crease pattern exposed to gravity loading combined with the constraint on facet rigidity, controlled horizontal displacement u_x of opposite nodes, and fixed vertical displacement in marked nodes. Configurations shown for selected time instances $t = [0.0, 0.4, 1.0]$.

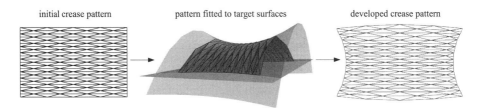

FIGURE 7. Form-finding example combining the target surface in Equation (5.2) with developability and flat-foldability conditions.

of the nearest point ξ within $\mathbf{s}(\xi, t)$. As a consequence, for each node $i \in S$, an isolated optimization problem needs to be solved:

$$(5.3) \qquad \mathcal{D}(\mathbf{u}_i, t) = \min_{\xi_i} \|\mathcal{D}_\xi(\mathbf{u}_i, \xi, t)\|,$$

where the function $\mathcal{D}_\xi(\mathbf{u}_i, \xi, t)$ evaluates the distance to a point ξ on the target surface

$$\mathcal{D}_\xi(\mathbf{u}_i, \xi, t) = \mathbf{x}_i^0 + \mathbf{u}_i(t) - \mathbf{s}(\xi, t).$$

The solution of the minimum distance problem in Equation (5.3) can be efficiently found using sequential least square quadratic programming provided in the `scipy.optimization` package. Analytical derivatives of the goal functions

$$\partial \mathcal{D}_\xi(\mathbf{u}, \xi, t)/\partial \xi$$

are derived symbolically *on the fly* using the `sympy` package [SymPy 13].

In order to provide the derivatives of the optimality condition in Equation (5.2) with respect to the nodal displacements $\mathbf{u}_i$ required for an efficient solution of the minimization problem in Equation (2.1), we apply the chain rule to obtain

$$\frac{\partial f(\mathbf{u}, t)}{\partial \mathbf{u}_i} = \frac{\mathcal{D}(\mathbf{u}_i, t)}{f(\mathbf{u})} \cdot \frac{\partial \mathcal{D}(\mathbf{u}_i, t)}{\partial \mathbf{u}_i}.$$

The code for the term $\partial \mathcal{D}(\mathbf{u}_i, t)/\partial \mathbf{u}_i$ is again generated symbolically on the fly.

EXAMPLE 5.2 (Crease Pattern Adaptation to Fit a Target Shape). By combining the developability and flat-foldability constraints with the criterion on the minimum distance to a target surface, the initial crease pattern can be optimized to achieve the best possible fit

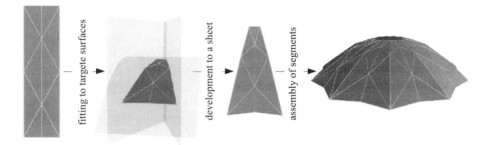

FIGURE 8. Form-finding of a segment and assembly of segments into a dome.

of the desired shape. An example of a crease pattern optimization with respect to a target surface is shown in Figures 7 and 8. In the example in Figure 7, both the developability and flat-foldability constraints were applied. Let us remark that the constraint of developability alone would be sufficient for the present case. However, the parametric studies have shown that simultaneous requirement of flat-foldability automatically renders more regular patterns with facets of similar size.

6. Modularization and Structural Performance

By combining the described form-finding use case with further constraints on the shape of the boundaries of a folded element, a modular structure can be designed as exemplified in Figure 8. In the present example, the rotational symmetry of a dome structure was required to achieve compatibility between the segment boundaries.

As an add-on module, a direct export of the object designed in oricreate to finite element packages (currently ABAQUS and RFEM) provides the possibility to evaluate the structural properties of the folded and segmented structure. An example of the parametric study of the folded and segmented dome is shown in Figure 9 with the comparison of the principle bending moments for 20, 40, and 60 segments. Furthermore, the maximum deflection for the applied vertical load has been calculated to compare the stiffness properties of the three studied segmentations. As expected, the larger number of segments leads to a stiffer structure with lower bending moments. The study indicates how the intended support of the individual steps of the design cycle with a seamless transitions between the simulation based on the criteria of foldability and the associated analysis of the structural behavior.

7. Conclusions

We have described the implementation and features of the oricreate package aiming to support a wide range of design cycles of folded-plate structures. It has been implemented as a general optimization framework and can be extended with several types of constraints reflecting the folding mechanisms and kinematics. The currently implemented goal functions and constraints have been briefly explained and exemplified using application examples. Based on the simulation, small-scale demonstrators have been realized using a combination of fine-grained cementitious matrix and textile fabrics, as demonstrated in Figure 10. Further criteria including the statically based optimization of the folded structure are currently being formulated and implemented using an open-source platform for code versioning and management [Oricreate 15].

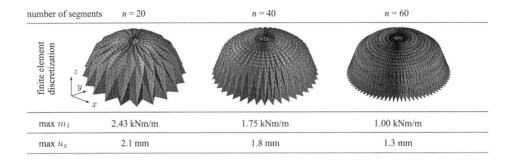

number of segments	$n = 20$	$n = 40$	$n = 60$
finite element discretization			
max m_1	2.43 kNm/m	1.75 kNm/m	1.00 kNm/m
max u_z	2.1 mm	1.8 mm	1.3 mm

FIGURE 9. Examples of FE models exported to ABAQUS for three versions of the the form-finding simulation. The sensitivity with respect to vertical load at the top of the dome was quantified in terms of the maximum principle moment m_1 and maximum deflection u_z.

FIGURE 10. Oridome realized using 16 folded segments.

Acknowledgments

The work was supported by the Deutsche Forschungsgemeinschaft in the framework of the priority program 1542: *Future concrete structures using bionic, mathematical and engineering form-finding principles*, Project No. CH276/3-2. This support is gratefully acknowledged.

References

[belcastro and Hull 02] sarah-marie belcastro and Thomas C. Hull. "A Mathematical Model for Non-flat Origami." In *Origami³: Proceedings of the Third International Meeting of Origami Science, Mathematics, and Education*, edited by Thomas Hull, pp. 39–52. Natick, MA: A K Peters, 2002. MR1955758 (2004a:52008)

[Chilton 10] John Chilton. "Heinz Isler's Infinite Spectrum: Form-Finding in Design." *Architectural Design* 80:4 (2010), 64–71.

[Chudoba et al. 14] Rostislav Chudoba, Jan D. van der Woerd, Matthias Schmerl, and Josef Hegger. "ORICRETE: Modeling Support for Design and Manufacturing of Folded Concrete Structures." *Advances in Engineering Software* 72 (2014), 119–127.

[Enthought 13] Enthought. "Scientific Computing Solutions." http://www.enthought.com, 2013.

[Gray et al. 11] Steven R. Gray, Nathan J. Zeichner, and Vijay Kumar. "A Simulator for Origami-Inspired Self-Reconfigurable Robots." In *Origami⁵: Fifth International Meeting of Origami Science, Mathematics, and Education*, edited by Patsy Wang-Iverson, Robert J. Lang, and Mark Yim, pp. 323–333. Boca Raton, FL: A K Peters/CRC Press, 2011. MR2866909 (2012h:00044)

[Hegger and Bruckermann 06] Josef Hegger and Oliver Bruckermann. "Aspects of Modeling Textile Reinforced Concrete (TRC) in 2D." In *Measuring, Monitoring and Modeling Concrete Properties*, edited by Maria S. Konsta-Gdoutos, pp. 769–776. Houten: Springer Netherlands, 2006.

[Hegger and Voss 08] Josef Hegger and Stefan Voss. "Investigations on the Bearing Behaviour and Application Potential of Textile Reinforced Concrete." *Engineering Structures* 30:7 (2008), 2050–2056.

[Isler 61] Heinz Isler. "New Shapes for Shells." *Bulletin of the International Association for Shell Structures* 8:3 (1961), 123–130.

[Kawasaki 91] Toshikazu Kawasaki. "On the Relation between Mountain-Creases and Vally-Creases of a Flat Origami." In *Proceedings of the First International Meeting of Origami Science and Technology*, edited by H. Huzita, pp. 229–237. Padova, Italy: Dipartimento di Fisica dell'Università di Padova, 1991.

[Klett and Drechsler 11] Yves Klett and Klaus Drechsler. "Designing Technical Tessellations." In *Origami^5: Fifth International Meeting of Origami Science, Mathematics, and Education*, edited by Patsy Wang-Iverson, Robert J. Lang, and Mark Yim, pp. 305–322. Boca Raton, FL: A K Peters/CRC Press, 2011. MR2866909 (2012h:00044)

[Konrad and Chudoba 09] Martin Konrad and Rostislav Chudoba. "Tensile Behavior of Cementitious Composite Reinforced with Epoxy Impregnated Multifilament Yarns." *International Journal for Multiscale Computational Engineering* 7:2 (2009), 115–133.

[Kraft 88] Dieter Kraft. "A Software Package for Sequential Quadratic Programming." Technical Report DFVLR-FB 88-28, DLR German Aerospace Center, Institute for Flight Mechanics, Koln, Germany, 1988.

[Lang 03] Robert J. Lang. *Origami Design Secrets: Mathematical Methods for an Ancient Art*. Natick, MA: A K Peters, 2003. MR2013930 (2004g:52001)

[Lang 09] Robert J. Lang (editor). textitOrigami^4: Fourth International Meeting of Origami Science, Mathematics, and Education. Wellesley, MA: A K Peters, 2009. MR2590567 (2010h:00025)

[Oricreate 15] Oricreate. "Tool for Modeling of Folding and Manufacturing of Thin-Walled Concrete Structures." http://github.com/simvisage/oricreate, 2015.

[Schenk and Guest 11] Mark Schenk and Simon D. Guest. "Origami Folding: A Structural Engineering Approach." In *Origami^5: Fifth International Meeting of Origami Science, Mathematics, and Education*, edited by Patsy Wang-Iverson, Robert J. Lang, and Mark Yim, pp. 291–303. Boca Raton, FL: A K Peters/CRC Press, 2011. MR2866909 (2012h:00044)

[Scholzen et al. 10] Alexander Scholzen, Rostislav Chudoba, and Josef Hegger. "Damage Based Modeling of Planar Textile-Reinforced Concrete Structures." In *Proceedings of the International RILEM Conference on Material Science*, edited by W. Brameshuber, pp. 283–291. Aachen, Germany: RILEM Publications SARL, 2010.

[Scholzen et al. 14a] Alexander Scholzen, Rostislav Chudoba, and Josef Hegger. "Thin-Walled Shell Structure Made of Textile Reinforced Concrete—Part I: Structural Design and Construction." *Structural Concrete* 16:1 (2014), 106–âĂŞ114.

[Scholzen et al. 14b] Alexander Scholzen, Rostislav Chudoba, and Josef Hegger. "Thin-Walled Shell Structure Made of Textile Reinforced Concrete—Part II: Experimental Characterization, Ultimate Limit State Assessment and Numerical Simulation." *Structural Concrete* 16:1 (2014), 115âĂŞ–124.

[SymPy 13] SymPy. "A Python Library for Symbolic Mathematics." http://sympy.org, 2013.

[Tachi 09] Tomohiro Tachi. "Simulation of Rigid Origami." In *Origami^4: Fourth International Meeting of Origami Science, Mathematics, and Education*, edited by Robert J. Lang, pp. 175–187. Wellesley, MA: A K Peters, 2009. MR2590567 (2010h:00025)

[Tachi 10a] Tomohiro Tachi. "Geometric Considerations for the Design of Rigid Origami Structures." In *Proceedings of the International Association for Shell and Spatial Structures (IASS) Symposium 2010, Shanghai, China*, pp. 771–782. Madrid: IASS, 2010.

[Tachi 10b] Tomohiro Tachi. "One-DOF Cylindrical Deployable Structures with Rigid Quadrilateral Panels." In *Symposium of the International Association for Shell and Spatial Structures*, pp. 2295–2305. Valencia, Italy: Editorial de la Universitat Politécnica de Valencia, 2010.

[Tarnai 01] Tibor Tarnai. "Origami in Structural Engineering." In *IASS Symposium 2001: International Symposium on Theory, Design and Realization of Shell and Spatial Structures, Nagoya, Japan, 9–13 Oct. 2001*, pp. 298–299. Madrid: IASS, 2001.

[Tysmans et al. 09] Tine Tysmans, Sigrid Adriaenssens, Heidi Cuypers, and Jan Wastiels. "Structural Analysis of Small Span Textile Reinforced Concrete Shells with Double Curvature." *Composites Science and Technology* 69:11–12 (2009), 1790–1796.

[van der Woerd et al. 13] Jan D. van der Woerd, Rostislav Chudoba, and Josef Hegger. "Single-Curved Shell Structure Made of Textile-Reinforced Concrete Plate Using a Folding Technique." Presented at IASS Symposium 2013, Wroclaw, Poland, September 23–27, 2013.

INSTITUTE OF STRUCTURAL CONCRETE, RWTH AACHEN UNIVERSITY, GERMANY
E-mail address: rostislav.chudoba@rwth-aachen.de

INSTITUTE OF STRUCTURAL CONCRETE, RWTH AACHEN UNIVERSITY, GERMANY
E-mail address: jvanderwoerd@imb.rwth-aachen.de

INSTITUTE OF STRUCTURAL CONCRETE, RWTH AACHEN UNIVERSITY, GERMANY
E-mail address: heg@imb.rwth-aachen.de

Rotational Erection System (RES): Origami Extended with Cuts

Yoshinobu Miyamoto

1. Introduction

Rotational Erection System (RES) is a design method to make a three-dimensional (3D) structure from a single sheet with systematic cuts and folds (see, for example, Figure 1). It is origami extended with cuts, or *kirigami* (Japanese: kiri = cut + gami = paper) folded into 3D shapes. RES would be an efficient production method for both artistic and industrial uses.

Pop-up techniques have been extensively developed for books and greeting cards over centuries. The single-sheet pop-up technique by cutting card stock was used for art education in Bauhaus in the 1920s by Josef Albers and became a common art/design teaching method in schools. In 1981 Masahiro Chatani named it *origamic architecture*, and Ramin Razani titled his 2006 book *Kirigami*.

In spite of the elaboration in paper engineering in the examples above, most of them are based on parallelogram transformations. In the case of a single-sheet construction with a 90-degree center fold, the 3D shapes stand at the corner of the center fold.

FIGURE 1. RES semi-domes (A4 paper).

This work is supported by JSPS KAKENHI Grant Number 25560012.

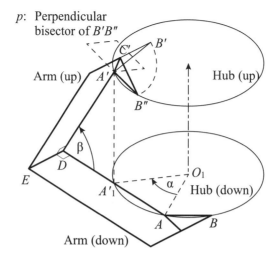

FIGURE 2. Primary element.

Effective use of systematic cuts to sheet material can be seen in expanded metal mesh. It also uses parallelogram transformations.

RES, on the other hand, enables one to bring the 3D shapes out of the plane without the need for a center fold. The rotational movement in RES resembles that of *nejiri-ori* (twist fold, seen in the works of Shuzo Fujimoto) but differs from it in the fact that RES keeps the margin area unfolded. The ease of local manipulation free from the over-all constraints provides flexibility in design and in production. RES has a single stable shape after erection, while a conventional design such as "Air Vase" [Torafu 10] with expanded slitted paper could take a variety of shapes with the plasticity of the hinges and of the paper itself.

Related research in pop-up card mechanisms deals with linkages connected to a center fold and opening actuation. Because RES does not use center-fold opening, there is little relation with recent works in the subject. One recent study concluded that "which 2D or 3D shapes are constructable using single sheet of material" is an open problem [Abel et al. 13]. In this work, RES is applied to shapes with rotational symmetry such as domes and towers. The generalization of RES to shapes without rotational symmetry is also described. Interactive RES pattern-making software tools are implemented with GeoGebra 5 [GeoGebra 14].

2. Geometric Principles

The primary element of RES is an arm linked to a hub with a triangular tab (Figure 2). The arm rotates vertically around the hinge DE on the ground, and the hub ascends with horizontal rotation following the tab linkage ABC. The structure is bistable due to the displacement of the arm's top end outward during the movement while there is no displacement on the ground and at the erected position.

The horizontal rotation angle α of the hub and the vertical rotation angle β of the arm are used as design parameters to obtain the coordinates and the pattern:

$$\alpha = \angle AO_1A_1', \qquad \beta = \angle ADA', \qquad A_1' = R_\alpha(A), \qquad H = O_1O_2,$$
$$A' = R_\beta(A), \qquad B' = R_\beta(B), \qquad B'' = (x(R_\alpha(B)), y(R_\alpha(B)), H),$$

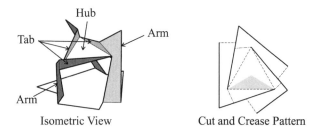

Isometric View   Cut and Crease Pattern

FIGURE 3. Tilted hub.

where R_α is rotation by angle α about O_1O_2 and R_β is rotation by angle β about DE.

At $\triangle A'B'B''$ (an isosceles triangle), the perpendicular bisector of $B'B''$, p, is the same as the bisecting plane of $\angle B'A'B''$ (therefore, $A'B' = A'B''$). Folding line $A'C'$ is obtained as the intersection of the arm (up) plane DEA' and p:

$$C = R_{\beta^{-1}}(C'),$$

where $R_{\beta^{-1}}$ is rotation by angle $-\beta$ about DE.

The following geometric relationship at $\triangle DA'A$ is used:

$$DA = DA'_1 + A'_1A, \qquad DA'_1 = DA' \cos\beta, \qquad A'_1A = 2O_1A \sin(\alpha/2),$$
$$L = 2R \sin(\alpha/2)/(1 - \cos\beta)$$
$$[\because L = L\cos\beta + 2R\sin(\alpha/2), \text{ where } R = O_1A, \ L = DA = DA'],$$
$$H = O_1O_2 = L\sin\beta.$$

Note that the only constraints are folding lines DE, AB, and AC. Cut lines/curves or the arm profile can be manipulated with substantial range. General 3D shapes with a tilted hub at the top without rotational symmetry can be designed with individual arm-tab calculations (Figure 3).

3. Design Development

Variations on the arm's outline define the shapes produced by the RES method (see examples in Figure 4). The general shape can be a part of a solid with rotational symmetry such as a sphere, ellipsoid, cone, or torus. A full sphere can be made of two hemispheres attached on both sides of glass plate (Figure 4, bottom left). A series of dome designs with short columns and broader margin areas were made for LED table lamp covers (Figure 4, bottom center and right). Tower shapes are made with multistage configurations. The reduced arc patterns nested in the hubs generate quasi-logarithmic spirals (Figure 5). The variety of designs has been shown at the author's Flickr albums [Miyamoto 08].

4. Angle Section Arms

Arms that are flat plate arms will easily buckle under compression. The stiffness of the arms can be improved with an *angle section* by folding a line along the arm. The angle section of the arm can be designed to make the tab plane extend to the hinge of the arm on the ground (Figures 6 and 7). The angle section can also be applied to tilted (nonparallel to the ground) hub geometries (Figure 7(b)). A group of the RES with angle-section arms can be used for the core element for sandwich panels (Figure 7(c) and (d)).

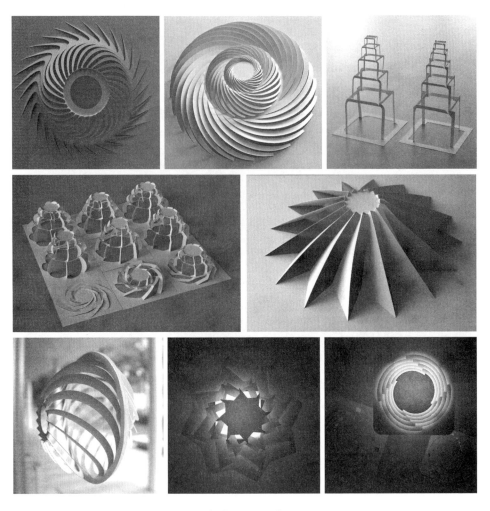

FIGURE 4. Domes and towers.

5. Design Tools and Work Flow

The free 3D software SketchUp [SketchUp 14] is useful for an initial design study.

For more interactive and flexible design, several software tools are implemented with GeoGebra 5. GeoGebra is a dynamic mathematics software that brings together geometry, algebra, spreadsheets, graphing, statistics, and calculus in one package. Parameters such as the number of arms and angles for horizontal and vertical rotations can be adjusted with sliders. Movable points on the 2D pattern give an intuitive interaction for a detailed design. The general 3D shape can be shown in the 3D view window (Figure 8). PDF files exported from the 2D pattern view are fed into a desktop cutting plotter through Adobe Illustrator CS6 with which cuts and creases are sorted to respective layers.

6. Meter Scale Samples

To study the applications of RES for display stands and playground toys, meter scale samples have been made from plastic sandwiched panels fabricated with an industrial CNC

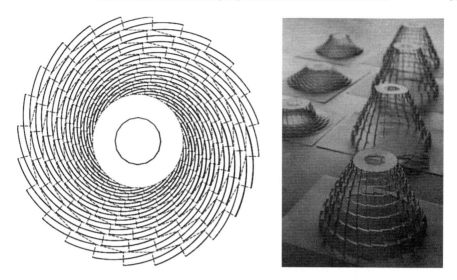

FIGURE 5. Quasi spiral cut-and-crease pattern (left) for towers (right).

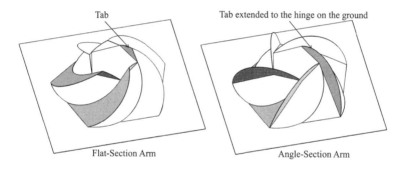

FIGURE 6. Flat-section arm (left) and angle-section arm (right).

cutting plotter (Figure 9). The panel is made of two surface sheets with an embossed core, all made of polypropylene. Angle-section arms working together with the bistable characteristics of the square plan produced a springy folding–unfolding action. The pattern consists of valley creases and cuts that are produced with half- and full-cut operations, respectively, from one side (bottom side) of the panel; the valley fold hinges are made with the top sheet uncut.

7. Conclusion

RES demonstrates the usefulness of the idea of extending origami with systematic and integrated cuts. It shall be used in multiple scales in the future. Photo-etched RES patterns on silicon plates could be a solution for 3D MEMS manufacturing. Chemical-etched ones on metal plates could be used for millimeter to centimeter scale mechanical elements and jewelry. RES with plywood sheets and sandwich panels fabricated with CNC routers could be used for furniture and building elements. A full architectural scale application could be a structure made with fiber reinforced concrete cast-in-situ on a flat floor with separators on cut curves where the concrete plate arms works as compression elements together with

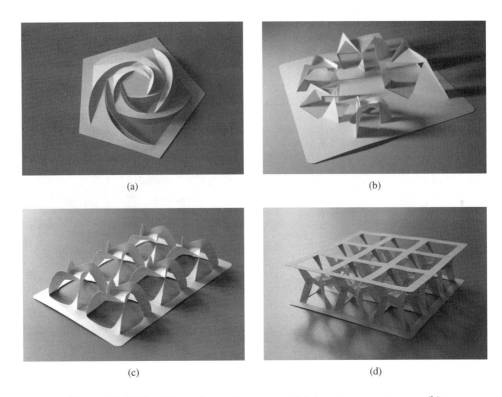

(a)   (b)

(c)   (d)

FIGURE 7. RES with angle section arms: (a) two-stage pentagon, (b) tilted hub triangles, (c) square cells, and (d) double square-cell core.

additional tension cables. The RES design software tool could be be improved to handle irregular shapes.

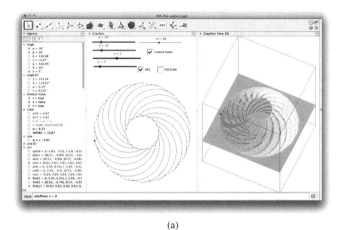

(a)

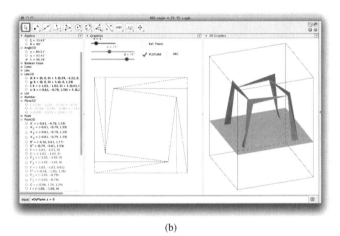

(b)

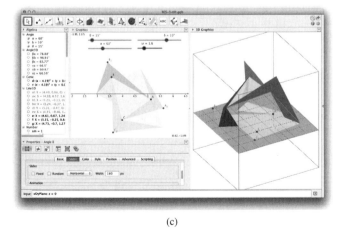

(c)

FIGURE 8. RES design tools with GeoGebra 5: (a) Dome with flat arc arms, (b) square with angle section arms, and (c) triangle tilted hub with angle section arms.

(a) (b)

FIGURE 9. Meter scale samples: (a) $120 \times 120 \times 120$, $t = 0.5$ cm, and (b) $57 \times 57 \times 37$, $t = 0.5$ cm.

References

[Abel et al. 13] Zachary Abel, Erik D. Demaine, Martin L. Demaine, Sarah Eisenstat, Anna Lubiw, Andre Schulz, Diane L. Souvaine, Giovanni Viglietta, and Andrew Winslow. "Algorithms for Designing Pop-Up Cards." In *30th International Symposium on Theoretical Aspects of Computer Science (STACS 2013), February 27-March 2, 2013, Kiel, Germany*, Leibniz International Proceedings in Informatics (LIPIcs) 20, edited by Natacha Portier and Thomas Wilke, pp. 269–280. Dagstuhl, Germany: Schloss Dagstuhl–Leibniz-Zentrum fuer Informatik, 2013. MR3137659

[GeoGebra 14] GeoGebra. "GeoGebra Homepage." http://www.geogebra.org/, 2014.

[Miyamoto 08] Yoshinobu Miyamoto. "Prof. YM Albums." *Flickr*, https://www.flickr.com/photos/yoshinobu_miyamoto/sets, 2008.

[SketchUp 14] SketchUp. "SketchUp Homepage." http://www.sketchup.com/, 2014.

[Torafu 10] Torafu Architects. "Air Vase." http://torafu.com/works/air-w, 2010.

AICHI INSTITUTE OF TECHNOLOGY, JAPAN
E-mail address: yoshinobu.miyamoto@gmail.com

Toward Engineering Biological Tissues by Directed Assembly and Origami Folding

Philipp J. Mehner, Tian Liu, Majid Bigdeli Karimi, Alyssa Brodeur,
Juan Paniagua, Stephanie Giles, Patricia Richard, Antoniya Nemtserova,
Sanwei Liu, Roger Alperin, Sangeeta Bhatia, Martin Culpepper, Robert J. Lang,
and Carol Livermore

1. Introduction

Human tissue engineering can save lives by providing donor tissues and organs, and by acting as a tool for screening new medical therapies before any human testing takes place. Tissue engineering has proven successful for certain types of tissue (e.g., skin [Wood et al. 07] and bladder [Atala et al. 06]) that have a more planar, sheet-like structure rather than a fully three-dimensional (3D) structure. The creation of more complex, fully 3D tissues has proven more challenging because of the need to create a functional (typically biomimetic) structure that is supported by appropriate vascular networks. Although some techniques have been demonstrated (e.g., bioprinting [Jakab et al. 10]), the current state of the art faces challenges in producing human tissue fast enough (i.e., with sufficient throughput), with complex human tissue structures suitable for transplantation or medical therapy testing (i.e., with sufficient control), and in a way that can be done to meet demand (i.e., with sufficient scalability). Origami offers potential to obtain well-controlled 3D structures for tissue engineering. Manual folding [Kuribayashi-Shigetomi and Takeuchi 11] and cell traction forces [Kuribayashi-Shigetomi et al. 12] have been used to fold nonbiodegradable parylene for tissue engineering. Nonbiodegradable polymeric microcontainers are folded to encapsulate biological specimens by a self-actuation process in [Azam et al. 11]. Patterned poly(ethylene glycol) (PEG) hydrogels are self-actuated and folded into structures with uniform radii of curvature for biological applications in [Jamal et al. 13]. In contrast to the previous demonstrations, the present work simulates and experimentally demonstrates actuated self-folding of biodegradable polymeric structures for tissue engineering in which well-defined hinges localize folding between the more rigid plates.

The present concept for tissue engineering combines the previously demonstrated ability to organize cells of different sizes (e.g., of different cell types) into hemispherical wells on a two-dimensional (2D) sheet [Agarwal and Livermore 11] with origami folding. In this approach, spherical cells suspended in a liquid medium are assembled onto a polymer surface; the surface may be precoated with collagen to better promote the survival and correct function of the cells. Although cells can adhere anywhere on the surface, external fluid forces ensure that they ultimately assemble only in wells that match the cells' diameters. The new element in this approach, and the focus of the present work, is the origami folding of the cell-seeded sheet to form the desired 3D tissue structure. The origami-folded structure will permit not only cell culture in static medium [Freshney 05] but also cell culture in a medium that flows through the folded origami channels. The scaffold material biodegrades through a process of surface erosion [Wang et al. 03], leaving behind the cells that have been organized through directed assembly and origami folding. The present results focus on the creation of potential origami-based folding architectures that mimic the structure of real human tissues and on the development of self-actuated polymer folding scaffolds for their implementation. Requirements for potential folding designs, material selection for polymer scaffolds, potential origami architectures, finite-element simulations, and experiments are demonstrated.

2. Requirements for Origami-Based Tissue Engineering

Each tissue in the human body has its own unique structure. Origami is a promising method for structuring tissues because of the wide diversity of forms that can be folded. An added layer of complexity may be introduced by controlling the pattern of cells on the 2D scaffold sheets. Despite origami's potentially broad applicability for tissue engineering, it is worthwhile to focus on a particular tissue structure for the original demonstrations. In this case, the chosen demonstration system is the liver. Although liver's macroscale structure appears complex, with four lobes, connective tissue, vasculature, etc., functional liver tissue comprises approximately 100,000 repeating units called liver lobules. Each liver lobule is about 1–2 mm in size and has an irregular hexagonal cross section with approximately sixfold symmetry; diagrams may be found in [Ho et al. 13]. Perpendicular to the cross section, each lobule is extruded to form a roughly hexagonal prism with nonplanar caps. Blood enters each lobule through six inlets organized around the lobule's periphery and fed by the portal vein and hepatic artery. Blood flows radially to the center of the lobule and exits through the central vein. Lobules are arranged in a rough array and are connected to common vascular inlets and outlets. The goal of this research is to replicate the structure and function of liver lobules in a modular origami system and to tile the repeated units together to form functional tissue.

For most tissues, including liver tissue, appropriate vasculature is one of the most challenging features to engineer. Not only must the network of blood vessels reach all of the parts of the tissue to supply nutrients and oxygen and to remove metabolic byproducts, but it must also meet requirements for vessel size, branching geometry, etc. In the origami tissue approach, the vascular architecture may be created in either of two main ways. If the folding sheets are pre-formed with holes in the appropriate locations, the vascular channels may cross folded sheets, with blood flowing through the holes. Alternatively, the fold pattern may be designed so that blood flows parallel to the sheets, in channels formed between adjacent folded plates (Figure 1). Liver lobules are well suited to the second approach, in which flow travels between radially oriented or partially radially oriented folds.

The design of the folds must meet additional requirements beyond achieving an (ideally hexagonal) radial fold structure. Because biological tissues are sensitive to contamination, it is important that the folding be achieved with a minimum of contact between the cell-seeded folding sheet and the outside world. An ideal fold design should therefore have one degree of freedom (1DOF), enabling the fold to be implemented with a minimum number of contacts with sterile actuators. Finally, the detailed design of the structure should be

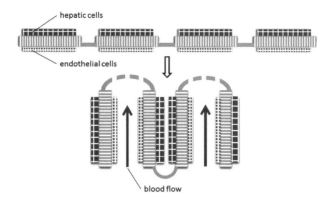

FIGURE 1. Conceptual design of a scaffold, showing a planar scaffold before folding (top) and after folding into three dimensions (bottom). The hinges may be made of the same material as the plates as long as each hinge's thickness and length are chosen to enable the desired folding architecture.

compatible with self-folding, in which biodegradable, biocompatible actuators integrated into the scaffold sheet itself drive the 1DOF folding with no contact with external actuators at all.

The research takes a multi-pronged approach to meeting the challenges of origami-based tissue engineering. Section 3 describes the design of candidate fold patterns that replicate the hexagonal structure of a liver lobule while maintaining few DOFs. Section 4 presents the concept and initial demonstrations of the proposed self-actuating polymer system for origami-based tissue engineering. Section 5 presents finite element analysis of the proposed polymer actuator system for a simple, well-controlled model system (the Miura fold). The Miura fold's well-understood architecture enables these models to highlight the mechanisms by which self-actuated folding can deviate from the design intent. Finally, Section 6 shows results to date on self-folded systems implemented in the target biocompatible polymer material system.

3. Candidate Fold Architectures

Figure 2 illustrates one candidate crease pattern for a group of lobules, as well as a photograph of the resulting folded structure implemented in paper. The pattern offers a hexagonal symmetry in each repeating unit, as well as the ability to tile multiple units together in a single sheet. The resulting folds form an approximately spiral structure, in which a radial inflow pattern is combined with a circumferential element. The hexagonal-spiral design is not a single-DOF structure like the idealized Miura-ori, but when facet bending and other real-world nonidealities are considered, it does have a single well-defined low-energy path in phase space from the unfolded to the folded state, which gives the same behavior as a single DOF: it folds easily in a single smooth motion. The proposed pattern deviates from biomimetic liver lobule structure in several ways. First, the spiral channels result in a longer flow length from the peripheral entry vessels to the central exit vessels. Second, the spiral folds are naturally wider at the periphery than near the center, unlike the more uniform dimensions of the vasculature in liver lobules. Third, liver lobules achieve these more uniform dimensions by increasing the number of vessels at larger distances from the

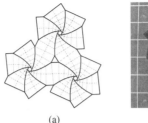 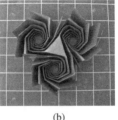

(a)   (b)

FIGURE 2. (a) Crease pattern and (b) paper demonstration of the hexagonal-spiral fold architecture.

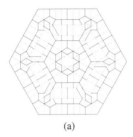 

(a)   (b)

FIGURE 3. (a) Crease pattern and (b) paper demonstration of the hexagonal-radial fold architecture.

lobule's center; the multiplication of vessels at larger radii is not included in the present fold pattern.

Figure 3 illustrates a second candidate crease pattern that allows radial flow through fixed-size channels, so that both the flow and sidewalls are purely radial, like those of a natural lobule. This pattern scales naturally to larger diameter, adding more sidewalls and more channels while keeping the channel size approximately fixed. This property is visible in the figure: The innermost ring contains 6 sidewalls, and the next ring contains 18; subsequent rings would add sidewalls linearly. Though this architecture more closely approximates that of the original lobule, this particular design does not yet have a smooth, low-bending-energy path from the unfolded to the folded state (unlike the hexagonal-spiral architecture). However, the concept has considerable potential for further development.

4. Self-Actuating Polymer Scaffolds

Choosing a material system for the self-actuated origami scaffold is nontrivial. The materials must be biocompatible to avoid harming the cells of the tissue or of the recipient of the tissue. Ideally the scaffold will biodegrade over time, leaving the cells to carry on the initial structure provided by the scaffold. The byproducts of biodegradation also must be biocompatible. The patterned scaffold must be able to withstand sterilization (increased temperature and pressure); be patternable by molding, printing, or lithography to define the necessary microscale tissue features; and have material stiffness and flexibility that enables folds of up to 180°. Finally, it must be possible to implement self-folding actuators in the material system.

A diverse range of biocompatible, biodegradable polymers has been created for medical applications and tissue engineering [Chen et al. 13]. This research is using members of the poly(polyol sebacate) (PPS) family of biocompatible polymers as the basic scaffold material, with an initial focus on poly(glycerol sebacate) (PGS). PPS polymers have stiffness ranging up to 0.38 Giga-Pascal (GPa, where $1 \, Pa = 1 \, N/m^2$) and failure strains ranging from 10% to 200% [Chen et al. 13]. The PGS synthesized in our laboratory has a Young's modulus (measure of stiffness of elastic material) of around 6.3 MPa and a failure strain of approximately 12%. The members of the PPS family are generally well studied and can be patterned in the prepolymer stage. They are chemically cross-linked polymers, and the byproducts from the degradation process are absorbable by the human body through metabolic processes. For comparison with the material properties, typical paper has a stiffness of a few GPa [Carson and Worthington 52] and thickness in the range of 50–100 μm; this suggests that PPS polymer sheets in the tens to hundreds of micrometer thickness range also have the potential to be origami folded.

Self-actuating origami scaffolds are implemented for this application by polymer bilayer actuators. One layer of the bilayer actuator is the basic PGS polymer. The second layer is polysuccinimide (PSI). PGS is essentially stable in water-based liquids, whereas PSI undergoes hydrolysis in physiological buffer solution, resulting in the formation of poly(aspartic acid) (PAA). The hydrolysis reaction causes an extreme volume change, with measured isotropic expansions of approximately 500% when cross-linked with 1,4-diaminobutane in 0.5 M imidazole buffer solution, consistent with literature reports of expansion of up to 600% [Zakharchenko et al. 11]. This cross-linked PSI has a measured Young's modulus of approximately 57 MPa and a measured failure strain of 9% in the unswollen state. When PSI is fabricated in a bilayer setup with PGS, the swelling of PSI creates powerful stresses that drive bending of the bilayer, potentially enabling folding of over 180°. The majority of the swelling reaction takes place in the course of 24 hours. It is therefore possible to first microfabricate the scaffold, then use directed assembly to locate the cells in their proper locations on the tissue scaffold (a process that takes 3–5 minutes) [Agarwal and Livermore 11], and finally permit the swelling of the PSI to fold the cell-seeded scaffold over the course of the following hours.

One of the first experiments tested the bilayer actuator behavior of the PSI/PGS combination. The concept is similar to the experiments of [Zakharchenko et al. 11], but the nonexpanding polymer is PGS rather than polycaprolactone. First, a PSI layer (0.7–1 μm) was spin-coated on a silicon substrate, followed by a PGS layer (several μm). A piece of the silicon substrate was then placed in deionized water. The resulting expansion of the PSI enables peeling of the bilayer, and the peeled material immediately forms into rolled tubes with radii of approximately 2 mm. The tubes are resistant to unrolling, indicating that the rolled structures reflect an equilibrium position for the intended bilayer bending.

Although fold patterns as in Figures 2 and 3 are potentially suitable for replicating the structure of liver lobules, the self-actuating folds are first designed and implemented in a simpler Miura fold. Because the Miura system is well-understood, the success of the self-actuated folding will be able to be readily assessed by comparing simulated and experimental results with expected folding outcomes.

5. Simulated Scaffold Self-Folding

In concept, the tissue scaffold should be designed with the geometry that best facilitates self-folding into the appropriate fold architecture. In practice, the scaffold's geometry

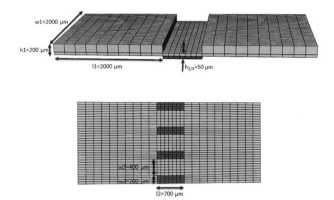

FIGURE 4. Two-rigid-plate system prior to folding, showing structure meshed in Abaqus.

is limited to structures that can readily be fabricated by casting from a mold to replicate the mold's geometry.

Given the microfabrication constraints, the scaffold design comprises thicker, more rigid plates connected by thinner, bilayer hinges. The thinner hinges help to localize the bending in the desired crease regions by reducing their stiffness relative to the more rigid plates. PSI is patterned on one or the other side of each hinge to ensure that it folds in the as-designed direction. The structures are simulated in ANSYS Parametric Design Language (ANSYS APDL) and in Abaqus. Two stages of simulation are carried out. In the first stage, qualitative simulations based on estimated material properties are executed to guide the design concept. A second stage of modeling utilizing experimentally determined material properties is then carried out to finalize the design parameters.

As an initial test of the simulation approach, a simple, two-rigid-plate system with one hinge is studied (Figure 4). The rigid plates and the top layer of the hinge consist of PGS, which is illustrated as a lighter layer. The bottom layer of the hinge is coated with strips of PSI, which is illustrated as a darker layer. When the strips of PSI undergo hydrolysis in physiological buffer solution, the PSI forms PAA, expands, and forces the hinge to bend. The hinge bending is driven by multiple parallel strips of PSI rather than a single uniform layer to minimize bending along the direction of the crease while driving bending perpendicular to the crease. Fixed boundary conditions are placed over 90% of all nodes of the first rigid plate. When the PSI expands, the hinge then bends upward like a cantilever beam, causing the second rigid plate to flip over the first rigid plate.

Each rigid plate has an area of $2000 \times 2000 \ \mu m$ and a height of $200 \ \mu m$. The hinge is $700 \ \mu m$ long and $2000 \ \mu m$ wide. Each layer of the hinge is $50 \ \mu m$ thick. In the future, hepatic cells will be patterned on the bottom of the rigid plates and endothelial cells will be patterned on the top of the rigid plates (Figure 1), and the hinges will be perforated to allow flow to cross the hinge region. The simulation omits these second-level features, focusing solely on the bilayer scaffold structure.

The models are manually meshed to ensure that the highly deformed hinges have a denser mesh than the nominally rigid plates. The nonuniform mesh decreases the computation time for the models and minimizes the required number of nodes and elements for the simulation. The simulation approach is constrained to use a mapped quadrilateral

FIGURE 5. Final configuration of the folded two-rigid-plate system simulated in Abaqus.

mesh. In order to avoid triangular transitions and cylindrical inflation, all discretization must spread out like a wave in all directions.

PSI expansion due to hydrolysis is not directly replicated in ANSYS or Abaqus. To create an equivalent mechanical result, the isotropic expansion of PSI in buffer solution is instead modeled as thermal expansion. The thermal coefficient α of PGS is set to zero so that it does not expand when the temperature is increased in the simulation; this mimics the stability of PGS in buffer solution. The thermal coefficient α and the temperature change ΔT together determine the engineering strain ε of the PSI if it were able to expand freely, as described in the following equation:

$$\varepsilon = \alpha \cdot \Delta T.$$

The expansion generates a residual stress σ in the PSI. For the case in which expansion effects may be approximated as uniaxial, residual stress is determined by the Young's modulus E and the engineering strain ε as follows:

$$\sigma = E\varepsilon = E\alpha\Delta T.$$

The residual stress is partially relieved by bending of the bilayer hinge. The simulation gradually increases the PSI's $\alpha \cdot \Delta T$ product, equilibrating the mechanics of the system at each stage until the target PSI expansion has been achieved and the system is in its final configuration.

Because the displacements are large, nonlinear simulations must be used instead of linear simulations. The nonlinear simulations permit displacements of the plates and hinges in the horizontal direction (along the axis of the neutral plane); linear simulations would not allow this key functionality for simulating 180° folding. For the case of Figure 4, a strain of 0.4 causes a folding of around 180°. The folded two-rigid-plate system is illustrated in Figure 5.

The simulation results of Figure 5 predict that folding will be successful when the actuating bilayer is patterned as a set of stripes oriented perpendicular to the fold. Simulations were also carried out with the bilayer patterned along the full length of the crease, so that actuating elements on the hinge are wider than they are long. In this case, the forces developed along the width cause a distortion, including some bending of nominally rigid plates. The thickness of the rigid plates serves to minimize this distortion, but distortion remains. Although actuation with a bilayer patterned along the full length of the hinge may be of interest for the creation of nondevelopable folding surfaces, it is not useful for the present designs.

Figure 6 shows results from a more-complex simulation of a system of nine angled rigid plates. This underlying crease pattern is a 77.5° Miura-ori [Miura 94], in which the creases have been expanded to allow the hinges to bend and holes have been added at the

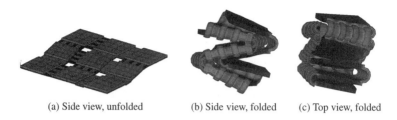

(a) Side view, unfolded   (b) Side view, folded   (c) Top view, folded

FIGURE 6. Final configuration of the Miura-fold system with nine angled rigid plates connected by hinges, as simulated in ANSYS.

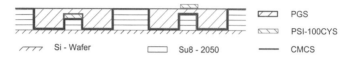

FIGURE 7. Conceptional sketch of the microfabrication process.

vertices where folding takes place in two directions. The holes minimize stretching, stress, and unwanted folding behavior at the vertices.

Figure 6 shows the Miura fold after actuation of the bilayer hinges. The constraints of the multilayer folded structure limit the final fold angle. The structures of Figure 5 achieve nearly 180° folding, whereas the Miura fold does not. The limited folding reflects the finite size of the hinges. For optimal folding, the lengths of the hinges need to be shorter for the inner layers than for the outer layers; this feature is being integrated into subsequent designs. Additionally, the plates of real polymer systems may experience adhesive contact during folding, which may affect the final folded geometry. The effects of interactions such as adhesive contact are best assessed through experimental demonstrations.

6. Experimental Scaffold Self-Folding

A polymer replication process is used to create the scaffold from a master mold. To create the master mold, a silicon wafer is first spin-coated with four layers of SU-8 epoxy (MicroChem Corp.). The SU-8 is patterned using photolithography to create a pattern of raised and lowered regions on the wafer surface; the heights of these regions will define the thicknesses of the hinges and plates, respectively. Details on microfabrication may be found in [Madou 02]. A thin release layer of carboxymethylcellulose sodium (CMCS) is coated over the surface. The CMCS is biocompatible, biodegradable, and water soluble. The polymers (first PSI in liquid, then liquid PGS prepolymer, then PSI in liquid) are applied to the master pattern and cured to form a solid. The PGS's upper surface is planar with the highest SU-8 feature, thereby creating 200 μm thick plates and 50 μm thick hinges (see Figure 7). The CMCS is then dissolved in water to release the scaffold.

When immersed in buffer solution, the hinges bend away from the PSI to accommodate the PSI's expansion. By patterning a first layer of PSI into the mold before the PGS is applied, and by patterning a second layer of PSI on top of the PGS, hinges that fold in either direction may be created. The PGS is cured prior to the addition of the final layer of PSI. Prior to its application onto the hinges, the PSI must be chemically cross-linked so that it will swell when it is exposed to buffer solution. Various chemicals may be used to chemically cross-link PSI, including cystamine dichloride (CYS) and diaminobutane (DAB). Additionally, the use of different physiological buffer solutions (e.g., phosphate

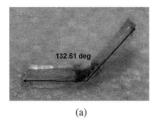
(a)

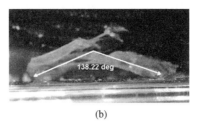
(b)

FIGURE 8. Manufactured two-rigid-plate system (a) before actuation of folding and (b) after actuation of folding.

buffer or imidazole buffer) will produce different expansion rates and times. The expansion can therefore be tailored to specific needs by adjusting the chemistry of the polymer bilayer actuator.

To demonstrate that folding is possible with a biocompatible, biodegradable tissue scaffold, a simple system comprising two rigid plates connected by one hinge was created, similar to the concept design in Figure 4. For simplicity in this first design, a single layer of PSI was applied to the full length of each hinge rather than in stripes along each hinge as shown in Figure 4. Applying the PSI expansion layer to the entire hinge area as in this example rather than to localized stripes can in principle result in distortion. The effects of the distortion are minimized in this case by the simplicity of the two-plate design and by the thickness of the plates.

For the present experiments, the synthesized PSI was cross-linked with diamino-butane, which produces a swelling of approximately 500% over 24 hours. In this first demonstration, the scaffold was first released from the mold, and PSI was applied to the hinge with a syringe. As the PSI solidifies from a liquid into a gel, it undergoes a volume shrinkage, causing the hinge to bend opposite from the desired actuation direction. The initial bending angle is therefore $-47°$. After the bilayer hinge structure is immersed in imidazole buffer for 12 hours, the bending direction reverses to a final angle of $42°$ as shown in Figure 8. The bending angle of the polymer bilayer actuator is therefore measured at $89°$. In the present case, the fold angle is limited by adhesion between the PGS and PSI layers; after $89°$, the PSI begins to delaminate from the PGS, limiting its ability to drive further folding. The $89°$ folding shown here is not a universal property of the system. For example, improved adhesion between the PGS and PSI layers, thinner hinges, and greater degrees of PSI expansion may all increase the fold angle, whereas thicker hinges or lesser PSI expansion may decrease the fold angle.

7. Conclusions

A new approach to engineering complex human tissues through a combination of directed cell assembly and origami folding of a two-dimensional scaffold is described. Two new fold patterns are presented as candidates to replicate the geometry of the target tissue (liver) in a 1DOF design that permits folding of the tissue scaffold with minimal contact and minimal potential for contamination. Modeling of the basic polymer system is presented, including results that validate a design in which actuation is driven by stripes of a bilayer actuator that runs perpendicular to the crease direction. Finally, an experimental demonstration of bilayer actuation in the proposed biodegradable, biocompatible system is presented, demonstrating that the present approach can be suitable for passive self-folding of an origami scaffold.

Acknowledgments

This research was supported by the National Science Foundation and the Air Force Office of Scientific Research through the EFRI-ODISSEI program (grant 1332249).

References

[Agarwal and Livermore 11] Gunjan Agarwal and Carol Livermore. "Chip-Based Size-Selective Sorting of Biological Cells Using High Frequency Acoustic Excitation." *Lab on a Chip* 11:13 (2011), 2204–2211.

[Atala et al. 06] Anthony Atala, Stuart B. Bauer, Shay Soker, James J. Yoo, and Alan B. Retik. "Tissue-Engineered Autologous Bladders for Patients Needing Cystoplasty." *The Lancet* 367:9518 (2006), 1241–1246.

[Azam et al. 11] Anum Azam, Kate E. Laflin, Mustapha Jamal, Rohan Fernandes, and David H. Gracias. "Self-Folding Micropatterned Polymeric Containers." *Biomedical Microdevices* 13:1 (2011), 51–58.

[Carson and Worthington 52] F. T. Carson and Vernon Worthington. "Stiffness of Paper." *Journal of Research of the National Bureau of Standards* 49:6 (1952), 385–392.

[Chen et al. 13] Qizhi Chen, Shuling Liang, and George A. Thouas. "Elastomeric Biomaterials for Tissue Engineering." *Progress in Polymer Science* 38:3 (2013), 584–671.

[Freshney 05] R. Ian Freshney. "Culture of Animal Cells." New York: Wiley-Liss, 2005.

[Ho et al. 13] Chen-Ta Ho, Ruei-Zeng Lin, Rong-Jhe Chen, Chung-Kuang Chin, Song-En Gong, Hwan-You Chang, Hwei-Ling Peng, Long Hsu, et al. "Liver-Cell Patterning Lab Chip: Mimicking the Morphology of Liver Lobule Tissue." *Lab on a Chip* 13:18 (2013), 3578–3587.

[Jakab et al. 10] Karoly Jakab, Cyrille Norotte, Francoise Marga, Keith Murphy, Gordana Vunjak-Novakovic, and Gabor Forgacs. "Tissue Engineering by Self-Assembly and Bio-printing of Living Cells." *Biofabrication* 2:2 (2010), 022001.

[Jamal et al. 13] Mustapha Jamal, Sachin S. Kadam, Rui Xiao, Faraz Jivan, Tzia-Ming Onn, Rohan Fernandes, Thao D. Nguyen, et al. "Bio-Origami Hydrogel Scaffolds Composed of Photocrosslinked PEG Bilayers." *Advanced Healthcare Materials* 2:8 (2013), 1142–1150.

[Kuribayashi-Shigetomi and Takeuchi 11] Kaori Kuribayashi-Shigetomi and Shoji Takeuchi. "Foldable Parylene Origami Sheets Covered with Cells: Toward Applications in Bio-implantable Devices." In *Origami^5: Fifth International Meeting of Origami Science, Mathematics, and Education*, edited by Patsy Wang-Iverson, Robert J. Lang, and Mark Yim, pp. 385–392. Boca Raton, FL: A K Peters/CRC Press, 2011. MR2866909 (2012h:00044)

[Kuribayashi-Shigetomi et al. 12] Kaori Kuribayashi-Shigetomi, Hiroaki Onoe, and Shoji Takeuchi. "Cell Origami: Self-Folding of Three-Dimensional Cell-Laden Microstructures Driven by Cell Traction Force." *PloS one* 7:12 (2012), e51085.

[Madou 02] Marc J. Madou. *Fundamentals of Microfabrication: The Science of Miniaturization.* Boca Raton, FL: CRC Press, 2002.

[Miura 94] Koryo Miura. "Map Fold a la Miura Style, Its Physical Characteristics and Application to the Space Science." In *Research of Pattern Formation*, edited by R. Takaki, pp. 77–90. Tokyo: KTK Scientific Publishers, 1994.

[Wang et al. 03] Yadong Wang, Yu Mi Kim, and Robert Langer. "In Vivo Degradation Characteristics of Poly (glycerol sebacate)." *Journal of Biomedical Materials Research, Part A* 66:1 (2003), 192–197.

[Wood et al. 07] Fiona M. Wood, Marie L. Stoner, Bess V. Fowler, and Mark W. Fear. "The Use of a Non-cultured Autologous Cell Suspension and Integra Dermal Regeneration Template to Repair Full-Thickness Skin Wounds in a Porcine Model: A One-Step Process." *Burns* 33:6 (2007), 693–700.

[Zakharchenko et al. 11] Svetlana Zakharchenko, Evgeni Sperling, and Leonid Ionov. "Fully Biodegradable Self-Rolled Polymer Tubes: A Candidate for Tissue Engineering Scaffolds." *Biomacromolecules* 12:6 (2011), 2211–2215.

TECHNISCHE UNIVERSITÄT, DRESDEN, GERMANY
E-mail address: philipp.jan.mehner@me.com

NORTHEASTERN UNIVERSITY, BOSTON, MASSACHUSETTS
E-mail address: t.liu@neu.edu

NORTHEASTERN UNIVERSITY, BOSTON, MASSACHUSETTS
E-mail address: a.karimi@neu.edu

TUFTS UNIVERSITY, BOSTON, MASSACHUSETTS
E-mail address: ali.brodeur@verizon.net

CARNEGIE MELLON UNIVERITY, PITTSBURGH, PENNSYLVANIA
E-mail address: juancamilopani@gmail.com

NORTHEASTERN UNIVERSITY, BOSTON, MASSACHUSETTS

MIDDLESEX COMMUNITY COLLEGE, LOWELL, MASSACHUSETTS
E-mail address: richardp@middlesex.mass.edu

NORTHEASTERN UNIVERSITY, BOSTON, MASSACHUSETTS
E-mail address: anemtserova@gmail.com

NORTHEASTERN UNIVERSITY, BOSTON, MASSACHUSETTS
E-mail address: liu.san@husky.neu.edu, sa.liu@neu.edu

SAN JOSE STATE UNIVERSITY, SAN JOSE, CALIFORNIA
E-mail address: roger.alperin@sjsu.edu

MASSACHUSETTS INSTITUTE OF TECHNOLOGY, CAMBRIDGE, MASSACHUSETTS
E-mail address: sbhatia@mit.edu

MASSACHUSETTS INSTITUTE OF TECHNOLOGY, CAMBRIDGE, MASSACHUSETTS
E-mail address: culpepper@mit.edu

LANG ORIGAMI, ALAMO, CALIFORNIA
E-mail address: robert@langorigami.com

NORTHEASTERN UNIVERSITY, BOSTON, MASSACHUSETTS
E-mail address: livermore@neu.edu

Cosmological Origami: Properties of Cosmic-Web Components When a Non-stretchy Dark-Matter Sheet Folds

Mark C. Neyrinck

1. Introduction

The formation of structure in the Universe proceeds somewhat like the origami-folding of a sheet. This concept is a Lagrangian fluid-dynamics framework (following the mass elements, not staying in a fixed spatial coordinate system). This approach in cosmology started with the Zel'dovich approximation [Zel'dovich 70]. Catastrophe theory has given some further understanding into the types of singularities that can occur when this sheet begins to fold [Arnold et al. 82, Hidding et al. 14]. Recently, many have realized the power of Lagrangian dynamics in general, and of explicitly following the dynamics of the sheet in a cosmological simulation, instead of considering the particles within it to be just fuzzy, isotropic blobs of matter [Shandarin et al. 12, Abel et al. 12, Falck et al. 12]. Figure 1 shows an example cosmic web [Bond et al. 96] folded from a collisionless dark-matter sheet that has distorted and moved around according to the Zel'dovich approximation.

2. An Origami Approximation to Structure Formation

Flat-foldable origami with paper is conveniently expressed as a continuous, piecewise isometry defined on a finite region, say $[0, 1]^2 \rightarrow \mathbb{R}^2$, encodable as a set of reflections (creases). Cosmological origami has similarities: It can be thought of as a mapping from a three-dimensional (dark-matter) sheet, which can cross itself without resistance in three dimensions (because dark matter is thought to be collisionless) but cannot cross itself in six-dimensional position-velocity phase space. The dark-matter sheet, and the universe in which it folds, are (as far as we can tell) infinite. To avoid dealing with an actual infinite space, often a finite domain with periodic boundary conditions (toroidal topology) is considered in cosmology, for example, in N-body gravitational simulations. To investigate how nodes interact with each other as they fold into a network, it might be interesting to look at origami in a region with periodic boundaries. But, for this introductory exploration, we concentrate on properties of isolated structures in an infinite space.

Here are some definitions: The analogy of a crease pattern in cosmology is called *Lagrangian space*, abbreviated $\mathcal{L}$. The *Lagrangian position*, $\mathbf{q} \in \mathcal{L}$, of a particle specifies its initial position on the "crease pattern." The usual position space is called *Eulerian*

The author is grateful for support from a New Frontiers in Astronomy and Cosmology grant from the John Templeton Foundation and from a grant in Data-Intensive Science from the Gordon and Betty Moore and Alfred P. Sloan Foundations.

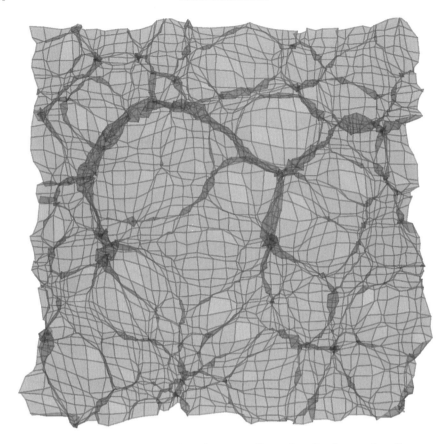

Figure 1. A dark-matter sheet in a two-dimensional universe that distorts and folds through an approximation to gravity, called the Zel'dovich approximation. The darkness of the color at each position gives the number of streams there. Initially, all vertices were nearly on a regular lattice. Then, gravity distorted the mesh, causing regions with a bit more matter than average to accumulate more matter around them. The patch shown is more than 10^8 light-years on a side; nodes correspond to galaxies or clusters of galaxies.

space, $\mathcal{E}$. After gravity folds $\mathcal{L}$ up into structures, the actual position of a particle at time t is called its *Eulerian position*, $\mathbf{x}(\mathbf{q}, t) \in \mathcal{E}$. All coordinates here are *comoving*, meaning that the homogeneous, isotropic expansion of the universe is scaled out; one can think of this as zooming out at the same time as the expansion happens. Initially, in $\mathcal{L}$, particles are arranged almost uniformly. They have vanishing velocity as $t \to 0$, so initially, in position-velocity phase space (3D position, plus 3D velocity), they were arranged on a flat sheet—flat (everywhere zero) as viewed in the velocity dimensions.

The *displacement field* $\boldsymbol{\Psi}$ gives the vector between the folded-up and initial positions of a particle, $\boldsymbol{\Psi}(\mathbf{q}, t) \equiv \mathbf{x}(\mathbf{q}, t) - \mathbf{q}$, and the *velocity* is just the time derivative of the Eulerian position, $\mathbf{v} = \partial \mathbf{x} / \partial t$. A *stream* is a region of $\mathcal{L}$ delimited by caustics, or folds [Neyrinck 12]. In an origami crease pattern, this would correspond to a polygon surrounded by creases.

A *void* is a single-stream region, i.e., a region in which the mapping from initial to final position, $\mathbf{x}(\mathbf{q})$, is one to one [Shandarin 11, Falck et al. 12].

The origami approximation imposes the following assumptions on the functions $\mathbf{\Psi}(\mathbf{q})$ or $\mathbf{x}(\mathbf{q})$. *Reality* means "the current cosmological structure-formation paradigm," which fits many observations quite well.

(1) $\psi(\mathbf{q}, t) \equiv |\mathbf{\Psi}(\mathbf{q}, t)|$ is bounded over all $\mathbf{q} \in \mathbb{R}^3$. This property holds in reality; the distribution of components Ψ_i over all particles is a roughly Gaussian distribution of dispersion $\sim 5 \times 10^7$ light-years—small compared to the radius of the observable universe, $\sim 5 \times 10^{10}$ light-years.

(2) $\mathbf{\Psi}$ is irrotational in a void. This holds in reality, since any initial vorticity decays with the expansion of the Universe, and since gravity is a potential force. However, in *multistream* regions (where $\mathbf{x}(\mathbf{q})$ is many-to-one), the flow, averaged among streams, often carries vorticity.

(3) The dark-matter sheet does not stretch, for a close analogy to paper origami. That is, $\mathbf{x}(\mathbf{q})$ is continuous and piecewise-isometric, i.e., $\nabla_{\text{Lagrangian}} \cdot \mathbf{\Psi} = 0$, except at creases, where it is undefined. This is the only assumption that is manifestly broken in reality, but we explore the consequences that it helps to establish, which we hope will apply more generally.

Collapsed structures in one dimension (1D) are simple. In 1D, a *node* is a connected region of $\mathcal{N} \in \mathcal{L}$, such that $\mathbf{x}(\mathcal{N})$ is multistream, but points immediately outside $\mathcal{N}$ map to voids. Figure 2 shows a schematic, but realistic, node in a 1D universe. For simplicity, hereafter we will restrict our attention to nodes without substructure. In 1D, nodes are simple pairs of crease points in $\mathcal{L}$, as shown at $t = 2$. We disregard added creases (e.g., present at $t = 3$) that leave the extent of the node after folding unchanged.

2.1. Two dimensions: Filaments and polygonal-collapse nodes. A 2D universe is useful to investigate; it is a step to 3D, and it also has some relevance in a 3D universe, where galaxies often form within the effective 2D universe of a "wall" (defined below). Under our assumptions, the structure foldable with the fewest creases in 2D is a *filament*, i.e., a pleat or pair of parallel crease lines. A one-crease structure is disallowed because any reflection of half the space would give an unbounded ψ. Why must a filament consist of parallel creases? Any crease must be a straight line in a piecewise-isometry [Demaine and O'Rourke 08]. And, the creases must be parallel, by both assumptions (1) and (2): (1) would be violated if nonparallel creases diverged arbitrarily far at infinity, giving an unbounded ψ. More importantly, (2) restricts even finite filaments to consist of parallel creases. This is because the two reflections produced by nonparallel creases would cause neighboring voids to be rotated with respect to each other.

Now consider a 2D node, a finite connected region that is *collapsing* (becoming multistream after folding). Note that circular (spherical) collapse is impossible with isometry, because creases must be straight lines, implying that a collapsing patch must be polygonal. Circular (spherical) collapse can be seen as a limiting case, with isotropy around the node, and in which the sheet stretches substantially. Polygonal (polyhedral) collapse can be seen as another limiting case, with anisotropy, but no stretching.

By Kawasaki's theorem [Kawasaki 91b] (the alternating sums of vertex angles in a flat-foldable 2D crease pattern add to $180°$), any vertex in a 2D crease pattern must join an even number (≥ 4) of creases. Thus, the node cannot form in complete isolation; other structures, e.g., filaments, must form together with it. Here, we confine attention to simple

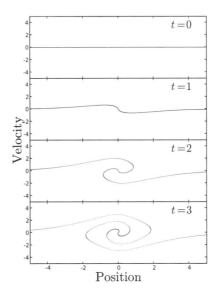

FIGURE 2. A schematic phase-space spiral that occurs in a 1D collapse of the dark-matter "string" (sheet in > 1D), on which vertices are represented as dots. Caustics, or creases, occur where the string goes vertical. Note that, here, the dark-matter string stretches, i.e., the particles vary in their distances. But, the same pattern of creases can be produced without stretching.

nodes in 2D with four vertices. Note that Kawasaki's theorem applies to a nonflat manifold, as well, if angles are measured arbitrarily close to a vertex [Robertson 78].

Angles at which filaments come off of the node's edges must equal each other (e.g., [Kawasaki 97]). Why? By Kawasaki's theorem, the angle opposite θ at a vertex in Figure 3 is $180° - \theta$. This angle is also opposite an angle in the next (going counterclockwise) vertex in a pair of parallel lines, so this angle must also equal θ. Continuing around the polygon, all angles labeled θ must be equal.

We have not yet discussed mountain or valley folds, or sheet-crossing (self-intersection). This is because these differ from the case of usual paper origami, in which folding occurs in 3D. Here, folding is in 4D symplectic phase space, where it is not clear that mountain-valley fold assignment is necessary, and the extra dimension makes sheet-crossing in 4D much more rare. To address possible sheet-crossing, and also to keep a close relation to physical flows, it is useful to adopt a kinematic flat-origami model, in which creases change continuously with time from an initial creaseless state. In polygonal collapse, if the shape of the polygon is held fixed, two parameters may be tuned: θ, as in Figure 3, and the scale (e.g., longest diameter) of the polygon. Either or both of these may be continuously changed from zero to yield a kinematic model. Alternatively, the shape of the polygon can be changed. We have determined velocity fields from many simple models changing either θ or the scale. In each case, streams overlapping in position have had different velocities, satisfying the no-sheet-crossing condition in 6D phase space. Examples are given in [Neyrinck 14]. The question of when the sheet-crossing condition might be violated in a kinematic model is an obvious question to answer more rigorously, though.

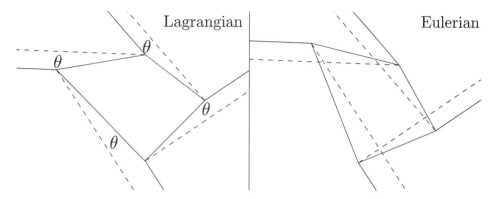

FIGURE 3. A node produced from a clockwise-twisting quadrilateral, before (left) and after (right) folding. Solid and dashed lines show mountain and valley folds, respectively, for a paper model. Mountain-valley crease assignment may not be meaningful in 4D phase space.

Note that, a bit unphysically, velocity fields in such kinematic models can be discontinuous spatially at caustics in $\mathcal{L}$, and also discontinuous in time, if the caustic is moving.

Any $\theta < 90°$ rotates the central polygon by 2θ; this provides a heuristic way to understand the prevalence of both rotating galaxies and filaments radiating from them. (This can also be seen as a rotation in the other direction by the larger, obtuse angle in the filament, by an angle $2(180° - \theta) = -2\theta$ in the opposite direction.) But, in the special case of $\theta = 90°$, shown in Figure 4, the collapse is an irrotational parity inversion. So, an interesting irrotational model keeps $\theta = 90°$ and increases the collapsing polygon's scale from 0. Irrotational collapse can occur with an arbitrarily-many-sided polygon; however, it is unlikely that an arbitrarily complicated such design can be folded from paper. Already, Figure 4 seems unable (based on failed attempts) to be folded with paper in a typical twist-fold manner, in which edges of the central polygon are mountain-folded and the polygon ends up on top. But, it can be folded up if one of the triangle's edges is valley-folded. After folding, all streams in the initial crease pattern overlap at the center, giving seven streams.

Another special case of polygonal collapse is worth mentioning: the intersection of filaments, forming sequentially. If two perpendicular filaments form sequentially, the result is simply a rectangular collapse, a four-sided version of Figure 4. If they are not perpendicular, though, the central parallelogram undergoes a rotation. Intersections of more than two sequentially-forming filaments do not generally produce simple nodes with four-crease vertices. It would be interesting to investigate the properties of 2D nodes, too, that fold on top of each other.

What are the topologies and shapes of voids and multistream regions in a piecewise-isometric origami cosmic web? Since filaments must consist of straight, parallel lines, they are either infinite, or they terminate at nodes. Thus, all voids are entirely enclosed by polygons (or are infinite); they form origami tessellations [Gjerde 08]. Angles between filaments are $< 180°$, since nodes consist of convex polygons, each vertex of which sprouts a filament. Thus, voids, too, must be convex in the origami approximation.

2.2. Three dimensions: Walls, polygonal-collapse filaments, and polyhedral-collapse nodes.
Origami-folding a 3D sheet is much less studied than that of a 2D sheet. But, the two-coloring of streams (regions bounded by creases) in $\mathcal{L}$ still applies

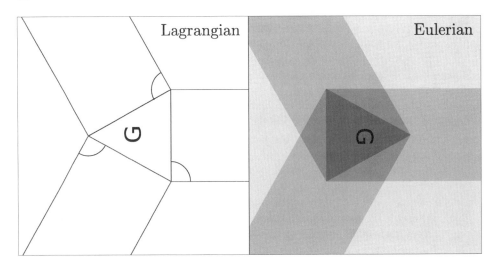

FIGURE 4. Irrotational triangular collapse. Eulerian regions exist with 1, 3, 5, and 7 (at the center) streams.

[Neyrinck 12]. In 2D, by the four-color theorem, the number of colors necessary to color arbitrary (non-origami) regions is four; in 3D, it is unbounded [Guthrie 80]. So, the two-colorability condition for streams in $\mathcal{L}$ is much more restrictive in 3D, reducing the number of colors from infinite to two, rather than from four to two.

In 3D, a *wall* is a parallel pair of creases (plane segments, in 3D). In the same way as in the 2D-universe filament, a wall's creases are constrained to be parallel by voids' mutual irrotationality. In 3D, a *filament* can be constructed by extruding a 2D polygonal node along an axis out of its plane (not necessarily perpendicular to the plane). As in 2D, to maintain mutual irrotationality between voids, the lines extruded from vertices of a 2D node that becomes a 3D filament must remain parallel. A 3D *node* lies at the intersection of filaments and consists of a convex polyhedron enclosed by creases. The 3D generalization of Kawasaki's theorem, discussed below, ensures convexity. As in 2D, 3D filaments and nodes cannot form in isolation; nodes sprout filaments and walls, and filaments sprout walls.

As in 2D sequential-filament intersections, a simple way to construct a node in 3D is by sequentially folding three intersecting walls. Three perpendicular, equal-width walls would give cubic collapse. A bit more complicated model involves a pair of nonorthogonal walls, collapsing along with a third wall, perpendicular to both. This is essentially a 2D collapse, occurring within the plane of the third wall, and would impart some rotation to the inner parallelepiped node. An intersection of three arbitrarily oriented walls would also be interesting to investigate.

However, an intersection of three walls produces a node terminating six filaments and 12 walls (double-counting pairs of collinear filaments, and quadruple-counting coplanar walls). This far exceeds the number of structures from nodes typically in a cosmological simulation; there are often as few as three filaments emerging from galaxies [Dekel et al. 09, Danovich et al. 12]. This suggests that many nodes form within previously formed walls and also motivates the following study of a minimal 3D collapse.

2.3. Tetrahedral collapse: A tetrahedral twist-fold. Imagine a point, with four rays coming from it that do not all point into the same half-space. This breaks space into four void regions, between triplets of rays. In tetrahedral collapse, the voids push together. Because the continuity of the displacement field Ψ must be preserved, a node (at the point), four filaments (along the rays), and six walls (between pairs of rays) arise as this happens.

We set up the problem by fixing the vertices of the central tetrahedral node in $\mathcal{L}$, and we constrain the properties of the filaments coming off of it. Denote the vertices of the tetrahedral node $\mathbf{g}_i$, for $i \in 1, 2, 3, 4$. Set $\mathbf{g}_1 = (0, 0, 0)$. This leaves nine degrees of freedom (DoFs), which can alternatively be assigned to one scale parameter, five parameters for the shape [Rassat and Fowler 04], and three angles that describe a three-dimensional rotation. The rotational DoFs control the relative rotation between the set of filaments and the node.

Filament 1 is an extrusion along direction $\hat{\mathbf{f}}_1$ of the triangle with vertices $\mathbf{g}_{2,3,4}$, and similarly for filaments 2–4. We set $\hat{\mathbf{f}}_1 = (0, 0, 1)$ along the z-axis, and $\hat{\mathbf{f}}_i = (\sin\theta_i \cos\phi_i, \sin\theta_i \sin\phi_i, \cos\theta_i)$ for $i = 2, 3, 4$, with $\phi_2 = 0$.

The problem reduces to finding five angles, given all $\mathbf{g}_i$. There are two meaningful sets of constraints. First, the angles at which walls come off of each filament i must equal each other; this is the triangular-collapse constraint applied in the plane perpendicular to $\hat{\mathbf{f}}_i$. Second, the creases coming from vertices must obey the 3D generalization of Kawasaki's theorem (Kawasaki-3D) [Robertson 78, Kawasaki 91a, Hull 10]: Two-color the corners of regions that meet in a vertex, such that one color represents original parity when folded and the other color represents opposite parity. The sum of solid angles of each color equals 2π steradians. In tetrahedral collapse, voids, walls, filaments, and the node have parities 1, -1, 1, and -1, respectively.

Looking down the barrel of a filament, in the plane perpendicular to each $\hat{\mathbf{f}}_i$, triangular collapse must happen, with walls coming off of vertices at equal angles. Considering Filament 1, shown in Figure 5, ϕ_4 and ϕ_3 come out easily from vectors involving $\mathbf{g}_{2\perp 1}$, $\mathbf{g}_{3\perp 1}$, and $\mathbf{g}_{4\perp 1}$, where $\mathbf{x}_{\perp 1}$ denotes the component of $\mathbf{x}$ perpendicular to $\hat{\mathbf{f}}_1$. This simplicity around Filament 1 comes from our choice of axes; ϕ_3 comes from Kawasaki's theorem used on the vertex labeled $\mathbf{g}_4$, together with the law of cosines on the triangle:

$$\cos\phi_3 = \text{coslaw}\left[(\mathbf{g}_4 - \mathbf{g}_2)_{\perp 1}, (\mathbf{g}_4 - \mathbf{g}_3)_{\perp 1}, (\mathbf{g}_3 - \mathbf{g}_2)_{\perp 1}\right],$$

where $\text{coslaw}(\mathbf{a}, \mathbf{b}, \mathbf{c}) \equiv (c^2 - \mathbf{a} \cdot \mathbf{b} - \mathbf{b} \cdot \mathbf{c})/(2ab)$. A similar equation gives ϕ_4. With these, a pair of simultaneous equations containing only θ_2 and θ_3 comes from using the law of cosines to relate $(\hat{\mathbf{f}}_{1\perp 3} \cdot \hat{\mathbf{f}}_{2\perp 3})$ and $(\hat{\mathbf{f}}_{1\perp 2} \cdot \hat{\mathbf{f}}_{3\perp 2})$ to $\mathbf{g}_i$. A similar pair of equations gives θ_2 and θ_4. We numerically solved these two pairs of equations with Mathematica, which did not find closed-form results. In all cases tried, single solutions were found, and the θ_2's found in both pairs of simultaneous equations agreed.

Irrotational regular-tetrahedral collapse is the simplest, most symmetric polyhedral collapse. Its filaments in Lagrangian space, each colored differently, are shown in Figure 6(a). Here, each $\hat{\mathbf{f}}_i$ points directly away from each $\mathbf{g}_i$. It obeys Kawasaki-3D: The solid angle subtended by a Lagrangian void region around a vertex of the tetrahedron is π steradians, since if the tetrahedron were not there, the four identical void regions would meet in a point, and the 4π steradians would be divided equally among the void regions. Each of the three filaments meeting at a vertex subtends $\pi/3$ steradians. So, the sum of solid angles subtended by odd-parity regions is 2π. As with irrotational equilateral-triangular collapse, all streams of the crease pattern overlap at the center, so voids, walls, filaments, and nodes characteristically have 1, 3, 7 (like a 2D node), and 15 streams, respectively.

Keeping the node regular-tetrahedral, but rotating it along $\hat{\mathbf{f}}_1$, produces rotations in all filaments; also, angles between filaments change from the equiangular $109.5°$. By symmetry around $\hat{\mathbf{f}}_1$, $\theta_3 = \theta_4 = \theta_2$, but we found that $\theta_2(\alpha_1) \approx \theta_2^{\text{approx}}(\alpha_1) \equiv$

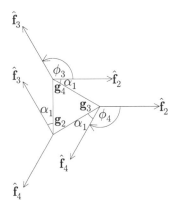

FIGURE 5. A cross section through Filament 1, with $\hat{\mathbf{f}}_1$ perpendicular to the page. All vectors should in fact have a "$\perp 1$" subscript, denoting the component of the vector perpendicular to $\hat{\mathbf{f}}_1$. Because of our choice of axes ($\hat{\mathbf{f}}_1 = \hat{z}$ and $\phi_2 = 0$), ϕ_3 and ϕ_4 come out simply, looking down the barrel of Filament 1.

$(109.5° − 90°)\sin\alpha_1 + 90°$, to within $0.5°$. Filament 1 remains equilateral in cross section, but the others elongate.

A particularly interesting rotational model retains $109.5°$ angles between filaments and equilateral filament cross sections. It involves an irregular tetrahedral node, with an equilateral face opposite (and perpendicular to) $\hat{\mathbf{f}}_1$, but with height $h = h_0 \sin\alpha_1$, where h_0 is the height if the tetrahedron were regular. A kinematic version of this model could have two parameters that vary with time: α_1, and an overall scale. The behavior is special at $\alpha_1 = \pi/6$, as shown in Figure 6(c) and (d). Here, the top filament, of side length s, rotates in one way by $\pi/3$ from its initial to final state. The bottom filaments, with cross sections of side length $s/\sqrt{3}$, rotate in the opposite way, by $2\pi/3$. The linear density ($\propto s^2$) of the top filament equals the sum of the linear densities of the three bottom filaments. Future work will further explore this model.

We also verified Kawasaki-3D numerically in several models specified with different $\mathbf{g}_i$. Kawasaki-3D takes the following form around vertex $\mathbf{g}_4$, summing solid angles subtended by all regions of odd parity (filaments and voids):

$$\Omega(\hat{\mathbf{f}}_1, \hat{\mathbf{f}}_2, \hat{\mathbf{f}}_3) + \Omega(\mathbf{g}_2 - \mathbf{g}_4, \mathbf{g}_3 - \mathbf{g}_4, \hat{\mathbf{f}}_1) + \Omega(\mathbf{g}_3 - \mathbf{g}_4, \mathbf{g}_1 - \mathbf{g}_4, \hat{\mathbf{f}}_2) + \Omega(\mathbf{g}_1 - \mathbf{g}_4, \mathbf{g}_2 - \mathbf{g}_4, \hat{\mathbf{f}}_3) = 2\pi,$$

where $\Omega(\mathbf{a}, \mathbf{b}, \mathbf{c})$ gives the solid angle subtended by a triangle with vertices along vectors $\mathbf{a}$, $\mathbf{b}$, and $\mathbf{c}$ [Van Oosterom and Strackee 83],

$$(2.1) \qquad \Omega(\mathbf{a}, \mathbf{b}, \mathbf{c}) = 2\tan^{-1}\frac{|\mathbf{a} \cdot (\mathbf{b} \times \mathbf{c})|}{abc + (\mathbf{a} \cdot \mathbf{b})c + (\mathbf{a} \cdot \mathbf{c})b + (\mathbf{b} \cdot \mathbf{c})a}.$$

A Mathematica notebook that solves for the five $\hat{\mathbf{f}}_i$ angles in terms of $\mathbf{g}_i$ is available from the author upon request.

2.4. Physical quantities. It is helpful to explicitly connect quantities in polyhedral collapse with physical quantities that one might measure, e.g., in a cosmological simulation. The *mass* of a node (or halo, or galaxy) is simply its volume V in $\mathcal{L}$ (times a constant density ρ_0). Note that other streams (for tetrahedral collapse, up to 15, the total number of streams) will overlap with the node once it is folded in $\mathcal{E}$; this could be added to the mass,

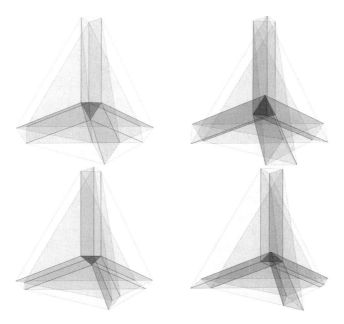

Figure 6. Tetrahedral-collapse models/tetrahedral twist folds. Filament creases are indicated by triangular tubes, intersecting at the central node. Wall creases extend from filament edges through the thin lines drawn between filaments. Left: Pre-folding/collapse (Lagrangian). Right: Post-folding/collapse (Eulerian). Top: An irrotational model ($\alpha_1 = \pi/2$). Each filament vector $\hat{\mathbf{f}}_i$ is perpendicular to a face of the central tetrahedron. Walls, filaments, and the node invert along their central planes, axes, and point, respectively, but remain connected as before. Void regions simply move inward. All 15 initial regions overlap at the center. Bottom: A rotational model ($\alpha_1 = \pi/6$). The top filament rotates counterclockwise by $\pi/3$, while the smaller, bottom filaments rotate clockwise by $2\pi/3$. See http://skysrv.pha.jhu.edu/~neyrinck/TetCollapse for an interactive 3D model.

as well. Similarly, the mass per unit length of a filament is its cross-sectional area A times ρ_0. An *angular momentum* can be defined for a node, $L = 2\alpha_{\text{node}}V$, where $2\alpha_{\text{node}}$ is the angle by which it rotates during collapse. For a filament, an angular momentum per unit length is $L/\ell = 2\alpha A$. In further work, we plan to give relations between these quantities in polyhedral-collapse models.

3. Conclusion

This origami approximation in a large-scale structure, a dark-matter sheet that does not stretch, gives an idealized cosmic web with convex voids and nodes. The no-stretch condition is generally false in reality, but it may hold closely enough in some regimes to give useful results. In this approximation, the convexity of the various shapes, as well as the inability to form a structure in isolation, gives a simple topology: Voids, as delineated by multistream regions, are convex and do not percolate through walls. Voids in "reality" (full cosmological N-body simulations) seem roughly convex only if using a density-based criterion to define them, but not by delineating them with multi-stream regions [Neyrinck et al. 13, Falck and Neyrinck 15]. (Note that density-based and multistream-based criteria exactly coincide in this origami approximation, where density can increase at an Eulerian point only by increasing the number of streams.) This is also qualitatively like a model in which voids are Voronoi cells [Icke and van de Weygaert 91].

Here we began to study the purely geometric "polyhedral collapse" model. The arrangement of filaments (one per face) around a polyhedral node determines the physical properties such as rotation of all of the pieces in the final conditions. This model could substantially aid the understanding of how filaments and galaxies rotate (or do not) based on their spatial arrangement, a field of much study [Aragón-Calvo et al. 07, Codis et al. 12, Aragon-Calvo and Yang 14, Dubois et al. 14]. There is even observational evidence for a correlation between galaxy spins and their arrangement in filaments and walls [Tempel and Libeskind 13]. This would give an "intrinsic alignment" between the observed ellipticities of nearby galaxies [Codis et al. 15], a systematic effect that must be overcome for weak lensing measurements to realize their full potential as a key test of cosmological questions, such as why the Universe seems to be accelerating in its expansion.

Many of the results given here, particularly in 3D, were numerical. This is fine for comparison to cosmological simulations, as we plan to do. But, there is much room for further rigorous mathematical study of polyhedral collapse, both of isolated nodes and of how networks of collapsed polyhedra behave together. For a more astronomical discussion of the origami approximation, including some explicit velocity fields, see [Neyrinck 14].

References

[Abel et al. 12] T. Abel, O. Hahn, and R. Kaehler. "Tracing the Dark Matter Sheet in Phase Space." *Mon. Not. Roy. Astr. Soc.* 427 (2012), 61–76.

[Aragon-Calvo and Yang 14] M. A. Aragon-Calvo and L. F. Yang. "The Hierarchical Nature of the Spin Alignment of Dark Matter Haloes in Filaments." *Mon. Not. Roy. Astr. Soc.* 440 (2014), L46–L50.

[Aragón-Calvo et al. 07] M. A. Aragón-Calvo, R. van de Weygaert, B. J. T. Jones, and J. M. van der Hulst. "Spin Alignment of Dark Matter Halos in Filaments and Walls." *Astrophys. J. Lett.* 655 (2007), L5–L8.

[Arnold et al. 82] V. I. Arnold, S. F. Shandarin, and I. B. Zeldovich. "The Large Scale Structure of the Universe: I—General Properties of One- and Two-Dimensional Models." *Geophysical and Astrophysical Fluid Dynamics* 20 (1982), 111–130.

[Bond et al. 96] J. R. Bond, L. Kofman, and D. Pogosyan. "How Filaments of Galaxies Are Woven into the Cosmic Web." *Nature* 380 (1996), 603–606.

[Codis et al. 12] S. Codis, C. Pichon, J. Devriendt, A. Slyz, D. Pogosyan, Y. Dubois, and T. Sousbie. "Connecting the Cosmic Web to the Spin of Dark Haloes: Implications for Galaxy Formation." *Mon. Not. Roy. Astr. Soc.* 427 (2012), 3320–3336.

[Codis et al. 15] S. Codis, R. Gavazzi, Y. Dubois, C. Pichon, K. Benabed, V. Desjacques, D. Pogosyan, J. Devriendt, and A. Slyz. "Intrinsic Alignment of Simulated Galaxies in the Cosmic Web: Implications for Weak Lensing Surveys." *Mon. Not. Roy. Astr. Soc.* 448 (2015), 3391–3404.

[Danovich et al. 12] M. Danovich, A. Dekel, O. Hahn, and R. Teyssier. "Coplanar Streams, Pancakes and Angular-Momentum Exchange in High-Z Disc Galaxies." *Mon. Not. Roy. Astr. Soc.* 422 (2012), 1732–1749.

[Dekel et al. 09] A. Dekel, Y. Birnboim, G. Engel, J. Freundlich, T. Goerdt, M. Mumcuoglu, E. Neistein, C. Pichon, R. Teyssier, and E. Zinger. "Cold Streams in Early Massive Hot Haloes as the Main Mode of Galaxy Formation." *Nature* 457 (2009), 451–454.

[Demaine and O'Rourke 08] E. D. Demaine and J. O'Rourke. *Geometric Folding Algorithms: Linkages, Origami, Polyhedra.* Cambridge, UK: Cambridge University Press, 2008. MR2354878 (2008g:52001)

[Dubois et al. 14] Y. Dubois, C. Pichon, C. Welker, D. Le Borgne, J. Devriendt, C. Laigle, S. Codis, D. Pogosyan, S. Arnouts, K. Benabed, E. Bertin, J. Blaizot, F. Bouchet, J.-F. Cardoso, S. Colombi, V. de Lapparent, V. Desjacques, R. Gavazzi, S. Kassin, T. Kimm, H. McCracken, B. Milliard, S. Peirani, S. Prunet, S. Rouberol, J. Silk, A. Slyz, T. Sousbie, R. Teyssier, L. Tresse, M. Treyer, D. Vibert, and M. Volonteri. "Dancing in the Dark: Galactic Properties Trace Spin Swings along the Cosmic Web." *Mon. Not. Roy. Astr. Soc.* 444 (2014), 1453–1468.

[Falck and Neyrinck 15] B. Falck and M. C. Neyrinck. "The Persistent Percolation of Single-Stream Voids." *Mon. Not. Roy. Astr. Soc.* 450 (2015), 3239.

[Falck et al. 12] B. L. Falck, M. C. Neyrinck, and A. S. Szalay. "ORIGAMI: Delineating Halos Using Phase-Space Folds." *Astrophys. J.* 754 (2012), 126.

[Gjerde 08] E. Gjerde. *Origami Tessellations: Awe-Inspiring Geometric Designs.* Wellesley, MA: A K Peters, 2008. MR2474884 (2009m:52001)

[Guthrie 80] F. Guthrie. "Note on the Colouring of Maps." *Proc. Roy. Soc. Edinburgh* 10 (1880), 727.

[Hidding et al. 14] J. Hidding, S. F. Shandarin, and R. van de Weygaert. "The Zel'dovich Approximation: Key to Understanding Cosmic Web Complexity." *Mon. Not. Roy. Astr. Soc.* 437 (2014), 3442–3472.

[Hull 10] Tom Hull. "Maekawa and Kawasaki's Theorems Revisited and Extended." http://courses.csail.mit.edu/6.849/fall10/lectures/L20.html, 2010.

[Icke and van de Weygaert 91] V. Icke and R. van de Weygaert. "The Galaxy Distribution as a Voronoi Foam." *Quart. J. Roy. Astr. Soc.* 32 (1991), 85–112.

[Kawasaki 91a] Toshikazu Kawasaki. "On High Dimensional Flat Origamis." In *Proceedings of the First International Meeting of Origami Science and Technology*, edited by H. Huzita, pp. 131–141. Padova, Italy: Dipartimento di Fisica dell'Università di Padova, 1991.

[Kawasaki 91b] Toshikazu Kawasaki. "On the Relation between Mountain-Creases and Valley-Creases of a Flat Origami." In *Proceedings of the First International Meeting of Origami Science and Technology*, edited by H. Huzita, pp. 229–237. Padova, Italy: Dipartimento di Fisica dell'Università di Padova, 1991.

[Kawasaki 97] Toshikazu Kawasaki. "$R(\gamma) = 1$." In *Origami Science and Art: Proceedings of the Second International Meeting of Origami Science and Scientific Origami*, edited by K. Miura, pp. 31–40. Shiga, Japan: Seian University of Art and Design, 1997.

[Neyrinck et al. 13] M. C. Neyrinck, B. L. Falck, and A. S. Szalay. "ORIGAMI: Delineating Cosmic Structures with Phase-Space Folds." ArXiv:1309.4787, 2013. (To appear in the Proceedings of the 13th Marcel Grossmann Meeting.)

[Neyrinck 12] M. C. Neyrinck. "Origami Constraints on the Initial-Conditions Arrangement of Dark-Matter Caustics and Streams." *Mon. Not. Roy. Astr. Soc.* 427 (2012), 494–501.

[Neyrinck 14] M. C. Neyrinck. "An Origami Approximation to the Cosmic Web." ArXiv:1412.6114, 2014.

[Rassat and Fowler 04] André Rassat and Patrick W. Fowler. "Is There a "Most Chiral Tetrahedron"?" *Chemistry: A European Journal* 10:24 (2004), 6575–6580.

[Robertson 78] S. A. Robertson. "Isometric Folding of Riemannian Manifolds." *Proceedings of the Royal Society of Edinburgh: Section A Mathematics* 79 (1978), 275–284. MR0487893 (58:7486)

[Shandarin et al. 12] S. Shandarin, S. Habib, and K. Heitmann. "Cosmic Web, Multistream Flows, and Tessellations." *Phys. Rev. D* 85:8 (2012), 083005.

[Shandarin 11] S. F. Shandarin. "The Multi-stream Flows and the Dynamics of the Cosmic Web." *J. of Cosmol. & Astropart. Phys.* 5 (2011), 015.

[Tempel and Libeskind 13] E. Tempel and N. I. Libeskind. "Galaxy Spin Alignment in Filaments and Sheets: Observational Evidence." *Astrophys. J. Lett.* 775 (2013), L42.

[Van Oosterom and Strackee 83] A Van Oosterom and J. Strackee. "The Solid Angle of a Plane Triangle." *IEEE Transactions on Biomedical Engineering* BME-30:2 (1983), 125–126.

[Zel'dovich 70] Y. B. Zel'dovich. "Gravitational Instability: An Approximate Theory for Large Density Perturbations." *Astronomy & Astrophysics* 5 (1970), 84–89.

DEPARTMENT OF PHYSICS AND ASTRONOMY, THE JOHNS HOPKINS UNIVERSITY, BALTIMORE, MARYLAND
E-mail address: neyrinck@pha.jhu.edu

VI. Origami in Art, Design, and History

Modeling Vaults in Origami: A Bridge between Mathematics and Architecture

Caterina Cumino, Emma Frigerio, Simona Gallina, Maria Luisa Spreafico, and Ursula Zich

1. Introduction

The starting point of our study is the double task of combining research and teaching in an experience that leads to the creation of reproducible models with the purpose to educate the perception of shapes and volumes: In fact, having a model in hand allows a tangible comparison between the idea of spatial visualization and its realization.

In real-world architecture, vaulted surfaces are intrinsically complex, as they are a synthesis of form, structure, and materials, and not all of them are suitable for realizing the structure in accordance with their geometric and formal properties. Ruled developable surfaces appear naturally in this context, for instance, in roofing systems: barrel vaults and their intersections such as groin vaults, cloister vaults, and barrel vaults with lunettes or with cloister heads.

Developable surfaces occur frequently both in traditional architecture and in architectural design, and they are classically well studied in mathematics (see e.g. [do Carmo 76].

Modeling with origami produces dynamic models, from a single sheet of paper to the realization of a three-dimensional shape, and the process, which respects the material, is reversible. When modeling curved surfaces with origami, we can hope to achieve a formal exactness in accordance with their geometric shapes only in the case of developable surfaces, whereas, for surfaces that cannot be unfolded flat, paper management imposes an approximation. This fact motivates the wide use of tessellations: polygonal facets connected by more or less flexible hinges allow us to visualize a smooth surface [Tachi 13, Casale and Calvano 12, Romor and Valenti 12].

Notice that, in architecture, there are many examples of structures appearing as a result of a tessellation process, e.g., barrel vaults with exposed brick: The faceted surface becomes smooth only with the addition of plaster that conceals the real structure.

At present, very little is known about origami models of vaults: to the best of our knowledge, paper models have been obtained only for groin vaults generated by circular barrel vaults.[1] In this work we aim to start filling this gap in the case of intersections of ruled surfaces; more precisely, of cylinders with any cross-section provided that their intersection is a piecewise planar curve with suitable hypotheses of symmetry.

The fourth author was partially supported by the "National Group for Algebraic and Geometric Structures, and Their Applications" (GNSAGA-INDAM).

[1] By P. Chapman-Bell at http://flickrock.com/oschene.

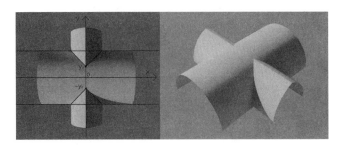

FIGURE 1. An example of the two cylinders C_1 and C_2.

The different scientific backgrounds inside our group have led us to use various methodological approaches. The mathematical formulation of our problem and its formal solution (Section 2) allow us to obtain both CAD modeling (Section 3) and crease patterns of different vaults somehow related to the same cylinder cross-section (Section 4); finally, the folded origami model gives a three-dimensional shape to our equations, with immediate educational and communicative applications.

Creating a shape from a simple sheet of paper allows us to grasp essential aspects as a synthesis of complexities: For example, the origami model of a vault formed by the intersection of two cylinders shows that the intersection is the structural element that constrains the shape of the roofing system and also that its paper model is subject to possible different execution methods (e.g., how to manage excess paper in a foldable way), depending on the different design intents.

As a consequence, we have developed our origami research project with the double purpose of a theoretical mathematical foundation as the essential support and with an interest in possible applications (Section 5).

2. A Mathematical Description

Let $C_1 \subseteq \mathbb{R}^3$ be the cylinder of equation $z = f(y)$; we can think of it as being obtained by translating the curve $\sigma_1 : z = f(y)$, $x = 0$, along the x-axis. Assume that the function $f : [-a, a] \to \mathbb{R}$ is continuous and satisfies the following properties:

$$f(y) \geq 0, \ \forall y \in [-a, a] \ \text{and} \ f(-a) = f(a) = 0;$$
$$f(-y) = f(y), \ \forall y \in [-a, a];$$
$$f \in C^2((-a, 0) \cup (0, a));$$
$$f'(y) \leq 0, \forall y \in (0, a), \ \text{and is monotonic.}$$

The assumption that $f'(y)$ is monotonic means that either $f''(y) \leq 0$ or $f''(y) \geq 0$, $\forall y \in (-a, 0) \cup (0, a)$; we call the first case *western type* (WT) and the second one *eastern type* (ET). Note that C_1 is symmetric with respect to the plane $y = 0$.

The parametric equations of C_1 are $C_1(u, v) = (u, v, f(v))$.

Consider now an analogous cylinder C_2 orthogonal to C_1, symmetric with respect to the plane $x = 0$, and require that the intersection curve $\gamma := C_1 \cap C_2$ is piecewise planar, i.e., it lies in the union of the four planes $y = \pm mx \pm y_0$, where $y_0 \in [0, a), m \in \mathbb{R}^+$, as in Figure 1.

Under the previous hypotheses, a straightforward calculation yields the following:

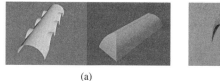 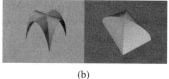

(a) (b)

FIGURE 2. (a) Barrel vault with lunettes and with cloister heads ($y_0 \neq 0$).
(b) Groin vault and cloister vault ($y_0 = 0$).

PROPOSITION 2.1. *The cylinder C_2 has Cartesian and parametric equations, respectively,*

$$z = f(m|x| + y_0) \quad and \quad C_2(u, v) = (u, v, f(m|u| + y_0)), |u| \leq \frac{a - y_0}{m}.$$

Figure 2 shows that, depending on the portions of cylinders we retain, C_1 and C_2 define two different architectural structures: a barrel vault with lunettes and a barrel vault with cloister heads, of which groin and cloister vaults are particular cases.

In order to create crease patterns for these vaults, we unroll the cylinders C_1 and C_2 on the planes $z = f(0)$ and $z = f(y_0)$, respectively, and we project their developments onto the plane $z = 0$.

From now on, we limit our description to points P in the first octant. For this choice, the unrolled cylinders lie in the first quadrant of the xy-plane, and the entire picture can be reconstructed by symmetry.

Recalling the arc-length formulas for the curves $\sigma_1 : z = f(y)$, $x = 0$, and $\sigma_2 : z = f(m|x| + y_0)$, $y = 0$, we get that the curve γ viewed as a curve on C_1 develops into the curve

$$(2.1) \qquad \gamma_1(v) = \left(\frac{v - y_0}{m}, \int_0^v \sqrt{1 + f'^2(t)} dt, 0 \right), \quad \text{with} \quad y_0 \leq v \leq a,$$

and viewed on C_2 develops into

$$(2.2) \qquad \gamma_2(u) = \left(\int_0^u \sqrt{1 + m^2 f'^2(mt + y_0)} dt, mu + y_0, 0 \right), \quad \text{with} \quad 0 \leq u \leq \frac{a - y_0}{m}.$$

From the previous description, we can deduce some properties of γ_1 that can help us to draw the crease patterns.

PROPOSITION 2.2. *The curve γ_1 has the following properties:*

(i) Its tangent line in $x = 0$ has slope $\alpha = m \sqrt{1 + f'^2(y_0)}$.
(ii) It is concave up if $f''(v) \leq 0$ (WT) and concave down if $f''(v) \geq 0$ (ET).
(iii) It has curvature

$$\kappa_{2D}(\gamma_1(v)) = \frac{|f'(v)f''(v)|}{m \sqrt{1 + f'^2(v)} (\sqrt{1 + \frac{1}{m^2} + f'^2(v)})^3}.$$

PROOF. From Equation (2.1) we easily deduce the intrinsic equation

$$y = \int_0^{mx+y_0} \sqrt{1 + f'^2(t)} dt, \quad 0 \leq x \leq \frac{a - y_0}{m},$$

of γ_1 in the xy-plane. Claim (i) follows by deriving the intrinsic equation one time. By deriving it twice, we get

$$y'' = \frac{m^2 f'(mx + y_0) f''(mx + y_0)}{\sqrt{1 + f'^2(mx + y_0)}}.$$

Now, $y'' \geq 0$ if and only if $f''(mx + y_0) \leq 0$, and claim (ii) follows.

To prove (iii), we use the parametric representation, because it is useful to express the curvature as a function of v. We get

$$\gamma_1'(v) = \left(\frac{1}{m}, \sqrt{1 + f'^2(v)} \right),$$

$$\gamma_1''(v) = \left(0, \frac{f'(v) f''(v)}{\sqrt{1 + f'^2(v)}} \right).$$

The claim follows by the curvature formula:

$$\kappa_{2D}(\eta(t)) = \frac{|\eta'(t) \times \eta''(t)|}{|\eta'(t)|^3},$$

for all regular curves $\eta(t)$ in $\mathbb{R}^3$. $\square$

Our aim is to produce crease patterns that allow us to fold barrel vaults (with lunettes or with cloister head). But, we would like to obtain the model, first of all, by folding along a straight line and then using easy curved folding and bending.

THEOREM 2.3. *Using the previous notation, in the plane $z = 0$ the curve γ_1 is symmetric to the curve γ_2, up to translation, if and only if one of the following holds:*

(1) $f(v) = \alpha x + q$;

(2) $m = \pm 1$.

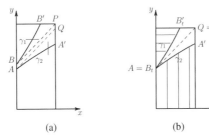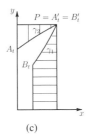

(a)   (b)   (c)

FIGURE 3. The creation of two different patterns from the same equations: (b) barrel vault with cloister heads and (c) barrel vault with lunettes.

Before proving the theorem, we sketch in Figure 3(a) the final situation relative to the first quadrant of the unrolled cylinders and their intersection curves γ_1 and γ_2 and show how to obtain the patterns. See Section 4 for the final crease pattern.

The movements take into account the cylinders' portions that we want to preserve. In both cases, the white paper inside the rectangle must disappear. Index t indicates that a point is translated.

(1) *Barrel vault with cloister heads:* (Figure 3(b)) Move γ_1 into $\gamma_1 - \overrightarrow{AB}$.

(2) *Barrel vault with lunettes:* (Figure 3(c)) Move γ_1 into $\gamma_1 + \overrightarrow{B'P}$ and γ_2 into $\gamma_2 + \overrightarrow{A'P}$.

PROOF. A computation for γ_2 analogous to Theorem 2.2(iii) yields

$$\kappa_{2D}(\gamma_2)(u) = \frac{|m^4 f'(mu + y_0) f''(mu + y_0)|}{\sqrt{1 + m^2 f'^2(mu + y_0)} \, (\sqrt{1 + m^2 + m^2 f'^2(mu + y_0)})^3}.$$

As the curves γ_1 and γ_2 are symmetric up to translation with respect to a line, they have the same curvature at corresponding points. In our case, $v = mu + y_0$, hence equating $\kappa_{2D}(\gamma_1)$ to $\kappa_{2D}(\gamma_2)$ implies

$$\frac{|f'(v) f''(v)|}{m \sqrt{1 + f'^2(v)} \, (\sqrt{\frac{1}{m^2} + 1 + f'^2(v)})^3} = \frac{m^4 |f'(v) f''(v)|}{\sqrt{1 + m^2 f'^2(v)} \, (\sqrt{1 + m^2 + m^2 f'^2(v)})^3}.$$

Recalling that $f'(v) \neq 0$ by hypothesis, we obtain

$$\frac{|f''(v)|}{m \sqrt{1 + f'^2(v)}} = \frac{m |f''(v)|}{\sqrt{1 + m^2 f'^2(v)}}.$$

If $f''(v) = 0 \, \forall v$, which happens if and only if $f(v) = \alpha x + q$, equality holds. Otherwise, we can simplify, obtaining

$$m^2 f'^2(v)(m^2 - 1) = 1 - m^4.$$

So, equality holds only if $m = 1$ (because we are interested in the first octant). Conversely, in case (1), the curves γ_1 and γ_2 are segments of the same length, so they are obviously symmetric up to translation. In case (2), the cylinder C_2 is obtained from C_1 by a rotation of $\pi/2$, so the curves γ_1 and γ_2 are symmetric up to translation. □

REMARK 2.4. In [Fuchs and Tabachnikov 99], the authors give a necessary condition about curvatures under which a planar curve φ can be folded in spatial curve ϕ: $\kappa_{2D}(\varphi) = \kappa_{3D}(\phi) \cos \alpha$, where α is half of the folding angle of the crease at each point. This means that $\kappa_{2D}(\varphi)/\kappa_{3D}(\phi) \leq 1$. With an easy calculation, we can show that in our case the above condition is fulfilled.

REMARK 2.5. Starting from a curve γ_2 in the plane $z = 0$, by the preceding method one may reconstruct the cylinder C_2 and so the portion of C_1 that intersects C_2. Here, we state only the result. Let $y = g(x)$ be the equation of a curve γ_2 in the first quadrant, with $x \in [0, d]$, and with $g(0) = y_0$; then,

$$f(y) = -\int_{y_0}^{y} \sqrt{g'^2(t) - 1} \, dt + \int_{y_0}^{d} \sqrt{g'^2(t) - 1} \, dt, \quad y_0 \leq y \leq d.$$

One can extend $f(y)$ arbitrary for $y \in [0, y_0]$, thus obtaining $\widetilde{f}(y) \in [-d, d]$ by symmetry. Note that γ_1 intersects the y-axis at the point $(0, \int_0^{y_0} \sqrt{1 + \widetilde{f}(t)} \, dt)$.

3. Virtual Modeling

The most commonly used software packages in architecture, such as AutoCAD, can easily provide two- and three-dimensional modeling of the vaults that result from intersections of cylinders obtained by extrusion of a defined curved path. However, the process of modeling is more complex for a cylindrical surface that is derived from curves such as catenaries or parabolas, for which AutoCAD does not provide the plot. In this case it is necessary to use applications that provide the virtual graph of any curve or surface, assuming that it can be expressed by a parametric equation.

FIGURE 4. Cloister vault: 3D model (left) and its unrolled pattern (right)

In order to represent in digital format the formal geometry of the vaults of interest, we therefore needed to define them mathematically. A first mathematical description, in Cartesian form, has led to experimentation with the Surfer software[2] that allowed a first assessment of the method's effectiveness. Subsequently, we conducted tests with AutoCAD installing the free applications 2DPlot[3] and 3DPlot.[4]

As anticipated, these applications enable AutoCAD users to graph mathematical functions that are not normally included in the classic menu of the software and to input their parametric equations transcribed in AutoLISP.

Once we obtained the curves, and therefore the cylinders, we conducted some tests on the optimum accuracy of parametric curves and surfaces to get the right compromise between accuracy of the curve and calculation speed of a regular computer. It was found that 200 iterations return a curve that is sufficiently precise and at the same time computable at a speed appropriate to the needs of the project.

To enable the rollout, it was required to produce a virtual model; two different modeling methods were tested. The first, aimed at modeling a vault with solids and boolean operations, did not lead to satisfactory results, and the second, more efficient and subsequently used, required the drawing of the given curve and its 3D processing with AutoCAD's surface modeler.

We intended to unroll the model with Pepakura Designer, hence it was necessary to get the virtualization of the vaults in a .obj file format (the model is a mesh generated using a parametric curve in AutoCAD).

This way, we produced the model in two different virtual formats, namely .obj and .ply. The latter is required to upload the model into the virtual viewer of MeshLab, which is a very useful application in education because it allows manual exploration of vaulted structures on tablets and smartphones. The model, imported into Pepakura Designer, had been easily and successfully unrolled, and the digital image thus obtained was saved into parametric .dxf format.[5] This graph, imported into AutoCAD, was used to draw the crease patterns for the folding of the vaults. (See Figure 4.)

The method we used has the advantage of producing comparable different representations of the same object and of leading to the production of a tool for the study, the analysis, and the production of crease patterns for the vaulted structures that are economical and easy in modeling, visualizing, and folding.

---

[2]http://imaginary.org/program/surfer

[3]http://www.cadstudio.cz/en/apps/2dplot/

[4]http://www.cadstudio.cz/en/apps/3dplot/

[5]The production of crease patterns in a .dxf format allows the import in numerical control machines that may allow the printing on different laminated materials and formats.

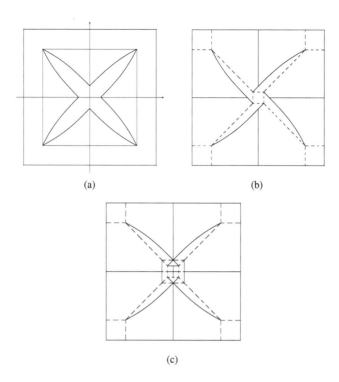

(a)   (b)

(c)

FIGURE 5. A WT groin vault: (a) pattern, (b) square twist crease pattern, and (c) double-squashed crease pattern.

4. Crease Patterns

The previous sections provide a unified method for obtaining the pattern of a vault satisfying our hypotheses. In all cases, the excess paper E is symmetric with respect to the x- and y-axes; however, the way we treat it, and more generally where to place the creases, depends on which kind of vault we want to fold. In this section, we will give some examples of the problems involved and their solutions; specifically, we will show how to obtain creases patterns for some vaults, both WT and ET, constructed from catenary cylinders.

Let us begin with a WT groin vault. Then, E has a four-petal flower shape having four axes of symmetry (Figure 5(a)); indeed, the corresponding three-dimensional real object has four planes of symmetry. To fold the model from the pattern, one has to identify the four base points of the petals with the center of the square; this is easily done by drawing the Voronoi diagram that has these five points as generating points. The result is a square, which may be twisted (Figure 5(b)) or double-squashed (Figure 5(c)) to manage excess paper E.

The two crease patterns proposed (Figure 5(b) and (c)) are less symmetric: The former has only rotational symmetries, and the latter has only two axes of symmetry. Although the models folded from them look the same from the outside, they are different on the inside, having only rotational symmetries and two planes of symmetry, respectively (Figure 6).

Both patterns work well if E is not too large compared to the square containing the pattern. If not, the amount of excess paper disturbs the vault perception and other easy

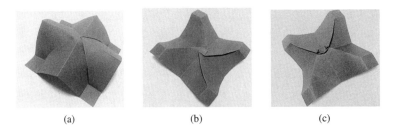

(a)   (b)   (c)

FIGURE 6. (a) Views of both models from the outside. Views from the
inside of folded crease patterns in (b) Figure 5(b) and (c) Figure 5(c).

folds must be added in order to reduce bulky protrusions. This is easier to achieve for the
crease pattern in Figure 5(c), while the one in Figure 5(b) is obviously more suitable for
generalization to groin vaults having nth order rotational symmetry for $n \neq 4$.

Observe that Figure 5 and Figure 6 illustrate the case in which the cylinders present
a ridge on their tops; with the same notation as in Section 2, this happens precisely when
$f'(0)$ is not defined (the right and left derivatives are nonzero). On the contrary, if $f'(0) = 0$,
the cylinders are smooth: in this case, the crease patterns are similar to the previous ones,
the only difference being that they do not have the long horizontal and vertical creases
parallel to the sides of the paper.

Now we turn to a WT barrel vault with lunettes. It is not difficult to show that, under
our hypotheses, the pattern can be easily obtained from that of the corresponding groin
vault: starting from a pattern similar to Figure 5(a), we delete two mutually orthogonal
rectangles and glue the four remaining parts to a suitable rectangle, as shown in Figure 7(b).

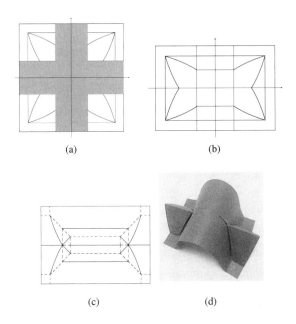

FIGURE 7. A WT barrel vault with lunettes: (a) deletion from original
pattern, (b) new pattern, (c) its crease pattern, and (d) a model.

Because, in this case, E has two lines of symmetry, we adapt the groin vault crease pattern with two lines of symmetry to this more general case: The example shown in Figure 7(c) and (d) refers to a case where C_1 is not ridged. As previously noted, only the smaller cylinder C_2 is completely determined in the folded model, while the mid-section of the crease pattern gives rise to a smaller rectangle that is simply bent, which can be done in infinitely many ways.

The corresponding ET groin vault and barrel vault with lunettes can be obtained in a similar way. The main difference is that, in their patterns, the petals of E are concave, instead of being convex. The ET groin vault is shown in Figure 8.

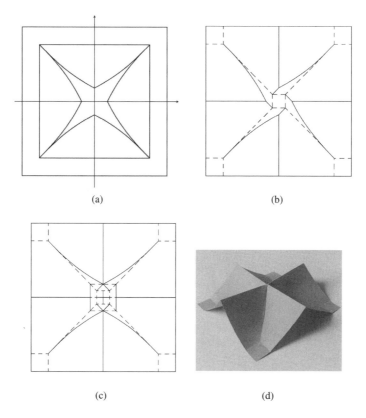

(a)   (b)

(c)   (d)

FIGURE 8. An ET groin vault: (a) pattern, (b) square twist crease pattern, (c) double-squashed crease pattern, and (d) a model.

Also, because of the shape of the cylinders' cross-section, it is necessary to add a few folds at the petals' junction in order to tuck in the excess paper.

We now illustrate ET cloister vaults and ET barrel vaults with cloister heads; their western counterparts are treated similarly.

Figure 9 shows the pattern, two different crease patterns, and a model of the cloister vault. In (b) some extra paper has been added along each petal's axis of symmetry, the result being a sort of (twisted) square capstone in the center of the folded model; this may be convenient particularly for WT cloister vaults whenever the curved lines in the pattern are very close to the diagonals of the square around its center.

The pattern, the crease pattern, and a model of an ET barrel vault with cloister heads are shown in Figure 10.

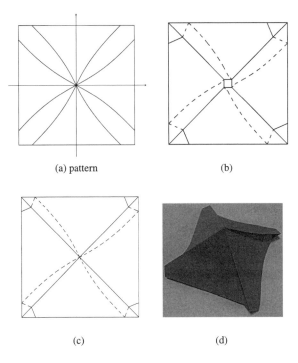

(a) pattern

(b)

(c)

(d)

FIGURE 9. An ET cloister vault: (a) pattern, (b) first crease pattern, (c) second crease pattern, and (d) a model of the crease pattern in (c).

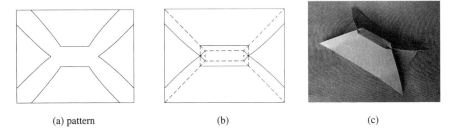

(a) pattern

(b)

(c)

FIGURE 10. An ET barrel vault with cloister heads: (a) pattern, (b) crease pattern, and (c) a model.

It must be noticed that, in all our models, the position of the excess paper depends not only on the type of vault we want to fold but also, to some extent, on the effect we want to achieve with the modeling.

REMARK 4.1. Let $f : [0, a] \to \mathbb{R}$ be the given half cross-section curve; recall (see Section 2) that we have assumed that $f'(y)$ is monotonic. To obtain vaults with a more elaborate shape, one could ask what happens if, in the considered interval $[0, a]$, a change of concavity occurs. In this case, even though drawing a pattern is an easy consequence of our investigations, managing excess paper is difficult when folding.

Consider, for example, a cloister vault such that its cross-section curve has inflection points: as we have shown, extra paper forms flaps lying outside the model, and, due to the change of concavity, these flaps tend not to adhere to the model. Origami models similar to this vault are known and present the same difficulties; different solutions have been proposed by various authors, as well (see, e.g., [Mitani 09b]).

5. Conclusions and Outlook

We showed how to design and realize, with mathematical rigor, origami models of vaults, relying on the knowledge of their equations. This way, scale models of significant architectural examples can be produced using the origami technique.[6] In the future we intend to explore other types of vaults and investigate mathematically how to fold extra paper.

When a rigorous mathematical description is lacking, we are forced to use a completely different process in order to obtain our model. In this case, starting from a real object, we need a metric survey, then we analyze the obtained data, and we select the significant elements to determine a theoretical model [Bertolini-Cestari et al. 13, Pancani 11]. Finally, we translate it into origami; it must be noted that, although we can achieve a high approximation quality, the model produced with this method is well away (as to accuracy) from a model that follows from equations.

The areas of possible applications of our work are various: educational purposes in architectural drawing courses, preliminary studies before beginning preservation work, creation of vaulted-roofed temporary architecture, and design for cultural merchandising.

References

[Bertolini-Cestari et al. 13] C. Bertolini-Cestari, F. Chiabrando, S. Invernizzi, T. Marzi, and A. Spanò. "Terrestrial Laser Scanning and Settled Techniques: A Support to Detect Pathologies and Safety Conditions of Timber Structures." *Advanced Materials Research* 778 (2013), 350–357.

[Casale and Calvano 12] Andrea Casale and Michele Calvano. "Castelli di carta: La piega per la costruzione di superfici articolate." *Disegnarecon* 5:9 (2012), 309–316.

[do Carmo 76] M. P. do Carmo. *Differential Geometry of Curves and Surfaces.* Englewood Cliffs, NJ: Prentice-Hall, 1976. MR0394451 (52:15253)

[Fuchs and Tabachnikov 99] D. Fuchs and S. Tabachnikov. "More on Paperfolding." *The American Mathematical Monthly* 106:1 (1999), 27–35. MR1674137 (99m:53009)

[Mitani 09a] J. Mitani. "A Design Method for 3D Origami Based on Rotational Sweep." *Computer-Aided Design and Applications* 6:1 (2009), 69–79.

[Mitani 09b] J. Mitani. *Spherical Origami.* Chiyoda, Japan: Futami-Shobo, 2009. (In Japanese.)

[Pancani 11] G. Pancani. "Lo svolgimento in vera grandezza delle volte affrescate delle sale dei quartieri al piano terreno di Palazzo Pitti a Firenze." In *Il Disegno delle trasformazioni, atti delle Giornate di Studio, Napoli 1–2 dicembre 2011.* Napoli: Clean Edizioni, 2011.

[Romor and Valenti 12] J. Romor and G. M. Valenti. "Geometria responsiva." *Disegnarecon* 9:1 (2012), 289–300.

[Tachi 13] T. Tachi. "Freeform Origami Tessellations by Generalizing Resch's Patterns." *Journal of Mechanical Design* 135:11 (2013), 111006.

---

[6]We warmly thank the Consorzio La Venaria Reale for giving us permission to test our modeling in the royal residence.

DIPARTIMENTO DI SCIENZE MATEMATICHE, POLITECNICO DI TORINO, ITALY
E-mail address: caterina.cumino@polito.it

DIPARTIMENTO DI MATEMATICA, UNIVERSITA' DEGLI STUDI DI MILANO, ITALY
E-mail address: emma.frigerio@unimi.it

DIPARTIMENTO DI ARCHITETTURA E DESIGN, POLITECNICO DI TORINO, ITALY
E-mail address: simona.gallina@polito.it

DIPARTIMENTO DI SCIENZE MATEMATICHE, POLITECNICO DI TORINO, ITALY
E-mail address: maria.spreafico@polito.it

DIPARTIMENTO DI ARCHITETTURA E DESIGN, POLITECNICO DI TORINO, ITALY
E-mail address: ursula.zich@polito.it

Folding Perspectives: Joys and Uses of 3D Anamorphic Origami

Yves Klett

1. Introduction

Finished origami in the artistic and recreational sense is very visual. Unless touching is allowed, the shape together with material and lighting generates the primary impression of an origami piece. With a large variety of mono-, duo-, or multicolored and patterned paper available, this allows for very appealing results.

The use of material is integral to real-world origami modeling. Color, texture, and behavior of the material used for an origami sculpture is one of the primary means to convey information in addition to the geometry of the model. Color is often used in a global fashion by the use of colored or patterned paper, the interplay between both sides of duo paper, or the combination of separate parts or modules made from different materials. In most cases, the coloring and geometry of the model are complementary and emphasize each other (see Figure 1).

We would like to demonstrate an additional possibility of combining color and images with crease patterns to design origami that produces precisely engineered visual impressions that are strongly dependent on the point of view and perspective of the observer and that uses the three-dimensional canvas of periodic tessellations in particular to generate visually pleasing and surprising interactive origami.

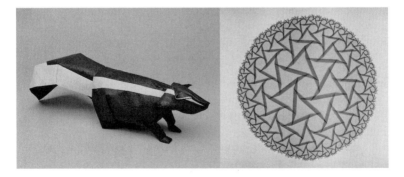

FIGURE 1. Two beautiful examples of the application of color and light. *Skunk (opus 47)* [Lang 03] (left) and 3^7 *Hyperbolic Limit (opus 600)* [Lang 11] (right). Courtesy of Robert Lang.

2. Anamorphosis and Origami

Anamorphosis describes the process of generating imagery that can only be seen properly from a certain perspective and/or with the help of a dedicated viewing device [Di Lazzaro and Murra 13, Hunt et al. 00]. Anamorphic images have a long history reaching back to the Early Renaissance and have been used extensively in architecture and art [Kenaan 02, Gagliardi 09, Kent 13]. A well-known application of anamorphosis is the CinemaScope film format, which uses special optics to realize large image aspect ratios on standard 35 mm film material. Road signs painted onto streets often are stretched to present a rectified image to drivers looking at them from low elevation angles, and so-called cam carpets are used for advertising on sport fields to present banner-like content from a specific camera vantage point [Privsek and Schnellhardt 14].

More pronounced examples of anamorphosis are images that can only be deciphered using a reflective cylinder or cone (catoptric anamorphosis) [Collection 95, Gardner 75] or street art that generates fascinating and perplexing trompe-l'œil effects [Honda 13].

In addition to these and other techniques categorized under the term *anamorphosis*, we propose to bring a new kind into the fold, using origami as a three-dimensional canvas. Since the morphological alignment of "anamorphic origami" is too good to pass up, we propose to describe this method by the portmanteau *anam-ori*.

For anam-ori as presented in this chapter, the intended visual impression is generated by partially collapsed crease patterns corresponding to tessellations of the plane and is produced by folding a precomputed printed image that precisely aligns with the faces (and crease pattern) of the piece.

Because tessellations (and rigidly foldable ones in particular) often exhibit a large number of predictably and spatially precisely oriented faces, the computation of the unfolded anamorphic image is a quite manageable process, as will be shown. Combining tessellations and specifically designed anamorphic imagery can result in drastic changes in the perceived image when the observer is moving relative to the object—an effect that is not attainable with flat-folded pieces, which are equivalent to any other flat surface in that respect.

Readily available modern printing and coating technologies remove nearly all limits on color, quality, and complexity even for homemade projects, and projects are scalable to any sensible size the folder would like to realize. Together with precreasing techniques, that facilitate precise alignment of the image and the crease pattern, producing anamorphic origami can become astonishingly easy and efficient.[1]

3. Examples of Anam-Ori with Discretely Colored Faces

One way to make effective anam-ori is the discrete, periodic coloring of individual faces of a given tessellation. An example for a bi-colored Miura-ori tessellation is shown in Figures 2 and 3 using two different perspectives. The coloring changes depending on the viewpoint of the observer.

Figure 2 uses a parallel perspective that is equivalent to a viewpoint far away from the object, with no perspective foreshortening. This results in a homogeneous color mix across the tessellation. In contrast, the perspective projection used in Figure 3 causes pronounced foreshortening, and the patterning does not appear uniform.

---

[1]On the software side, all rendered figures were created using Mathematica, building on existing origami design and simulation packages [Klett and Drechsler 07, Klett and Drechsler 08, Klett and Drechsler 11, Klett 13a, Klett 13b].

FIGURE 2. Miura-ori with coloring of diametrically opposed faces as seen from far away: top view (left), and a 360° orbit with 45° inclination (right). The patterning appears uniform across the field, and the floor tiles show no foreshortening.

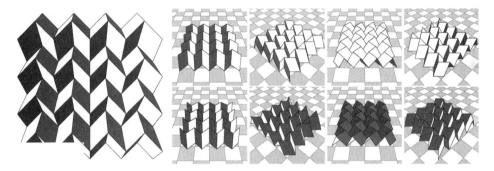

FIGURE 3. The piece from Figure 2 as seen from closer up: top view (left), and a 360° orbit with 45° inclination (right). The impression of the patterning is not uniform across the field, and the floor tiles show pronounced foreshortening.

FIGURE 4. Orbit of a real-world anam-ori with alternatingly colored rows. The images were taken with a focal length of 44 mm (35 mm equivalent) at 45° inclination.

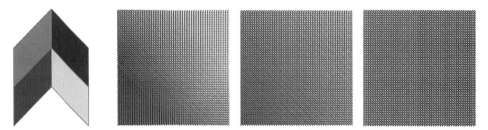

FIGURE 5. Four-colored unit cell (left) and a panel made up by 50×50 of these cells as seen from differing distances (from near to far). The effect of perspective on the perceived uniformity of the coloring in analogy to Figures 2 and 3 is clearly visible.

FIGURE 6. A 360° orbit of the periodically four-colored panel from Figure 5 with 45° inclination. The perspective implies an observer fairly close to the structure.

Figure 4 shows a set of photographs of a real-world bi-color anam-ori featuring alternatingly colored rows. The chosen focal length results in a perspective similar to the one used in Figure 3.

With a growing number of faces within the visual field (or with diminishing visual angle of any given face), the impression moves from clearly discernible separate faces to a more homogeneous, color-dominated view. Figure 5 shows the top view of a large four-colored Miura grid. The changing hue on the top view is caused by perspective effects; with growing viewing distance, the coloring becomes more uniform. Moving close to the same structure and orbiting at 45° inclination results in the changing—and quite dazzling—impressions in Figure 6.

A structure with rotational symmetry is shown in Figure 7 with viewpoint-dependent inner and outer coloring. During a 180° rotation of the viewpoint, the inside and the outside seem to reverse their coloring.

FIGURE 7. Prismatic tube analogue to the plane structure in Figure 3: Developed pattern (top), and changing inner and outer color impressions during a 180° rotation (middle and bottom).

4. Examples of Anam-Ori Using Textured Faces

The basic principle of textured anam-ori is illustrated in Figure 8 for a Miura-ori geometry. A checkerboard pattern is placed under the tessellation and is projected vertically onto the individual faces by parallel rays. Seen from far away and looking into the projection direction, the undistorted square checkerboard pattern is visible, but both a change of perspective and the unfolding show that a vertically perceived square is in fact a parallelogram in the paper plane. In consequence, the flat pattern consists of a number of periodically arrayed parallelograms, as shown in the bottom-right corner of Figure 8.

While the discrete coloring of individual faces does not depend on a preprinted template and can easily be carried out after folding, the application of more-complex images (like, for example, photographs) across different folded faces may not be straightforward at all. To realize more-complex anam-ori, a suitably distorted image needs to be applied in the flat state and the actual creases must be aligned precisely to generate the rectified image for a given three-dimensional (3D) state of the model. In the following we will demonstrate one way to use basic linear algebra to compute the necessary distortions.

For a parallel projection approach as shown in Figure 8, the transformation between the projected 3D image and the corresponding developed pattern can, in general, be described piecewise using a two-dimensional affine transformation for each face that maps the rectified image as seen in three dimensions into its distorted developed counterpart.

Figure 9 shows a unit cell of the tessellation from Figure 8 and overlays the developed pattern with a vertical projection of the 3D faces. Using the nomenclature from Figure 9,

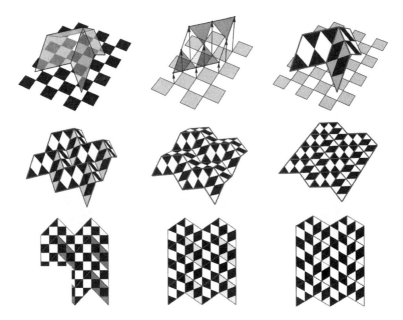

FIGURE 8. Vertical parallel projection of a checkerboard pattern onto a Miura grid. In the top row, from left to right: Miura-ori unit cell on checkerboard pattern, projection of the pattern on one face by parallel rays, and textured unit cell. In the middle row, perspective views of the unfolding sequence of a 2×2 unit cell grid. In the bottom row, top views of the unfolding sequence.

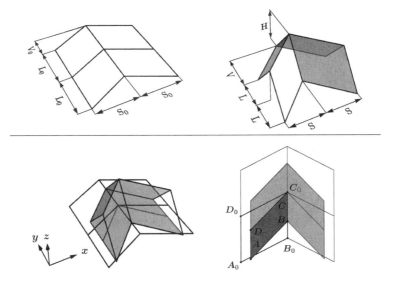

FIGURE 9. Dimensions of the developed Miura unit cell (top left), and dimensions of the 3D cell (top right). Overlay of the developed and 3D cells (bottom left), and vertical projection of the overlay into the xy-plane with two sets of points (bottom right): A to D for the lower-left projected 3D face, and A_0 to D_0 for the corresponding developed face.

the transformation necessary to compute the anamorphic image maps the projected 3D parallelogram $ABCD$ onto the developed parallelogram $A_0 B_0 C_0 D_0$.

Putting the origin at $C = C_0$, the plane coordinates for A to D and A_0 to D_0 can be described by

$$A = \{-S, -L - V\}, \qquad A_0 = \{-S_0, -L_0 - V_0\},$$
$$B = \{0, -L\}, \qquad B_0 = \{0, -L_0\},$$
$$C = \{0, 0\}, \qquad C_0 = \{0, 0\},$$
$$D = \{-S, -V\}, \qquad D_0 = \{-S_0, -V_0\}.$$

The choice of origin has the additional benefit of reducing the generally affine solution to a simpler linear one. Using the relations between the 3D parameters L, S, V, and H and their developed counterparts L_0, S_0, and V_0 [Klett and Drechsler 11] results in

$$A_0 = \left\{ -\sqrt{\frac{H^2 V^2}{H^2 + L^2} + S^2}, \ -\frac{LV}{\sqrt{H^2 + L^2}} - \sqrt{H^2 + L^2} \right\},$$
$$B_0 = \left\{ 0, \ -\sqrt{H^2 + L^2} \right\},$$
$$C_0 = \{0, 0\},$$
$$D_0 = \left\{ -\sqrt{\frac{H^2 V^2}{H^2 + L^2} + S^2}, \ -\frac{LV}{\sqrt{H^2 + L^2}} \right\}.$$

An affine transformation that maps $\vec{x}$ onto $\vec{x_0}$ can be described by a linear transformation of $\vec{x}$ by a 2×2 matrix M plus a translation by $\vec{b}$:

$$(4.1) \qquad \vec{x_0} = M \vec{x} + \vec{b} = \begin{bmatrix} m_{11} & m_{12} \\ m_{21} & m_{22} \end{bmatrix} \begin{bmatrix} x \\ y \end{bmatrix} + \vec{b}.$$

If we apply Equation (4.1) to any three of the four 2D/3D coordinate tuples, the translation represented by $\vec{b}$ cancels out because $C = C_0 = \{0, 0\}$. The result can be solved in general for the four components of M and in particular for the unit cell parameters of the structure from Figure 8 with $L = S = V = H = 1$:

$$(4.2) \qquad M = \begin{bmatrix} m_{11} & m_{12} \\ m_{21} & m_{22} \end{bmatrix} = \begin{bmatrix} \dfrac{\sqrt{\frac{H^2 V^2}{H^2 + L^2} + S^2}}{S} & 0 \\ -\dfrac{H^2 V}{LS \sqrt{H^2 + L^2}} & \dfrac{\sqrt{H^2 + L^2}}{L} \end{bmatrix} = \begin{bmatrix} \sqrt{\dfrac{3}{2}} & 0 \\ -\dfrac{1}{\sqrt{2}} & \sqrt{2} \end{bmatrix}.$$

Using this result for M, any coordinate of a projected image on the lower-left surface of the unit cell from Figure 9 can now be transformed directly into its developed shape. The transformations for the remaining three faces of the unit cell can be derived likewise. For a tessellation consisting of multiple of these unit cells, the linear transformations for each of these cells only need to be augmented with a translation (resulting in the general affine case) that depends on the 2D cell dimensions determined by even multiples of S_0 and L_0. In other words, the developed image is stitched together from one periodically applied set of transformations.

Going from the coarse checkerboard pattern to a bitmap image of arbitrary resolution works with the very same algorithm, only with a larger number of elements to be distorted. Figuratively, every square pixel of the image is distorted in analogy to the bigger squares in Figure 8. As an example for this process, Figure 10 shows the affine transformation

FIGURE 10. Application of the affine transformation defined in Equation (4.2) to a coarse checkerboard pattern (left) and a bitmap image (right).

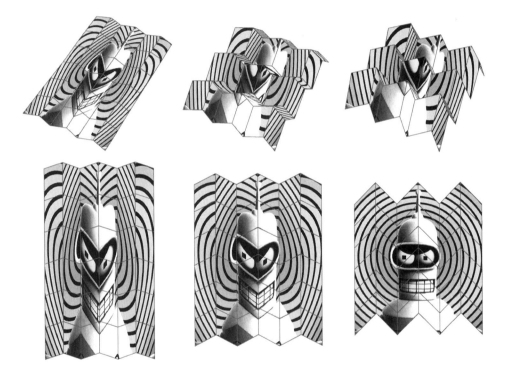

FIGURE 11. Folding of one of our favorite robots on a Miura grid: perspective view (top), and top view as intended for the undistorted final image (bottom). See also [Klett 13b].

of a checkerboard pattern and a bitmap. Finally, Figure 11 shows the application of the projection method by mapping a more complex bitmap onto a larger tessellation.

The presented, necessarily static imagery can only convey a very limited impression of the actual, dynamic nature of anam-ori interaction. For the interested reader, we provide an interactive Mathematica demonstration [Klett 15] that is based on the principles presented here (see Figure 12). In addition, we vehemently advocate real-world experimenting, which naturally offers the richest anamorphic experience, for example by using a few of the provided developed anam-ori patterns as folding templates.

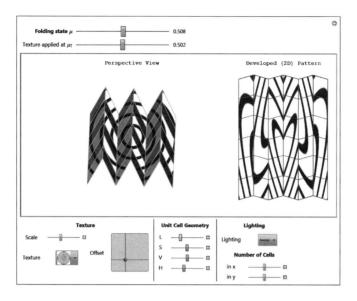

FIGURE 12. Screenshot of the interactive demonstration available at [Klett 15]. The user can apply different textures to variable Miura-ori and manipulate and fold/unfold the resulting structure in real time.

5. Parallel versus Perspective Projection

The simplest case for textured anam-ori is a parallel projection of an image onto the structure. As shown in Section 4, for this case the computation of the developed image is a fairly straightforward process.

The drawback is that parallel projection assumes a viewpoint infinitely far away from the object. Most observers will not be that far away, though, so the parallel projection will result in distorted images for observers within finite eyeshot. Fortunately, parallel projection still retains its usefulness for reasonable definitions of "far away" as demonstrated in Figure 13: While for viewpoint V_1 (very close to the piece) large distortions occur, this effect quickly and nonlinearly diminishes for greater distances—already from viewpoint V_4 the remaining distortions are difficult to spot.

For any application that assumes observers are relatively close to the object, parallel projection is of limited use, and the influence of perspective and foreshortening must be taken into account. The principle to generate perspective anam-ori stays the same: an image is projected onto faces of a tessellation, but using perspective projection instead [Carlbom and Paciorek 78]. This does result in non-affine distortions for the squares in the developed pattern. The computations necessary to project the perspective patterns are considerably more complex than for the parallel case.

Figure 14 shows an example of perspective anam-ori for the tessellation from Figure 13 with an adapted checkerboard pattern, again from differing distances. This time, the undistorted pattern is only observed from the design viewpoint V_2. Moving farther away results in significant distortion. The developed pattern and the folding process are shown in Figure 15.

Anamorphic designs with a strong perspective component, as in Figure 14, can also be used to lure an observer into the sweet spot (here, V_2) where there is a global, three-dimensionally defined distortion minimum. For anam-ori generated by parallel projection

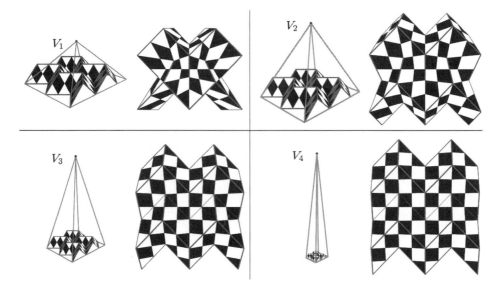

FIGURE 13. Anam-ori from Figure 8 generated by parallel projection, seen from different viewpoints V_1 to V_4: for each viewpoint, its position in relation to the tessellation (left) and the view as seen from that point (right).

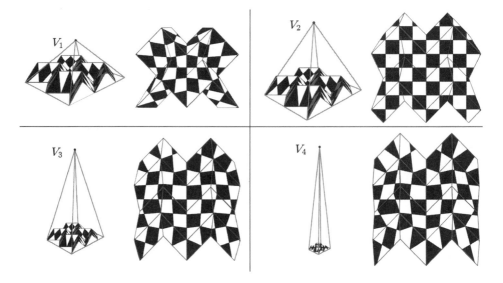

FIGURE 14. Anam-ori generated by perspective projection using the tessellation and viewpoints from Figure 13. The rectified checkerboard can only be seen from position V_2.

and an observer sufficiently far from the object, only an angular difference between the viewing vector and the projection direction produces a noticeable change in distortion, while there is no distinct sweet spot concerning translation (and distance) relative to the object. In consequence, the choice of parallel or more or less pronounced perspective

FIGURE 15. The folding process for the object from Figure 14: perspective view (top), and top view using viewpoint V_2 from Figure 14 (bottom).

projection will greatly influence the character and accessibility of a piece of anam-ori, especially if more than one observer is involved. Stronger perspective will result in a closer, more intimate experience, while a parallel projection will be accessible to multiple, more distant observers.

6. Anam-Ori Variations

The possibilities for using the described techniques to combine geometry, color, images, perspective, and lighting are endless. This section will highlight a few interesting aspects of anam-ori, and the corresponding images have been rendered to demonstrate or emphasize certain aspects of a given idea.

In contrast to the computed images, real-world anam-ori will not only be influenced by the choice of pattern, viewpoint, and perspective but also by the folded material, lighting conditions, and manufacturing precision. Perfect precision, however, is not called for most of the time because the observer does not care about or unconsciously corrects for slight imperfections and immediately recognizes the underlying pattern. The sensitivity to deviations from the rectified image will also vary with the image type: Distortions are more easily spotted in highly regular geometric patterns like the checkerboard than in more-complex images or photographs.

All presented structures are foldable, and flat patterns can be extracted from the lower-left corners of Figures 16–21, which have been generated using parallel projection. Even though the use of complex bitmaps like the one in Figure 11 would result in more spectacular and entertaining results, the generic monochrome checkerboard pattern has been used for Figures 16–19 to give a good impression of the resulting distortion in the developed patterns.

To add some variety to the tessellation zoo, Figure 16 uses a curved eggbox tessellation. For the case of curved origami, the projection method used for planar surfaces can be used as well, as long as the curved surfaces are approximated by a sufficient number of

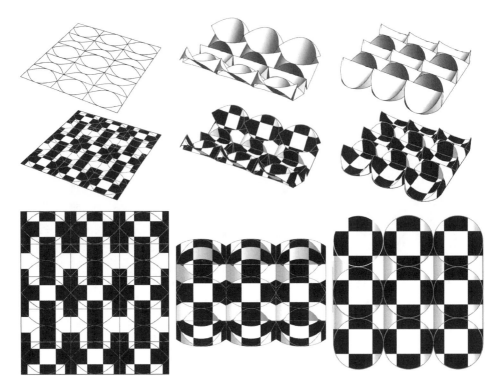

FIGURE 16. Checkerboard anam-ori on a curved eggbox tessellation: perspective views of three folding states (top), the same with applied texture (middle), and top views of the folding states (bottom).

smaller plane polygons. Influenced by the chosen pattern and position, the black squares develop into fairly rectangular cross shapes.

A combination of the same tessellation with a rotation of the checkerboard texture by 45° in Figure 17 produces a much more complex flat pattern, which also shows more influence of the curvature of the underlying structure.

Another tessellation made up of joined truncated circular cone sections of differing heights is exposed to the familiar checkerboard in Figure 18. Unsurprisingly, the resulting flat pattern shows a high degree of rotational symmetry and somehow reminds one of a hyperbolic tiling. Even though the geometry of the tessellation is ultimately very simple, the shape of the resulting developed checkerboard does not seem to be very intuitive.

Taking the conical topic one step further is Figure 19: the projection direction for the checkerboard pattern is inclined to the horizontal plane and the main axis of the ellipse that defines the footprint of the conical surfaces. This causes a complete loss of symmetry in the developed pattern and in the visual impression when moving around the piece.

In Figure 20, a run-of-the-mill waterbomb rascally tries to camouflage as a Miura-ori—and manages to do so only from the top view. The prominent black faces of the developed pattern are only seen in small part and enhance the virtual crease impression, while the darker and lighter shades emulate basic lighting conditions.

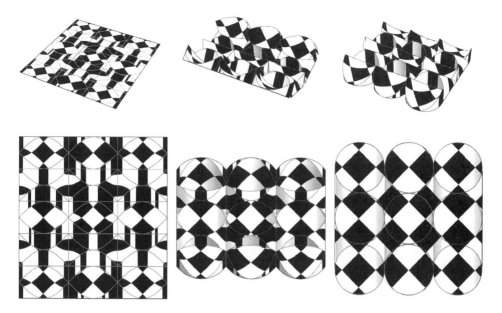

FIGURE 17. The tessellation from Figure 16 with texture rotated by 45°. The developed anamorphic image shows more curvature-related distortion and has certain Rorschach-esque qualities.

FIGURE 18. Checkerboard pattern on circular cones.

7. Possible Applications

One of the main applications (and the original motivation to delve into the idea) of anam-ori is the generation of visually pleasing structures with a strong interactive aspect. On a deeper level, anam-ori can be used to add another layer of information or artistic intent to origami. Given a piece of anam-ori, the recipient will try to find the correct folding

FIGURE 19. Obliquely projected checkerboard pattern on elliptic cones: flat pattern (left), and folding process and views from an orbit with 60° inclination (right).

FIGURE 20. Origamimicry: Waterbomb camouflaged as Miura-ori. The textured crease pattern also enhances the virtual black creases and emulates basic lighting effects.

FIGURE 21. Two different images projected obliquely from opposite directions onto alternating face rows of a tessellation. The flat pattern (left) looks tousled, but it straightens out just fine when folded and—depending on the viewpoint—reveals either a bull's-eye pattern or a mystery message (right).

state and point of view to arrive at the implied rectified image, and thus the viewer is much more consciously engaged than by static or flat images [Collins 92a, Collins 92b]. Consequently, advertising and packaging may well profit from anam-ori applications. Drastically changing colors or images work as (peripheral) eye-catchers and actively invite potential customers to interact with a display or package, resulting in a memorable and enjoyable encounter.

For the very same reasons, anam-ori can also be used as a playful means of conveying a broad range of mathematical concepts in education—concepts that can be verified quickly and without need for expensive material or infrastructure in an entertaining, hands-on fashion that is quite unique to origami [Golan and Jackson 09, Winckler and Wolf 11]. The range of addressable topics is broad and can be tailored to cater to all education levels.

Carefully designed anam-ori show potential for use in interior design and architecture—e.g., as three-dimensional, interactive wallpaper or as a subtle means of crowd control. Possible technical applications might concern, e.g., optics, spatial alignment, or the adding of functional and informational layers to folded structures in general. Some of these aspects can be found in Figure 21 (first trials to decode anam-ori 2D barcodes [ISO 14] with standard smartphones have been encouraging). Just as important, developing new methods and algorithms to generate anam-ori is a rewarding task with strong ties to mathematics, geometry, and computer science.

8. Conclusions

We have illustrated the principle of the combination of anamorphosis and origami. The resulting anam-ori use tessellations as the canvas to project images whose perceptions strongly depend on the spatial relationship between object and observer. A number of examples demonstrate different methods to apply this principle, using elements of color, lighting, perspective, and origami geometry.

The presented topic has proven to be a lot of fun, but it also shows potential for application in many different fields. We hope that the shown examples may serve as a starting point for further exploration, and we look forward to encountering more anam-ori in the future.

References

[Carlbom and Paciorek 78] Ingrid Carlbom and Joseph Paciorek. "Planar Geometric Projections and Viewing Transformations." *ACM Computing Surveys* 10:4 (1978), 465–502.

[Collection 95] Collection. *Secrets des anamorphoses*, Collection Secrets 12. Paris: Gallimard Jeunesse, 1995.

[Collins 92a] Dan Collins. "Anamorphosis and the Eccentric Observer: Inverted Perspective and Construction of the Gaze." *Leonardo Journal* 25:1 (1992), 73–82.

[Collins 92b] Dan Collins. "Anamorphosis and the Eccentric Observer: History, Technique and Current Practice." *Leonardo Journal* 25:2 (1992), 179–187.

[Di Lazzaro and Murra 13] Paolo Di Lazzaro and Daniele Murra. "Figurative Art, Perception and Hidden Images in Inverse Perspective." *Energia, Ambiente e Innovazione* 1–2 (2013), 42–51.

[Gagliardi 09] Raffaele Gagliardi. "Perception as the Raw Material of the Plan: Felice Varini's Works." *Colore* 62 (2009), 61–67.

[Gardner 75] Martin Gardner. "The Curious Magic of Anamorphic Art." *Scientific American* 232:1 (1975), 110–116.

[Golan and Jackson 09] Miri Golan and Paul Jackson. "Origametria: A Program to Teach Geometry and to Develop Learning Skills Using the Art of Origami." In *Origami^4: Fourth International Meeting of Origami Science, Mathematics, and Education*, edited by Robert J. Lang, pp. 459–470. Wellesley, MA: A K Peters, 2009.

[Honda 13] Honda. "Honda Illusions, An Impossible Made Possible." YouTube video, https://www.youtube.com/watch?v=UelJZG_bF98, 2013.

[Hunt et al. 00] J. L. Hunt, B. G. Nickel, and C. Gigaul. "Anamorphic Images." *American Journal of Physics* 68:3 (2000), 232–237.

[ISO 14] ISO. "Information Technology—Automatic Identification and Data Capture Techniques—Aztec Code Bar Code Symbology Specification." Technical Report ISO/IEC 24778, International Organization for Standardization, 2014.

[Kenaan 02] Hagi Kenaan. "The Unusual Character of Holbein's Ambassadors." *Artibus et Historiae* 23:46 (2002), 61–75.

[Kent 13] Phillip Kent. "Art of Anamorphosis." http://www.anamorphosis.com/index.html, 2013.

[Klett and Drechsler 07] Yves Klett and Klaus Drechsler. "Design of Multifunctional Folded Core Structures for Aerospace Sandwich Applications." In *1st CEAS European Air and Space Conference Proceedings*, pp. 903–908. Berlin: Deutscher Luft- und Raumfahrtkongress, 2007.

[Klett and Drechsler 08] Yves Klett and Klaus Drechsler. "Cutting Edge Cores: Aerospace and Origami." In *Electronic Proceedings of the 9th International Mathematica Symposium, Maastricht*, http://south.rotol.ramk.fi/IMS/IMS2008/IMS%2708%20eProceedings/IMS%2708%20eProceedings/WWW/IMS_2008_e-Proceedings.html, 2008.

[Klett and Drechsler 11] Y. Klett and K. Drechsler. "Designing Technical Tessellations." In *Origami^5: Fifth International Meeting of Origami Science, Mathematics, and Education*, edited by Patsy Wang-Iverson, Robert J. Lang, and Mark Yim, pp. 305–322. Boca Raton, FL: A K Peters/CRC Press, 2011. MR2866909 (2012h:00044)

[Klett 13a] Y. Klett. "Realtime Rigid Folding Algorithm for Quadrilateral-Based 1-DOF Tessellations." In *ASME 2013 International Design Engineering Technical Conferences and Computers and Information in Engineering Conference*, paper no. DETC2013-12659. ASME 2013.

[Klett 13b] Yves Klett. *Auslegung multifunktionaler isometrischer Faltstrukturen für den technischen Einsatz.* Munich: Verlag Dr. Hut, 2013.

[Klett 15] Yves Klett. "Anamorphic Origami." *Wolfram Demonstrations Project*, http://demonstrations.wolfram.com/AnamorphicOrigami/, 2015.

[Lang 03] Robert J. Lang. "Skunk, Opus 47." http://www.langorigami.com/art/gallery/gallery.php?name=skunk, 2003.

[Lang 11] Robert J. Lang. "3^7 Hyperbolic Limit, Opus 600." http://www.langorigami.com/art/gallery/gallery.php?tag=tessellations&name=hyperbolic_limit, 2011.

[Privsek and Schnellhardt 14] Joerg Privsek and Guenther Schnellhardt. "Display Mat." Patent WO 2014075820 A1, 2014.

[Winckler and Wolf 11] Michael J. Winckler and K. Wolf. "Hands-On Geometry with Origami." In *Origami^5: Fifth International Meeting of Origami Science, Mathematics, and Education*, edited by Patsy Wang-Iverson, Robert J. Lang, and Mark Yim, pp. 219–231. Boca Raton, FL: A K Peters/CRC Press, 2011. MR2866909 (2012h:00044)

INSTITUTE OF AIRCRAFT DESIGN, UNIVERSITY OF STUTTGART, GERMANY
E-mail address: yves.klett@ifb.uni-stuttgart.de

Master Peace: An Evolution of Monumental Origami

Kevin Box and Robert J. Lang

1. Introduction

Origami is traditionally thought of as being made of folded paper, as ephemeral and fragile, and as existing only at the hand-held scale. However, the art form has expanded to encompass other materials and other sizes, and it has incorporated themes and concepts that arise from a wide range of influences. While paper is, of course, the traditional medium, a wide variety of materials may be used, including plastics, cloth, edibles [Lang 15], and metal (in the form of thin foils and foil-backed paper). While directly foldable metals have been the most common usage of metal in origami, artists have explored it in other forms, e.g., ceramic clay [Fire Mountain Gems 15], fabricated steel [Spear 15], and even curved-folded sheet metal [Epps and Verma 13].

In 2008, the authors began working together to render origami in metal using a variety of techniques. In this paper, we[1] present some of our individual and collaborative origami sculptures and their evolution from the traditional paper-based art to monumental works enlarged, cast, and fabricated in metal.

We use three distinct techniques for rendering origami in metal. First, there is *one-to-one*: direct casting from paper and wax originals. This method precisely captures the surface texture of paper down to the watermarks and is usually used on smaller pieces. Second, there is *monumental*: we laser scan the paper/wax original, digitally enlarge it, mill it from foam using CNC, and hand-finish the surface in clay. This method captures the essential shape and surface texture of the piece for large outdoor works. Third, there is *fabrication*, used for heroic scale: we deconstruct the exterior shapes by hand using the unfolded crease pattern, then recreate the surfaces using cut shapes that are welded back together along fold lines.

We present several case studies. We begin with one-to-one casting, which then led to the development of a 24-foot origami Pegasus, whose design evolution begins in 1960s-style Bird-Base–based forms but evolved through several different origami bases. It was ultimately deconstructed into a series of mild steel fabricated shapes that were reassembled on its final pedestal. Last, we present *Master Peace*, an hommage to the legend of 1000 cranes and the story of Sadako. *Master Peace* is a stainless steel cast *tsuru* sculpture in which all 1000 cranes exist in both reflection and physicality. Along the way, we will present several other examples of origami translated into bronze and steel, at scales ranging from desktop to monumental.

---

[1]Throughout this paper we use first-person plural ("we") to describe our collaboration. Individual activities and thoughts are described using third-person singular ("Box" and "Lang").

2. Kevin Box's Sculpture

Kevin Box's relationship with paper began with a paper-making kit in childhood. Throughout high school, Box studied graphic arts and apprenticed summers at an uncle's design firm in Atlanta, Georgia; he then studied graphic design on scholarship at the School of Visual Arts in New York City. After graduating with a BFA, he left paper behind and began working in foundries in Atlanta and Austin, Texas. For three years he labored under a self-imposed apprenticeship to become proficient in metal casting, attaining an exhaustive knowledge of casting techniques and fabrication processes. The artists he worked for mentored him through his exploration of style as well as the business of art, leading, eventually, to management of one of the largest fine art foundries in Texas—and, crucially, casting rights, which allowed him the freedom to experiment and explore.

However, paper had not entirely lost its hold upon him, and he began pioneering a technique for capturing all the delicate details of paper into bronze using the lost wax process. In the beginning his work was more geometric and architectural with no references to origami. As Box began exhibiting his castings, people immediately identified it with origami. Intrigued by these references, Box began researching origami and found that the relationship lay in the unfolded crease patterns from origami models that looked very similar to his works. His first origami-related work was *Crane Unfolding*, which depicts the traditional *tsuru* (crane) unfolding through five stages into the crease pattern, or "tar" as Box describes it, at the base of the sculpture. This sculpture achieved great success and recognition as well as an invitation to an origami festival in Houston in 2004, where he met Te Jui Fu and Linda Tomoko Mihara, who introduced him to the work of Robert Lang. His first origami collaboration emerged from that experience in his *Painted Pony* series that he created with Te Jui Fu, a few of which are shown in Figure 1.

Over the following years, Box continued to integrate origami forms into his own work. Eventually he had ideas that he wanted to realize but were too complex, which is when he reached out to Lang for help.

3. Collaborations with Lang

In 2006, Box contacted origami artist Lang to suggest possible collaborations; an email correspondence ensued over the next few years. In 2008, Lang visited Santa Fe in connection with a showing of the film *Between the Folds* at the Santa Fe Film Festival, and the two met for discussions. By the end of the evening, they had resolved to develop joint origami/bronze collaborations in which each could contribute artistically and creatively. As far back as 1999, Lang had worked with a foundry to transform original origami designs into bronze for a redevelopment project for the city of Santa Monica. That relationship had been one of "handing off" the origami to the foundry; the prospect of working closely with Box, as well as the compatibility of their artistic sensibilities, was both intriguing and inspiring to Lang.

For our first collaboration, we chose to take on a subject of long-time interest to Box: the White Bison, a subject of deep significance to native Americans, particularly those of the Great Plains and Oklahoma, where Box was raised. Lang took on the initial challenge of developing an origami design. One of the artistic goals he sought was to emphasize the contrast between the shaggy front of a bison relative to its hindquarters. After exploring several textured fold patterns, he decided to fold in the "inside-out" style, i.e., making use of contrasting colors on the two sides of the paper for the front and rear of the bison (as well as contrasting horns and eyes). The initial origami design is shown in Figure 2.

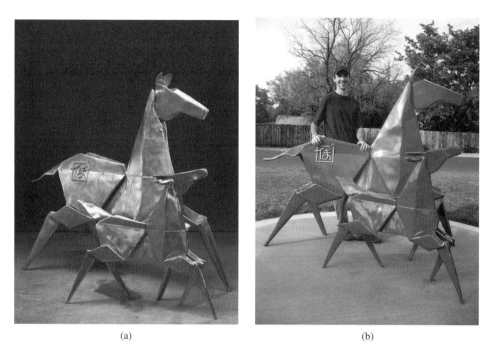

(a)   (b)

FIGURE 1. (a) *Painted Pony*, cast bronze, based on an origami design by T. J. Fu. (b) Artist Box with *Painted Pony* in stainless steel.

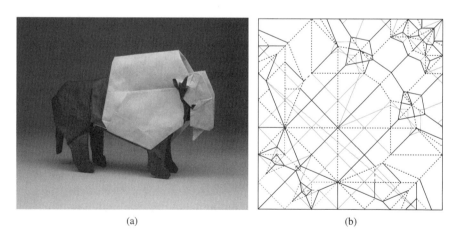

(a)   (b)

FIGURE 2. (a) The paper origami bison. (b) The crease pattern of the bison.

Once the folding design was completed, we shifted the focus from paper to bronze. Casting an origami figure in bronze inevitably alters the origami work, not just in the obvious way of replacing paper with metal but also due to changes that must be made for the form to be compatible with the design rules of casting, by augmenting the paper model with wax to prepare it for casting. Wax is used in several ways: to add stiffness, to build

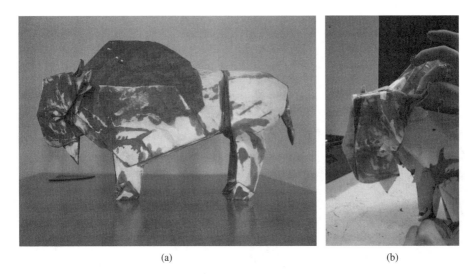

(a)   (b)

FIGURE 3. (a) The waxed bison. (b) Close-up of the head and fine shaping.

up thickness, and, in general, to modify the form in ways that accommodate the unique requirements of casting.

For example, there are constraints on minimum wall thickness, to avoid holes in the casting. Thin sections are built up with wax to reach a minimum thickness that corresponds to a minimum flow channel width within the ceramic mold, typically a few millimeters. The figure is typically designed to be cast as a hollow sculpture, to reduce the thickness of cast metal, and so there must be strategically placed openings to allow inserts that displace excess metal. Cracks between layers of paper are filled in with wax, to avoid creating entrapped mold material, but then they are cut back to a defined angle (called "drafting")) to restore the visual impression of the multiple layers that are part of the paper original.

At the same time, the wax work and preparation allows additional shaping and personality. Both artists went "hands on" in the final shaping, which was carried out during the wax work. As the wax cools, it holds the shape of the paper in place, enabling the artists to better capture the gesture and character of the paper model (Figure 3).

At this point, the process can take one of several different paths. It is possible to make a ceramic mold directly from the wax/paper model, which is called *direct investment casting*. In most cases, though, we go through a two-stage mold-making process. A silicone rubber mold is made from the wax/paper model; this mold is then used to cast wax submasters. This process allows the creation of an edition, which allows the one-time cost of casting and mold-making to be amortized over multiple sales.

The wax submaster is further modified by the attachment of sprues to form channels for the molten metal; it is then coated in a ceramic layer, which will serve as the mold for the molten metal. The ceramic mold is then baked, which allows the wax to melt and run out (and any residue is burned out by the 2000° oven). The heated mold is then ganged together with other molds, and a previously prepared crucible of molten bronze is poured into the mold (Figure 4).

After cooling, the ceramic is removed, excess metal is cut away, points of attachment are carefully ground off and textured, if necessary, to match their surroundings, and a patina is applied to give the desired finish.

FIGURE 4. (a) Pouring the bronze. (b) Applying the patina.

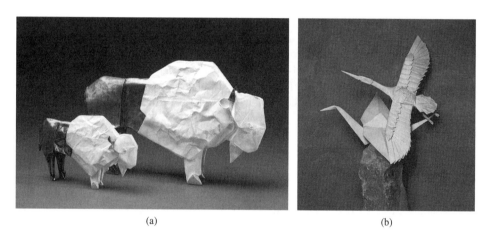

FIGURE 5. (a) *White Bison* in 12-inch and 20-inch lengths. (b) *Flight of Folds*, with a 24-inch wingspan.

The *White Bison* was successful, leading to a second version in a larger size (cast from a newly folded original) and to *Flight of Folds*, a design that combined the traditional Japanese crane with a modern feathered design by Lang (Figure 5).

Box also recognized early on that the creases in an origami figure had their own artistic appeal that was distinct from the folded form. In an early work, *Temple Mandala*, shown in Figure 6(a), Box created a free-form crease pattern to resemble a mandala and incorporated it into a cast wall hanging in which the mandala pattern of the creases evolves from the chaos of irregular folds to crumpling around the edges. This work was very successful.

After we began working together, we explored ways of representing the crease patterns of our collaborative designs to demonstrate that our models were folded from uncut squares. Initially, we tried laser-burning crease patterns into paper for display in a fashion

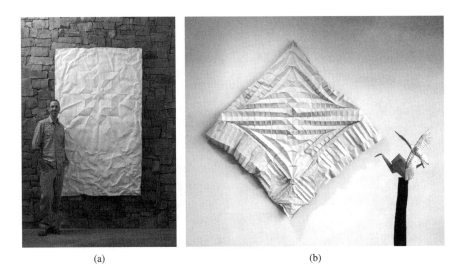

FIGURE 6. (a) *Temple Mandala*, cast aluminum. (b) *Unfolded Crane*, cast aluminum.

similar to prints, but we were unsatisfied by the results. In 2013, we cast a piece directly from an origami model that we unfolded as a demonstration at an art gallery. This crease pattern from an actual folded model had far more character and detail than the sterile line art of an idealized crease pattern. The approach was very successful, particularly when the unfolded pattern was not smoothed out but instead left with deep relief in the folds, as illustrated in Figure 6(b).

4. Monumental Collaborations

Although Box had previously created several monumental works of public art, *Star Unfolding* (2004) and *Folding Planes* (2005–2012), our first monumental collaboration came about through a stroke of serendipity. Box had worked with TMC foundry in Thailand for many years, and they often experimented on each other in the research and development of new techniques or materials. TMC and Box were working to establish new techniques for casting stainless steel, and TMC offered to create a monumental work "on spec." Specifically, they offered to create a life-size version of *White Bison* that would be cast in stainless steel. We took them up on the offer and selected an edition size of 4.

Our previous origami castings had been one-to-one, in which molds are made directly from a paper origami original prepared with wax. Making a one-to-one casting from a life-size bison would be highly problematic, though. Beyond about 24 inches in size, the scaling of paper size, weight, strength, and foldability breaks down; large-scale origami installations almost always require an extensive support structure, and even then, they remain extremely fragile. Rather than attempting a one-to-one casting, we elected to go with *digital enlargement*. This is the current standard technique for most artists working in monumental scale. In this process, a three-dimensional scan is taken of a smaller model (we used *White Bison II*), and then computer numerically controlled (CNC) machining is used to mill a larger replica from large blocks of foam to make the full-size model from which molds would be made. The CNC process is not exact, however; after the model is

(a)   (b)

FIGURE 7. (a) *White Bison*, full size. (b) *Flight of Folds*, full size.

roughed out by CNC, artisans go back in and re-sculpt the fine detail of the paper layers using wax and clay, restoring edges (and even wrinkles) to the model. From this model, molds are then made; wax submasters are cast, and then these are used to carry out the final full-scale casting. The finished piece is shown in Figure 7(a).

Our second monumental collaboration was also the result of a stroke of serendipity—although "result of a mistake" was our first characterization. After the success of *Flight of Folds* in sizes of 8-inch and 18-inch wingspans, we decided to move to larger versions: a 30-inch wingspan (cast one-to-one, i.e., from a full-size origami figure folded from a 6-foot square), and a 5-foot wingspan (digitally enlarged from a 30-inch model). Somewhere along the way, an extra factor of 2× made its way into the instructions, and our first knowledge of this came when the foundry said "it's done" and sent photos—revealing a massive *Flight of Folds* with a 10-foot wingspan, standing over seven feet high!

This presented a number of problems including the higher cost of casting, the logistics of moving, and most importantly the higher retail value that reduced the number of potential clients significantly. However, since the piece was almost finished and so impressive, Box and TMC elected to take the risk and continue the production process, resulting in the work shown in Figure 7(b). It is now part of the "Origami in the Garden" traveling exhibition, whose debut show was at the Santa Fe Botanical Garden in 2014.

5. Hero's Horse

Serendipity and monumental seem to go together; our largest monumental collaboration also incorporated a stroke of the former. Box was in discussions with a client interested in a still larger origami sculpture: something 20 or more feet tall. Discussions focused initially on a design based on the Box–Fu horse, but as the discussion drew to closure, the customer asked: "If I change my mind, rather than a horse can you make a Pegasus?" As any professional artist knows, the answer to such questions is always "why yes, of course," and Box sketched a drawing of a Box–Fu pony with added wings. The customer agreed to proceed, and Box considered simply adding wing elements to the existing pony. But, he realized it would be a better sculpture if it was constructed from an uncut square, so

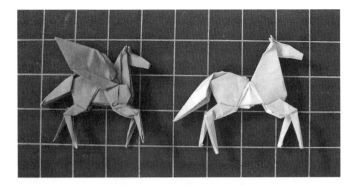

FIGURE 8. Uncut-square Pegasus from a Blintzed Frog Base (left). Uncut-square horse from a "six-sided square" (right).

he called Robert: "Hey Robert, do you think you could reverse-engineer the Box–Fu pony designed with four cuts out of an uncut square? Oh, and can you add wings to that?"

To Lang, this challenge had a particular resonance: several of Lang's designs from the 1980s and 1990s were uncut-square renderings of "classic" designs that had been originally folded from multiple sheets and/or used cuts (e.g., Yoshizawa's monkey and Honda's fox). The Box–Fu pony was folded from a bird base with a few cuts (similar to Fred Rohm's *Circus Pony* [Harbin 71]), and Lang had been tempted for some time to fold an uncut-square version of same. This provided the opportunity to do so: using a Montrollian "six-sided square" structure for the basic horse, then augmenting it with two more flaps for wings. Fortuitously, this could be accomplished with an "eight-sided square," better known as the classic Blintzed Frog Base—both augmented by numerous decidedly un-classic 3-through 8-sided multiple open sink folds.

Figure 8 displays paper design prototypes, but the final design needed to have a particular character and pose tied to both Box's sketches and his past *Painted Pony* artworks (see Figure 9). Lang folded several origami designs to the near-finished state and then turned them over to Box for further shaping, pose definition, and the all-important waxing and preparation for casting. Box then cast two different sizes, both using one-to-one casting (molds made directly from origami figures): 6-inch and 12-inch versions, with finishes of silver nitrate and paper-white, respectively, shown in Figure 10.

The full-scale commission had to be over 20 feet tall. This is too large even for digital enlargement, so yet another technique was called into play.

Box developed a process of fabrication specifically for origami enlargement, using the crease patterns as templates for large sheets of metal. The origami work is deconstructed into the relevant surface shapes, which are then traced into digital line art. (See Figure 11.) These shapes can then be scaled, cut out from mild steel (ranging in thickness from 1/4 inch to 1 inch, depending on its location within the structure), and welded together.

Because this was public art to be mounted outdoors, it was not sufficient to simply design for appearance; the figure had to be designed so that it could be disassembled for powder-coating and transportation to the installation site for assembly on location. Furthermore, because it was exposed to the elements, it had to be designed and analyzed to withstand the extreme weather of the Texas plains. Box had previous experience with the engineering firm of Gregory P. Luth and Associates (GPLA) of California. They were contracted to design a multi-piece rendition of the pattern, working with Box to preserve the artistic lines of the design while ensuring that the result could be built, transported, and

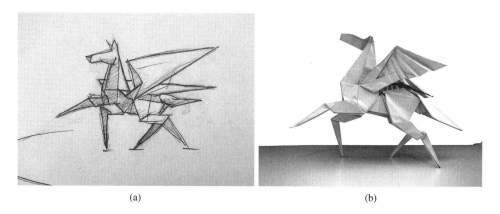

(a)   (b)

FIGURE 9. (a) Box's sketch. (b) The folded origami reference model.

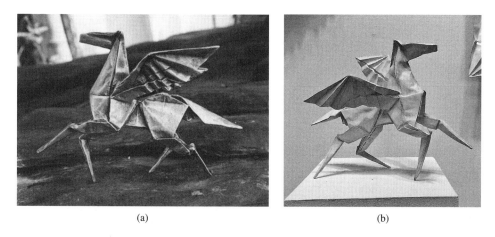

(a)   (b)

FIGURE 10. (a) The 6-inch Pegasus with silver nitrate finish. (b) The 12-inch Pegasus with paper-white finish.

installed in a practical fashion. Fabrication was carried out by Damon Chefchis of CMY, Inc., in Albuquerque, New Mexico.

For the engineering, a full digital model was constructed and subjected to various loading conditions, including wind loads of up to 95 mph winds (those of a small tornado—a not unreasonable condition, considering its location in Tornado Alley). Under such simulated load, the digital model remained fixed (a truly flying Pegasus would not be desirable), with its wings flapping up to 6 inches (thereby proving the adage that any origami model can be an action model with sufficient applied force). Having passed all design tests, the model was then "value engineered" to reduce material thickness to save weight and money, re-tested, and sent to fabrication. Fabrication took over 1600 man-hours of welding and grinding each of the 87+ pieces. Once complete, the steel was sandblasted and powder-coated with a zinc-rich primer followed by a durable outdoor satin white coating. The pieces were loaded and transported to the site (via two flatbed trucks) and then assembled at the Cypress Waters development in Irving, Texas, in April of 2014. (See Figure 12(a).)

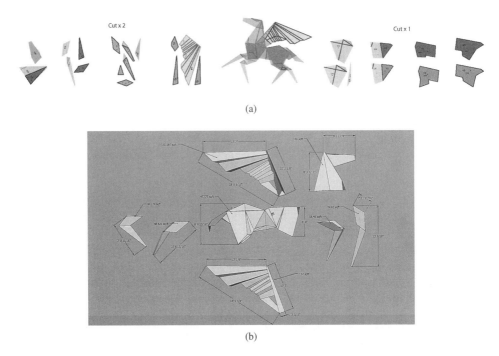

FIGURE 11. (a) Cut plans for the fabricated Pegasus. (b) The parts in their proper orientation.

FIGURE 12. (a) Final assembly on site. (b) The finished *Hero's Horse*.

The completed *Hero's Horse* is shown in Figure 12(b). (N.B.: It is clearly visible from airplanes on approach from the north to DFW airport.)

(a)

(b)

FIGURE 13. (a) *Master Peace*, cast stainless steel. (b) Individual cast cranes from *Master Peace*.

6. Master Peace

Master Peace is a sculpture created by Kevin and his wife Jennifer Box, inspired by the legend of 1000 cranes (Figure 13(a)). It took approximately nine years to bring all the elements together to realize this monumental origami sculpture. It consists of 1000 origami cranes cast in stainless steel. 500 of the cranes are gathered together in a 25' tall monument while 500 of the cranes are scattered into the world as individual collector pieces. The monument stands on a 20'x20' polished black granite base that keeps all 1000 cranes together in the reflection.

This monument had to be engineered to come apart for transportation and to withstand 95 mph sustained wind loads. Two critical problems had to be solved to make this sculpture possible: the engineering and the financing. Box worked with GPLA engineering for two years trying different approaches for stacking so many cranes into the sky. The engineers suggested adding structural components and cables to the work that would satisfy the wind loads but these were unsatisfying to the aesthetic of the artist. The final solution came when Box realized an approach that combined four different sizes of cranes, larger at the base and smallest at the top, along with engineered cables that he saw as the strings that held a traditional Japanese *sembazuru* together. A flagpole-like structure in the center of the sculpture enabled it to come apart into multiple pieces for transportation.

The problem of financing the sculpture was solved by the "gathering and scattering" concept held together by the reflection. By scattering 500 cranes as individual collector pieces that are for sale (Figure 13(b)), each sale of an individual crane paid for its twin crane in the monument. Many of the cranes have been purchased by collectors and enthusiasts in support of this monument to peace, and many of them are still available as of this writing (2014). The finished work is currently on display as the center piece of the "Origami in the Garden" public garden exhibition.

7. Conclusions

While origami is traditionally simple and fragile, the last half-century has seen it change in many ways and grow into fields it had never been associated with, both functional fields and artistic ones. Origami can be combined with metal sculpture to realize a unique combination of delicacy and robustness. It has allowed our collaboration to merge our artistic visions and talents. The horizon of possibilities lies far, far, away, with much beauty and satisfaction on the journey ahead of us.

References

[Epps and Verma 13] Gregory Epps and Sushant Verma. "Curved Folding: Design to Fabrication Process of RoboFold." In *Shape Modeling International 2013*, pp. 75–83. Bournemouth, UK: Bournemouth University, 2013.

[Fire Mountain Gems 15] Fire Mountain Gems. "Art Clay." http://www.firemountaingems.com/shop/kw1cml318h75yfv, retrieved January 19, 2015.

[Harbin 71] Robert Harbin. *Secrets of Origami*. London: Octopus Books, 1971.

[Lang 15] Robert J. Lang. "Paper." http://www.langorigami.com/paper/paper.php, retrieved January 19, 2015.

[Spear 15] Joe Spear. "Metal Origami." http://metalorigami.carbonmade.com/, retrieved January 19, 2015.

BOX STUDIO LLC, CERRILLOS, NEW MEXICO
E-mail address: boxstudio@sbcglobal.net

LANG ORIGAMI, ALAMO, CALIFORNIA
E-mail address: robert@langorigami.com

Wearable Metal Origami

Tine De Ruysser

1. Introduction

The art of paper folding has possible applications in design and engineering, but paper itself is often too weak as a material for real-life applications. Durable materials that can be folded with the intricacy of origami patterns are needed but not easily available. This chapter describes one way of making a textile-metal laminate, developed especially for the creation of tessellating origami structures. The material draws upon the knowledge of various design fields and is suitable for the creation of different types of objects. It is particularly relevant to jewelry for its visual character, its flexibility (almost organic movement that easily adjusts to the human body), and the possibility to use precious metals.

2. Context

Folding and pleating are well-known techniques applied within fashion and textiles. They have been used through the centuries to make fabrics drape elegantly on the body. *Folding* in this context is used to describe how folds are pressed into the fabric to make them more permanent. This process is more commonly referred to as *pleating*. The pleats are kept in shape by heat-setting or locally stitching the pleats together in a technique called *smock*. Sometimes the result is a textile version of origami. Several artists have used this to create textile origami pieces. Chris Palmer has described how to fold fabric into tessellating origami patterns [Rutzky and Palmer 11]. Matthew Gardiner makes moving origami "robots," which use pleated polyester textiles and ingenious mechanisms to provide movement [Gardiner 15]. However, the material described in this work has stiff, metalized areas that create a different sort of movement and unique appearance. The way the material moves on the body is more like chain mail or deployable structures. Illan Garibi makes metal origami in both small and large panels by etching metal sheets [Garibi 15]. These stunning pieces do not remain flexible like wearable metal origami (see Section 7).

3. History

The development of this material started 16 years ago and came about for practical reasons: as a jewelry designer, I had discovered a tessellating origami pattern (Figure 1), and I wanted to make it in a material suitable for the creation of jewelry.

I developed two solutions:

The first one, stitching a layer of plastic or paper in between two layers of fabric, allowed me to construct clothing with one layer and to permanently attach an accessory with the other layer. The stitching was done with a computer-aided embroidery machine,

FIGURE 1. Paper structure at the basis of Wearable Metal Origami (1998).

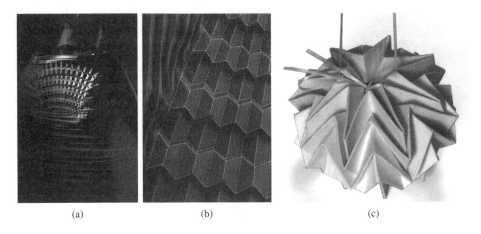

(a)   (b)   (c)

FIGURE 2. Origami pattern applied to clothing and accessories through stitching paper in between two layers of textile. (a) Dress with scarf (2001), and (b) detail of stitching (2001). (c) White Bag (2002) made on sewing machine.

with the aid of textile technicians at the Royal College of Art in London and the Textile Museum in the Netherlands (Figure 2(a,b)). This combination of stitching and folding was continued in a range of bags and objects, made by hand on a regular sewing machine (Figure 2(c)).

The second solution was more appropriate to the purpose of making jewelry, and the method that was the basis for further research. It consists of a layer of copper platelets applied to a piece of fabric, creating a material that looks like copper, yet can fold on the bare textile folding lines (Figure 3). This is done through the process of electroforming.

4. Electroforming Fabric for the Creation of Metalized Folding Textiles

Electroforming is an electrochemical process in which a layer of metal is deposited on an object. To make this possible, the object is made electrically conductive and is suspended in a solution containing metal particles (Figure 4). An electrical current is run through the solution and the object, so that the metal particles in the solution move toward the object and adhere to the surface. A metal layer forms, and the process continues

(a)   (b)

FIGURE 3. Early work in electroformed textiles (2001). (a) Sample and (b) bag, copper on black fabric.

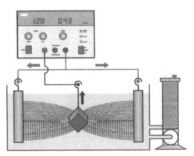

FIGURE 4. The electroforming process [Curtis 04].

FIGURE 5. Electroformed platelets on textile, with bare fabric hinges.

until the desired thickness is achieved. This process is mostly used on a mold, which is completely covered and later removed so that a metal piece remains.

In contrast to the traditional method, I only applied metal to certain areas of a piece of fabric, and I left the fabric "mold" in place. This allowed me to recreate tessellating origami patterns, with bare fabric hinges for the folding lines and stiff metalized platelets in between (Figure 5). This laminated fabric is called *Metalized Folding Textile* (MFT).

To allow the build-up of metal platelets, the fabric has to be made locally conductive, according to the chosen folding pattern: Platelets have to be conductive on the surface of

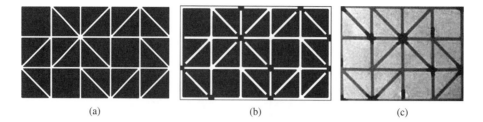

(a)   (b)   (c)

FIGURE 6. (a) Folding pattern is drawn; folding lines are given a certain width. Black areas will be printed in conductive ink, so metal can adhere there. (b) Connections are drawn, so that an electrical current can run through each platelet. (c) Connections are covered with a lacquer to prevent metal from building up in these places.

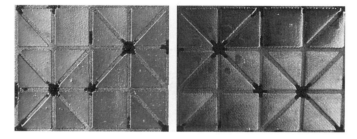

FIGURE 7. The fabric with metal platelets after electroforming, front (left) and back (right).

the fabric; folding lines should not be conductive. The process described here is one of many processes tested, and even though it was the first, it still gives the best results. The chosen images are of a square, "boxy" pattern, but the same principle can be applied to any folding pattern. Fabric is stretched over a frame, which will keep it flat when it is submerged in the solution. Conductive ink is applied where the platelets will be through screen-printing or spray-painting with the aid of a stencil. In both cases, the same basic pattern is drawn (Figure 6(a)). To enable the current to run through all platelets, they have to be electrically connected, so connections are added to the drawing (Figure 6(b)). The pattern is then transferred onto a silk-screen and printed with conductive ink; or, a stencil is cut from self-adhesive vinyl, and the ink is applied with an airbrush through the stencil. The connections between the platelets should not have any metal build up, or the hinges will not be foldable. So, they are covered by hand with a layer of lacquer, which forms a protective layer that cannot be penetrated by the solution (Figure 6(c)). This lacquer is applied to both sides of the fabric.

The fabric is then wired up to electric cables and submerged in the electroforming solution, and a current is sent through it until a metal layer of chosen thickness is achieved (Figure 7).

The fabric is removed from the frame, and the cables and lacquer are removed. Now the material can be folded into shape (Figure 5).

Most of my work is made in copper for practical reasons, but it is possible to use silver or even gold instead.

(a)   (b)

FIGURE 8. Shoulder cape (2009), boxy pattern, (a) when on a flat surface and (b) taking the shape of the shoulders of the wearer.

5. Working with Metalized Folding Textile as a Material

5.1. Weight and support. Folded paper is very light, and most types of paper keep their folded shape well. In contrast, MFT is quite heavy because of the metal parts, and the textile does not have a good capacity for keeping its shape. Some folding patterns in MFT will remain folded more easily than others. The first pattern I designed (Figures 1 and 3) keeps it shape well under normal gravitational forces and only unfolds if extra forces are applied through pushing or pulling on the fabric. Boxy patterns will not remain folded unless extra support is given. All patterns need extra support if they are used for the creation of wearable pieces, or pieces that will be handled by non-origami experts. Mostly, it is sufficient to add a few stitches to critical locations to keep the patterns folded. Sometimes the weight and chosen pattern work together for a wearable piece to shape itself to the body of the wearer (Figure 8)

5.2. Metal thickness. The platelets have a certain thickness, greater than that of the average paper. It varies depending on the size of the platelets (larger platelets need to be thicker to remain stiff; smaller platelets need less thickness) and on the location of the platelets in the whole pattern (platelets closest to the electric cables in the electroforming tank build up a thicker layer than those further removed). Even though the thickness is generally never more than 0.8 mm, it still means that even flat-foldable patterns can create considerable thickness in a folded piece. To ensure the pattern folds well, the hinges are given a width of at least twice the thickness of the platelets (Figure 9).

5.3. Metal stiffness. Paper can bend slightly, whereas metal platelets have no such flexibility. They behave like rigid origami: rigid plates connected by hinges [Tachi 09]. Certain tessellating folding patterns rely on the flexibility of paper to go from unfolded to folded state. For these patterns, extra folding lines have to be added in the pattern of MFT to allow for it to be folded like rigid origami (Figure 10).

5.4. Edges. Because MFT has a textile core, extra care needs to be taken to the edge-finish (Figure 11). If all surrounding fabric is removed, this has to be done neatly and in such a way that the risk of tearing is kept to a minimum. For copper electroforming the most suitable choice of textile is polyester because the electroforming solution does not corrode it. The extra advantage is that it can be cut with a hot tool, so that the fibers at the

FIGURE 9. The width of
the textile hinge is twice
the platelet thickness to
allow for folding.

FIGURE 10. The hexagons
do not need creases to be
folded in paper, but they
need hinges in the loca-
tion of the black lines to
be foldable in MFT.

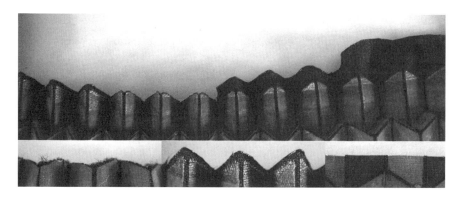

FIGURE 11. Different ways of finishing the edge (top) with close-ups
(bottom). Copper on polyester fabric.

edge are melted together and do not fray. The distance to keep from the metal edge is an
aesthetic choice, and for a really sharp edge it is even possible to cut through the metal.

5.5. Colors. Apart from the obvious color choices that can be made by selecting colored fabrics and the color of the chosen metal (Figure 12), there is also the option of
coloring the metal surface. Both silver and copper can be chemically treated to change
their surface color, although copper has a wider range of possibilities than silver. The entire surface can be treated to become one uniform color (often black) or to show a color
pattern. By using stencils, selective coloring of certain platelets is also possible (Figure 13)

6. Designing with Metalized Folding Textile

The whole process of making MFT is time consuming, making the creation of pieces
in MFT a costly process. For this reason, the design of the finished piece has to be well
considered before it is executed in MFT. Critical for the design process is an understanding
of how MFT behaves. As mentioned in the previous section, this depends on the specific
characteristics of this material, but of course the folding pattern also takes a central role.

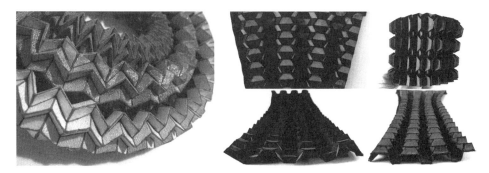

FIGURE 12. Three bracelets. Inside-out: copper, gold-plated silver, and silver.

FIGURE 13. By coloring half the platelets, the material seems to change color when seen from different angles.

To understand the different aspects that influence the design process, they were each investigated separately.

6.1. Folding patterns. MFT is developed to transform tessellating origami patterns into wearable pieces that are more durable than paper. Both the shape-change from flat material to folded object and the shape of the folded object are important. An overview of how different patterns behave during the folding process was needed, so that a selection could be more easily made when I had a final design in mind.

When I started this process, useful tools such as the Rigid Origami software [Tachi 09] were not available, so most expertise was built by experimenting with paper and through reverse-engineering the patterns of images I found on the internet [Flickr 14].

All folding patterns were classified based on their crease pattern into groups and mapped out on a family tree (Figure 14). The classification is made on the appearance of the folded model and on how the material moves from the folding pattern to the folded model. Yet, the descriptions on the tree are based on the folding pattern because this is the clearest way of defining them: it is hard to distinguish between two folded models with minor differences, but their folding patterns show differences in angles and size of platelets more easily.

6.1.1. *Accordion models.* These behave like an accordion: the simplest would be a row of parallel folding lines, equal distance apart, alternating valley and mountain folds. All accordion folds have a set of long straight lines running through them, often from one edge of the paper to another, dividing it into strips. They are most useful for objects that need extreme size change or great flexibility. This group can be subdivided in different subcategories. I will describe the different steps as grades (°), following the example of Ray Schamp [Schamp 14]. The first subcategory is whether the straight lines of the first grade (1°) that create a simple accordion when folded are parallel or not and, if they are not parallel, whether they all fan out from a single point or from several points (Figure 15).

This will determine whether in a given pattern the platelets will be the same size throughout the whole piece or whether they will gradually increase and decrease in size.

The second grade (2°) is formed by zig-zag creases going across the first grade creases. This determines whether the pattern will fold into a flat or curved surface—or a combination of both (Figure 16).

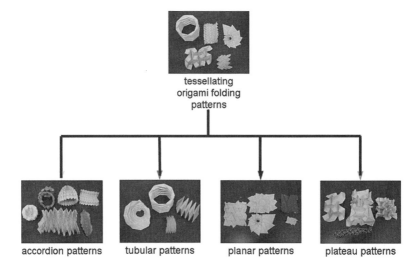

FIGURE 14. Division of tessellating origami patterns in main groups. Each group is further divided.

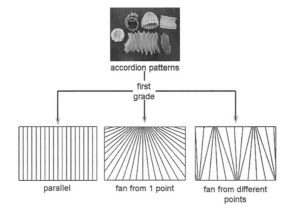

FIGURE 15. First grade division of accordion patterns.

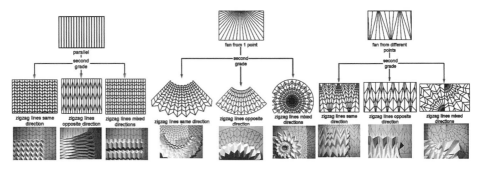

FIGURE 16. Second grade division of accordion patterns.

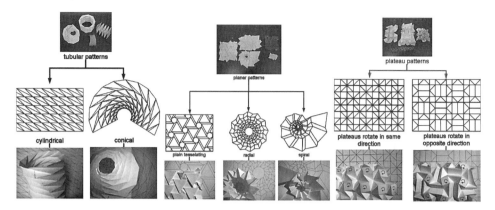

FIGURE 17. Tubular models.   FIGURE 18. Planar models.   FIGURE 19. Plateau models.

6.1.2. *Tubular models.* This group of patterns (Figure 17) distinguishes itself from the others in that the two sides of the folded material are fixed together to form a tube in both unfolded and folded form. The tube can be cylindrical or conical in shape. These patterns are most useful for making a tubular object collapse into a shape with roughly the same circumference but diminished height, or for creating a design that converts from a flat sheet to a tubular object and back again. Cylindrical patterns are also a subgroup of the accordion models.

6.1.3. *Planar models.* This group (Figure 18) consists of tessellations of clearly recognizable geometric forms, fitting together like Arabic decorations. They are true flat-foldable patterns: The models fold flat into a plane. This group is subdivided depending on whether the tessellated units are all of the same size or if they increase in size as they rotate around a center to form concentric circles or a spiral pattern. Planar models are useful for decreasing the plane of visible area when the object is folded, without creating too much thickness. Unlike the other groups of patterns, they do not curve flexibly in the folded state.

6.1.4. *Plateau models.* This group (Figure 19) resembles the planar models because they are also constructed of tessellating units of geometric forms. They are not flat-foldable but have platelets (plateaus) that rise up to a higher plane, or sink to a lower plane, while the platelets in between form walls perpendicular to the plateaus. This way, a sort of box is created by each of the units, explaining why these patterns are often called *boxy patterns.* Plateau folds create visual depth, and the empty spaces inside the boxes can be used to set stones without hindering the folding. When partly folded, they form spherical shapes, returning to a flat surface when fully folded.

6.1.5. *The use of the family tree.* The family tree makes it possible to quickly develop a pattern for a specific application based on the shape it should be and how it should move. This is done by finding a pattern in the tree that behaves more or less like the one needed and then adjusting it to make it behave exactly as wanted. This reduces the time spent on the trial-and-error process of developing a new pattern.

As more folding patterns are created both by others and me, I keep on discovering new aspects and relationships. The family tree described here is not a final version; it will be adapted as my understanding of the behavior of folding patterns deepens.

FIGURE 20. One of the first samples for a model-making material: laser-cut veneer glued on textile.

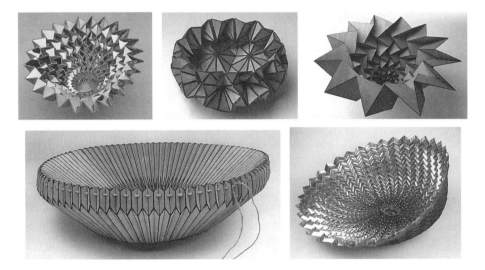

FIGURE 21. Various decorative objects made in textile-plywood, textile-mirror foil, or textile-flock foil laminates.

6.2. Sample materials. Folding paper samples is effective for determining the crease pattern needed. But, as described above, MFT behaves differently from paper because of its weight and the flexibility of the hinges. New model-making materials were developed to more accurately mimic the behavior of MFT. These new materials also consist of a textile base layer and have platelets of different materials applied. The platelets can be laser-cut or cut with a vinyl cutter, and then they are glued onto the fabric (Figure 20).

These new materials are very useful for the design process for MFT. On top of that, they are beautiful in their own right and can be used to create autonomous decorative objects (Figure 21).

7. Wearable Metal Origami

Wearable pieces can be made in Metalized Folding Textiles. A few examples of the most successful pieces made in MFT so far are shown in Figures 22–25.

8. Conclusion

The MFT material is suitable for the creation of a range of applications, especially for jewelry, wearable pieces, and decorative "tableware" objects. It could only be developed

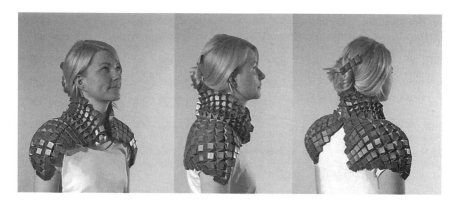

FIGURE 22. Shoulder cape.

FIGURE 23. Silver bracelet.

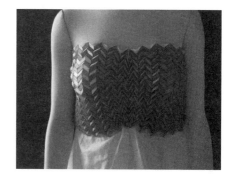

FIGURE 24. Design for a dress.

FIGURE 25. Bracelet that can be converted into a carrier bag.

through a multidisciplinary approach, revolving around tessellating origami and incorporating printing, electroforming, design methodology, and CAD drawing, as well as the study of material properties and existing folding and flexible structures. All this knowledge is currently brought together in one person, and collaborations with experts in these specific fields would carry it a lot further.

MFT is still difficult to produce, and its use will remain limited to unique art pieces unless the production process can be improved and scaled up. For this, experts in printing and the electroforming process are needed. For the creation of wearable pieces, further knowledge of fashion and textiles should be explored. And last but not least, to expand the range of shapes and applications, further development in knowledge of folding patterns is needed.

This can partly be gained through the use of available software [Lang 14, Tachi 14], but it would improve even more through collaborations with origami experts.

References

[Curtis 04] Lesley Curtis. *Electroforming*. London: A & C Black, 2004.

[Flickr 14] Flickr Group. "Origami Tessellations." *Flickr*, http://flickr.com/groups/origamitessellations/pool/, accessed July 27, 2014.

[Gardiner 15] Matthew Gardiner. "On Oribotics." http://www.matthewgardiner.net/art/On_Oribotics, accessed February 14, 2015.

[Garibi 15] Illan Garibi. "Garibi Origami." http://www.garibiorigami.com/, accessed February 14, 2015.

[Lang 14] Robert J. Lang. "Origami Flanged Pots." *Wolfram Demonstration Project*, http://demonstrations. wolfram.com/OrigamiFlangedPots/, accessed July 28, 2014.

[Rutzky and Palmer 11] Jeffrey Rutzky and Chris K. Palmer. *Shadowfolds*. New York: Kodansha USA, 2011.

[Schamp 14] Ray Schamp. "Origami, Collections, Theory." *Flickr*, http://www.flickr.com/photos/miura-ori/ collections/72157600013526866/, accessed July 28, 2014.

[Tachi 09] Tomohiro Tachi. "Simulation of Rigid Origami." In *Origami⁴: Fourth International Meeting of Origami Science, Mathematics, and Education*, edited by Robert J. Lang, pp. 175–187. Wellesley, MA: A K Peters, 2009. MR2590567 (2010h:00025)

[Tachi 14] Tomohiro Tachi. "Freeform Origami Software." http://www.tsg.ne.jp/TT/software/, accessed July 28, 2014.

UNIVERSITY OF HASSELT, HASSELT, BELGIUM
E-mail address: info@tinederuysser.com

Crowdsourcing Origami Sculptures

Jeannine Mosely

1. Introduction

In 1994, I learned to make a traditional origami model of a cube using six rectangular cards [Leeming 34]. These can be almost any kind of card: playing card, index card, business card, etc., provided that the ratio of the sides is (roughly) greater than 1.5:1 and less than 2:1. Though many modular origami designs rely on units having both flaps and pockets to insert the flaps into, the business card cube has only flaps, and the model is only stable when all the flaps are on the outside. While playing with these cubes, I discovered a method of linking the cubes together by interlocking the flaps. I also devised a method of using additional cards to cover the exposed flaps, making the model stronger and letting you pattern the surface of the structure. (See Figure 1.) In the years since then, I have made several very large origami models from these cubes, with the help of hundreds of volunteers.

2. The Sculptures

2.1. The Menger Sponge. One of the first designs that I built was a level-one approximation of the Menger Sponge, made from 20 cubes. It uses 120 cards in the base

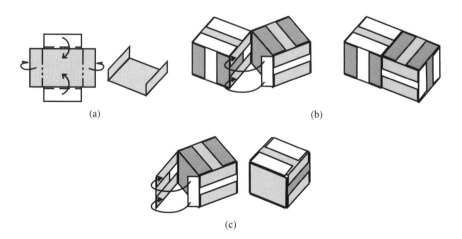

(a)   (b)

(c)

FIGURE 1. (a) Building, (b) linking, and (c) paneling cubes.

©2015 American Mathematical Society

FIGURE 2. Level-three Menger Sponge.

structure with 72 additional paneling cards. The Menger Sponge is a famous fractal named for mathematician Karl Menger [Peitgen and Richter 86]. To understand this shape, imagine a cube divided into $3 \times 3 \times 3$ smaller cubes. Now, discard the cube at the center and the 6 cubes in the middle of each face, keeping the 8 corner cubes and 12 edge cubes. Repeat this process with each of the remaining cubes, and repeat again, ad infinitum.

This inspired me to make a level-three Menger Sponge from 8000 cubes, using 48,000 cards in the base with 18,048 additional paneling cards [Institute for Figuring 06]. I acquired the base cards from my co-workers after the company we worked for changed its name and, soon after, moved. The colored paneling cards were misprints donated by a local printer. I decided to crowdsource the project (though the word had not yet been coined) and gathered as many volunteers as possible to help me with it. I found volunteers at origami conventions, by visiting school classrooms, by lecturing on college campuses, and by holding parties in my home. The model was finished in 2005, and more than 200 people participated during the 10 years that it took to build. (See Figure 2.)

2.2. Union Station. The second large cube sculpture that I crowdsourced was a model of Union Station in Worcester, Massachusetts. This was built in 2008 for a community arts organization, First Night Worcester. Their purpose is to organize exhibitions and performances throughout the city on New Year's Eve each year. The director of First Night Worcester, Joyce Kressler, chose to hire teaching artists to guide the children of Worcester in creating as many of the exhibits as possible. We decided to build a model of a local architectural landmark—the train and bus terminal—that everyone would recognize. During the fall of 2008, around 300 school children and their teachers, 150 college students from

FIGURE 3. Union Station.

Worcester Polytechnic Institute, and another 50 or so members of the community coop-
erated to build the sculpture from around 60,000 misprinted business cards provided by a
local printer [Jacobs 10]. (See Figure 3.)

2.3. The Snowflake Sponge. Next I led a project to build a model of another fractal
that I designed and named the *Snowflake Sponge*. Consider a cube divided into 27 smaller
cubes. Now suppose that we keep the 12 edge cubes and the 6 cubes in the middle of
each face, while discarding the 8 corner cubes and the cube at the center. The resulting
fractal is full of diagonal holes whose cross sections resemble a snowflake. The Snowflake
Sponge was built from 49,000 specially printed cards in 2012 by nearly 300 members of
the University of Southern California community. The project was sponsored by the USC
Libraries and curated by their Discovery Fellow, Margaret Wertheim [Wertheim 12]. (See
Figure 4.)

3. Design Considerations

When embarking on any project to build such a massive origami model, a number
of questions must be considered. How many cards are needed and where can they be
obtained? What will the sculpture weigh and will the design support its own weight?
How large will the model be, and can it be moved, either whole or in pieces? Where will
the model be built and/or exhibited? Who will build it and how will the volunteers be
recruited and organized? What is the schedule for its completion? How will the project be
documented? What is the budget to pay for supplies, instructional materials, transportation,
pedestals, advertising, artist's honorarium, and opening-night refreshments?

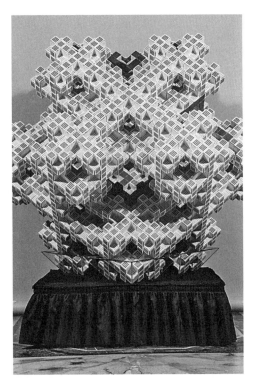

FIGURE 4. Level-three Snowflake Sponge.

3.1. The Menger Sponge. When I set out to build the Menger Sponge in 1995, I had little idea of the challenges that lay ahead. I had already procured the cards I needed, and I knew that the sculpture would weigh around 66 kg. (Business cards weigh roughly 1 g each.) I built a cube and loaded it with weights to see what it would bear—it held up several kilograms—and I concluded that the Menger Sponge could support its own weight. American business cards measure $2'' \times 3.5''$ (50.8 mm $\times$ 88.9 mm), so the model was going to measure $56'' \times 56'' \times 56''$ (140 cm $\times$ 140 cm $\times$ 140 cm). It clearly would not fit through most doorways! I did not have a venue where it could reside while volunteers came to work on it, so I needed to find a way to break it up into smaller pieces that people could make and deliver to me, which could be assembled into the whole in a suitable location.

The obvious decomposition of the Menger Sponge is into smaller Menger Sponges. Could 400 volunteers each make a level-one sponge, so that 20 of them could be linked to make a level-two sponge, and then 20 of them could then be linked into the level-three sponge? Unfortunately, this approach does not work because you cannot get at all of the flaps to interlock when you bring two smaller sponges together face to face. However, separate cube structures can be joined by building linking cubes to place between them, one card at a time. This kind of linking is slower and requires more expertise than the usual method, so it was important to find a decomposition of the sponge that allowed for a large percentage of the required cubes to be built as part of smaller units, with as few linking cubes as possible.

After grappling with this problem for some time, I came up with what I call the *tripod decomposition*. The sponge is broken up into units that are either a simple tripod—a cube

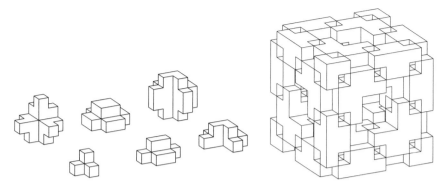

FIGURE 5. The six different kinds of tripod units.

FIGURE 6. Tripod decomposition of a level-two Menger Sponge.

with three additional cubes attached to three adjacent faces—or a compound of 2, 3, 4, or 6 tripods. (See Figure 5.) The level-three Menger Sponge decomposes into 4 single tripods, 84 double tripods, 156 triple tripods, 84 non-planar quadruple tripods, 48 planar quadruple tripods, and 72 hextuple tripods, accounting for 80% of the total number of cubes in the sponge. (See Figure 6.)

The tripod modules were then linked together to form eight (almost) identical octants. The octants are small enough to fit through most doorways, can fit in the back of a station wagon or van, and can be easily packaged for shipping. They can be assembled into the whole by linking a small number of cubes (192) in a reasonably short period of time (8–10 hours) by just one or two people.

I decided that I wanted to panel each face of the Menger Sponge with a different color. Business cards are rarely printed on brightly colored stock, and the colors that I eventually used were rather muted: pale gray and dark gray, beige and tan, light blue and pink. I could have aquired brighter colors if I paid for the cards, but I wanted the project to be made entirely from recycled materials. One of the benefits of the tripod decomposition was that it allowed each module to be paneled prior to final assembly. Other approaches to building sponges, such as simply building layer by layer from the ground up, leave you with tunnels that are difficult, if not impossible, to panel.

3.2. Union Station. Initially, I was doubtful that I would be able to create a design for the train station that would simultaneously provide enough detail for the building to be recognizable without being too large too build. I started with a photograph of the building's facade and superimposed different sized grids on it. (See Figure 7.) After developing a suitable layout for the facade, I used additional photos to create a three-dimensional computer model for the rest of the building, eliminating the parking garage at the back of the building. This became the blueprint for a model that was around 10′ (3 m) wide, 6′ (2 m) high, and 7′ (2.5 m) deep and that used around 60–70 thousand cards.

Because the building had arches and domes, I designed a business card origami *half cube*: a cube cut in half on one of its diagonals, with flaps that could link it to its neighboring cubes. (See Figure 8.) I also developed a way to make some small peaks that attached to the building's towers.

The bulk of the structure was built by school children in grades 3–8 (ages 8–14), meeting after school one or twice a week in groups of 12–25 students. The cubes made by

FIGURE 7. Union Station with grid overlay.

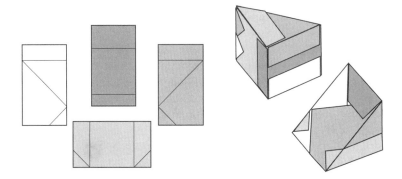

FIGURE 8. Folding half cubes.

the children were not of uniform quality and their ability to create complex shapes from them was limited. So, we taught the children to build rectangular blocks of various sizes: 2×3, 2×4, 3×4, etc. These could be used as sections of the roof or wall. (See Figure 9.) It proved impractical to properly link these panels together into sizes larger than 11×18 cubes; however, there were sections of roof that needed to be even larger, so I used cards folded like hairpins to clip the sections together.

Because the building itself is made from white stone, it was natural to make the model out of white cards. But, to raise funds for First Night Worcester, which is a nonprofit organization, we sold businesses the opportunity to have their cards incorporated into the structure with their logos showing. These were attached to one of the side walls.

The more-complex towers at the front of the building were constructed in an all-day folding event at Worcester Polytechnic Institute by members of the university's three sororities.

3.3. The Snowflake Sponge. Like the Menger Sponge, the Snowflake Sponge needed to be broken into smaller pieces for assembly. I designed two small units called X and Y modules, each consisting of 14 cubes. These were essentially level-one Snowflakes with

FIGURE 9. Worcester children with a wall section.

four cubes missing. They could be joined together by building in the missing cubes. They comprised approximately 78% of the total number of cubes. The X and Y modules were then linked to make six "towers," which were combined to make the finished sponge. The X and Y modules were simple enough for all the volunteers to make, but linking them together required the help of master folders.

Initially, I imagined that the Snowflake Sponge would rest on one of its faces, like the Menger Sponge. But, from my computer renderings I knew that people needed to be able to look down the length of the diagonal tunnels. This would require the viewer to either stand on a ladder or lie on the floor. So, I decided to mount the sponge tilted, resting on its corners to bring the diagonals to eye level. A level-one Snowflake rests on 3 corners, a level-two rests on 9, and a level-three rests on 27. This is not very many corners over which to distribute the full weight of the sponge (120 lbs/50 kg). To help distribute the weight over more cubes, I designed three cradles that were made out of plexiglass to hold the corners of the tilted sponge. They worked very well and prevented the bottom cubes from being crushed. (See Figures 10 and 11.)

The cards we used were specially designed and printed for this project. The base cards were printed on yellow with official project logos. The paneling cards were printed in USC school colors, red and gold, with designs taken from a mathematics book in the libraries' collection. The gold cards were used to line the tunnels of the sponge while the red cards paneled the exterior. In addition, a handful of solid colored red and gold cards were applied here and there to break the symmetry and add visual interest.

4. Educational Approaches

There are many mathematics and engineering lessons that can be taught using business cards models—especially the fractals. I have taught classes from second grade (7–8 years old) through high school and college.

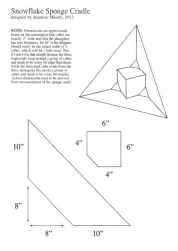

Snowflake Sponge Cradle
designed by Jeannine Mosely, 2012

FIGURE 10. Cradle design.

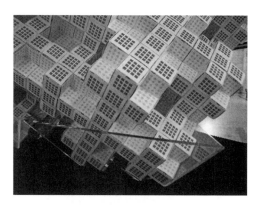

FIGURE 11. Sponge in
the cradle.

At the lowest levels, I focus on teaching mathematical language, counting, and simple geometry: This is a cube. It is folded from six rectangular pieces. When assembling the cards we match the short edge of one rectangle to the long edge of its neighbor. A cube has six faces, twelve edges, and eight corners.

With slightly older students, I introduce arithmetic: addition, multiplication, and possibly exponents. A level-one sponge is made of 20 cubes: 8 corner cubes and 12 edge cubes. A level-two sponge is made of 20 level-one sponges so it has $20 \times 20 = 400$ cubes total. How many cubes are in a level-three sponge? There are three cubes along the edge of a level-one sponge and $3 \times 3 = 9$ cubes along the edge of a level-two sponge. How many cubes are there along the edge of a level-three sponge?

Middle school students can be introduced to the idea of chirality. While individual cubes do not have handedness, some compounds of cubes (like the tripod units) do. All of the tripod units in the Menger Sponge must have the same handedness!

High school students can be introduced to recursions through the fractal sponges. How many cards are needed to panel a level-one sponge? A level-two? A level-n? Let P_n be the total number of cards needed to panel a level-n sponge, and let F_n be the number of cards needed to panel one face of a level-n sponge. It is easy to see that $F_n = 8^n$ and that

$$P_n = 20 \times P_{n-1} - 24 \times F_{n-1}.$$

Can you find a nonrecursive expression for P_n?

Convergent and divergent series can be demonstrated with the sponge. If the different-level sponges are considered to have the same starting size, with ever more and smaller tunnels through them, it can be shown that the volume of a level-n sponge goes to 0 as n goes to infinity, while the surface area increases without bound!

In addition, the concept of fractional dimension, for which fractals are famous, can be explained while teaching students about logarithms. In ordinary geometry, suppose you start with an object that has a volume of 1. When you scale it up by a factor of 2 on all sides, the resulting object will have volume $2^3 = 8$, and if you scale it by a factor of 3, the result has volume $3^3 = 27$. The power to which the scale factor is raised, 3, is the dimensionality of the object. But, if you scale a Menger Sponge by a factor of 3 on all sides, the result is another Menger Sponge whose volume is only 20 times that of the original. Hence, the dimensionality of the Menger Sponge is $\log_3(20) = 2.7268$.

An important engineering lesson for all ages is the problem of quality control. Many school children are obsessed with speed of production and strive to make as many cubes as quickly as possible with the result that many are too poorly folded to be used. Getting them to slow down and pay attention to quality without discouraging them is crucial. To begin, put everyone's cubes into the same box so that no one knows whose work is being critiqued. Then take out several cubes with varying degrees of "goodness." Ask the children to examine them and rate them, explaining the criteria. They quickly discern that the best cubes are tight with crisp creases and right angles. When a student asks you, "Is this cube good enough?" make them answer the question themselves.

5. Project Planning Lessons

I learned a lot about project planning during these endeavors.

It helps enormously to have an organization or institution backing you, especially if there are one or more invested individuals within that organization who want to see the endeavor succeed. The sponsor can provide a source of volunteers, a place for them to gather to work, a place to store the work under progress, and a place to exhibit the final sculpture. The sponsor will also help promote the project in the press and the community. It makes the difference between taking years to finish and taking months.

No matter how you break down the sculpture into smaller pieces that are easy to make, a certain amount of work will need to be done by specially trained people. While the tripods and X and Y modules of the Menger and Snowflake Sponges, respectively, represent around 80% of the volume of each, the remaining 20% of the assembly requires an expert. Most people are capable of learning these skills, but many of them don't want to make the commitment of time to do so. Making sure you have a team of capable lieutenants to perform this work is both a challenge and a necessity.

While it is very rewarding to work with younger children on projects like these, there are two major drawbacks that I have found. Their product is often too poor for inclusion in the final sculpture. While it is fairly easy to discard poorly made cubes, if a group has been working on a larger structure and has built it out of good cubes mixed with bad ones, the entire structure may be compromised and have to be thrown out. An even larger problem, though, is getting them to part with their cubes! As soon as they realize the possibilities of cube constructions, they start devising their own projects and don't want to give you their work.

Acknowledgments

I want to thank my husband and children—Allan, Martha, and Simon Wechsler—for their inspiration, encouragement, and support and for their enduring patience when the Menger Sponge took over our home for so many years. Special thanks go to Anne LaVin, Elsa Chen, and Alasdair Post-Quinn for their extraordinary contributions to the project. Jeff DelPapa helped me build the original display table for the sponge. Peg Primak drove the second van carrying four octants to New York City for the Sponge's first exhibition at the OUSA convention in 2005. My undying gratitude goes to Margaret Wertheim, of the Institute for Figuring, and Mark Allen, of Machine Project gallery, who arranged for the sponge's second exhibition in Los Angeles in 2006.

Joyce Kressler of First Night Worcester was the primary mover and shaker that made the Union Station project possible. Matt Hagopian and Grace Chan brought in last-minute volunteers to see the project through to completion when an untimely ice storm threatened our schedule.

The Snowflake Sponge would never have been built without the tireless help, planning, and promotion of Margaret Wertheim and her colleagues at the USC Libraries: Hugh McHarg, Tyson Gaskill, and Timothy Stanton. Howard Smith's extraordinary graphics helped elucidate and promote the project.

And, of course, a big thanks to all of the nearly one thousand volunteers who folded all those cards.

References

[Leeming 34] Joseph Leeming. *Fun with Paper*. New York: Lippincott, 1934.

[Peitgen and Richter 86] Hans-Otto Peitgen and Peter Richter. *The Beauty of Fractals*. Heidelberg: Springer-Verlag, 1986. MR852695 (88e:00019)

[Institute for Figuring 06] The Institute for Figuring. "The Business Card Menger's Sponge." http://theiff.org/exhibits/iff-e4.html, 2006.

[Jacobs 10] Jonathan Jacobs. "An Analysis of You Cubed as an Example of Collective Creativity." http://www.wpi.edu/Pubs/E-project/Available/E-project-060710-012032/unrestricted/jjacobsIQP.pdf, 2010.

[Wertheim 12] Margaret   Wertheim.   "An   Origami   Moment: Mathematics   Meets   Paper   Folding   in   Los   Angeles."   http://www.kcet.org/arts/artbound/counties/los-angeles/an-origami-moment-mathematics-meets-paper-folding-in-los-angeles.html, 2012.

ORIGAMI ARTIST
E-mail address: j9mosely@gmail.com

On the Aesthetics of Folding and Technology: Scale, Dimensionality, and Materiality

Matthew Gardiner

1. Introduction

The question "What is a fold?" produces simple and complex answers. Origami provides a simple answer that we can demonstrate; make a crease in a sheet of paper and there it is, done. However, this answer does not address the infinite possibilities of folding that origami artists, scientists, mathematicians, and educators know and relish, nor does it even begin to explain folds in Deoxyribonucleic Acid (DNA) chains [Rothemund 05], pleats embedded in haute couture fashion [Van Herpen 14, Miyake 15], creases in the façades of new architectural icons [Delugan Meissl Associated Architects 12], or analogies for the shape of dark matter [Abel et al. 12].

As a result of these artistic and scientific advances, the meaning of *origami* is shifting from its association as an art and craft. This is evident in the title of OSME, that origami is a science as well as an art form. The term *origami* is used in the fields of computation, biology, soft-matter, design, and fabrication to describe folding operations, functions, and stylistic approaches. *Origami* is often used as a metaphor, as very few cases literally involve the folding of a sheet of paper: DNA origami [Rothemund 05], for example. The term *origami* is being borrowed for its culturally associated image of a complex of folds, from which the materiality of paper is no longer necessary, but rather for the functional aesthetic of folding. Rather than contest or try to compartmentalize the term *origami* into its literal meaning, this paper investigates this shift through the proposition of three interdependent aesthetic and functional characteristics: dimensionality, scale, and materiality.

2. Background and Related Works

The philosophy of thought surrounding the universality and complexity of folding began in earnest with Gilles Deleuze in *The Fold: Leibniz and the Baroque* [Deleuze 06]. Treatments prior to this were principally engineering and design approaches, focused on developing systems and equations, constructed as tools for solving the mathematical problems of folding. The impact of computation in architecture and design shifted to a more theoretical landscape when Deleuze's article was reprinted in *Folding in Architecture* [Lynn 93] alongside a set of essays and example projects that evoked a more ephemeral architectural theory to address the *Free Form* or *Digital Baroque* [Eekhout 02]. These theories enveloped space structures: folded plate structures, shell structures, space frames and tensegrity structures; once inventions of the latter half of the 20th century, they are

FIGURE 1. Concrete Dürer tiles with subtle fold patterning on the upper surface.

now matured design systems. Architecture was not the only beneficiary of these theoretical advances; the structural language of origami informing theory in construction also informed tinier design targets—in materials other than paper, other than concrete, glass, and steel, but and rather in DNA or in silicon as Micro Electro Mechanical Systems (MEMS) [Pickett 09].

My efforts here are to reflect on the broad diversity of origami as the "science of matter" [Deleuze 06] and to use the process of artistic research—including speculation, computational design, and fabrication—as part of a process to address the question, "What is a fold?"

3. Dimensionality

At the beginning of my practice-led research, my intentions were focused on developing an understanding of the visual aesthetics of folds. Origami has many differing visual aesthetics, ranging from the artistic-organic "Akira Yoshizawa" style to the geometric-faceted "Tomoko Fuse" style of models. Style is a topic loaded with opinion in the broader origami community, and in my view these two artist's works bookend the stylistic extremes of origami language: one is figurative, emotive, and defined by approximations; the other is abstract, pristine (equally emotive to some), and informed by strict mathematical rules. Trends in fashion, architecture, and design have adopted folding as a stylistic language and tend toward the unit-style, geometric-faceted, aesthetic of folding, such as the *Bao Bao* bag by Issey Miyake [Miyake 15].

The aesthetic of origami and technology combines the futuristic abstracted style of mathematic–organic intersections, the wireframe and polygon views of three-dimensional modeling, and the attraction of the techno-organic in catwalk fashion [Van Herpen 14]. My examination of these stylistic shifts began with the consideration of two-dimensional tessellations, the tiling patterns, and the history of complex interlocking polygons. This research led to the idea of designing a concrete tile with a subtle folded surface. While making the drawings for a tiling design (Figure 1) of interlocking concrete blocks, I realized that the lines on the page were one-dimensional, constrained to the two dimensions of the page, and the corners were folds. My vision extended to the realisation that a fold separated each additional step toward a higher dimension (Figure 2): the fourth dimension being expansion and contraction (folding and unfolding) of all lower dimensions. The folds form the structure of each dimension.

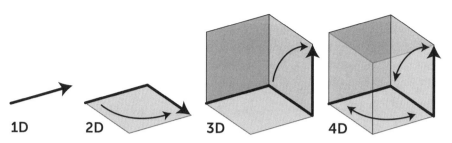

FIGURE 2. Folds define dimension, each dimensional is created by the folding/unfolding of a new dimension.

The criteria of dimensionality is used in mathematical models of origami. For DNA origami, the model is a one-dimensional string. Sheet fabrication consists mostly of two-dimensional models of crease patterns and their influence on three- and four-dimensional geometries. Several research projects have also investigated four-dimensional printing [Tibbits 14]—a fabrication process using three-dimensional printing to produce larger products in the small volume of three-dimensional printers. An object is designed and then pre-folded, using a tessellation of the surface, so that it fits into the build dimensions. The resulting three-dimensional print can then be unfolded to a larger form outside the three-dimensional printer. Research into rigid origami [Tachi 09] is an investigation into the four-dimensional (time-based morphology) and requires computational assessment of the three-dimensional folded model. In addition, the notion of architecture as manifestation of the folded surface intersects with Deleuzian architectural notions of *The Fold* [Deleuze 06], as the angular variations at the intersection of two or more planes in a building's surface is visually interpreted as "folded."

4. Scale

In the natural world, folds can be found at all scales, from the nanoscopic scale of DNA origami and protein folding [Rothemund 05] all the way up to an analogy for the dark matter sheet at the cosmological scale [Abel et al. 12]. We find folds, buckling in structural geology [Hunt 10], in Earth's topography: One can the perceive folds of landscapes (in the language of origami, the terms *mountain* and *valley* evoke such landscapes) formed by tectonic movements, a mountain range with ragged peaks, and the worn-down folds of rolling hills. Depending on the scale of magnification, a fold can appear soft and curved close up, while far away it appears sharp and pointed.

The introductory essay for my publication on the topic of origami design and materials, *Designer Origami* [Gardiner 13], attempted to position origami across scales with a diagram illustrating the scales of origami as follows: nano, origami, interior, exterior, and space. (See Figure 3.) This diagram and concept was intended for a nontechnical audience. Miyamoto's *Origami Powers of Ten* [Miyamoto 12] takes this concept even further, tabulating the scale in meters, materials, hinges, and actuators from 106–11 m up to 10^{20} m, covering DNA, proteins, MEMS, art/crafts (origami), furniture, machines, buildings, Earth, and the Solar System. This concept, based on Eames' famous *Powers of Ten* video, clearly illustrates the idea that scale is indeed an important factor in understanding what is a fold.

Scale is not simply a matter of size; it shares interdependence to the amount of force required to program a given material with a fold and the force that binds the material.

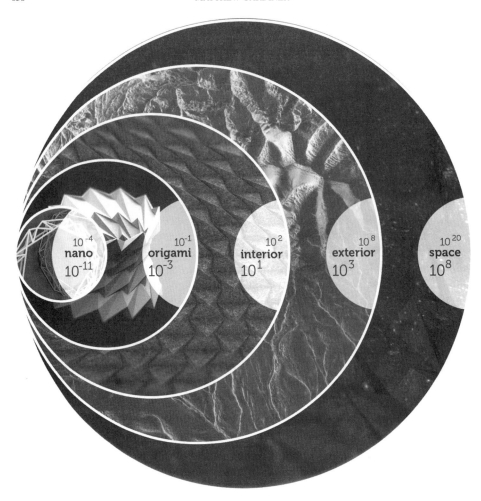

FIGURE 3. The scale of folds, from the nanoscale of DNA to the macroscale of the cosmos.

Scale also determines the structural stability of the material to resist gravity and maintain its structural integrity. For example, paper functions reliably as a material for folding from as small as 10^{-4} m up to around the 1 m scale. Any smaller or larger and the fibrous structure and the bonds between them become compromised, being either too small to fold or too large to cope with the forces of gravity.

5. Materiality

In the case of the materiality for origami scales, qualities like strength, thickness, elasticity, and plasticity equate to what we can call *foldability*. A series of paper reviews published in *The Fold* [Garibi and Vishne 10] detail qualities relevant for expert paper folding. The materiality concerns in folding and technology include foldability, but the attention in contemporary scientific circles is on the actuation and programming of kinetic material properties: the focus is on materials and material hybrids that offer actuation through shape memory, elasticity, or chemical or mechanical hinging and that allow self-folding, programmable shape-changing. Hybrid material solutions such as *Elastomeric Origami* [Martinez et al. 12] in fields like soft matter show how simple material combinations afford new possibilities for soft robotics and mechanism design. The use of traditional methods of pleating can be applied to woven materials such as polyester fabric in artistic contexts, such as *Oribotics* [Gardiner 11]. Shape-memory actuators hinging a tessellated plate structure affords the reprogrammabilty of folded sheet structures [Hawkes et al. 10], and the use of shape-memory polymer/paper composite allows self-folding by heating [Felton et al. 13]. In these applications, it is the bonding of rigid and flexible materials with differing rates of change to stimuli, such as chemistry and temperature, that affords actuation. The combination of rigid and flexible materials is exemplified by the quality of production, such as the variety of shapes afforded by the design of Issey Miyake's *Bao Bao* [Miyake 15] series of bags. This materiality can be seen as either giving "life" as movement or extending the life of the living hinge. The knowledge required for fabricating these material composites is process-based and requires experimentation and significant expertise for high-quality results. The materiality of these origami mechanisms can be generalised as material hybrids that afford the following properties: structural rigidity across the planar faces, hinged flexibility along the fold lines, and, where present, embedded actuation between adjacent folded planes.

6. Folding = Force + Matter

Folds are formed when the material and dimensional natures of an object are influenced by a force. We can categorize the intent of these forces as being either chaotic or designed.

6.1. By-chance folding. Chaotic or chance processes are produced as the result of buckling and bifurcation when a sheet is compressed by a force. Miura established a mathematical basis for studying the nature of folding by showing a set of patterns that can be found through compression [Miura 97]. The easiest kind of buckling to imagine, though difficult to predict, is the crushing of a sheet of paper into a ball. When the crumpled sheet is flattened out, we see folds made by chance and the surface has a topographical aesthetic, as if the crumpled sheet were a tiny landscape. Despite the chaotic appearance of such folds, when taken as a source of inspiration, studies of crushing and buckling have aided the discovery and generalization of well-known origami patterns such as the Yoshimura [Yoshimura 51] and Miura [Miura 70] patterns.

6.2. By-hand folding and by-code folding. Designed processes in origami are forces applied with specific intent, such as the pinching actions of fingers in shaping a sheet of paper. Artists and designers use the origami axioms to reliably make the same sequence of folds, often resulting in symmetrical geometric aesthetics, which Engel attributes to the perfection of the square and its latent symmetries [Engel 97]. Figure 4 illustrates a simple diagram of three possible approaches to making folds: *by-chance*, *by-hand*, and *by-code*. The latter example, by-code, has been derived and expanded upon in several directions depending on the design problem: specific software tools such as Treemaker [Lang 98], Origamizer [Demaine and Tachi 10, Tachi 10b], and Freeform Origami [Tachi 10a], among others allow a user to tackle specific design problems, while bespoke software applications like Grasshopper for Rhino allow a user to construct their own parametric solutions using an extensible set of components. The aesthetic of these forms dates back to the pre-computational works of Ron Resch [Resch 73] and earlier to the Bauhaus school [Wingler et al. 69]. More recent contemporary research such as Tomohiro Tachi's rigid

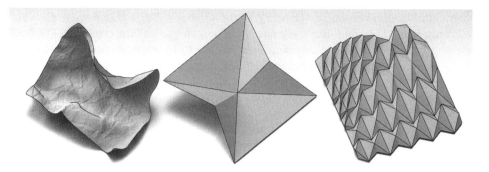

FIGURE 4. From left to right, by-chance folding (a crumpled sheet), by-hand folding (Ananas (waterbomb) base), and by-code folding (felt wall section).

FIGURE 5. A lightweight "wireframe" fold mapped around a toroid, printed in silver.

origami works, Gregory Epps' works at Robofold [Tachi and Epps 11], Daniel Piker's development of Kangaroo for Grasshopper [Piker 13], and the works of Erik and Martin Demaine—for example, *Computational Origami* as part of the exhibition "Design and the Elastic Mind" at the Museum of Modern Art [Antonelli 08]—have been pushing the definitions of what is foldable.

The aesthetic of folding and technology is by-code, infinite, developable approximations of continuous sculpted surfaces, reminiscent of tectonic topography. We find algorithmically iterated, faceted, asymmetric, dynamic forms that evoke the organic origins of buckling patterns and the undeniable precision of calculated order.

7. Fold Mapping By-Code

My recent aesthetic experiments (see Figures 5, 6, 7, 8, and 9) apply design by-code. The experiments are based on mapping discrete folding units, such as open corrugations (like the Yoshimura, Miura, and Ananas patterns), onto designed surfaces. The units can

FIGURE 6. The mapping of a folded pattern around a twisted cylinder: Queen of Diamonds 5.24.42, mesh and wireframe versions.

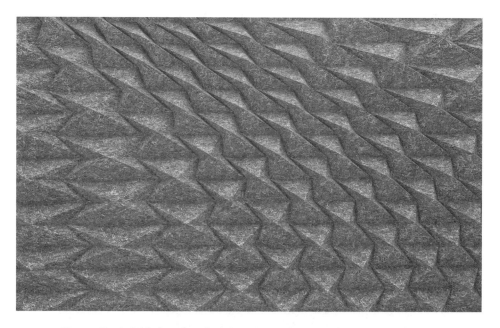

FIGURE 7. A folded surface in felt-resin composite. The base surface is a flat plane, sculpted with curved valleys and mountains of expansion and contraction.

be either designed by-hand with a specific aesthetic or functional intent, or adopted from by-chance studies of buckling. The results are continuums of discrete folded elements that form an approximation of the surface.

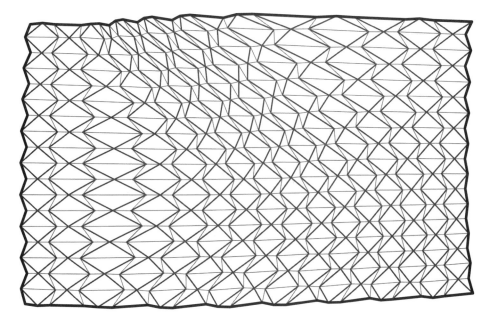

FIGURE 8. This crease pattern is a near approximation of a developable pattern of the folded surface in Figure 7 generated using the developable constraint in Freeform Origami.

FIGURE 9. Stills Fallen Future, a giant origanic leaf falls backward through time into Ho Chi Minh City, researchers mine the the artifact for future technologies.

These works differ from existing folding processes, such as those enabled by Freeform Origami [Tachi 10a], that involve interactive manipulation of a folded surface, and they begin with the design of the object and retrospectively map the folds across the design. The process takes advantage of the modeling of surfaces in Rhino, and it is combined with the PanelingTools plug-in. "PanelingTools plug-in helps generate two- and three-dimensional

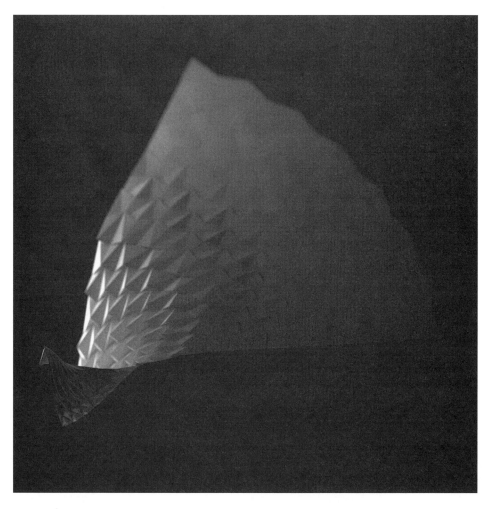

FIGURE 10. This spiral blossom explores the idea of recursive infinity through by-code fold-mapping across an algorithmically generated spiral.

cellular patterns and populate them over rectangular grids" [Issa 14]. The folding units are defined by a sets of vertices to make up the edges and faces of the folded unit in an open state. To overcome limitations in the software and to ensure the vertices of adjacent units are aligned, the folded unit is generalized such that the vertices are positioned only on positive integer (x, y, z) coordinates. The pattern mapped onto Figures 5–10 was defined as shown in Figure 11. These figures are indicative of my artistic response to the notions explored above. They explore dimensionality, materiality, and scale, and they were created with the by-code design method. Further work will involve exploration of the kinetic functions through material experimentation and fabrication.

8. Conclusion

These aesthetic experiments and theoretical statements will form the basis for further investigation. The criteria of scale, dimensionality, and materiality are shown to be relevant

VERTEX (X,Y,Z)
(4,0,0)(0,0,0)(2,1,1)(4,0,0)
(4,2,0)(0,2,0)(2,1,1)(4,2,0)
(3,1,0)(7,1,0)(5,2,1)(3,1,0)
(7,1,0)(3,1,0)(5,0,1)(7,1,0)
(5,0,1)(3,1,0)(4,0,0)(5,0,1)
(5,2,1)(4,2,0)(3,1,0)(5,2,1)
(2,1,1)(3,1,0)(4,2,0)(2,1,1)
(3,1,0)(2,1,1)(4,0,0)(3,1,0)
(6,0,0)(5,0,1)(7,1,0)(6,0,0)
(5,2,1)(6,2,0)(7,1,0)(5,2,1)
(1,1,0)(2,1,1)(0,2,0)(1,1,0)
(2,1,1)(1,1,0)(0,0,0)(2,1,1)

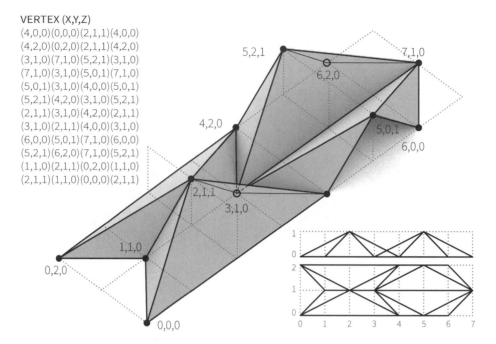

FIGURE 11. Set of faces defined by a string of (x, y, z) vertex coordinates (top left). The open folded pattern with annotated vertex points (center). Side and top views showing vertices constrained to a grid (bottom right).

in understanding the aesthetics of folding and technology. In addition, the aesthetics of folding and technology are deeply informed by the methods of fold programming: by-chance, by-hand, and by-code. These criteria and methods continue to be a rich field for studies in new aesthetics for the artist, researcher, engineer, and scientist alike.

References

[Abel et al. 12] Tom Abel, Oliver Hahn, and Ralf Kaehler. "Tracing the Dark Matter Sheet in Phase Space." *Monthly Notices of the Royal Astronomical Society* 427:1 (2012), 61–76.

[Antonelli 08] Paola Antonelli, curator. *Design and the Elastic Mind.* Art exhibition, The Museum of Modern Art, New York, NY, 2008

[Delugan Meissl Associated Architects 12] Delugan Meissl Associated Architects. "EYE Film Institute Netherlands." http://www.dmaa.at/projekte/detail-page/eye-film-institute.html, 2012.

[Deleuze 06] Gilles Deleuze. *The Fold: Leibniz and the Baroque.* London: Continuum, 2006.

[Demaine and Tachi 10] Erik Demaine and Tomohiro Tachi. "Origamizer: A Practical Algorithm for Folding Any Polyhedron." Manuscript, 2010.

[Eekhout 02] M. Eekhout. "Design, Engineering, Production and Realisation of Spatial Glass Structures for 'Digital Baroque' Architecture." *Space Structures* 5:1 (2002): 123.

[Engel 97] Peter Engel. "Breaking Symmetry: Origami, Architecture, and the Forms of Nature." In *Origami Science and Art: Proceedings of the Second International Meeting of Origami Science and Scientific Origami,* edited by K. Miura, pp. 119–130. Shiga, Japan: Seian University of Art and Design, 1997.

[Felton et al. 13] Samuel M. Felton, Michael T. Tolley, ByungHyun Shin, Cagdas D. Onal, Erik D. Demaine, Daniela Rus, and Robert J. Wood. "Self-Folding with Shape Memory Composites." *Soft Matter* 9:32 (2013), 7688–7694.

[Gardiner 11] Matthew Gardiner. "Oribotics: The Future Unfolds." In *Origami⁵: Fifth International Meeting of Origami Science, Mathematics, and Education,* edited by Patsy Wang-Iverson, Robert J. Lang, and Mark Yim, pp 127–137. Boca Raton, FL: A K Peters/CRC Press, 2011. MR2866909 (2012h:00044)

[Gardiner 13] Matthew Gardiner. *Designer Origami*. Melbourne: Hinkler Books PTY, Limited, 2013.

[Garibi and Vishne 10] Ilan Garibi and Gadi Vishne. "Paper Review #1: Elephant Hide." *The Fold* 1 (2010), https://origamiusa.org/thefold/article/paper-review-1-elephant-hide.

[Hawkes et al. 10] Elliot Hawkes, B. Nadia Benbernou, Hiroto Tanaka, Sangbae Kim, Erik D. Demaine, Daniella Rus, and Robert J. Wood. "Programmable Matter by Folding." *Proceedings of the National Academy of Sciences* 107:28 (2010), 12441–12445.

[Hunt 10] Giles W. Hunt. "Reflections and Symmetries in Space and Time." *IMA Journal of Applied Mathematics*, 76:1 (2010), 2–26. MR2764271 (2011k:74045)

[Issa 14] Rajaa Issa. "Panelling Tools." *McNeel Wiki*, http://wiki.mcneel.com/labs/panelingtools, 2014.

[Lang 98] Robert J. Lang. "Treemaker 4.0: A Program for Origami Design." http://www.langorigami.com/science/computational/treemaker/TreeMkr40.pdf, 1998.

[Lynn 93] Greg Lynn. *Folding in Architecture*. Chichester: Academy Press, 1993.

[Martinez et al. 12] Ramses V. Martinez, Carina R. Fish, Xin Chen, and George M. Whitesides. "Elastomeric Origami: Programmable Paper-Elastomer Composites as Pneumatic Actuators." *Advanced Functional Materials* 22:7 (2012), 1376–1384.

[Miura 97] Koryo Miura (editor). *Origami Science and Art: Proceedings of the Second International Meeting of Origami Science and Scientific Origami*. Shiga, Japan: Seian University of Art and Design, 1997.

[Miura 70] Koryo Miura. "Proposition of Pseudo-Cylindrical Concave Polyhedral Shells." *ISAS Report* 34:9 (1970), 141–163. (Available at http://ci.nii.ac.jp/naid/110001101617/en/.)

[Miyamoto 12] Yoshinobu Miyamoto. "Expanded/Extended Origami Design." Talk given to Japanese Origami Academic Society, Tokyo, Japan, December 16, 2012.

[Miyake 15] Issey Miyake. "Bao Bao Issey Miyake." http://www.baobaoisseymiyake.com/, 2013.

[Pickett 09] G. T. Pickett. "Origami-Inspired Self-Assembly." In *Origami^4: Fourth International Meeting of Origami Science, Mathematics, and Education*, edited by Robert J. Lang, pp. 101–116. Wellesley, MA: A K Peters, 2009. MR2590567 (2010h:00025)

[Piker 13] Daniel Piker. "Kangaroo: Form Finding with Computational Physics." *Architectural Design* 83:2 (2013), 136–137.

[Resch 73] Ronald D. Resch. "The Topological Design of Sculptural and Architectural Systems." In *Proceedings of the June 4–8, 1973, National Computer Conference and Exposition*, pp. 643–650. New York: ACM, 1973.

[Rothemund 05] P. W. K. Rothemund. "Design of DNA Origami." In *Proceedings of the 2005 IEEE/ACM International Conference on Computer-Aided Design, ICCAD '05*, pp. 471–478. Los Alamitos, CA: IEEE Computer Society, 2005.

[Tachi and Epps 11] Tomohiro Tachi and Gregory Epps. "Designing One-DOF Mechanisms for Architecture by Rationalizing Curved Folding." Paper presented at International Symposium on Algorithmic Design for Architecture and Urban Design (ALGODE-AIJ), Tokyo, Japan, March 14–16, 2011.

[Tachi 09] Tomohiro Tachi. "Generalization of Rigid-Foldable Quadrilateral-Mesh Origami." *Journal of the International Association for Shell and Spatial Structures (IASS)* 50:3 (2009), 173–179.

[Tachi 10a] Tomohiro Tachi. "Freeform Variations of Origami." *Journal for Geometry and Graphics* 14:2 (2010), 203–215. MR2799369

[Tachi 10b] Tomohiro Tachi. "Origamizing Polyhedral Surfaces." *IEEE Transactions on Visualization and Computer Graphics* 16:2 (2010), 298–311.

[Tibbits 14] Skylar Tibbits. "4D Printing: Multi-Material Shape Change." *Architectural Design* 84:1 (2014), 116–121.

[Van Herpen 14] Iris Van Herpen. "Iris van Herpen—Magnetic Motion." http://www.irisvanherpen.com/womenswearmagnetic-motion, 2014.

[Wingler et al. 69] H. M. Wingler, J. Stein, W. Jabs, and B. Gilbert. "The Bauhaus Dessau: 1925–1932" In *The Bauhaus: Weimar, Dessau, Berlin, Chicago*, edited by H. M. Wingler, pp. 430–435. Cambridge, MA: MIT Press, 1969.

[Yoshimura 51] Yoshimaru Yoshimura. "On the Mechanism of Buckling of a Circular Cylindrical Shell under Axial Compression." Technical report, No. NACA-TM-1390, National Advisory Committee for Aeronautics, 1951.

ARS ELECTRONICA FUTURELAB, LINZ, AUSTRIA AND SCHOOL OF CREATIVE ARTS, UNIVERSITY OF NEWCASTLE, NEWCASTLE, AUSTRALIA

E-mail address: hello@matthewgardiner.net http://matthewgardiner.net

Computational Problems Related to Paper Crane in the Edo Period

Jun Maekawa

1. Historical Background

First, I will briefly explain some background history of Japan from the seventeenth to the nineteenth centuries and provide an outline of Wasan.

In the early seventeenth century, the civil wars that had lasted over a century in the Japanese Islands all but ended and the feudal regime of the Tokugawa clan was established. That regime lasted about 250 years, until the political restoration around 1870 (Meiji Ishin). The period is commonly called the Edo era because the practical capital was placed at Edo (now Tokyo). Its policies included prohibitions against Christianity missionary activities and overseas traffic and severe restrictions on foreign trade, a policy later called Sakoku (National Seclusion). Sakoku had a great influence on Japanese culture. Many elements of what is now regarded as Japanese culture matured in this protected environment. One of these cultural elements is Wasan.

Wasan is a type of mathematics whose notations, constructions of logic, and configurations of problems came from China. Some suggest it also includes influence of the mathematics that was introduced by Christianity missionaries of the late sixteenth and the early seventeenth centuries; however, the details of this influence are not clear. The word *Wasan* became commonly used after Western mathematics was imported in the nineteenth century, with Wasan describing the Japanese mathematics to distinguish it from its Western counterpart (Yo-san).

Wasan was highly developed owing largely to a genius named Seki Takakazu (1642?–1708).[1] His achievements, including invention of the concept equivalent to the matrix determinant, yielded a big leap in Wasan. Seki was deified after his death, and the mainstream of Wasan came to be called Seki-ryu (the Seki school), which led to a factionalism wherein the Seki school's accomplishments were kept secret.

Wasan maintained little connection with sciences besides calendar-making and measuring—that is, in contrast to its counterpart in the West, which became the basis for the scientific and industrial revolutions of that time. Other shortcomings of Wasan are a lack of systematization and disinterest in logical proofs.

In 1855, the Tokugawa regime founded the Nagasaki Naval Training Center, where Western mathematics was adopted. The centralized government that was established later also accepted Western mathematics for elementary education in the course of their swift modernization program. Thus, Wasan rapidly became obsolete.

---

[1] The Japanese names in the text and bibliography of this paper are written in the order of Family name then given name.

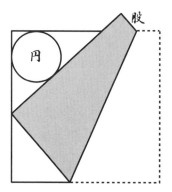

FIGURE 1. Problem on a Sangaku at Kuroiwa Kokuzo-do Temple: the length of the segment labeled with a Chinese character equals the radius of the circle.

One of the positive aspects of Wasan is that it spread widely across societal classes. It was taught in private schools all over Japan as not only practical calculations or measurements but also sophisticated problems purely for fun. There was little distinction between the classes, and there were female students. The practitioners of Wasan sometimes offered to a shrine or a temple a board on which they colorfully described geometric or other mathematical problems along with their solutions. Such offerings are called *Sangaku*. Sangaku represents the penetration of mathematics into the general public. There still remain about 1,000 examples of Sangaku.

For details on Wasan in English, see, for example [Ogura 93].

2. Origami-Related Problems in Wasan

Around 30 problems in Wasan that (in my subjective judgment) relate to origami can be found in Sangaku and some books. They can be classified in several types, each of which is shown here with a representative example.

2.1. Type 1: Problems on shapes of folded paper. The first type embraces problems about the properties of figures that are made by folding square or simple-shaped paper. A prominent example of this type is the problem on a Sangaku at Kuroiwa Kokuzo-do Temple, Fukushima (Nakamura Kumajiro, 1893) [Fukushima 89]. Fold a corner of a square to a point on one of the edges that does not include the corner, and inscribe a circle in one of the triangles. Then, the radius of the circle equals the length of a line segment that is made by the fold (Figure 1).

In this problem, the circle is not brought into contact with the crease line. By doing that, further investigation is possible [Maekawa 11].

2.2. Type 2: Problems on centroids of folded planes. The second type includes problems on centroids of folded planes. In one example that was on a Sangaku at Okunitma Shrine, Fuchu, Tokyo (Tomizawa Rinkichi, 1865, now missing), the goal is to place a string to hang a folded square paper so that the crease line will be horizontal (Figure 2) [Sato 79, Maekawa 12b].

2.3. Type 3: Problems on numerical computations about origami models. The third type contains problems on numerical computations about known origami models or similar shapes. A problem on a Sangaku at Kitano Shrine, Fujioka, Gunma (Kishi Juho?,

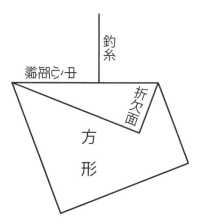

FIGURE 2. Problem on a Sangaku at Okunitma Shrine: locate the point to make the edge horizontal.

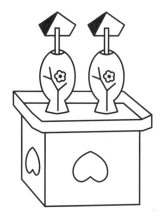

FIGURE 3. Problem on a Sangaku at Kitano Shrine: Find the ratio of the rectangle when the colored face is the largest for a given length of the long side of the rectangle.

1891) is an example (Figure 3) [Gunma 87, Maekawa 12a]. This problem about a decoration for sake bottles (rectangle sheets folded in half) asks one to calculate the ratio of the sheet when the largest area of the colored side is seen in front for a given length of the long side of the rectangle.

3. Problems about Paper Crane and Similar Problems

I have identified eight problems about the paper crane and three similar problems (on the frog instead of the crane) among the problems of the third type described in the previous section. Table 1 shows a list of them. Every problem asks one to compute the length of a part of an origami model.

These problems are presumed to have come into existence in the following way. The origin of Problem A is that it was created by Watanabe Kazu (1767–1839). Watanabe created the problem shortly after 1800, according to his biographical facts [Fukushima 77a, Fukushima 77b]. Problems B, C, and D are quotations from A. They are essentially the

Prob.	Type	Title/Location	Creator of Problem	Author	Year	Fig.	Note/Reference
A	Manuscript	Sanpo Nento Shoshi Shu	Watanabe Kazu	Aida Yasuaki	1805?		Missing
B	Manuscript	Sanpo Mi no Kagen	Watanabe Kazu	Watanabe Kazu	1830	4	[Fukushima 77a, Fukushima 77b]
C	Scrapbook	Sanpo Kenbun Shu	Watanabe Kazu	Saito Shozen	1850	5	Yamagata University Kojirakawa Library
D	Book	Toyo Sanpo	Watanabe Kazu	Sakuma Tsuzuki	1853	6	Tohoku University Library
E	Manuscript	Sanpo Shogaku Senmon Ki	–	Hodoji Zen	1859?	–	[Fujii 97]
F	Manuscript	Sanpo Zatsumon Kidai	–	Hodoji Zen	1859	–	[Fujii 97] Problem of frog
G	Manuscript	Jurinji Hogaku Sandai	–	Hodoji Zen	1865?	–	[Fujii 97] Problem of frog
H	Sangaku	Ryuko Temple (Inzai, Chiba)	–	Kojima Takakazu	1861	–	Missing [Hirayama et al. 70, Maekawa 12c]
I	Sangaku	Ichinomiya Shrine (Inzai, Chiba)	–	Itokawa Keizaburo	1877	7	[Hirayama et al. 70, Maekawa 12c]
J	Sangaku	Ichida Shrine (Yamagata, Yamagata)	–	Komazawa Seijiro	1917	8	The text is illegible. [Hirayama and Matsuoka 66]
K	Sangaku	Ohara-Katori Shrine (Kasama, Ibaraki)	–	Hagiwara Teisuke	1927	9	[Matsuzaki 97] Problem of frog

TABLE 1. Problems about the paper crane and problems alike.

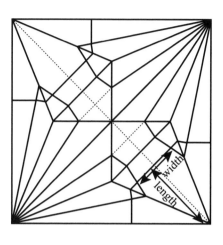

FIGURE 4. Problem in "Sanpo Mi no Kagen" (traced, not photocopied): B in Table 1 (left), and the crease pattern of the paper crane explaining the problem (right).

same in terms of being problems that ask the relation between the width and the length of the paper crane's wing. The figures are different in shape from the common paper crane, as described in Section 4.

The followings is the content of this document literally translated, but using modern mathematical notation. The notation of Wasan is different from what we imagine, being written in Chinese characters.

Question: When the width of the wing is 1, what is the length of the wing?
Answer: It is 1.74830287 and a fraction.

Procedure: $\dfrac{\sqrt{2 - \sqrt{2}} \cdot \sqrt{2 + \sqrt{2}} + 1}{2}$

Figure 5 is part of a scrapbook assembled by Sakuma, the author of Problem D (Figure 6). The author of Problem C, Saito, dated it as February in the year of the Dog, in the lunisolar calendar used at that time. Though Sakuma assumed the year to be 1862, I believe it is 1850 because Saito perished in January 1862.

Sakuma Tsuzuki (1820–1896) studied mathematics under Watanabe and became a leading educator. He belonged to a school of Saijo-ryu, scholars of which tended to dislike the idea of concealing problems and answers, which was the practice of the Seki-ryu school. I speculate that Problems E to K were some results of Sakuma's diffusion across schools, but we only have weak evidence for this presumption.

Problem J was dedicated on the centennial of the death of Aida Yasuaki, author of Problem A. Its answer appears to contain an error, according to my calculations. It was written in a period when Wasan was almost obsolete, which shows that the custom of Sangaku had continued in a reduced scale.

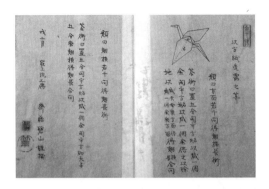

FIGURE 5. Crane problem described by Saito Shozen (Yamagata University Koji-rakawa Library, photographed by Maekawa): C in Table 1.

FIGURE 6. Crane problem in *Toyo Sanpo* (Tohoku University Library): D in Table 1.

FIGURE 7. Sangaku at Ichinomiya Shrine (photographed by Maekawa). The problem is illegible: I in Table 1.

FIGURE 8. Sangaku at Ichida Shrine (part; photographed by Maekawa): J in Table 1.

4. Solution to the Crane Problem and Inference on Creation

Here we present the basic idea to solve the problem of the crane wing dimensions. First of all, people at that time must have known how to fold the paper crane. It is reasonable to assume that they used the crease pattern shown in Figure 4.

The key to the solution is the computation of trigonometric functions of $11.25°$, one-eighth of the right angle. Only the Pythagorean Theorem will be needed for the calculation if we draw additional lines to make an isosceles triangle as shown in Figure 10. To solve this problem, as well as many problems in Wasan, no technical knowledge was required, which makes them useful in today's education.

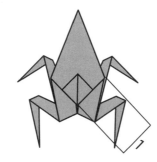

FIGURE 9. Trace from Sangaku at Ohara-Katori Shrine: Asks the length of a side of the square when the length in the figure of the origami frog is 1: K in Table 1.

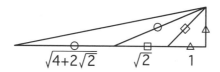

$$\sqrt{4+2\sqrt{2}} \qquad \sqrt{2} \qquad 1$$

FIGURE 10. Calculating trigonometric functions of 11.25° using the Pythagorean Theorem.

It is also straightforward to solve the problem with the trigonometric half-angle formulas. These formulas were known in Wasan. Watanabe himself is likely to have used them, considering their relation to the problem on π mentioned in Section 5.

Now I would like to infer where Watanabe got the idea for the problem. As stated above, it appears that Watanabe got the idea somewhere within a few years after 1800. *Senbazuru Orikata* (Akisato Rito, 1797)[2] had been published a few years before. This book shows how to fold various connected cranes from rectangular sheets with cuts. So, it is a kind of puzzle book themed on the paper crane. In addition, it contains the crease pattern of the crane. This synchrony is interesting, though we do not have enough evidence to conclude that *Senbazuru Orikata* directly related to Watanabe's problem.

In Wasan, both mathematical content and sophistication of the idea were important. The reason why this problem was repeatedly reproduced is likely because the connection between mathematics and craft was thought to be surprising and in good taste. As said in the introduction, Wasan had an aspect as recreation that is not necessarily practical.

On the other hand, Watanabe was a scientist/engineer aiming at rational thought, and he emphasized the importance of natural observation in his *Sugaku Hyouri Ben* (Watanabe, 1812)[3] and other books. In this respect, the figure of the crane is notable. The paper crane is depicted with its "tail" horizontal (see Figures 4, 5, and 6). It is raised upward in most books of today and in older texts. From the viewpoint of realism, we cannot tell whether the "tail" flap represents legs or a tail in that design. I suspect that Watanabe drew it horizontally because of his inclination to realism, aiming at expressing the lined-up legs to agree with those of an actual flying crane.

---

[2]Belongs to Japan Origami Academic Society Library.
[3]Belongs to Yamagata University Kojirakawa Library.

FIGURE 11. Problem on π in *Sanpo Min no Kagen* by Watanabe.

5. Relation between the Crane Problem and π

Fukagawa Hidetoshi, a scholar specialized in Wasan, points out the relationship between the crane problem and a formula for π in *Toyo Sanpo* [Fukagawa 98]. To summarize his assertion, he wondered if Sakuma independently discovered the formula (equivalent to the formula of Franciscus Vieta (1540–1603) [Hirayama 61]), but became convinced that Sakuma surely did when he solved the crane problem that was placed next to the formula of π in *Toyo Sanpo*.

I have two comments on this. As mentioned above, the crane problem, as well as the formula for π in Sakuma's *Toyo Sanpo*, was created by Watanabe. Sakuma just quoted them. Adding to Sakuma's honor, Sakuma made it clear that he quoted them. Second, the two problems are not placed next to each other in Watanabe's book. However, as Fukagawa points out, questions seeking to calculate trigonometric functions of $90°/(2n)$ have something in common with Watanabe's formula of π.

The crane problem is in the supplement of *Sanpo Min no Kagen* (which consists of five volumes, one additional volume, and a supplement), whereas the π problem is in Volume 4 (Figure 11).

The following is the content of this document literally translated, but (again) using modern mathematical notation. The table in Figure 11 shows the calculated values of every step.

Question: What is $\pi/4$?
Answer: It is 0.78539816339744830961566084581987572104929234984377 and a fraction.
Procedure: Repeat the following calculation:

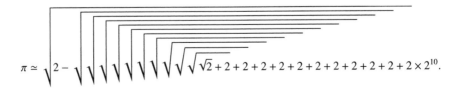

$$\pi \simeq \sqrt{2 - \sqrt{\sqrt{\sqrt{\sqrt{\sqrt{\sqrt{\sqrt{\sqrt{\sqrt{\sqrt{\sqrt{2} + 2} + 2} + 2} + 2} + 2} + 2} + 2} + 2} + 2} + 2} + 2 \times 2^{10}}}.$$

The serial structure of the derivation of this formula is easily understood by using the half-angle formula:

$$\sin 45 = \frac{\sqrt{2}}{2}, \qquad\qquad \cos 45 = \frac{\sqrt{2}}{2}$$

$$\sin 22.5 = \sqrt{\frac{1 - \cos 45}{2}} = \frac{\sqrt{2 - \sqrt{2}}}{2}, \qquad \cos 22.5 = \sqrt{\frac{1 + \cos 45}{2}} = \frac{\sqrt{2 + \sqrt{2}}}{2}$$

$$\sin 11.25 = \sqrt{\frac{1 - \cos 22.5}{2}} \qquad\qquad \cos 11.25 = \sqrt{\frac{1 + \cos 22.5}{2}}$$

$$= \frac{\sqrt{2 - \sqrt{2 + \sqrt{2}}}}{2}, \qquad\qquad = \frac{\sqrt{2 + \sqrt{2 + \sqrt{2}}}}{2}.$$

As stated above, the crane problem can also be solved using the half-angle formula. It is reasonable to suppose that Watanabe related the crane problem to the formula of π. The crane problem was possibly not only witty and attractive but also important for Watanabe and Sakuma.

There is, however, a problem with Watanabe's description. The forty-digit value for $\pi/4$ is, though accurate, difficult to calculate using his method. His formula was inductively derived from the calculation of perimeters of regular n^2-gons, a method that dates back to Archimedes. With this method, however, we can only be precise to at most the sixth decimal place, even if we use an 8192-gon as calculated in Figure 11. It is obvious that the forty digits were not computed with the formula.

The value appears to have been quoted from the result of Tatebe Katahiro (1664–1739). Tatebe was a mathematician whom Seki directly taught, and who calculated π to the 41st decimal place by considering perimeters of regular 2^n-gons as a sequence that is getting progressively more accurate and inferring its limit inductively. The number of digits is the same as Watanabe's description. This computing method is equivalent to Romberg's method [Ogawa and Hirano 03]. Tatebe also obtained the following formula in 1722, which is the same as that of Leonhard Euler (1707–1783) [Hirayama 61]:

$$\pi^2 = 9 \left(1 + \frac{1^2}{3 \cdot 4} + \frac{1^2 \cdot 2^2}{3 \cdot 4 \cdot 5 \cdot 6} + \frac{1^2 \cdot 2^2 \cdot 3^2}{3 \cdot 4 \cdot 5 \cdot 6 \cdot 7 \cdot 8} + \cdots \right).$$

This formula converges much faster than Watanabe's and is easy to calculate. Watanabe probably presented this method as his own discovery. I assume Watanabe meant the following by his description:

> We need to compute infinitely to obtain the value of π. I present a value computed by Tatebe as a relatively accurate one. We can calculate the value of π infinitely with my procedure, too. The results will be the same at infinity.

6. Conclusion

Over 200 years ago, when origami made great strides, there were some pioneers who studied origami mathematically. The problems they created can be categorized into several types. In this paper, I have examined a problem seeking the length of a part of the paper crane. The problem is a numerical calculation using trigonometric functions, and it is interesting because it relates to the calculation of π. It would be a pity if this problem becomes buried in history, as it can be useful even today as a mathematics educational tool.

Origami has an aspect as a mathematical puzzle, solved for fun. The same is true for Wasan. In the Edo era, Japan had many problems from the viewpoint of modern values such as human rights and liberty. So, the assertion that the past was a utopia, which is occasionally observed, is not true. We can appreciate, however, research carried out for fun by many people who directed their efforts to cultural pursuits partly because they had few civil wars. Origami and Wasan are examples of such explorations as recreation.

Acknowledgments

In writing this paper in English, I had help from Hatori Koshiro and Robert J. Lang. In addition, I obtained the support of Tohoku University Library, Yamagata University Kojirakawa Library, Ryuko Temple, and Sakuma Motomu, a descendant of Sakuma Tsuzuki.

References

[Fujii 97] Fujii Sadao. "Origami to Wasan." *Sanyo Wasan Kenkyukai Kaishi* 32 (1997), 30–36. (In Japanese.)

[Fukagawa 98] Fukagawa Hidetoshi. *Reidai de Shiru Nihon no Sugaku to Sangaku.* Tokyo: Morikita Shuppan, 1998. (In Japanese.)

[Fukushima 77a] Fukushima-ken Wasan Kenkyu Hozon Kai. *Sanpo Mi no Kagen.* Fukushima: Fukushima-ken Wasan Kenkyu Hozon Kai, 1977. (In Japanese.)

[Fukushima 77b] Fukushima-ken Wasan Kenkyu Hozon Kai. *Sanpo Mi no Kagen ni Tsuite.* Fukushima: Fukushima-ken Wasan Kenkyu Hozon Kai, 1977. (In Japanese.)

[Fukushima 89] Fukushima-ken Wasan Kenkyu Hozon Kai. *Fukushima no Sangaku.* Fukushima: Soki Shuppan, 1989. (In Japanese.)

[Gunma 87] Gunma-ken Wasan Kenkyu Kai. *Gunma no Sangaku.* Takasaki: Gunma-ken Wasan Kenkyu Kai, 1987. (In Japanese.)

[Hirayama 61] Hirayama Akira. *Wasan no Rekishi—Sono Honshitsu to Hatten.* Tokyo: Chikuma Shobo, 2007. (Original published in 1961; in Japanese.)

[Hirayama and Matsuoka 66] Hirayama Akira and Matsuoka Motohisa. *Yamagata no Sangaku.* Yamagata: Hirayama, 1966. (In Japanese.)

[Hirayama et al. 70] Hirayama Akira, Ohno Seiji, and Mihashi Aiko. *Chiba-ken no Sangaku.* Narita: Narita-san Shiryokan, 1970. (In Japanese.)

[Maekawa 11] Maekawa Jun. "Origami Theorems from WASAN." *Science of Origami* 1:1 (2011), 23–30. (In Japanese.)

[Maekawa 12a] Maekawa Jun. "Orikata Sanpo Sanpo Part 1." *Origami Tanteidan Magazine* 23:2 (2012), 14–15. (In Japanese.)

[Maekawa 12b] Maekawa Jun. "Orikata Sanpo Sanpo Part 2." *Origami Tanteidan Magazine* 23:3 ïijĹ2012ïijĽ, 14–15. (In Japanese.)

[Maekawa 12c] Maekawa Jun. "Orikata Sanpo Sanpo Part 3." *Origami Tanteidan Magazine* 23:4 ïijĹ2012ïijĽ, 14–15. (In Japanese.)

[Matsuzaki 97] Matsuzaki Toshio. *Ibaraki no Sangaku.* Ushiku: Tsukuba Shorin, 1997. (In Japanese.)

[Ogawa and Hirano 03] Ogawa Tsukane and Hirano Yoichi. *Sugaku no Rekishi—Wasan to Seiyo Sugaku no Hatten.* Tokyo: Asakura Shoten, 2003. (In Japanese.)

[Ogura 93] Ogura Kinnosuke (translated by Ise Norio). *Wasan: Japanese Mathematics.* Tokyo: Kodansha, 1993.

[Sato 79] Sato Ken-ichi. *Tama no Sangaku.* Tokyo: Kensei-sha, 1979. (In Japanese.)

NATIONAL ASTRONOMICAL OBSERVATORY OF JAPAN, TOKYO, JAPAN
E-mail address: jun.maekawa@nao.ac.jp

Mitate and Origami

Koshiro Hatori

1. Introduction

In his series of articles titled "Schemes of Origami Criticism" [Nishikawa90], Nishikawa Seiji insists that origami involves *mitate*,[1] which roughly means "likening a thing to something else." As an example, he considers an origami elephant: its long, narrow flap will be seen as a trunk; its lower, shorter flaps as tusks; and the four flaps at the bottom as legs—thus, the whole artwork will be seen as an elephant.

Nishikawa's series was published in the first issues of *Origami Tanteidan Newsletter* (now *Origami Tanteidan Magazine*). Three years later, he also published a series of articles in the first issues of the now-defunct *Oru*. In this series, "Creatures Design Courses," he maintains that origami is an art of mitate [Nishikawa93].

Nishikawa argues that origami designers look for novel shapes or patterns in folded paper. When a designer finds a shape, he or she sees it as something—a bird's head, an insect's leg, an elephant's trunk, and so forth. Then, the designer combines such patterns to complete an origami work representing a crane, an insect, an elephant, etc. [Nishikawa93]. He asserts, in short, that mitate plays an important role in designing origami models. This view of origami design is now popular among Japanese paper folders.[2]

The notion of mitate itself, however, is sufficiently complex that careful analysis is required when applying it to origami. In fact, whereas Nishikawa mentions caricature portraits and shadow pictures as examples of mitate expression [Nishikawa90], mitate can be identified in other traditional Japanese arts such as *haiku*, *ukiyo-e*, and *kabuki*.

2. Mitate in Traditional Japanese Arts

If you look up the word *mitate* (見立て) in a Japanese dictionary, you will find several different meanings: choosing something good-looking (clothes, prostitutes,

---

In this paper, Japanese names are written with the surname first and the given name last.

[1]In an interview, Nishikawa recalls that he became aware of this idea around 1990 while talking to Okamura Masao, who might have been the first to apply the concept of mitate to origami [Sojusha95].

[2]See, for example, Kasahara Kunihiko's *Joy of Origami* [Kasahara96] and Maekawa Jun's *Genuine Origami* [Maekawa07].

etc.); diagnosis, identification, or judgment by an expert; seeing someone off; or likening a thing to something else. This study is concerned with the latter definition. This usage of the word originally came from *haikai* poetry[3] [Hayakawa95].

Mitate in haikai is a rhetorical device that can be compared to simile and metaphor. It was frequently used by Matsunaga Teitoku and his followers (the Tei-mon school) in the seventeenth century. As an example, Amagasaki Akira identified Shōi's haikai 散る花は音なしの滝と言ひつべし [Amagasaki88] from *Kefukigusa*, an anthology assembled by Matsue Shigeyori, a member of the Tei-mon school.[4] This haikai translates literally as "The falling cherry blossoms should be claimed to be a soundless waterfall." When cherry blossoms are in full bloom, large amounts of petals fall continuously to the ground. The poet observed such a scene (in actuality or imaginarily) and likened it to a waterfall.

Mitate, or metaphor, plays a significant role in the Japanese garden (*nihon teien*), which dates back to at least the seventh century. Japanese gardens often have ponds with islands, which are metaphors for oceans and mountains [Isozaki90]. In a typical *karesansui*-style garden (commonly called a Zen garden), the sea is represented by white sand instead of a pond, and the mountains are not islands but rocks.[5] In general, Japanese gardens are miniature representations of landscapes with mountains and bodies of water.

The islands or rocks in Japanese gardens often represent Mount Shumi[6], the center of the universe in Buddhist cosmology, or Mount Hōrai[7], a legendary island in Chinese mythology where immortals are said to live [Tanaka94]. A virtual Mount Hōrai is often accompanied by cranes and turtles—symbols of immortality—which are also represented by islands or rocks.

The form of mitate found in tea ceremonies (*chanoyu*, *chadō*, or *sadō*) differs somewhat from metaphor in that two things are compared not visually but functionally. That is, ordinary objects are not only seen but actually used as tea utensils.[8] Sen no Rikyū, who perfected the modern tea ceremony in the sixteenth century, utilized a bamboo creel or a gourd bottle as a vase [Sen10], while his mentor Takeno Jōō used a well bucket or a wooden pail as a carafe [Tsutsui08].

Rakugo, or traditional Japanese vernacular comedy, also relies on mitate. Rakugo is a form of storytelling entertainment performed by one person who sits on a cushion (*zabuton*) and uses hand props consisting of only a fan (*sensu*) and a towel (*tenugui*). The rakugo actor depicts a long story (sometimes up to an hour) in this very limited stage setting. As such, the performer has to express many things using only the fan and towel. A closed fan, for example, is seen as a sword, pipe, or pair of chopsticks; a half-open fan as a tray or wine glass; and a folded towel as a purse or notebook [Amagasaki95].

---

[3]*Haikai* is the original form of *haiku*. Haikai emerged in the sixteenth century, from which haiku was derived in the late nineteenth century.

[4]Shigeyori listed *mitate* and *tatoe* among the good styles of haikai composition [Matsue43]; these are equivalent to simile and metaphor, respectively. I do not, however, discriminate between simile and metaphor since the distinction only makes sense in literature.

[5]*Karesansui* translates literally as "dry mountains and waters."

[6]It is called Mount Meru in India. *Shumi* (*Xumi* in Chinese) is the phonetic transliteration of the Sanskrit word *Sumeru*, which means "Great Meru."

[7]It is equivalent to Mount Penglai in Chinese.

[8]Here, the meaning of "mitate" is closer to "choosing something good-looking."

Mitate-e (literally, "mitate picture") is a genre of *ukiyo-e* woodprint where Japanese or Chinese classics are depicted with the characters replaced by contemporary townspeople. In the context of ukiyo-e, mitate is often translated as "parody" since mitate-e prints typically have a humorous tone. In fact, such pictures were often described in the eighteenth century not as mitate but *yatsushi*, which means "reworking to be informal or vulgar" [Clark97].

The most notable eighteenth-century mitate-e artist was Suzuki Harunobu. His *Mitate of Meng Zong*[9] (figure 1[10]) depicts a courtesan digging out bamboo shoots in the snow. The viewer is expected to understand that the beautiful woman actually represents Mōsō (Meng Zong in Chinese), one of the Twenty-Four Paragons of Filial Piety (*Nijūshikō*) [Waterhouse97]. In the story explaining the Confucian ideal of filial devotion, Mōsō goes into the bamboo grove in winter to answer his mother's desire for bamboo shoots. After praying to heaven, he is able to dig out some shoots despite the deep snow.

FIGURE 1

Replacing characters is also common in *kabuki* drama. Kabuki playwrights typically add certain clever ideas (*shukō*: literally, "device") to the main plot (*sekai*: literally, "world"), with the most typical shukō being mitate, or changing characters and settings [Miura96]. For example, the most popular kabuki, *Kanadehon Chūshingura*[11], is based on an actual incident from the early eighteenth century, though its story ostensibly comes from *Taiheiki*, a historical fiction written in the fourteenth century.[12]

In 1701, Asano Takuminokami failed to kill Kira Kōzukenosuke in Edo Castle and was ordered to commit *seppuku* (commonly, *hara-kiri*) that same day. Led by Ōishi Kuranosuke, Takuminokami's 47 vassals killed Kōzukenosuke the following year [Oishi07]. *Kanadehon Chūshingura* depicts this incident using *Taiheiki* as its sekai. Takuminokami and Kōzukenosuke are replaced with Enya Hangan and Kō no Moronō, respectively, and Kuranosuke's name is changed to Ōboshi Yuranosuke.

3. Mitate as Metaphor

Above, I provided some examples of mitate in various Japanese arts. A salient feature of mitate is that it always involves two distinct subjects—in these examples, flowers and a waterfall, a creel and a vase, a courtesan and Mōsō, and so forth. In his now-classic analysis of metaphor, Max Black calls these two subjects the *principal subject* and the *subsidiary subject* [Black55]. In our examples, the principal subjects are flowers, a creel, and a courtesan; the subsidiary subjects are a waterfall, a vase, and Mōsō.

Any account of mitate must explain how these subjects relate to each other. We might think of the relationship as substitution: a pond in a garden substitutes

---

[9]Many of Harunobu's mitate-e were untitled because the paintings are, in a sense, intellectual plays or puzzles. This title has been supplied by present-day art historians [Clark97].

[10]The image is taken from *Ukiyo-e Search* site at http://ukiyo-e.org/image/mia/8881.

[11]*Kanadehon Chūshingura* was originally a script for *bunraku* puppet theater. Kabuki and bunraku have many scripts in common.

[12]One reason why mitate was used is that depicting real events in theater was prohibited at that time.

for an ocean, a rakugo actor's fan substitutes for a sword or chopsticks, and so on. The relationship might also express similarities: Shōi's haikai suggests the similarity between falling flowers and a waterfall.[13]

Black characterizes these accounts using the terms *substitution view* and *comparison view*, respectively [Black55]. Regarding mitate, however, both views have the same problem: neither can account for all the examples mentioned in the previous section. Falling flowers do not substitute for a waterfall, and an eighteenth-century Japanese woman does not resemble Mōsō, a third-century Chinese bureaucrat.

Black proposes a more adequate account: the *interaction view* [Black55]. Consider the metaphorical expression, "Man is a wolf." Black calls the word that is used metaphorically—in this case, "wolf"—the *focus* of the metaphor; the rest of the sentence, which should be read literally, is the *frame*. In the interaction view, through the interaction between the primary subject and the subsidiary subject, the focal word "wolf" obtains a new meaning that can fit in the frame—that is, it can be applied to the man.

Black suggests the interaction involves filtering. The word "wolf" is associated with being fierce, carnivorous, treacherous, and so on. When a man is called a "wolf," that system of association is evoked and filtered so it can also apply to a man. Thus, we create new implications regarding the principal subject. The wolf metaphor, Black insists, organizes our view of man by suppressing some details and emphasizing others [Black55].

However, since Black only deals with linguistic metaphor, this argument must be extended to effectively analyze mitate. The first consideration is that the construction of metaphor in literature contrasts with its use in other arts [Amagasaki88]. In Shōi's haikai, the primary subject (falling blossoms) appears in the frame, and the subsidiary subject (a waterfall) is the focus. In Harunobu's mitate-e, however, the primary subject (a courtesan) is the focus, and the subsidiary subject (Mōsō) is suggested in the frame.[14]

In the interaction view, the meaning of the focal word is filtered and applied to the primary subject. This account cannot be generalized to mitate because the primary subject *is* the focus in nonliterary arts. Instead, Amagasaki argues that the effect of interaction in mitate is that it changes our attitudes toward the primary subject. Mitate evokes our attitude toward the subsidiary subject and directs it toward the principal subject. As a result, our way of seeing the primary subject changes [Amagasaki88].

This revised interaction view also holds for mitate in literature. What Shōi's haikai changes is not the meaning of the word "waterfall" but our impression of falling petals [Amagasaki88]. The haikai is not a statement about falling flowers but a command that the reader should view falling flowers as a waterfall. Because we are forced to evoke our impression of a waterfall and direct it toward falling flowers, we might then experience awe, fear, or a chill when we see the petals of cherry blossoms falling.

---

[13]Many Japanese scholars and writers seem to favor the similarity account. See Nakamura Yukihiko's *Gesakuron* [Nakamura66], for example.

[14]Whether the subject is explicit or implicit in the frame corresponds to the difference between simile and metaphor, which is insignificant here.

Rakugo serves as another example. When the rakugo actor uses his or her fan as a sword, the actor orders the audience to see the fan as a sword. Moreover, the actor demands that he or she be seen as a *samurai* warrior and the stage as a street in Edo. Here, the frame is not expressed in words: the actor never says the fan is meant to be a sword. The frame for the fan is the context in which it is used—that is, the world the actor expresses [Amagasaki95].

4. Mitate as Aspect Change

To summarize the previous section, an instance of mitate is a command to see one thing (the primary subject) as another thing (the subsidiary subject). The interaction between the two subjects causes us to see the primary subject differently, though we know it has not changed. Ludwig Wittgenstein calls such experience *seeing an aspect* [Wittgenstein09].

Consider the famous duck-rabbit drawing (figure 2). Sometimes we see a rabbit, other times a duck, even though the picture itself does not change. We can see a picture in different ways because what we see is an aspect of the picture. The picture does not change, but its aspect does. In addition, because seeing an aspect is, as Wittgenstein notes, subject to the will, there is such a command as, "Now see the figure as a rabbit" [Wittgenstein09]. The resulting aspect change we may call mitate.

FIGURE 2

Suppose the drawing is surrounded by several pictures of rabbits or is titled "Rabbit." Then, the frame (the surrounding pictures or the title) orders us to see the drawing as a rabbit. This phenomenon is identical to mitate. Generally, as Sasaki Ken'ichi argues, the title of an artwork functions as a "seeing-as" command [Sasaki01].[15] As such, every artwork relies on mitate in its broadest sense.[16]

Though we are usually unaware of it, we can easily recognize this seeing-as structure by looking at René Magritte's *The Treachery of Images* (figure 3[17]). What looks like a pipe appears in the upper part of the painting with *Ceci n'est pas une pipe* ("This is not a pipe") written below it. The brown paint on the canvas would be seen as a pipe if it were not for the sentence. Magritte, however, orders us not to see it as a pipe by situating the paint within an ingenious frame.[18]

FIGURE 3

Within this broad sense of mitate, the statement "origami is an art of mitate" is meaningless because all art that expresses something would be an art of mitate. Nishikawa's assertion is equivalent to saying origami is a form of expression, which

---

[15] A title may be provided by the artist, an art historian, an art critic, or others. Hence, the command is not necessarily the artist's. This implies that the argument is also valid for the names of natural objects such as rocks and constellations.

[16] Amagasaki suggests that every play depends on mitate [Amagasaki88]. It is easy to extend this claim to visual art in general.

[17] The image is taken from a University of Alabama site "Approaches to Modernism" at http://www.tcf.ua.edu/Classes/Jbutler/T311/Modernism.htm.

[18] One might recall Maurice Denis's statement here: "Remember that a picture—before being a battle horse, a nude woman, or some anecdote—is essentially a plane surface covered with colors assembled in a certain order" [Denis45].

is too obvious to be worth pointing out. For the assertion to be significant, mitate must be understood in a narrower sense.

Recall that mitate-e is a genre of ukiyo-e. We could say every piece of ukiyo-e is mitate-e in the broadest sense. However, the fact that not all ukiyo-e are mitate-e implies that the notion of mitate in ukiyo-e is different from just "seeing-as." In other words, there is another meaning of mitate besides expression.

We see a portrait of a beauty as a beauty and a landscape of Mount Fuji as Mount Fuji. In Harunobu's mitate-e, however, we not only see the picture as a courtesan but also the courtesan as Mōsō. As Hattori Yukio notes [Hattori75], the beauty is *superimposed* on the story of Mōsō. Here, we observe two instances of mitate at once: one in the broadest sense and the other in a narrower sense.

Mitate as superimposition is observed in kabuki as well. In *Kanadehon Chūshingura*, the story of *Taiheiki* is superimposed on an actual event that occurred at the beginning of the eighteenth century. As a result, we not only see the actor as Enya Hangan but also Hangan as Asano Takuminokami. The fictional seppuku of Hangan is represented on the stage, yet we see the actual seppuku of Takuminokami "behind" the stage.

To my knowledge, few origami works involve mitate in this sense. Trivial exceptions would be the human figures in *Orikata-tehon Chūshingura*, popular in the nineteenth century, which depict the characters in *Kanadehon Chūshingura* (figure 4 shows Hangan [left] and Moronō [right] [Okamura93]). Besides these, mitate as superimposition is rare in origami.

FIGURE 4

Thus, if we interpret mitate in this narrow sense, origami is *not* an art of mitate. However, this interpretation is so narrow that it would also exclude mitate in rakugo and Japanese gardens. The account of mitate as superimposition is inappropriate for analyzing mitate in general.

Let us return to the notion of aspect. Wittgenstein said, "I cannot try to see a conventional picture of a lion *as* a lion" [Wittgenstein09]. That is because we *view* such a picture as a lion, and viewing *always* occurs. In contrast, seeing-as, or mitate in its "medium" sense, requires aspect change, and since aspect depends on the will, mitate "occurs only while I am actually concerning myself with the picture as the object represented" [Wittgenstein09].

It should be emphasized that whether we view or see a picture as something depends on whether the picture is conventional. Mitate differs from other types of expression in that the subsidiary subject is not a conventional aspect of the primary subject. Therefore, when mitate causes us to see the primary subject as the subsidiary subject, the aspect must change. When we see a conventional picture, however, we experience no aspect change.

This counterconventional characteristic of mitate, or metaphor, is described by various scholars in different ways. Nakamura Yukihiko insists that mitate is about two things, "which on the face of it are not similar, or are not generally thought to be similar. ... It is better to make them as different as possible"[19] [Nakamura66].

---

[19]The English translation is quoted from Clark's paper [Clark97].

Nelson Goodman said, "Where there is metaphor, there is conflict" [Goodman76], while Hattori noted that a drastic leap is essential for mitate [Hattori75].

We cannot, however, see something as anything. The rakugo actor's fan cannot be seen as, say, a chair or a dog. Mitate requires, as Goodman notes, "attraction as well as resistance—indeed, an attraction that overcomes resistance" [Goodman76]. Such attraction should result from interaction between the focus and frame of mitate. That is, the focus of mitate should in some way agree with the frame.

5. Mitate in Origami

Applying the arguments presented thus far to origami, the geometric shape of the folded paper is the focus—which is also the primary subject—and the subject the shape represents is the subsidiary subject defined by the frame. To be an instance of mitate, the focus needs to agree in some way—and at the same time disagree—with the frame. In other words, the geometric shape should represent the subject in an unconventional way.

The origami crane (*orizuru*, figure 5) is clearly an instance of mitate. It somehow resembles an actual crane: it has a long neck, a long beak, and a pair of wings. Yet, it does *not* resemble a crane: no actual crane has an upward pointy appendix at its back, like the orizuru. The appearance of the orizuru is quite different from that of a crane, and that is why we can *see* the orizuru as a crane.[20]

FIGURE 5

It should be noted that an orizuru resembles a stork, heron, or even a dragon as much as it resembles a crane. A paper crane could be a paper stork or dragon. We see an orizuru as a crane via our will, probably because of the folkloric idea that cranes live for one thousand years. In contrast, Kamiya Satoshi's *Crane* [Kamiya10] (figure 6) cannot be seen as a crane because it represents the crane in a conventional way.

Other examples of mitate can be found in Nishikawa's works. His *A Simple Lion* [Nishikawa03] (figure 7) consists of a triangular pyramid "head" and a rectangular "body." Since it is not a conventional representation of a lion, we never *view* it as a lion. Still,

FIGURE 6

we *see* it as a lion because it somehow resembles a lion and the word "lion" is in the title. If it were titled *Chowchow*, we would see it as a chowchow [Nishikawa03].

Nishikawa's other *Lion* [Nishikawa03] (figure 8) represents the lion in a more conventional way. As sculpture, the expression is unusual because the origami work is virtually flat. No actual lion is flat. However, flat pieces are common in origami, and the leap from two to three dimensions is shared with every piece of painting, drawing, and relief. The flatness of many expressive origami pieces does not imply

---

[20]Modern people, especially modern Japanese, almost *view* an orizuru as a crane because, as Goodman suggests, instances of metaphor or mitate "become more literal as their novelty wanes" [Goodman76]. Yet, they remain metaphor or mitate.

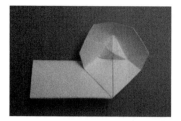

FIGURE 7

FIGURE 8

that they are unconventional or rely on mitate.[21] After all, origami is a different medium from sculpture in that the material is completely flat.

Most contemporary technical origami works, such as Kamiya's *Crane*, represent their subjects in conventional ways and hence do not involve mitate as a whole piece.[22] Such representational pieces are not found in nineteenth-century European origami, most of which was based on the so-called double blintz fold. Interestingly, this means traditional Western origami depended heavily on mitate.[23]

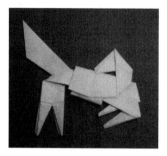

FIGURE 9

FIGURE 10

More interestingly, Japanese origami of that time did include conventionally representational pieces. For example, compare these two origami horses, both of which were originally folded in the first half of the nineteenth century and reproduced by the author: one from the former collection of the Moriwaki house in Japan [Takagi99] (figure 9), the other from the Museum of Saxon Folk Art in Germany (figure 10). The representation of the Japanese horse is obviously more conventional than that of the German counterpart.[24]

There are other types of origami work that do not involve mitate. As we have seen, Mitate results from the interaction between primary and subsidiary subjects, and for interaction to occur, as Black argues, we need to share common ideas about what the subsidiary subject is [Black55].[25] Without common ideas, mitate cannot occur.

Nishikawa asserts that the subject of an origami work is either something that exists (e.g., an elephant) or something depicted by another method of expression

---

[21]They depend on mitate in the broadest sense, of course.

[22]Some parts of such a piece may be instances of mitate if we consider the parts to be the foci and the whole piece the frame.

[23]This is not entirely surprising considering we have analyzed mitate using the concepts of Western philosophers.

[24]Also, compare the soldier in figure 10 with the kabuki actors in figure 4.

[25]Black calls the common ideas the *system of commonplaces* [Black55].

(e.g., a unicorn) [Nishikawa90]. We certainly have common ideas for such subjects. Such is not the case, however, with abstract works such as Yoshizawa Akira's *Hope* and *Despair* [Yoshizawa98] and Paul Jackson's "One Crease" pieces [Jackson94].[26] We have no common ideas about the shape of hope or despair, and Jackson's origami work represents no subject.

Like conventionally representational origami, abstract works have a long history. Fröbelian forms of symmetry (also known as forms of beauty; figure 11 shows examples [Kraus-Boelte and Kraus 77]) date back to the first half of the nineteenth century when Friedrich Wilhelm August Fröbel established the world's first kindergarten in Germany [Hatori11]. Clearly, these pieces involve no mitate at all.[27]

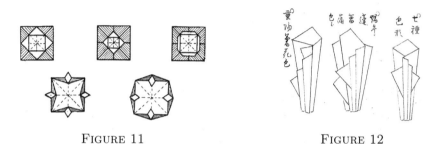

FIGURE 11   FIGURE 12

Moreover, Japanese *noshi*, as well as other wrappers of the nineteenth century and before (figure 12 shows, left to right, chrysanthemum wrapper for the Chōyō Festival, mugwort and iris wrapper for the Tango Festival, and seven spring herbs wrapper for the Jinjitsu Festival [Brossman and Brossman 61]), are purely decorative and represent no subject.[28] They are said to have started in the fourteenth century; in fact, they are thought to represent the origins of origami in Japan [Hatori11]. In other words, origami most likely began without mitate.

References

[Amagasaki88] Amagasaki Akira. *Nihon no Rhetoric.* Tokyo: Chikuma Shobō, 1988.

[Amagasaki95] Amagasaki Akira. *En no Bigaku: Uta no Michi no Shigaku II.* Tokyo: Keisō Shobō, 1995.

[Black55] Max Black. "Metaphor." *Proceedings of the Aristotelian Society* 55 (1955) 273–294.

[Brossman and Brossman 61] Julia Brossman and Martin Brossman. *A Japanese Paper-folding Classic: Excerpt from the "Lost" Kan no mado.* Santa Ana: The Pinecone Press, 1961.

[Clark97] Timothy T. Clark. "*Mitate-e*: Some Thoughts, and a Summary of Recent Writings." *Impressions* 19 (1997) 6–27.

[Denis45] Maurice Denis. "Paris, August, 1890." In *Artists on Art: from the XIV to the XX Century*, edited by Robert Goldwater and Marco Treves, pp. 380–381. New York: Pantheon Books, 1945.

[Goodman76] Nelson Goodman. *Languages of Art: An Approach to a Theory of Symbols.* Indianapolis: Hackett Publishing Company, 1976.

[Hatori11] Hatori Kōshirō. "History of origami in the East and the West before interfusion." In *Origami*[5], edited by Patsy Wang-Iverson, Robert J. Lang, and Mark Yim, pp.3–11. Boca Raton: CRC Press, 2011.

---

[26]Nishikawa was not unaware of abstract origami when he wrote the articles for *Oru*, but his analysis is restricted to representational origami works [Nishikawa93].

[27]Only one such piece is well known in Japan; it is usually called *medal*. Interestingly, the piece became an example of mitate after being imported to Japan.

[28]The only exception is *Ochō Mechō*, or male and female butterflies.

[Hattori75] Hattori Yukio. "'Mitate' Kō." In *Hengeron: Kabuki no Seishinshi*, pp. 176–192. Tokyo: Heibonsha, 1975.

[Hayakawa95] Hayakawa Monta. "Mitate-e ni tsuite: 'mitate' no kōzō to imi." In *Bijutsushi no Danmen*, edited by Takeda Tsuneo Sensei Koki Kinen-kai, pp. 420–445. Osaka: Seibundo Shuppan, 1995.

[Isozaki90] Isozaki Arata. *Mitate no Shuhō*. Tokyo: Kashima Shuppankai, 1990.

[Jackson94] Paul Jackson. "One Crease Origami: Less is More." In *Origami Science & Art*, edited by Koryo Miura, Tomoko Fuse, Toshikazu Kawasaki, and Jun Maekawa, pp. 431–440. Otsu: Seian University of Art and Design, 1994.

[Kamiya10] Kamiya Satoshi. *Kamiya-ryū Sōsaku Origami ni Chōsen!* Tokyo: Soshimu, 2010.

[Kasahara96] Kasahara Kunihiko. *Joy of Origami*. Tokyo: Sōjusha, 1996.

[Kraus-Boelte and Kraus 77] Maria Kraus-Boelté and John Kraus. *The Kindergarten Guide*. New York: E. Steiger, 1877.

[Maekawa07] Maekawa Jun. *Genuine Origami: 43 Mathematically-Based Models, from Simple to Complex*. Tokyo: Japan Publications Trading, 2007.

[Matsue43] Matsue Shigeyori ed. *Kefukigusa*. Tokyo: Iwanami Shoten, 1943.

[Miura96] Miura Hiroko. "Kabuki ni okeru Mitate: 'Sakurahime Azumabunshō' no Baai." *Nihon no Bigaku* 24 (1996) 104–120.

[Nakamura66] Nakamura Yukihiko. *Gesakuron*. Tokyo: Kadokawa Shoten, 1966.

[Nishikawa90] Nishikawa Seiji. "Origami Hihyō Taikei." *Origami Tanteidan Shimbun* 1:3–4 (1990).

[Nishikawa93] Nishikawa Seiji. "Seibutsu Zōkei Kōza." *Oru* 1:1–4 (1993-94).

[Nishikawa03] Nishikawa Seiji. *Works of Seiji Nishikawa*. Tokyo: Origami House, 2003.

[Oishi07] Ōishi Manabu. *Genroku Jidai to Akō Jiken*. Tokyo: Kadokawa Gakugei Shuppan, 2007.

[Okamura93] Okamura Masao. "Koten Kenkyū: 'Orikata-tehon Chūshingura'." *Oru* 1:3 (1993) 76–81.

[Sasaki01] Sasaki Ken'ichi. *Title no Maryoku*. Tokyo: Chūō Kōron Shinsha, 2001.

[Sen10] Sen Sōoku. *Cha: Rikyū to Ima o Tsunagu*. Tokyo: Shinchōsha, 2010.

[Sojusha95] Sōjusha ed. "Origami Sakka Interview: Nishikawa Seiji." *Oru* 3:10 (1995) 42–45.

[Takagi99] Takagi Satoshi. "Moriwaki-ke Kyūzō no Origami Shiryō ni tsuite." In *Oru Kokoro*, edited by Ichimura Kōki, pp. 67–74. Tatsuno: Tatsuno-shi Rekishi Bunka Shiryōkan, 1999.

[Tanaka94] Tanaka Yūko. "Edo no Mitate." In *Gendai Mitate Hyakkei*, pp. 4–12. Tokyo: Inax Shuppan, 1994.

[Tsutsui08] Tsutsui Kōichi. "Karamono to Mitate no Jidai." In *Sen no Rikyū: "Wabi" no Sōzōsha*, edited by Yuhara Kimihiro, pp. 39–68. Tokyo: Heibonsha, 2008.

[Waterhouse97] David Waterhouse. "Some Confucian, Buddhist, and Taoist *Mitate-e* by Harunobu." *Impressions* 19 (1997) 28–47.

[Wittgenstein09] Ludwig Wittgenstein. *Philosophical Investigations*. Chichester: Wiley-Blackwell, 2009.

[Yoshizawa98] Yoshizawa Akira. *Origami Tokuhon II*. Tokyo: New Science-sha, 1998.

VII. Origami in Education

The Kindergarten Origametria Program

Miri Golan and John Oberman

1. Introduction

The Kindergarten Origametria (KO) program (KOP) is a program to train kindergarten teachers to work with the geometry curriculum of the Israeli Ministry of Education, using origami as a learning tool. The program uses the imagination of kindergarten-age children (aged 4–6 years) as the focus of the activity, involving them in a series of creative folding activities that acknowledge their limited motor skills. The KOP is a tool for the kindergarten teacher to make an activity in a creative environment that builds a strong mathematical base for the children.

The emphasis on imaginative play and experimentation as a means to learn, though common in many kindergarten activities, is historically uncommon as an approach to using origami as a learning tool, where teaching named models is the norm. In this way, the KOP may be considered an unorthodox approach to origami.

This chapter describes the progress of the KOP since the brief account of the pilot KOP eight years ago given in *Origami⁴* [Golan and Jackson 09].

2. Structure of the KOP Courses for Kindergarten Teachers

The first KO pilot course began in 2005. In 2010, the program was rewritten with supervisors from the Israeli Ministry of Education and with input from specialist teachers and professors of mathematics and mathematics education. To date (summer 2014), the KOP has been studied by teachers in 120 state kindergartens, mainly in Tel Aviv. The program is ongoing and will continue to expand in the foreseeable future, supervised and funded jointly by the Ministry of Education and by local departments of education in different cities.

Each course runs for a total of 30 hours, over eight sessions, spread over a period of several months. Each course accepts 20 kindergarten teachers (KTs). Each KT is required as part of her Terms of Service to undertake a minimum number of courses each year, and attending the KO course contributes to meeting this requirement. Some KTs choose to take the course, while others are recommended to participate by their supervisors.

The KO course divides into three parts:

(1) *Learning Topics of Geometry According to the Kindergarten Curriculum (10 hours):* The KTs are taught basic geometric knowledge, which many did not know, had forgotten, or had misremembered. They are taught the terminology and definitions they will need when teaching the KOP, and later, they are taught

additional terminology and definitions in advance of what they will need in order to feel they are teaching within their knowledge.

This knowledge is learned by folding, led by the teacher. The learning is thus folding-based and not lecture-based. During the process of folding, the geometry of the paper is described and analyzed by the KTs.

(2) *The Method of Using the KOP Activity in Kindergarten (12 hours):* The KTs are introduced to the method of how to conduct KOP activities (three sample activities are described below in Section 5). Between each course session, every KT introduces what she has recently learned as an activity in her kindergarten and reports back to the class on her experiences. They are encouraged to take photographs and to make short movies, to assist with the description of their experiences. Feedback is given by the teacher and other KTs.

(3) *Additional Geometric Information (10 hours):* The KTs are taught basic three-dimensional geometry (cubes, cuboids, and pyramids) and the relationships between members of the triangle and quadrilateral families (for the quadrilateral family, for example, the similarities and differences between a square, rectangle, rhombus, parallelogram, trapezium, and more).

The KTs are also introduced to the theories of Piaget [Piaget et al. 99], van Hiele [van Hiele 99, Crowley 87], and Vygotsky [van der Veer and Valsiner 91], regarding how children learn and how this is applied to the KOP.

After the course has concluded, visits are made by the course teacher to each KT's kindergarten to observe a KO activity and to help the teacher fine-tune her implementation of the program. It is important that with these visits the program is tailored to fit the individual circumstances of each kindergarten, not vice versa.

The KOP method is based on encouragement, curiosity, and learning through experimentation, allowing the children to play with their paper as an imaginative and fun activity. The geometric research undertaken by the children during the KOP activity develops strong mathematical thinking skills.

In the past year, the program has received input from Dr. John Oberman, PhD, MSc, DipEd, Director of Pre-service Mathematics Training, Shaanan Academic College, Haifa, Israel, who has helped relate the open-ended folding experiments undertaken by the children during the KOP activities to the kindergarten geometry curriculum.

3. Distinctive Contributions of the KOP to Geometric Education in Kindergarten

The KOP repositions origami as an activity that uses the imagination of young children aged 4–6 as the basis of the teaching method. This focusing of an activity around a child's imagination and on discovery through experimentation is not new in kindergarten education—indeed, it is the basis of well-established methodologies such as the Montessori and Steiner systems—but is an unorthodox use of origami, where teaching named models is the norm.

The KOP, along with many other constructing activities such as working with Plasticine and wooden bricks, helps with developing a child's imagination, fine motor control, spatial awareness, group work, and communication skills. However, there are two aspects to the KOP that may be considered distinctive contributions to geometry education in kindergarten.

(1) The KOP helps young learners differentiate between different polygons by asking them during the process of folding to count the number of corners and sides, to name different polygons, to intuitively recognize right angles in squares and

rectangles, and to create and identify simple mirror symmetry. These concepts are developed by asking the children questions such as, "What is the same and what is different with the shapes you have made?" or "Which shapes would you like to put together?" After discussions between the KT and the children, the formal language of geometry will develop as a need for communication. The children are not given knowledge or asked to learn definitions "by rote"; they are given methods to observe and explore, from which definitions can be deduced. This method, once learned and practiced, can be used at any time.

Many KTs report that after running the activity, the children from the group will teach other children in the kindergarten what they had learned, using correct geometric terminology.

(2) During the process of folding, the paper will change its shape many times: from a square to a rectangle, then perhaps to a triangle or hexagon, and back to a square. This continual process of creation, change, and re-creation allows the child to identify a polygon in different circumstances, at different rotations, and at different sizes. Further, at times the teacher will hold her paper deliberately askew and ask, for example, if her square is still a square. In this way, the children learn to recognize polygons in diverse and unfamiliar situations and thus gain a stronger understanding of the individual characteristics of the shapes.

4. Four Ways to Develop Creative Thinking

These four ways guide the structure of the KOP courses for kindergarten teachers and the approach of the teachers to their KO activities. They are based on the research of Guilford, Christensen, and Torrance [Guilford 67, Guilford and Christensen 73], [Torrance 80].

(1) *Fluency:* The ability of the child to make a few samples, cases, or situations within the limits of the task.
(2) *Flexibility:* The ability of the child to move from one way of thinking to another and to produce samples and solutions that relate to a different category.
(3) *Elaboration:* The ability of the child to expand their knowledge, to add detail, and to develop it in combination with other ideas.
(4) *Originality:* The ability of the child to relate to certain problems in a new way, in a different way, so he can produce unexpected situations.

5. Three Examples of KOP Activities

During their KO course, the KTs are taught twelve KOP activities that relate to different topics within the geometry curriculum. Here are three sample activities, described step by step. The full twelve topics can be found in the appendix (Section 8).

ACTIVITY 5.1 (Researching Squares and Rectangles).

(1) The KT gives a sheet of square origami paper to each child.
(2) The children count how many sides and vertices they can find and check the lengths and angles with a straight edge. (Usually a square of paper is folded in half, long edge to long edge, three times.)
(3) The KT asks the group to assemble the squares to make one big square (composition and decomposition). See Figure 1.

FIGURE 1. Children discovering the characteristics of a large square.

FIGURE 2. An example of an arrangement of rectangles made by a group.

(KT questions: Do all the squares always make a big square? What are the characteristics of the big square? These questions provoke much discussion and research about what is a square.)

(4) The KT shows the children how to fold the square in half to make a rectangle.

(5) She asks the children to count the number of sides and vertices and to measure the lengths of the edges.

(6) The children are asked to assemble the rectangles without overlapping to create an imaginative shape. See Figure 2.

(7) The KT asks each child what he or she can see in the arrangement, asking for a detailed description. (For example, if the answer is "a robot," the child is asked to show the arms, head, legs, etc.) Usually each child sees a different subject (robot, butterfly, spider, etc.).

(8) The KT asks the children what is the difference between a square and a rectangle and how many of these rectangles will make a square. (Note: It is recommended that before this KO activity, the KTs run activities that teach concepts such as *long* and *short*.)

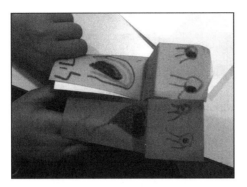

FIGURE 3. Children playing with their finished work.

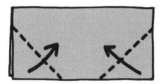

FIGURE 4. Activity 5.2, Step 2.

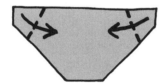

FIGURE 5. Activity 5.2, Step 5.

(9) The KT asks the children to fold a long side to the opposite side. The children again check the polygon.

(10) The KT asks the children to fold one short side to the opposite and parallel short side and to check the polygons that creates.

(11) The KT inserts her finger into the short side of the rectangle and asks each child what it is. The children draw on their own paper. See Figure 3.

ACTIVITY 5.2 (Defining and Finding Polygons).

(1) The KT begins the activity by repeating Steps 1–8 of Activity 5.1.

(2) The KT asks the children to fold back the open corners as shown in Figure 4. The position of the folds is not important.

(3) Turn over.

(4) The children count the number of edges and vertices and discover the shape of the paper is a hexagon.

(5) The children fold in the corners of the long edge as shown in Figure 5. Again, the position of the folds is unimportant.

(6) Turn over.

(7) The children fold back the corners to reveal white paper. See Figure 6.

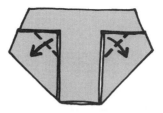

FIGURE 6. Activity 5.2, Step 7.

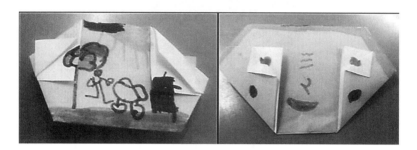

FIGURE 7. An example of how differently two children saw their finished work.

FIGURE 8. An example of an arrangement of triangles made by a group.

(8) The KT inserts her finger into the pocket and asks each child what it is. The children draw on their own paper. See Figure 7.

ACTIVITY 5.3 (Defining and Researching Triangles).

(1) The KT gives a sheet of square origami paper to each child.
(2) Each child folds the square in half, corner to corner, to make a triangle.
(3) The children are asked to assemble the triangles without overlapping, to create an imaginative shape.
(4) The KT asks each child what he or she can see in the arrangement, asking for a detailed description. See Figure 8.
(5) Each child takes back their triangle and checks with the KT how many sides and vertices it has.

FIGURE 9. Collage of six examples of the same folded shape, perceived as different subjects by different children.

(6) The KT asks the children to try to make a big triangle from four individual triangles (composition and decomposition).

   (*KT questions: Do the four triangles always make a big triangle? What are the characteristics of the big triangle?* These questions provoke much discussion and research about what is a triangle.)

(7) Each child takes back his or her triangle. The KT asks the children to fold vertex to vertex to make a smaller triangle and then to open the fold.

(8) The KT asks the children how many triangles they can see. (The answer is three: one large and two small triangles.)

(9) The KT asks the children to fold the apex to the base, to create a trapezium.

(10) Turn over.

(11) The KT asks the children to count the sides and corners to check if the polygon is still a triangle.

(12) Turn over again. The KT asks the children to fold the bottom corners to the middle of the base.

(13) The KT asks the children to name what they have made and to draw on it. See Figure 9.

6. The KOP and Friedrich Froebel

The KOP is often compared to the well-documented use of origami (*papierfalten*) by the German educator Friedrich Froebel (1782–1852), including his concept of Folds of Life [Brosterman 97]. While there are similarities between the two, there are also many differences. Table 1 makes a comparison between the programs.

Froebel	KOP
Origami was taught as the 18th of 20 Gifts, when the children were 7 years old.	The KOP is taught to children aged 4–6.
Froebel's 20 Gifts were all geometric in concept. So, by the 18th Gift, the children were well used to working with geometrical shapes and forms.	For many children, the KOP is their first experience of working with geometric shapes and forms.
An emphasis of Folds of Life is on making recognizable models of objects familiar to the children (furniture, utensils, boxes, etc.).	An emphasis is on imaginative play, with the children naming what they have made.
An emphasis is on the achieving of a final model.	An emphasis is on geometrical analysis and group discussion during the folding.

TABLE 1. A comparison between Froebelian paper folding and the KO program.

7. Conclusion

Although unorthodox in its use of origami, the KOP has quickly established itself as a program for the teaching of the Israeli Ministry of Education's geometry curriculum for kindergarten, proving itself popular with ministry officials, the teachers, and also the children. Formal assessments of the KO courses for KTs written by participating teachers consistently rate the courses very highly for didactic relevance and for consistent success within the demanding real-world circumstances of different kindergartens with different population groups.

The key elements of the program are the emphasis on imaginative play with folded paper and group analysis of a geometric topic or open-ended problem. At no point in the activity can a child consider himself to have failed, thus encouraging participation and a willingness to experiment without limits. This approach, although puzzling to many people familiar with origami and the teaching of origami to older children and to adults, relates to the educational level of kindergarten-age children and their predisposition to learn through imaginative play [Clements and Sarama 09, Cramond et al. 05, Ginsburg 06, Pandisco and Orton 98, Torrence 67].

Further, the structure of the 30-hour courses undertaken by KTs to learn the KOP and the follow-up visits to each teacher's kindergarten to see the program in action, ensure that the philosophy of the program is translated into a successful activity.

Since the relationship between the Ministry of Education (MoE) and the KOP is new and its place within the national curriculum has yet to be fully determined, there is as yet no formal quantitative assessment regarding the comparative effectiveness of the program. However, it is a requirement of the MoE that KTs study and document the progress of each child in each area of the curriculum, including mathematics. From this documentation, it is evident that the KOP makes an effective contribution to the learning of the geometry curriculum and is a popular activity. It is this positive assessment of the KOP that has led directly to rapid growth in the support given to it by the MoE. Many future KOP courses are planned.

Finally, the KOP is best assessed by the teachers who have been trained to use it. Here is a testimonial from one KT who took the KOP course:

At the beginning I thought Origametria was just folding paper models, but then I saw it was really about geometry and I was afraid to introduce it as an activity in my kindergarten because I don't know much about geometry. Although we learned the basics of geometry in the course, I was still afraid and began the activity with a lot of fear, but I saw the children enjoyed it. They loved it! They were excited and waited for their activity.

I didn't have enough time to work with all the children, so I worked only with the oldest group. Afterward, they introduced the activity to the younger children without my involvement and using correct geometric language. It was very beautiful to see!

I feel I'm only at the beginning and I need more time to work with it, but I feel the program is important and makes a valuable contribution to geometry in the kindergarten.

8. Appendix

These are the twelve topics studied on the KOP course for KTs.

Shape:

(1) Identify and research each polygon according to the number of sides and vertices.

(2) Identify and research the difference between long and short sides.

(3) Identify and research quadrilaterals according to the number of sides and vertices.

(4) Create a paper ruler and learn to measure long and short sides and vertices and to identify right angles.

(5) Identify and research squares according to the number of sides, vertices, and right angles.

(6) Identify and research squares and rectangles according to the number of sides, vertices, and right angles.

(7) Identify and research different quadrilaterals such as a square, rhombus, and rectangle according to the lengths of the sides and the number of vertices.

Mirror Symmetry:

(1) Identify and research mirror symmetry in triangles.

(2) Identify and research mirror symmetry in quadrilaterals.

Solids:

(1) Identify and research cubes by building cubes and learning about the structure.

(2) Identify and research three-sided pyramids.

Composition and Decomposition:

(1) Build different polygons from a large number of triangles and research topics studied previously.

References

[Brosterman 97] N. Brosterman. *Inventing Kindergarten*. New York: Harry N. Abrams, Inc., 1997.

[Clements and Sarama 09] D. H. Clements and J. Sarama. *Learning and Teaching Early Math: The Learning Trajectories Approach*. New York: Routledge, 2009.

[Cramond et al. 05] B. Cramond, J. Matthews-Morgan, D Bandalos, and L. Zuo. "A Report on the 40-year Follow-up of the Torrence Tests of Creative Thinking: Alive and Well in the New Millennium." *Gifted Child Quarterly* 49 (2005), 283–291.

[Crowley 87] M. L. Crowley. "The van Hiele Model of the Development of Geometric Thought." In *Learning and Teaching Geometry—K–12: 1987 Yearbook of the National Council of Teachers of Mathematics*, edited by Mary Montgomery Lindquist, pp. 1–16. Reston, VA: National Council of Teachers of Mathematics, 1987.

[Ginsburg 06] H. P. Ginsburg. "Mathematical Play and Playful Mathematics: A Guide for Early Education." In *Play = Learning: How Play Motivates and Enhances Children's Cognitive and Social-emotional Growth*, edited by D. Singer, R. M. Golinkoff, and K. Hirsh-Pasek, pp. 145–168. New York: Oxford University Press, 2006.

[Golan and Jackson 09] M. Golan and P. Jackson. "Origametria: A Program to Teach Geometry and to Develop Learning Skills Using the Art of Origami." In *Origami⁴: Fourth International Meeting of Origami Science, Mathematics, and Education*, edited by Robert J. Lang, pp. 459–469. Wellesley, MA: A K Peters, 2009. MR2590567 (2010h:00025)

[Guilford 67] J. P. Guilford. *The Nature of Human Intelligence*. New York: MacGraw-Hill, 1967.

[Guilford and Christensen 73] J. P. Guilford and P. R. Christensen. "The One-way Relation between Creative Potential and IQ." *The Journal of Creative Behavior* 7:4 (1973), 247–252.

[Pandisco and Orton 98] E. Pandisco and R. E. Orton. "Geometry and Meta-cognition: An Analysis of Piaget's and van Hiele's Perspectives." *Journal of Focus on Learning Problems in Mathematics* 20:2–3 (1998), 78–87.

[Piaget et al. 99] J. Piaget, B. Inhelder, and A. Szeminska. *The Child's Conception of Geometry*. London: Routledge, 1999.

[Torrence 67] E. P. Torrance. *Creativity*, What Research Says to the Teacher 28. Washington, DC: National Education Association, 1967.

[Torrance 80] E. P. Torrance. "Growing Creatively Gifted: The 22-year Longitudinal Study." *The Creative Child and Adult Quarterly* 3 (1980), 148–158.

[van Hiele 99] P. van Hiele. "Developing Geometric Thinking through Activities that Begin with Play." *Teaching Children Mathematics* 5:6 (1999), 310–316.

[van der Veer and Valsiner 91] R. Van der Veer and J. Valsiner. *Understanding Vygotsky: A Quest for Synthesis*. Oxford, UK: Blackwell, 1991.

DIRECTOR, ISRAELI ORIGAMI CENTER, RAMAT-GAN, ISRAEL
E-mail address: `origami@netvision.net.il`

DIRECTOR OF PRE-SERVICE MATHEMATICS TRAINING, SHAANAN ACADEMIC COLLEGE, HAIFA, ISRAEL

Area and Optimization Problems

Emma Frigerio and Maria Luisa Spreafico

1. Introduction

Origami is perhaps the most versatile tool for hands-on mathematical activities. According to the van Hiele model, geometric thinking develops through five successive levels [Cagle 09]:

(1) *Visualization:* Children recognize figures by their appearance.

(2) *Analysis:* Children discern some characteristics of figures but cannot see interrelationships between figures.

(3) *Informal Deduction:* Children can derive relationships among figures and follow simple proofs, though they don't understand them completely.

(4) *Formal Deduction:* Students understand the significance of deduction and the role of postulates, theorems, and proofs.

(5) *Rigor:* Students are able to work in an axiomatic system and can understand non-Euclidean geometry.

Although origami may be used effectively for the last two levels of the van Hiele model as well [Cagle 09, Frigerio 02, Hull 06, Pope and Lam 09], it is mainly used for teaching mathematics in primary and middle schools, which roughly correspond to the first three levels [Golan 11]. In some East Asian countries, and in Israel as well, origami is extensively used in early mathematics education, and many geometrical issues are investigated with the aid of paper folding.

When we explain mathematics, certainly we could fold directly a geometric figure (such as a triangle or a rhombus) and study its properties; however, especially with younger students, often it is preferable to give a geometry lesson while folding a non-mathematical object (such as an animal or a plane). The latter is Miri Golan's approach in her Origametria program [Golan and Jackson 09], and of others as well.

Following some occasional experiences of teaching mathematics lessons in Italian elementary schools, in 2010–2011, when the son of one of us was in first grade, we started in his school a five-year-long program, which will end in 2015, when his class will conclude primary school. We give about four lessons per year, usually reinforcing the regular teacher's lessons, sometimes anticipating them. The aim is to promote a deeper understanding of the mathematical concepts involved, to improve the students' communication

The second author was partially supported by the National Group for Algebraic and Geometric Structures and Their Applications (GNSAGA-INDAM).

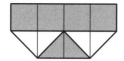

FIGURE 1. Fractions in an origami model.

skills, and, we hope, to improve their long-term retention. In Italian primary school mathematics, usually the emphasis is on arithmetic, with geometry playing a secondary role. Also, quite often geometry is reduced to a mere application of formulas so that, in a sense, it is a pretext for arithmetic calculations rather than being a gymnasium for reasoning. On the contrary, our lessons are based on geometry, even though the main topic is of an arithmetical nature. For instance, in the lesson on fractions, at several steps of the folding process, students are asked to determine which fraction of the whole is constituted by the colored parts and which by the white parts (see Figure 1 for one of these steps); this makes a good exercise on complementary and equivalent fractions, while also having fun making an origami model (a tropical fish in this case; see http://en.origami-club.com/sea/tropical %20fish/index.html for the folding diagrams).

We usually start from the real world. Thus, if the lesson is, say, on hexagons, we ask children where they see hexagons around them, either in nature, in art, or in everyday life. When teaching the origami model, we basically follow the Origametria method, with its rules for students and for the teacher [Golan and Jackson 09]. In particular, we do not tell the students in advance what we are folding, and we check that all have executed the requested fold correctly before going on. The questions we ask are varied, depending on the lesson topic; some examples are the following:

- How many triangles can you see?
- Can you see rectangles of different shapes?
- Which fold could you do in order to get an axis of symmetry in your model?
- Can you see a new rhombus (or a right angle, or a pair of parallel lines) that did not exist in the previous step?

In some instances, we invite children to cooperate both in folding and in finding answers to the questions. Also, we encourage children to use different strategies, we make sure that everyone gives some answers aloud, and we use wrong answers in a positive way.

The topics we have chosen include diagonals; triangles; squares and rectangles; axes of symmetry of some polygons (square, rectangle, hexagon, rhombus (see Figure 2(a)); parallel and incident lines; right, acute, and obtuse angles; fractions; classification of triangles; angle measurement; the Tangram; and area.

We also had the class work together in the construction of some modular models; here the main point was to foster cooperation among the students and, in one case, to connect mathematics to history (see Figure 2(b)).

To illustrate our work, we present here a set of three lessons—suitable for fifth graders in the Italian school system—that take children from an introduction of the concept of area and its measure to an optimization problem.

2. Lesson 1: The Need of a Unit

We prefer to give our first lesson before students are taught area formulas. We begin with a very simple activity, aimed both at promoting critical thinking and at showing the need of a unit of measure. Students will be asked to compare how "big" certain shapes

(a) The model used for the lesson on the rhombus

(b) The Egyptian pyramid

FIGURE 2. Examples of origami in the classroom.

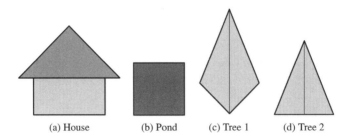

(a) House (b) Pond (c) Tree 1 (d) Tree 2

FIGURE 3. Comparing areas with origami models.

are without performing any calculation. Each group of four students receives five square sheets of the same size (and of appropriate colors), then we show them how to fold the house and the pond (see Figure 3(a,b)). The two shapes that constitute the house are obtained respectively by folding a vertex onto the opposite one (the roof) and a side onto the opposite one (the walls) of two separate squares, while the pond is obtained by folding all four vertices to the center of the square.

At any point, the three shapes (triangle, rectangle, square) have two layers of paper, hence they have the same area; however, most children perceive the roof in Figure 3(a) as having the greatest area and the pond Figure 3(b) the smallest one. Things get more complicated when two trees are folded and added to the scene. Figure 3(c) is just a kite base, and Figure 3(d) has an extra fold that hides the bottom part of it. Although we cannot tell exactly the areas of the trees, certainly, among the five shapes, one of them has the greatest area (its layers are two or one) and the other the smallest (its layers are two or three). This kind of reasoning is not so obvious for children, who tend to disregard how they obtained a certain shape and to estimate its area visually.

Then, we proceed with the mystery model, which is the classical water-bomb cube (see http://www.mathematische-basteleien.de/oricube.htm). Again, each group gets five sheets, one for each student and one "for the table." On each square, first we have students fold a 4 × 4 square grid, so as to have a convenient unit of measure, then we start to give

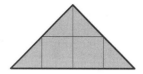

FIGURE 4. Water-bomb base.

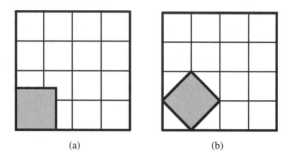

(a)   (b)

FIGURE 5. The (a) wrong and (b) correct ways to put the shape onto the grid.

instructions for the model. Following most folds, we ask the class to determine the area of the shape obtained, and we invite students to find different ways to obtain the answer. For instance, once the water-bomb base is folded, as shown in Figure 4, they have at least four strategies to determine its area:

(1) The shape is made of two unit squares and four small triangles, each of which is a half-square; hence, its area is 4 units.
(2) Four copies of the shape entirely cover the table's (unfolded) square, whose area is 16 units; hence, each shape has area 4 units.
(3) The shape has four layers everywhere, hence its area is $16/4 = 4$ units;
(4) The shape obtained at the previous step had area 8 units, and we have halved it, thus obtaining a 4-unit shape.

The next step has proven to be the most difficult for fifth graders: when students are asked to find the area of the new shape obtained, most of them put it on the grid as shown in Figure 5(a) and do not know what to say; eventually, one places it as in Figure 5(b) and gets the correct answer.

Getting the cube by blowing into the hole comes as a pleasant surprise to most children, who easily determine that the total surface area is 6 units.

3. Lesson 2: Using Different Units to Determine Areas

In the second lesson, the mystery model is a collapsible variation of the traditional *masu* box; the result resembles very much another traditional box, the *orisue*, which is folded from a rectangle (folding instructions can be found at http://www.origami-cdo.it/ modelli/models.htm). See Figure 6.

Students are given square sheets colored on one side only and work individually. At several steps, we ask them to compare the areas C and W of the colored and white parts, respectively, on one side of the model.

FIGURE 6. The collapsible box: inside (left) and outside (right).

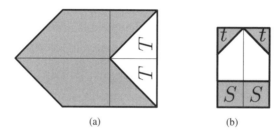

(a)   (b)

FIGURE 7. Different units at different steps.

Different units that naturally appear in the folding process are used by different students, which leads to the observation that if the unit is changed, areas generally change in value, but their ratio remains constant. For instance, in Figure 7(a), $C = 4W$, no matter which unit is used (the most popular being the triangle T or the entire white triangle).

We constantly encourage children to use various methods and to explain their reasoning; for instance, in Figure 7(b), either t or S could be used to determine C and W; but, if we just want to compare them, it is enough to observe that each of the white trapezoids can be decomposed into a square and a triangle congruent to S and t, respectively.

The model is flat until the end, when unexpectedly it becomes three dimensional; at this point students are asked to cooperate in pairs and compare C and W, looking both from inside and from outside (and including the flaps); see Figure 6. Here, the most commonly used unit is S, but some children use a rectangle $R = 2S$, which is a lateral face of the box, or even t. In any case, if they count everything correctly, they find that $C = W$.

A final observation is in order. In this lesson we give students 15×15 cm sheets, while we use a 30×30 cm sheet. At the end, we make them observe that any segment in our model is twice as long as the corresponding segment in their model, while our areas are four times theirs. At present, volumes are not studied in Italian primary schools; nevertheless, we like to hint at this topic. Thus, we ask the students how many times we could fill their box with water and pour it into our box in order to fill it. Having the real objects in front of them helps students to get the correct answer.

4. Lesson 3: An Optimization Problem

In the last lesson, we use origami to solve a simple problem of area optimization. Starting from a rectangular sheet, a traditional envelope model is folded; then, it is reopened and the associated crease pattern is studied.

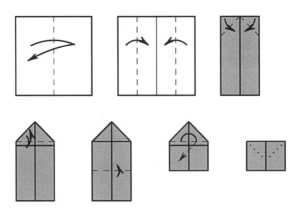

FIGURE 8. Folding diagrams for the envelope.

The required work is twofold: construct the crease pattern when the sizes of the envelope are known and establish the most economical solution.

The activity consists of the following three steps.

Step 1—Folding: We give each student a rectangular sheet. To point out that the crease pattern is essentially independent of the sheet used, it is preferable to hand out rectangles of different shapes and sizes.

Then we teach the class how to fold the model (see Figure 8).

Step 2—Worksheet: We divide students into groups of four, and we give each group the worksheet in Figure 9. We invite each group to work at their own pace. In this phase we have a maieutic attitude: Whenever we notice that a group is not making any progress, we pose appropriate questions to promote new ideas among the students.

Step 3—Discussion: Once students have completed their work, we discuss their answers with them. Then, we end the lesson with some important remarks. Here we point out two of them.

- In discussing item 8 on the worksheet, we turn the question into a real-life problem: If a company wants to produce a large number of these envelopes, which model is most economical (i.e., minimizes paper consumption)? This is significant in the Italian school, where mathematics problems are too often unrelated to real situations.
- If we want to understand where the area difference comes from, we have to look again at the crease patterns. The area of the paper that folds in the closing triangle, CT, is four times the CT itself. Hence, we need more paper if the CT is bigger, which occurs when the CT is attached to the long side of the envelope. On the contrary, the remaining part of the paper is the same in both cases (four times the final envelope). This can be shown to the class simply by opening both models, rotating one by 90°, and overlapping one onto another as in Figure 10).

This activity is quite challenging for ten-year-old students, both due to the difficulty of some questions and the working time required. In particular, they find it difficult to answer item 6, because they have to make an abstraction from the rectangle in the picture to the square in the question.

1. On both sides of your model, color the outline of the closed envelope.

2. Take out the triangle which closes the envelope (*CT, in the following*) and color its outline on both sides.

3. Now, reopen the model completely; fold lines form a crease pattern similar to the following figure.

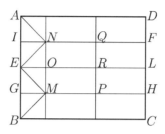

4. Recognize the following polygons:

the quadrangle *EGMO* is a _____ ;

triangles *EOM* and *EON* are _____ .

5. Now, suppose that *AB* is 16 *cm* long. Looking at the picture, and recalling how you folded the envelope, compute the lengths of the following segments:

$AE = $ _____ *cm* $IE = $ _____ *cm* $EG = $ _____ *cm*

$MN = $ _____ *cm* $GM = $ _____ *cm*

6. Imagine you started with a square sheet whose sides *AB* and *BC* are 16 *cm* long. In this case compute $MH = $ _____ *cm* and $MP = $ _____ *cm*. Show your work (hint: recall the length of the segment *GH*).

_____

7. In conclusion, if the initial sheet is a square of side length 16 *cm*, the closed envelope is a rectangle whose sides measure _____ *cm* and _____ *cm*. On squared paper, draw a 16 by 16 *cm* square and complete the crease pattern according to your computations. Then ask the teacher for a 16 *cm* square origami sheet and fold the envelope with it. Finally, reopen the new envelope and check whether the crease pattern you drew is exact; correct it otherwise.

8. Problem. In the second envelope, the CT (see 2) is attached to the long side of it. If you wanted an envelope of the same size, but with the CT attached to the short side, which sheet should you start from? To solve this problem, first you may draw a rectangle with the same side lengths you found in 7. Then add the CT in the right position and complete the crease pattern. Write you answer below.

_____

9. Looking at your crease patterns, which of the two sheets looks bigger, the first one (square) or the second (rectangular)?

_____

Compute their areas and check your answer.

Area (square) $= $ _____ cm^2;

Area (rectangle) $= $ _____ cm^2.

FIGURE 9. Worksheet for Lesson 3.

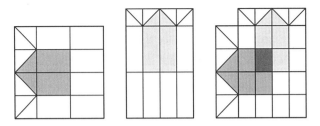

FIGURE 10. Comparing the two crease patterns via overlapping.

Other questions could be posed in a subsequent lesson or assigned as homework. For instance, we mention the following:

- Find the side lengths of a sheet if you want to fold a square envelope whose side is 8 cm long.
- If you want an envelope with final size 8×18 cm, is it possible to have the CT along the shorter side? And along the longer side? Why?

5. Conclusion

During the last four years, we constantly worked in two parallel classes and sometimes we gave just one lesson in other classes.

As expected, children who worked with us each year improved their manual skills, level of concentration during the activities, and cooperation among themselves.

In particular, they understood how to help friends, explaining and showing some difficult folding step without completing it for them.

This sense of cooperation was also increased by folding modular models such as the pyramid in Figure 2(b): Only a great number of children folding simple modules can obtain a big and beautiful result.

From the point of view of learning mathematics, these children progressed in understanding mathematical concepts, increased spatial perception, and greatly enhanced their use of specific language, thus improving their communication skills [Pope and Lam 09]. Moreover, having a physical object in hands helps students to "touch" mathematics, which is very important for this age bracket when the transition from concrete to abstract is not completely developed.

We also observed that students with some fragility in learning mathematics in a traditional way are stimulated by this hands-on approach and do not hesitate to answer questions or solve problems.

References

[Cagle 09] M. Cagle. "Modular Origami in the Secondary Geometry Classroom." In *Origami⁴: Fourth International Meeting of Origami Science, Mathematics, and Education*, edited by Robert Lang, pp. 497–505. Natick, MA: A K Peters, 2009.

[Frigerio 02] E. Frigeriol "In Praise of the Papercup: Mathematics and Origami at the University." In *Origami³: Proceedings of the Third International Meeting of Origami Science, Mathematics, and Education*, edited by Thomas Hull, pp. 291–298. Natick, MA: A K Peters, 2002. MR1955754 (2003h:00017)

[Golan and Jackson 09] M. Golan and P. Jackson. "Origametria: A Program to Teach Geometry and to Develop Learning Skills Using the Art of Origami." In *Origami⁴: Fourth International Meeting of Origami Science, Mathematics, and Education*, edited by Robert Lang, pp. 459–469. Natick, MA: A K Peters, 2009.

[Golan 11] M. Golan."Origametria and the van Hiele Theory of Teaching Geometry." In *Origami⁵: Fifth International Meeting of Origami Science, Mathematics, and Education*, edited by Patsy Wang-Iverson, Robert J. Lang, and Mark Yim, pp. 141–150. Boca Raton, FL: A K Peters/CRC Press, 2011. MR2866909 (2012h:00044)

[Hull 06] T. Hull. *Project Origami: Activities for Exploring Mathematics*. Wellesley, MA: A K Peters, 2006. MR2330113 (2008d:00001)

[Pope and Lam 09] S. Pope and T. K. Lam."Using Origami to Promote Problem Solving, Creativity, and Communication in Mathematics Education." In *Origami⁴: Fourth International Meeting of Origami Science, Mathematics, and Education*, edited by Robert Lang, pp. 517–524. Natick, MA: A K Peters, 2009.

DIPARTIMENTO DI MATEMATICA, UNIVERSITÀ DEGLI STUDI DI MILANO, ITALY
E-mail address: emma.frigerio@unimi.it

DIPARTIMENTO DI SCIENZE MATEMATICHE, POLITECNICO DI TORINO, ITALY
E-mail address: maria.spreafico@polito.it

Mathematics and Art through the Cuboctahedron

Shi-Pui Kwan

1. Introduction

One of the many reasons for attending the OSME meetings (International Meeting of Origami in Science, Mathematics and Education) is the invaluable opportunity to see and learn about the design of very creative origami models. I still remember the set of lively origami insects by Robert Lang at 3OSME and the twisting origami lamp by Tomoko Fuse at 5OSME. But they can hardly be integrated into the formal school curriculum. For learning of mathematics through origami, ideas are either elementary or they are too advanced for the age group 11–15 years old. This paper focuses on the integration of mathematics, art, and origami through the cuboctahedron. The term *cuboctahedron* may be strange to these children, so our exploration begins with regular solids. A *regular* polyhedron is a polyhedron with congruent faces and identical vertices. There are only five regular convex polyhedra, known as the *Platonic solids*. Among them, the regular tetrahedron, the cube, and the regular octahedron are familiar to pupils of this age group.

2. Cuboctahedron and Cut Sections

Educators understand that solid dissections help children to develop spatial sense [Obara 09]. Examine a cube; each vertex is connected to three mutually perpendicular edges. Using their midpoints to construct a dissecting plane, a "corner" can be cut off from the cube. Can you imagine the shape of the solid left behind? Teachers can guide students to visualize the geometric figure by actually building the origami model (see Figure 1). Please refer to the folding of the Columbus cube [Mitchell 99].[1]

What will happen to the cube when more "corners" are trimmed off? How about the final situation when all eight vertices are dissected? Can you modify David Mitchell's method and create the solid so obtained? (See Figure 2.)

By truncating the vertices of a cube at half-edge length, we end up with a cuboctahedron. This solid has six square and eight triangular faces with equilateral edges.

Real objects are valuable teaching aids for the study of geometry. Their manipulation provide children with concrete experiences and help them to visualize abstract concepts. Paper models contribute a lot in this area. The folding instructions for the cut-off triangular pyramid are shown in Figure 3.

---

[1]The model does not actually "cut away" the corner but "turns it inside" for locking purposes. Nevertheless it is a simple and tight model easily learned by origami beginners.

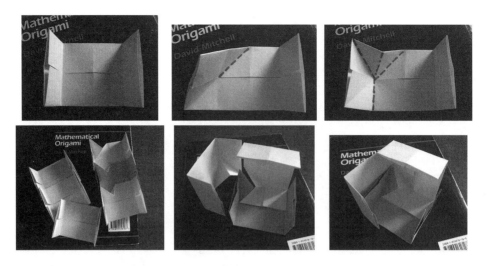

Figure 1. David Mitchell's method.

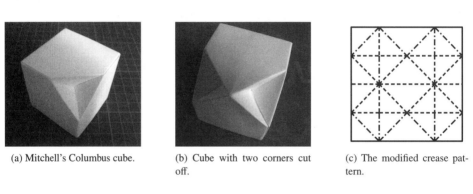

(a) Mitchell's Columbus cube.

(b) Cube with two corners cut off.

(c) The modified crease pattern.

Figure 2. A cube with more corners cut off.

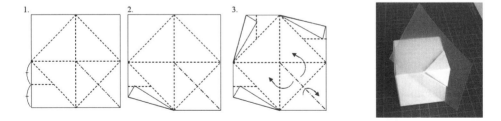

Figure 3. The origami triangular pyramid.

Now take a regular octahedron and repeat the above process in a similar manner. This time we cut through the midpoints of the four neighboring edges connected to each vertex.[2] What will be the solid left behind?

___

[2]Three noncollinear points determine a plane. It is interesting for pupils to investigate, make conjectures, and prove that the fourth midpoint always lies on the plane passing through the other three.

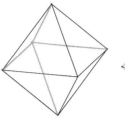

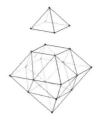

(a) A regular octahedron.   (b) Half-edge dissection.   (c) A square face is produced.

FIGURE 4. The WisWeb applet animation [Freudenthal Institute 08] of creating a cuboctahedron.

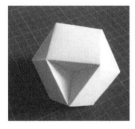

FIGURE 5. A cuboctahedron and its cut-off "corners."

Let us do the dissection in our minds. The three dissection planes cutting through each (triangular) face will leave a smaller equilateral triangle behind. For every cut a right square pyramid is detached from the octahedron, creating new square surface. (See Figure 4.) Therefore, the remaining solid has six square and eight triangular faces with equal edges. It is again a cuboctahedron!

3. Cuboctahedron and Volume

Finding the total surface area of a cuboctahedron is straightforward. How do we determine its volume?

Consider the eight congruent triangular pyramids dissected from a cube of edge length x (units). (See Figure 5.) For each pyramid, the base area is $\frac{1}{8}x^2$ (square units) and the height is $\frac{1}{2}x$ (units). Hence, the volume of the cuboctahedron is

$$V = x^3 - 8\left(\frac{1}{3}\left(\frac{1}{8}x^2\right)\left(\frac{1}{2}x\right)\right)$$

$$= \frac{5}{6}x^3 \text{ (cubic units)}.$$

Is there any alternate approach to solving the problem? It can be done by purely dissecting the cuboctahedron into four congruent rectangular pyramids and a central cuboid.

FIGURE 6. Alternate solution for volume of a cuboctahedron.

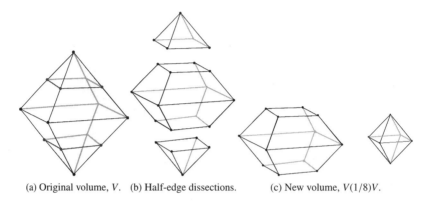

(a) Original volume, V.   (b) Half-edge dissections.   (c) New volume, $V(1/8)V$.

FIGURE 7. Octahedron dissection.

(See Figure 6.) With the same notation above, the volume of the cuboctahedron is

$$V = 4\left(\frac{1}{3}(x)\left(\sqrt{2}\left(\frac{1}{2}x\right)\right)\left(\frac{1}{2}\left(\sqrt{2}-\sqrt{2}\left(\frac{1}{2}x\right)\right)\right)\right) + x\left(\sqrt{2}\left(\frac{1}{2}x\right)\left(\sqrt{2}\frac{1}{2}x\right)\right)$$

$$= \frac{1}{3}x^3 + \frac{1}{2}x^3$$

$$= \frac{5}{6}x^3 \text{ (cubic units).}$$

Knowing that the volume of a regular octahedron is $\frac{\sqrt{2}}{3}$ (edge length)^3, and supposing that we start with a regular octahedron with edge length $\sqrt{2}x$ (units), the volume of the cuboctahedron obtained from dissections is

$$\frac{\sqrt{2}}{3}\left(\sqrt{2}x\right)^3 - 3\left(\frac{1}{8}\left(\frac{\sqrt{2}}{3}\left(\sqrt{2}x\right)^3\right)\right) = \frac{5}{6}x^3 \text{ (cubic units).}$$

The same value is obtained.

Take a closer look at the above calculation. Is it a complicated formula substitution or a simple result of solid decomposition? Figure 7 serves as an illustrative idea similar to "proofs without words" [Nelsen 93]. The expression has just described the action applied to the octahedron three times.

Starting with a cube or a regular octahedron of suitable dimension and carrying out the half-edge dissection process, we get exactly the same cuboctahedron as our final product. That is why the name *cuboctahedron* comes from the combination of *cube* and *octahedron*.

FIGURE 8. Business card cuboctahedron.

4. Business Card Cuboctahedron

Rethinking our modified origami method for constructing the cuboctahedron, we note that the folding is actually carried out on half of a square sheet in double layers. Ordinary origami sheets are too weak for constructing the model. A better option is to replace paper sheets by cards, which are stiffer. With a little research it is easy to find that such a folding method for a cuboctahedron is well established in business card origami by Jeannine Mosely, Kenneth Kawumara, and Paul Jackson [Origami Resource Center 15].

Business cards are usually rectangular in shape with edge ratio 4:7. Names and logos are two common features found in the printing. Depending on the design, they are placed in various positions of the printout. Sometimes it is impossible to have a particular feature appear properly in the cuboctahedron that is folded. Note, for example, the card in Figure 8: the fish appears on the face of the cuboctahedron but the name of the sushi restaurant is hidden.

Furthermore, business card shapes are getting more and more creative. Some of them are squares and cannot be used for the origami instructions mentioned above. Are they still useful in constructing the cuboctahedron?

5. Cuboctahedron Lantern

At 5OSME I joined a workshop on Akari Origami by Miyuki Kawamura. She introduced the construction of a lovely model, a Checkered Lantern, using square sheets. Being a mathematics and physics teacher, I recognized that an LED lamp had been inserted into a folded model of a cuboctahedron. Her idea inspired my study of this solid. I have found various folding algorithms (ranging from elementary to sophisticated methods) for the model and reviewed its mathematics properties. Kawamura and Moriwaki chose an LED chip with 120-degree irradiation angle and a type of translucent paper for constructing their lantern [Kawamura and Moriwaki 11]. (See Figure 9(a).) In Kawamura's words, "The Checkered Lantern is an easy model for beginners. Advanced folders/professional people who like challenges can design their own origami polyhedra." As a teacher I asked myself, "Can it be done in other simple ways with materials easily accessible to us? Would it be possible for age 11-15 kids to complete the model while maintaining Kawamura's ideas in designing the lantern?"

Considering the use of a much weaker (and cheaper) lamp for the lantern, we have to select a transparent sheet for the cuboctahedron construction. The plastic folder was a good choice. Just like a business card, the folder sheet is rigid but transparent. (See Figure 9(b–c).) Its major drawback is the conspicuous crease produced by folding. So we have to avoid and reduce unnecessary fold lines. Below is the revised origami instructional procedure:

(a) Kawamura's model.   (b) Modules from plastic folder.   (c) The modified model.

FIGURE 9. A modification of Kawamura's model.

(1) Take a 60 mm × 100 mm plastic folder rectangular sheet.
(2) Estimate the midpoint of the longer side.
(3) Fold both sides as indicated to obtain a right angle symmetrically situated at the mid-point (Figure 10(a–b)).
(4) Unfold one side (Figure 10(c)).
(5) Valley fold the opposite longer edge to meet the original folded edge (Figure 10(d)).
(6) Repeat steps 4 and 5 on the other side to complete a creased square in the middle of the rectangular sheet (Figure 10(e)).
(7) Unfold, and mountain fold at both the left and right square vertices to obtain the required crease pattern (Figure 10(f)).
(8) Repeat steps 1-7 with a new plastic folder sheet and prepare six total modules (Figure 10(g).
(9) Assemble the modules as before (Figure 10(h)).
(10) Insert the lamp (Figure 10(i)) into the cuboctahedron at one of the concave vertices.

6. Cuboctahedron Lantern and Error Estimation

Two estimations affecting the final lantern are the accuracy of (1) the location of the midpoint and (2) the construction of the square at 45 degrees to the longer sides. With GeoGebra [GeoGebra 15], we can guide children visually to explore the errors made. The first error will merely shift the crease pattern linearly on the card while the second error will deform the original square into a rectangle, thus not achieving the interlocking mechanism. (See Figure 11.)

Meanwhile, it is a good exercise for older children to prove that the origami procedure in Section 5 will produce a creased rectangle lying in between two given parallel lines (the longer sides of the rectangle).

The new model can hardly be compared with Kawamura's design. But, the finished lantern, excluding the dry cells, costs only eight Hong Kong dollars (about one US dollar)! This price is affordable for art classes in schools.

7. Cuboctahedron Souvenir

Since the interlocking structure can hold a piece of paper firmly inside the square face, a message (motto, greeting, photo, and the like) can be left inside as a souvenir. Given a

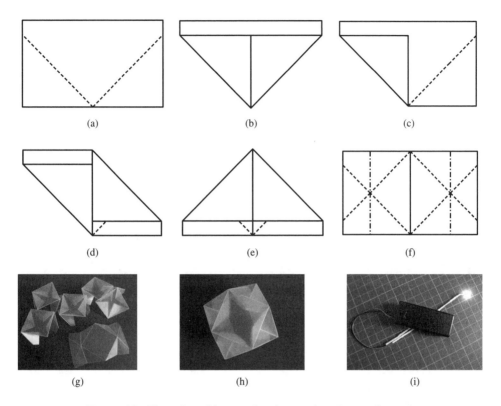

FIGURE 10. The origami instructional procedure for our lantern.

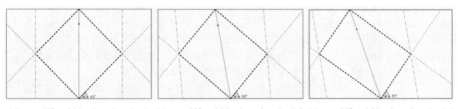

(a) $\alpha = 45°$, width : length = 1 : 1. (b) $\alpha = 50°$, width : length = 1 : 1.2.(c) $\alpha = 55°$, width : length = 1 : 1.4.

FIGURE 11. Error due to angle (α) estimation.

photo of a particular square size, what dimensions of the plastic folder sheets should be prepared for the construction of an origami cuboctahedron photo frame? (See Figure 13.)

Given a rectangular sheet $a \times b$ ($a \leq b$), the square surface generated by origami is independent of b. The side of the square surface produced is $a/\sqrt{2}$. Hence, the ratio of the message/photo length to the width (namely, a) of the transparent plastic sheet is $1 : \sqrt{2}$. Bearing this relationship in mind and looking back in our previous discussion of displaying both the name and the logo of a business card, it is easy to determine the appropriate plastic sheet size for holding the square sushi card[3] (see Figure 12).

---

[3]This idea can be developed into a mini project for pupils' home study.

FIGURE 12. Sushi card cut to a square.

FIGURE 13. Cuboctahedron souvenirs.

The cuboctahedron is an Archimedean solid, and the concave vertices can hold a smaller cuboctahedron (the *baby*) within the larger (the *mother*). This idea brings about the *pregnant mother* model. What is the minimum baby size that can be held firmly by its mother without slipping? (A more challenging problem!)

8. Cuboctahedron Pop-Up Card

The cuboctahedron as a birthday present brings about a new thought: Can it be placed flat inside a card and pop up when it is opened? This question is clearly related to the net of the solid (Figure 14(a)). With regard to the card design, each of the four lateral squares is cut (along the vertical diagonals) into halves (two isosceles right angle triangles) so as to yield two identical and symmetrical nets (Figure 14(b)) that can be overlaid flat on a surface. The horizontal diagonals are hinges between the bottom and the top layer [Walser 00]. A tiny paper strip is attached to the top square for pulling up the model (Figure 14(e). Figure 14 shows the nets and the card made. Does it look like a pumpkin?

9. Cuboctahedron Earrings and Necklace

Upon my return from 6OSME, I shared with my colleagues many of the interesting ideas learned. Josie Lee suggested that the cuboctahedron could be made into attractive earrings and a pendant. After weeks of discussions and trials, we were happy and amazed to have produced the earrings and necklace set shown in Figure 15.

10. Epilogue

To be rigorous, the model discussed so far is a *cubohemioctahedron*,[4] which is a faceted version of the cuboctahedron. Also, the origami methods described above do not

---

[4]Following the previous discussion, the volume of a cubohemioctahedron equals the volume of the cube minus the total volume of sixteen congruent triangular pyramids.

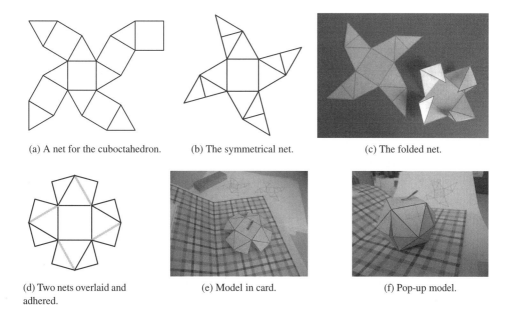

(a) A net for the cuboctahedron.   (b) The symmetrical net.   (c) The folded net.

(d) Two nets overlaid and   (e) Model in card.   (f) Pop-up model.
adhered.

FIGURE 14. A cuboctahedron pop-up card.

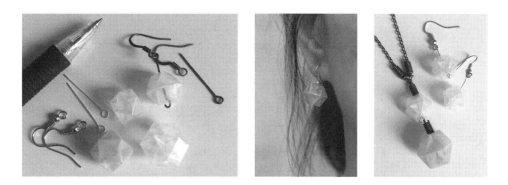

FIGURE 15. Cuboctahedron earrings and necklace set.

constitute the best design. These instructions are selected because they are simple algorithms that can be implemented effectively in classrooms. They are meant to be a means
and not an end for learning mathematics and art. Children motivated by the activities may
be guided toward the study of more advanced designs. Figure 16 presents models designed by renowned origami artists. They are suitable for extension study/discussion and
self-learning.

The cuboctahedron has long attracted the attention of our ancestors. Hakan Hisarligil
discovered that this solid seems to be an icon with special meaning. Cuboctahedral structures and decorations are found in Kayseri, Turkey and in Kyoto, Japan [Hisarligil 12].
Maybe the Checkered Lantern belongs to this category.

Lanterns are popular among the Chinese, too. The fifteenth day of the first month
in the Lunisolar Year and the Mid-Autumn Festival in China are also called the Lantern

(a) [Stern 11]

(b) [Fuse 90]

(c) [Montroll 09]

FIGURE 16. More sophisticated cuboctahedron designs.

Festival. They are usually in early March and mid-September. Don't miss the opportunity to introduce the origami cuboctahedron to your pupils!

Acknowledgments

I would like to express my gratitude to Miyuki Kawamura, who first introduced me to the origami cuboctahedral lantern, and Josie Lee, who inspired me to design the cuboctahedron earrings and pendant.

Lastly, I would like to thank Haruo Hosoya who shared with me his envelope model of the cuboctahedron after my 6OSME presentation.

References

[Freudenthal Institute 08] Freudenthal Institute. "Overview of WisWeb-applets." *WisWeb*, http://www.fi.uu.nl/wisweb/applets/mainframe_en.html, 2008 (retrieved February 12, 2015).

[Fuse 90] Tomoko Fuse. *Unit Origami: Multidimensional Transformations*. Tokyo: Japan Publications, 1990.

[GeoGebra 15] "GeoGebra: Dynamic mathematics for learning and teaching." http://www.geogebra.org/, 2015 (retrieved February 12, 2015).

[Hisarligil 12] Hakan Hisarligil "Cuboctahedron as a Potential Evidence of the 'Cultural Bridge' between Kyoto and Kayseri." In *Proceedings of 2nd International Conference*, pp. 20–25. Nishinomiya, Japan: Mukogawa Women's University, 2012.

[Kawamura and Moriwaki 11] Miyuki Kawamura and Hiroyuki Moriwaki. "New Collaboration on Modular Origami and LED." In *Origami 5: Fifth International Meeting of Origami Science, Mathematics, and Education*, edited by Patsy Wang-Iverson, Robert J. Lang, and Mark Yim, pp. 89–97. Boca Raton, FL: CRC Press, 2011. MR2866909 (2012h:00044)

[Mitchell 99] David Mitchell. *Mathematical Origami: Geometrical Shapes by Paper Folding*. Stradbroke, UK: Tarquin Publications, 1999.

[Montroll 09] John Montroll. *Origami Polyhedra Design*. Natick, MA: A K Peters, 2009. MR2567429 (2010i:52001)

[Obara 09] Samuel Obara. "Decomposing Solids to Develop Spatial Sense." *Mathematics Teaching in the Middle School* 14:6 (2009), 336–343.

[Origami Resource Center 15] Origami Resource Center. "Business Card Origami Cuboctahedron." http://www.origami-resource-center.com/business-card-cuboctahedron.html, 2015 (retrieved February 12, 2015).

[Nelsen 93] Roger B. Nelsen. *Proofs Without Words: Exercises in Visual Thinking*. Washington, DC: Mathematical Association of America, 1993.

[Stern 11] Scott Wasserman Stern. *Outside the Box Origami: A New Generation of Extraordinary Folds*. Singapore: Tuttle Publishing, 2011.

[Walser 00] Hans Walser. "The Pop-up Cuboctahedron." *The College Mathematics Journal* 31:2 (March, 2000), 89–92. MR1766157 (2001c:52008)

SHATIN TSUNG TSIN SCHOOL, HONG KONG
E-mail address: spkwan@hotmail.com

Origami-Inspired Deductive Threads in Pre-geometry

Arnold Tubis

1. Introduction

The use of origami in the informal geometry or pre-geometry phase of mathematics education (grades K–7 or 8 in schools in the United States) enables students to (1) do hands-on (versus computer-aided) constructions such as line/angle bisection, perpendicular and parallel lines, and golden sections—constructions that usually require substantially more steps when made with a straight edge and compass; (2) directly verify the congruence of line segments, angles, and polygons by folding these elements (or portions of them) on top of one another; (3) discover and/or verify the Pythagorean theorem and various properties of polygons such as the sum of the angle measures of a triangle and area formulae; and (4) derive pleasure and satisfaction from the synergy of discovering the many ways in which a popular art and craft activity has relevance for, and can supplement, the study of geometry. The article [Coad 06] presents an excellent overview of how paper folding has been typically used in the classroom to introduce some standard elements of school geometry.

In this paper, we propose in rough preliminary outline, a program that incorporates origami in pre-geometry as part of an engaging prelude to the type of deductive arguments that are a staple of geometry at higher levels. As will be seen, some of the deductive threads introduced may be considered rather idiosyncratic in that they do not closely mimic the classical Euclidean ones (e.g., we do not make use of the standard sufficiency conditions such as the Side-Angle-Side one for triangle congruence). Nevertheless, we hope that this work will spur efforts to develop similar (and perhaps more pedagogical) instructional units in which origami plays a dual role—as a catalyst for making basic geometrical assertions, and, as a means of demonstrating or verifying the implications of these assertions.

Our proposal may be most effective as part of an end-of-unit review of pre-geometry, after students in their first seven or eight years of school have developed an elementary working knowledge of some important geometric results (but not the deductive threads connecting them). In brief, it consists of (1) focusing on five key assertions or postulates about single, perpendicular, and parallel lines, and about parallelograms that are strongly suggested/supported by easy folding explorations; (2) showing how these can be used to logically infer, or at least make very plausible, a substantial body of geometric knowledge; and finally (3) showing, in turn, how most of the inferred results could be made more vivid and memorable by demonstrating/verifying them by folding. The inferred geometric results include the equality of measures of alternate interior, alternate exterior, and corresponding angle pairs, the specific sum of the angle measures of a triangle, area formulae for various polygons, and the Pythagorean theorem and its converse. The fairly straightforward deductive threads of the program should hopefully establish strong and clear connections among some very important practical geometric facts—connections that sometimes tend to be fuzzy and clouded in the minds of students when they are later encapsulated in the more precise frameworks of higher-level geometry.

In the various folding explorations/demonstrations described in this paper, the use of translucent wax ("patty") paper will give the clearest and most satisfactory results.

2. Assumed Geometric Background of the Students

We assume that the student group involved has had some experience with guided explorations in paper folding geometry like, e.g., those in [Serra 94] or [Tubis and Mills 06], and have been informally introduced to a body of geometric concepts without excessively detailed sets of definitions, axioms, propositions, or theorems. We assume that these geometric concepts include all or most of the following: line, length measure of a line, intersecting lines, angle and angle measure, line and angle bisection, perpendicular lines, parallel lines, right and straight angles and their unique nature, supplementary and complementary angles, vertical angle pairs, corresponding and alternate interior and exterior angle pairs, polygons (triangles, rectangles, parallelograms, trapezoids, and other quadrilaterals, etc.), area, perimeter, and volume.

In the spirit of informal geometry, we also assume that the students have achieved an intuitive working understanding of the various equalities involving geometric and numerical entities that are traditionally considered *self-evident* (e.g., things that are equal, or congruent, to the same thing are equal, or congruent, to each other; if equals are added to equals, the sums are equal; corresponding angles and sides of congruent polygons are congruent; and polygons with congruent corresponding sides and angles are congruent). For simplicity of presentation in this short paper, we assume that students will apply this understanding when needed in the deductive threads even though it is not always explicitly mentioned.

3. Geometric Postulates Motivated by Folding Rectangular and Parallel Line Patterns

Students with only a modicum of origami experience soon learn that normally folding and creasing a sheet of paper produces a unique straight-line segment connecting two given points, with the line having the same geometric features as a stretched string or a line drawn with a conventional straight edge. They also note that the straight line is uniquely and indefinitely extendable beyond the segment at both ends, and that a straight line connecting two points on the line lie totally on the original line. Therefore (within the realm of Euclidean planar geometry), two lines either never intersect (i.e., are parallel), or intersect at only a single point. (If they intersected at two points, the two lines would then completely coincide). Students also learn how to fold a portion of a crease line onto an adjacent portion to produce another unique crease line perpendicular to the initial line and passing through a given point on the line or a point outside the line. (It may be a perpendicular bisector if half a creased line segment is folded onto the other half by bringing the ends of the segment together and creasing). Finally, they learn how to verify by folding a major hallmark of these perpendicular lines: the formation of four congruent right angles at their intersection [see Figure 1(a)]. One of the first papers on the modern foundations of origami geometry [Frigerio and Huzita 89] contains a somewhat profound observation [see Figure 1(b)]. Consider the following constructions: (1) folding an initial crease line

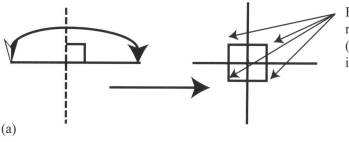

Four congruent right angles (verified by folding).

(a)

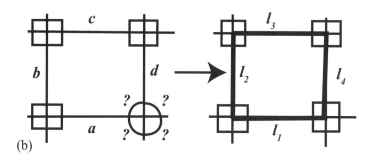

(b)

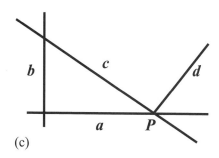

(c)

If lines a and c intersect (at P), there could be two different lines (a and c) perpendicular to line d at the same point P on d. This is not possible because of the assumed uniqueness of the perpendicular to a line at a given point on the line.

FIGURE 1. Folding experiences that give support for assertions P2, P3, and P4. In (b), l_1, l_2, l_3, and l_4 denote the lengths of the bold line segments.

a, (2) folding a onto itself to give another line b perpendicular to a, (3) similarly folding b onto itself to give a line c perpendicular to b, and finally (4) folding c onto itself to give line d perpendicular to c. Now, if we did not know about the exact nature of the paper that is being folded, we could not in principle say anything specific about the intersection of lines d and a.

The fact that in the case of conventional paper, d and a will also be found to be perpendicular to one another and produce four congruent right angles at the point of intersection [see Figure 1(b)] reflects the basic (planar) geometry of the paper. The findings just described and summarized in Figure 1 suggest that it may be useful to make the following assertions or postulates (loosely stated in the spirit of informal geometry):

P1: A unique line segment may be constructed between two given points and extended indefinitely at both ends of the segment, and a line segment between any two points on it will lie completely on it. (Based on the experiences of folding straight line creases.)

P2: There is a unique constructible line perpendicular to a given line that passes through a specific point on the line or a point outside the line, with the intersecting lines forming four congruent right angles. (Based on the experiences of folding right angles as described in Figure 1(a).)

P3: Lines perpendicular to the same line at two different points are parallel (i.e., never meet no matter how far extended). (Based on the experience described in Figure 1(b) and elaborated on in Figure 1(c).)

P4: If two lines are parallel, a line perpendicular to one is also perpendicular to the other. (Based on the experience described in Figure 1(b).)

Note that we have not stated anything yet about relations among the lengths of the line segments l_1, l_2, l_3, and l_4 in Figure 1(b).

4. Geometric Assertion Supported by Congruence of Two Triangles Made by Diagonal of Parallelogram

Instead of considering the various sufficiency conditions for the congruence of two triangles (Side, Angle, Side; Angle, Side, Angle; Side, Angle, Angle; and Side, Side, Side) as is done in higher-level geometry, we simplify our logical framework and focus just on the specific congruence (verified by folding) of the two triangles formed when the diagonal of a general parallelogram is constructed (Figure 2). This congruence, and the congruence of corresponding sides and angles of congruent triangles, will be the basis for our final assertion or postulate:

P5: The two triangles formed when the diagonal of a general parallelogram is constructed are congruent.

Limiting our assertions about triangle congruence to just P5 reduces considerably the range of possible deductions in our simplified introduction to logical geometrical arguments. Nevertheless, as we shall see, the deductions do include valuable practical knowledge, such as area formulae.

5. Some Inferences Following from the Assertions Easily Demonstrated by Folding

We list here eleven of the many inferences that can be derived from P1–P5, all of which can easily be demonstrated or verified by folding. The main ingredients (except for the congruence relations mentioned at the end of Section 2) used in the proofs are indicated in parenthesis.

I1: Vertical angles pairs are congruent. (Use P1 and P2.)

I2: If two parallel lines are intersected by a transversal, then the alternate interior angle pairs, the corresponding angle pairs, and the alternate exterior angle pairs are congruent. (Use P2, P3, P4, P5, and I1.)

I3: If two lines are parallel, the distance from one line to the other along any line perpendicular to them is constant. (Use P5 in the special case of a rectangle and one of its diagonals.) Hence, $l_1 = l_3$ and $l_2 = l_4$ in Figure 2(b).

I4: The opposite sides of a parallelogram are equal in length. (Use P5.)

I5: The area of a rectangle is equal to the product of its base and height. (Construct a rectangular grid of equal-spaced parallel lines using P1–P4 and I3 to produce a rectangle divided into congruent square units.)

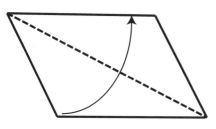

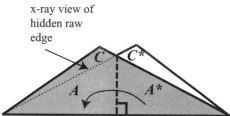

1. Make a patty paper parallelogram, and valley fold to give two triangles.

2. The front (shaded) triangle has sections A, A^*, and C. The rear one has section C^* and sections congruent to A and A^*. Valley fold.

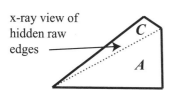

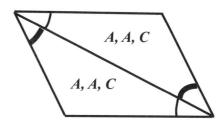

3. Sections A and A^* are seen to be congruent, as are sections C and C^* ones. Unfold completely.

4. The congruency of the two triangles implies that each of the two pairs of alternate interior angles are congruent, that the opposite sides of a parallelogram are equal in length, and that the area of each triangle is half the area of the parallelogram.

FIGURE 2. Folding verification of the congruence of the two triangles separated by the diagonal of a parallelogram.

I6: The sum of the angle measures of a triangle is two right angles. (Use P2, P3, and I2.)

I7: The area of a triangle is one half the base times the height. (Use P2, P5, I5, and I7.) See Figures 5(b) and 6(a).

I8: The area of a parallelogram is the base times the height. (Use P2, P5, and I5.) See Figures 5(c) and 6(b).

I9: The area of a trapezoid is [length of base + length of top)/2] times height. (Use P2, I3, I5, and I7.) See Figures 5(d) and 6(c).

I10: The Pythagorean theorem is true. (Use P2, P3, P5, I5, and I7.) See Figure 7.

I11: The converse of the Pythagorean theorem is true. (Use P2 and I10.) See Figure 8.

These particular inferences are presented here because they have traditionally been the basis for many of the problems in standardized tests. Since the details of their proofs are generally well known, we will not give an extended presentation of the proofs in this short paper. Instead, we briefly illustrate here the nature of the informal proofs of the statements in I2, I3, and I4.

Consider a line transverse to two parallel lines, l_1 and l_2. From P2, we may construct a line from the intersection point of the transversal and l_1 (respectively l_2) so that it is perpendicular to l_2 (respectively l_1). By P4, these constructed lines are perpendicular to both lines. By P3, these constructed lines are also parallel to each other, so that the original parallel lines and the two constructed ones define a parallelogram (actually a rectangle) with the transversal being a diagonal of it. The congruence of the two parts of the rectangle separated by the diagonal (according to P5), the congruence of corresponding angles of congruent triangles (considered *self-evident*, as was previously mentioned), and the use of I1 then give the statements of I2.

The statements of I3 follow if two perpendiculars are constructed between parallel lines (using P2 and P4), thus forming a rectangle. Constructing the diagonal of the rectangle and then using P5 gives I3. I4 follows from using P5 and the congruence of corresponding sides of congruent triangles (considered *self-evident*).

6. Folding Demonstration/Verification of Some of the Inferences

Figure 3 contains the well-known formal proof as well as the folding verification of I1, and Figure 4 shows the folding verification of the congruence of alternate interior angles and corresponding angle pairs (I2). Similar demonstrations may easily be given for the congruence of alternate exterior angle pairs.

The folding demonstration for the area of a rectangle in Figure 5(a) is, of course, only valid for the case of a rational number value for the length/width ratio. However, it is in line with typical school mathematics discussions of area. The limits arguments required for dealing with the case of an irrational number value for the ratio is generally considered beyond the scope of pre-geometry.

The folding demonstration of I6 in Figure 5(b) has been incorporated in a number of textbooks and is certainly more elegant than the practice of tearing off the vertex sections of a triangle and combining the angles so that they sum to two right angles.

Special attention should be directed at the folding verifications of the areas of a triangle, parallelogram, and trapezoid (I7, I8, and I9, respectively). One of the reviewers of the original draft of this paper pointed out that the specific protocols used to determine area in almost all school mathematics texts are not applicable as they stand for the cases of (1) triangles oriented so that one of the base angles is obtuse; (2) parallelograms oriented so that the top side lies fully to the right or left of the bottom side (taken as the base); and (3) trapezoids in which the top member of the parallel sides is longer than the bottom one. We show, however, in Figure 6 that simple modifications of the folding procedures can easily be used to demonstrate the area formulae in these cases. The general procedure for demonstrating area formulae is to fold the starting shape into a double-layered rectangle whose dimensions are simply related to those of the triangle, parallelogram, or trapezoid.

Finally, we show respectively in Figures 7 and 8 one of the many possible folding demonstrations of the Pythagorean theorem and its converse.

7. Summary

A major aspect of pre-geometry is the honing of skills in solving missing-angle and area problems—problems in which perpendicular and parallel lines, the angle relationships in the case of parallel lines intersected by a transversal, the sum of angle measures of a triangle, area formulae for triangles and various quadrilaterals, and the Pythagorean theorem play an important role. We have tried to show how origami can be used to motivate basic assertions from which many practical results of Euclidean geometry follow as logical implications and can thus be advantageously part of the transition to the more intensive and formal deductive emphasis in higher-level geometry.

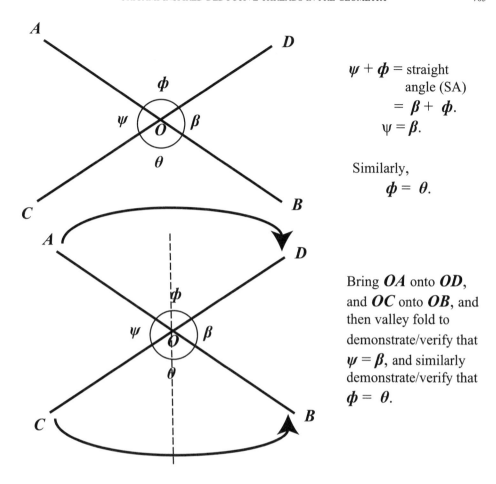

$\psi + \phi$ = straight
            angle (SA)
    = $\beta + \phi$.
  $\psi = \beta$.

Similarly,
    $\phi = \theta$.

Bring **OA** onto **OD**, and **OC** onto **OB**, and then valley fold to demonstrate/verify that $\psi = \beta$, and similarly demonstrate/verify that $\phi = \theta$.

FIGURE 3. Proof and folding verification of the congruence of vertical angle pairs.

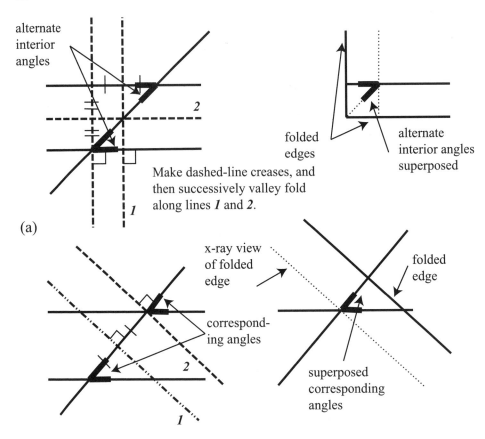

(a)

(b)

FIGURE 4. Folding verification of the congruence of alternate interior and corresponding angle pairs.

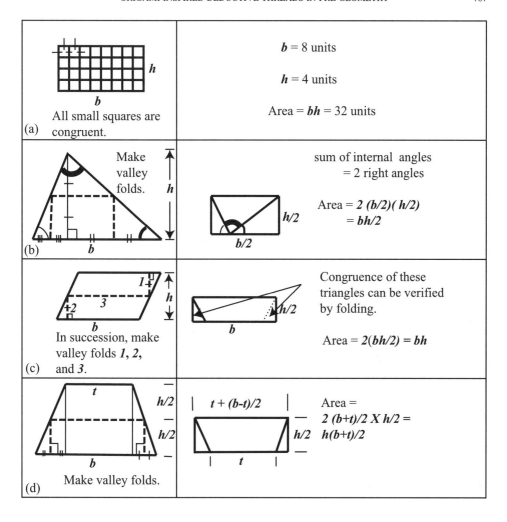

FIGURE 5. Folding verifications of (a) the area formulas for a rectangle (I5), (b) the sum of angle measures (I6) and area (I7) of a triangle, (c) the area of a parallelogram (I8), and (d) the area of a trapezoid (I9). As discussed in the text, the specific folding protocols in (b), (c), and (d) are not as they stand applicable to all cases. The required changes in folding procedures for other possible cases are shown in Figure 6. The folding demonstrations are best done with patty (translucent waxed) paper.

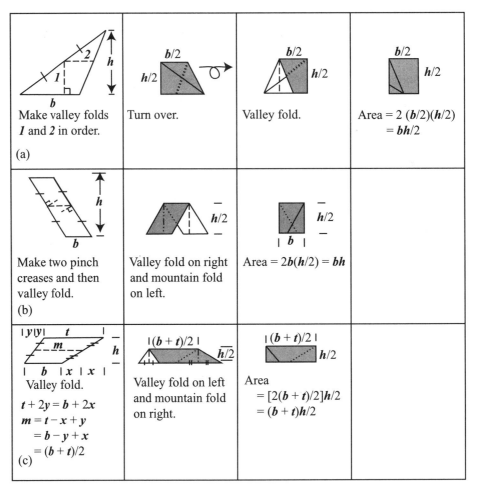

FIGURE 6. Modified folding procedures for demonstrating area formulae for (a) triangles oriented so that one of the base angles is obtuse, (b) parallelograms oriented so that the top side is fully to the right or left of the bottom one, and (c) trapezoids in which the top member of the parallel sides is longer than the bottom one. As the top side of the parallelogram recedes further and further to the right or left of the bottom side, extra folds will be required to produce the final double-layered rectangular piece whose dimensions are *b* and *h*/2. These extra folds can easily be implemented in a straightforward manner, but the specific details will not be given here. Note that in all three cases, the final configuration is a double-layered rectangular piece whose area is *half* that of the starting polygon.

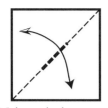

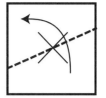

1. Make a pinch crease along the diagonal.

Use patty paper.

2. Make a pinch crease along the other diagonal.

3. Valley fold. The crease is not parallel to any side of the square.

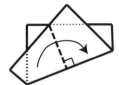

4. Valley fold.

5. Valley fold/unfold.

6. Valley fold. The side lengths of the extra bold right triangle are b, h, and c.

Verify congruence of four quadrilateral ($ABCD$) and triangular (ABD) sections.

7.

quadrilateral $ABCD$

triangle ABD

8.

area of large square
$$= (h + b)^2$$
$$= c^2 + 4(1/2)hb$$

$$h^2 + b^2 = c^2$$

FIGURE 7. Origami demonstration of the Pythagorean theorem (most effectively done with patty paper). In step 3, the crease line may be any line passing through the center that is neither horizontal nor vertical. Although the basic crease lines (of length c) may be made with just four folds, this method enables the congruence of the four hbc right triangles to be directly verified by folding. (Folding scheme adapted from [Tubis and Mills 06, p. 90].)

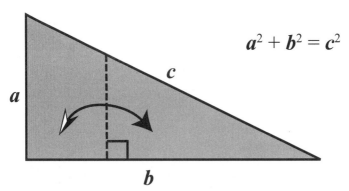

$$a^2 + b^2 = c^2$$

Valley fold and unfold (crease) at right angle to base.

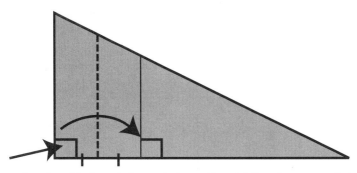

Verify that this is a right angle by valley folding it on top of right angle formed in the first step.

FIGURE 8. Folding verification of the converse of the Pythagorean theorem.

Acknowledgments

I wish to thank Patsy Wang-Iverson for stimulating and maintaining my interest in the use of origami in pre-geometry, and Patsy, Robert Orndorff, as well as two anonymous reviewers of the original manuscript for constructive criticism.

References

[Coad 06] Lance Coad. "Paper Folding in the Middle School Classroom and Beyond." *Australian Mathematics Teacher* 52:1 (2006), 6–13. (Available at https://www.questia.com/library/1G1-164525454/paper-folding-in-the-middle-school-classroom-and-beyond.)

[Frigerio and Huzita 89] Emma Frigerio and Humiaki Huzita. "Axiomatic Development of Origami Geometry." In *Proceedings of the First International Meeting on Origami Science and Technology*, edited by Humiaki Huzita, pp. 143–158. Padova, Italy: Dipartimento di Fisica dell'Università di Padova, 1989.

[Serra 94] Michael Serra. *Paper Patty Geometry*. Berkeley, CA: Key Curriculum Press, 1994.

[Tubis and Mills 06] Arnold Tubis and Crystal Elaine Mills. *Unfolding Mathematics with Origami Boxes*. Emeryville, CA: Key Curriculum Press, 2006.

PURDUE UNIVERSITY, WEST LAFAYETTE, IN (RETIRED)
E-mail address: tubisa@aol.com

Using Paper Folding to Solve Problems in School Geometry

Yanping Huang and Peng-Yee Lee

1. Introduction

In this paper, we shall illustrate how problems in school geometry can be solved by means of paper folding. The objective is to demonstrate possible ways of solving problems in school geometry.

First, we introduce six standard paper-folding methods. In the literature of origami, they are known as the six axioms [Justin 89]. However, we have no intention to develop it as an axiomatic system. In current grade school geometry, we assume the congruence of triangles as given, then we prove other properties of parallel lines, triangles, quadrilaterals, and circles, using congruent triangles [Lee 09]. Here, in place of congruent triangles, we assume the six folding methods as given. Then, we solve other problems using the six folding methods and some basic properties of triangles, parallel lines, as well as two key lemmas, namely, the perpendicular lemma and the parallel lemma, which are discussed in Section 1.

We do not suggest that we teach geometry as presented in this paper. We merely demonstrate the capabilities of paper folding. We make explicit for secondary school teachers how this can be done in the classroom. These axioms are well-known in the origami community, but in the literature, there has not been a systematic application of these axioms to grade school geometry, following the syllabus in China or Singapore, and done within the curriculum time.

Note that the key folding steps will be highlighted in boldface in the solutions.

2. Six Paper Folding Methods

We shall introduce the six paper folding methods with illustrative examples.

AXIOM 2.1 (A1). *Given two points P_1 and P_2, we can fold a line passing through the two points. (See Figure 1.)*

In symbols, we write $P_1 \leftrightarrow P_2$.

$$P_1 \qquad\qquad P_2$$

FIGURE 1. Illustration of Axiom 2.1.

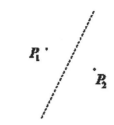

FIGURE 2. Illustration of Axiom 2.2.

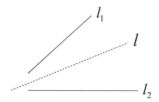

FIGURE 3. Illustration of Axiom 2.3.

PROBLEM 2.1. Given three points P_1, P_2, and P_3, fold a triangle with vertices P_1, P_2, and P_3.

SOLUTION. **Apply A1** to the pairs $P_1 P_2$, $P_1 P_3$, and $P_2 P_3$, respectively. The folded lines form a triangle $\triangle P_1 P_2 P_3$.

AXIOM 2.2 (A2). *Given two points P_1 and P_2, we can fold a line such that P_1 coincides with P_2.*

In symbols, we write $P_1 \to P_2$.

PROBLEM 2.2. Given two points P_1 and P_2, fold an isosceles triangle with base $P_1 P_2$.

SOLUTION. **Apply A2**: $P_1 \to P_2$. Choose a point P_3 on the folded line not on line $P_1 P_2$. If necessary, refer to Figure 2. As in Problem 2.1, we can fold a triangle from the three points P_1, P_2, and P_3. The triangle $\triangle P_1 P_2 P_3$ is isosceles with base $P_1 P_2$.

Note that if we apply A1: $P_1 \leftrightarrow P_2$ and A2: $P_1 \to P_2$, then we obtain two folded lines that are perpendicular to each other. This may serve as a definition for two lines being perpendicular. Conceptually, perpendicular lines come before parallel lines. Two lines are parallel if they are perpendicular to the same line.

AXIOM 2.3 (A3). *Given two lines ℓ_1 and ℓ_2, we can fold a line such that ℓ_1 coincides with ℓ_2. (See Figure 3.)*

In symbols, we write $\ell_1 \to \ell_2$.

PROBLEM 2.3. Given an isosceles triangle $\triangle ABC$ with $AB = AC$, fold an angle bisector that bisects the vertex angle, bisects the base, and is perpendicular to the base. (See Figure 4.)

SOLUTION. Let AB be ℓ_1 and AC be ℓ_2. **Apply A3**: $\ell_1 \to \ell_2$. Then, the properties follow by symmetry.

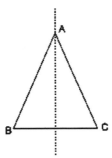

FIGURE 4. Illustration of Problem 2.3.

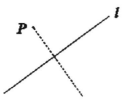

FIGURE 5. Illustration of Axiom 2.4.

In Problem 2.3, the two given lines intersect at a point. It is possible that if the two given lines are parallel, A3 still applies. In Problem 2.3, we also verify that the base angles are equal.

AXIOM 2.4 (A4). *Given a line ℓ and a point P, we can fold a line such that ℓ coincides with itself and the folded line passes through P.*

In symbols, we write $\ell \to \ell(P)$.

PROBLEM 2.4. Given a line ℓ and a point P, fold a line parallel to ℓ that passes through P.

SOLUTION. **Apply A4**: $\ell \to \ell(P)$. Denote the folded line by ℓ_1. Here, ℓ_1 is perpendicular to ℓ. If necessary, refer to Figure 5. Next, **apply A4**: $\ell_1 \to \ell_1(P)$. Denote the new folded line by ℓ_2. Here, ℓ_2 is perpendicular to ℓ_1. Hence, ℓ_2 is parallel to ℓ.

Note that in A4 the point P may or may not lie on ℓ.

AXIOM 2.5 (A5). *Given a line ℓ and two points P_1 and P_2, we can fold a line such that P_2 lies on ℓ and the folded line passes through P_1. (See Figure 6.)*

In symbols, $P_2 \to \ell(P_1)$.

PROBLEM 2.5. Given two points P_1 and P_2, fold an equilateral triangle with side P_1P_2.

SOLUTION. **Apply A2**: $P_1 \to P_2$, and obtain a folded line ℓ. Then, **apply A5**: $P_2 \to \ell(P_1)$. See Figure 7. The image of P_2 is Q_2 on ℓ. By A5, we have $P_1P_2 = P_1Q_2$. By A2, we have $P_1Q_2 = P_2Q_2$. Hence, $\triangle P_1P_2Q_2$ is an equilateral triangle.

Note that in Problem 2.5, P_1 and P_2 lie on different sides of ℓ. It is possible that P_1 and P_2 may lie on the same side of ℓ when we apply A5.

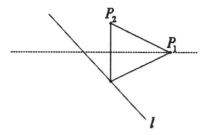

FIGURE 6. Illustration of Axiom 2.5.

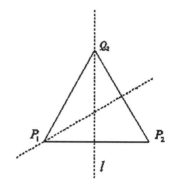

FIGURE 7. Illustration of Problem 2.5.

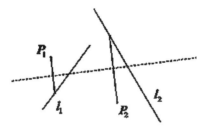

FIGURE 8. Illustration of Axiom 2.6.

AXIOM 2.6 (A6). *Given two lines ℓ_1, ℓ_2 and two points P_1, P_2, we can fold a line such that P_1 lies on ℓ_1 and P_2 lies on ℓ_2. (See Figure 8.)*

In symbols, $P_1 \to \ell_1 \wedge P_2 \to \ell_2$.

In what follows, we shall not make use of A6. We include it for completeness. In the literature, A6 is used to trisect some acute angles [Huang and Lee 12]. See also https://www.math.lsu.edu/~verrill/origami/trisect/. It is known that trisection of an acute angle is not possible using a straightedge and compass.

3. Perpendicular and Parallel Lines

We shall solve some problems involving perpendicular and parallel lines.

PROBLEM 3.1. Given two lines ℓ_1 and ℓ_2 that intersect at a point, fold a pair of perpendicular lines such that each line is a bisector of an angle between ℓ_1 and ℓ_2. (See Figure 9.)

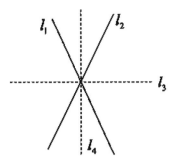

FIGURE 9. Illustration of Problem 3.1.

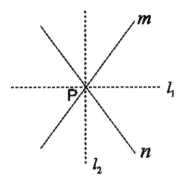

FIGURE 10. Illustration of the perpendicular lemma.

SOLUTION. **Apply A3**: $\ell_1 \rightarrow \ell_2$. There are two ways of folding ℓ_1 onto ℓ_2. The resulting folded lines ℓ_3 and ℓ_4 are the required perpendicular lines.

LEMMA 3.1 (The perpendicular lemma). *Let ℓ_1 and ℓ_2 be two lines perpendicular to each other that intersect at a point P. Given a line m passing through P, fold along ℓ_1 and afterward fold along ℓ_2. If the image of m after the first folding is n, then the image of n after the second folding is m.*

SOLUTION. As seen from Figure 10, by symmetry the image of n after folding along ℓ_2 is m. Note that A1 allows us to fold a line. We fold along ℓ_1 then along ℓ_2. Here we **apply A1** twice.

To understand the perpendicular lemma visually, draw Figure 10 on a sheet of paper and fold twice accordingly. Punch a hole at a point on m through all four layers of paper. Unfold it. Then we should be able to see the result clearly from the punched holes.

PROBLEM 3.2. Given three lines ℓ_1, ℓ_2, and m such that ℓ_1, ℓ_2 are parallel and m intersects ℓ_1, ℓ_2 at A, B, respectively, then $\angle 1 = \angle 2$ as shown in Figure 11. In words, alternate interior angles are equal.

SOLUTION. **Apply A2**: $A \rightarrow B$. We obtain the midpoint P of AB. **Apply A4** involving P twice, and obtain line ℓ_3 perpendicular to ℓ_1 and passing through P and line ℓ_4 perpendicular to ℓ_3 and passing through P. In view of the perpendicular lemma, the image of PA after folding along ℓ_3 and then along ℓ_4 is PB. Hence, $\angle 1 = \angle 2$.

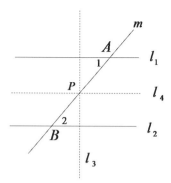

FIGURE 11. Illustration of Problem 3.2.

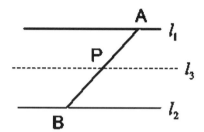

FIGURE 12. Illustration of the parallel lemma.

As a consequence of Problem 3.2, we can verify other angle properties involving parallel lines.

LEMMA 3.2 (The parallel lemma). *Given two lines ℓ_1 and ℓ_2 parallel to each other, fold ℓ_1 onto ℓ_2. Then, the folded line cuts any line segment connecting ℓ_1 and ℓ_2 into two equal halves. (See Figure 12.)*

SOLUTION. Let AB be the line segment with A on ℓ_1 and B on ℓ_2. **Apply A3**: $\ell_1 \rightarrow \ell_2$. Since ℓ_1 and ℓ_2 are parallel, there is only one way to fold ℓ_1 onto ℓ_2. The folded line ℓ_3 cuts AB at P. Following the proof of the perpendicular lemma, we obtain $AP = PB$.

Note that in the case of Problem 3.2, the point P is taken initially as the midpoint of AB, whereas in the case of the parallel lemma, the point P is taken initially as the intersection point of the folded line ℓ_3 and AB.

4. Triangles and Quadrilaterals

The following problem is known as the mid-segment theorem for a triangle.

PROBLEM 4.1. In a triangle $\triangle ABC$, the midpoint of AB is E and the midpoint of AC is F. Verify by paper folding that EF is parallel to BC and that the length EF is half of that of BC. (See Figure 13.)

SOLUTION. Let BC be ℓ_1. By Problem 2.4, we can fold a line ℓ_2 parallel to ℓ_1 that passes through A. **Apply A3**: $\ell_2 \rightarrow \ell_1$. By the parallel lemma, the folded line passes through E and F. Let the image of A be D on ℓ_1. **Apply A3**: $FC \rightarrow FD$. Then, $DF = AF = FC$. Similarly, **apply A3**: $EB \rightarrow ED$. The rest follows.

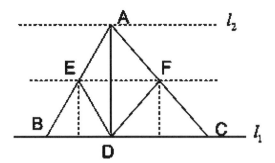

FIGURE 13. Illustration of Problem 4.1.

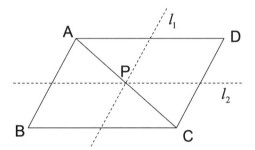

FIGURE 14. Illustration of Problem 4.2.

Note that Problem 4.1 holds true for an obtuse triangle $\triangle ABC$. Though the diagram may look different, the solution process is the same. In other words, the solution does not depend on the diagram. Furthermore, Problem 4.1 shows that the angle sum of a triangle is equal to two right-angles.

PROBLEM 4.2. Given a parallelogram, verify by paper folding that the diagonals bisect each other.

SOLUTION. Let $ABCD$ be a parallelogram where AB is parallel to CD and AD is parallel to BC. See Figure 14. For convenience, we use AB to denote the line passing through A and B as well as the line segment AB, and similarly for BC, CD, and AD. **Apply A3**: $AB \to CD$. Then, by the parallel lemma, the folded line ℓ_1 passes through the midpoint P of AC. Next, **apply A3**: $AD \to BC$. Again by the parallel lemma, the folded line ℓ_2 also passes through the midpoint P of AC. In fact, P is the intersection point of ℓ_1 and ℓ_2. By the same argument, the intersection point P is also the midpoint of BD. Hence, AC and BD bisect each other at P.

5. Circles

We define a circle by a center and a radius. Alternatively, a circle can be defined by three given points as shown in Problem 5.1 and Problem 5.2 below. In other words, three points determine a circle.

PROBLEM 5.1. Given a right-angled triangle $\triangle ABC$ where $\angle C$ is a right angle, fold the center of the circle passing through the vertices of the triangle.

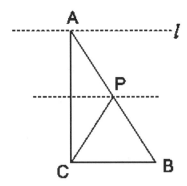

FIGURE 15. Illustration of Problem 5.1.

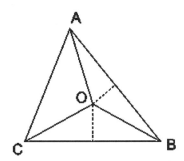

FIGURE 16. Illustration of Problem 5.2.

SOLUTION. By Problem 2.4, we can fold a line ℓ parallel to BC and passing through A. (See Figure 15.) **Apply A3**: $\ell \to BC$. By the parallel lemma and the mid-segment theorem (Problem 4.1), the midpoint of AB is the center of the circle, and the circle passes through points A, B, and C.

PROBLEM 5.2. Given a triangle $\triangle ABC$, fold the center of the circle passing through the vertices of the triangle.

SOLUTION. **Apply A2**: $A \to B$ and **apply A2**: $B \to C$. (See Figure 16.) The two folded lines, intersecting at O, are respectively the perpendicular bisectors of AB and BC. We obtain that $OA = OB = OC$. Hence, O is the center, OA is the radius, and the circle passes through A, B, and C.

Note that if we apply A3: $OA \to OC$ in the solution of Problem 5.2, by Problem 2.3 we obtain that the three perpendicular bisectors of the sides meet at a point. Similarly, the three angle bisectors of a triangle meet at a point. It shows that three lines also determine a circle. In this case, the circle is tangent to each of the three lines.

PROBLEM 5.3. Verify by paper folding that an inscribed angle of a circle is half of the corresponding central angle.

SOLUTION. Let the circle be determined by three points A, B, and C. Its center is O. Let $\angle BAC$ be an inscribed angle and $\angle BOC$ its corresponding central angle. **Apply A1**: $A \leftrightarrow O$. The folded line ℓ_1 cuts BC at D. By Problem 2.4, we can fold a line ℓ_2 parallel

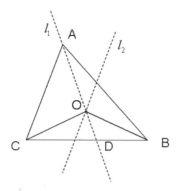

FIGURE 17. Illustration of Problem 5.3.

to AC and passing through O. (See Figure 17.) By the properties of parallel lines and isosceles triangles, $\angle CAO$ is half of $\angle COD$. Similarly, $\angle BAO$ is half of $\angle BOD$. Hence, the result is verified.

In Figure 17, O lies inside $\angle BAC$. The solution still applies if O lies outside $\angle BAC$.

More problems involving circles can be solved. For example, using A5 we can fold the intersection points, if any, of a circle and a line.

6. Conclusion

We have demonstrated how some problems in school geometry can be solved by means of paper folding. In fact, more problems can be solved in this way. The problems often are solved by applying one or two of the paper folding methods. The presentation given above is brief. In fact, the solution can be presented in more detail in the form of two columns: one column for stating the paper folding methods used, and another for the results obtained. The current approach is designed for teacher training. The basic tools are the perpendicular lemma and the parallel lemma. The process is mainly geometric. More materials for teacher training can be found in [Huang and Lee 12]. For more references, see *Project Origami*, for undergraduates [Hull 06], and *How to Fold It*, which also targets secondary students [O'Rourke 11].

References

[Huang and Lee 12] Yanping Huang and Peng-Yee Lee. *Paper Folding and Mathematics* (in Chinese). Beijing: Science Press, 2012.

[Hull 06] Thomas Hull. *Project Origami: Activities for Exploring Mathematics*. Wellesley, MA: A K Peters, 2006. MR2330113 (2008d:00001)

[Justin 89] Jacques Justin. "Resolution par le pliage de l'equation du troisieme degre et applications geometriques." In *Proceedings of the First International Meeting of Origami Science and Technology*, edited by H. Huzita, pp. 251–261. Ferrara: Comune di Ferrara and Centro Diffusione Origami, 1989.

[Lee 09] Peng-Yee Lee. "Why Do We Teach What We Teach in Schools?" *Maths Buzz* 10:2 (2009), 5–8. Available at http://math.nie.edu.sg/ame/.

[O'Rourke 11] Joseph O'Rourke. *How to Fold It*. Cambridge, UK: Cambridge University Press, 2011.

SOUTHWEST UNIVERSITY, CHONGQING, CHINA
E-mail address: pengyee.lee@nie.edu.sg

FORMERLY NATIONAL INSTITUTE OF EDUCATION, SINGAPORE
E-mail address: kouenpe@sina.cn

Using Origami to Enrich Mathematical Understanding of Self Similarity and Fractals

Ali Bahmani, Kiumars Sharif, and Andrew Hudson

1. Introduction

Throughout history, infinity has been a concept that people have a hard time getting their heads around—Zeno's Paradoxes being a particularly infamous example [Zeno 14]. And yet, an understanding of infinite sequences and the infinitesimal are central to skills we use every day. Driving a car safely, if you think about it, implies a basic understanding of infinite sequences—estimating the speed and size of distant objects means that, on some level, you have an intuitive grasp of the inverse-square law and the limit of the ratio of corresponding distance and time increments even if you don't know it mathematically. Or, to use another example, financial planning in the modern era is made much easier if one understands how interest compounds. And, of course, as origami designers, the authors have been particularly interested in recursive sequences in origami, from the flower towers of Chris Palmer [Palmer 14] to the substitution systems used in Andrew Hudson's work with nonsquare polygon grids [Hudson 11].

As teachers of mathematics and origami, the authors have noticed that our students often have difficulty understanding concepts related to fractals and infinite sequences. We wondered if we might be able to use our enthusiasm for origami, and our expertise in working with these concepts in an origami context, to design some curriculum that might help students by giving them a hands-on experience that might allow them to better understand some of these concepts.

In this paper, we present a unit of study that we developed for a group of schools in Iran, and we discuss our experiences implementing this curriculum with several classes of students. Because our classes took place in Iran, we also drew connections to Iran's cultural heritage, which is rich with geometric forms in art and architecture, such as the dome from the Sheikh Lotfollah mosque shown in Figure 1. We will discuss the background and structure of our unit, then present four activities we designed, and close with our observations about how the program was received.

2. Structure of the Curriculum

The National Organization for Development of Exceptional Talents (NODET) is a system of secondary schools in Iran whose purpose is to educate high-achieving students, and prepare them for university education, particularly in STEM fields. NODET was first established in 1967. After Iran's Revolution in 1979, the organization was closed for several years. After its re-establishment in 1987, NODET expanded and developed its schools in

Tehran, as well as other cities [Ghahremani 13]. Alumni of this program include Maryam Mirzakhani, who was educated in the Tehran Farzanegan School and was a 2014 recipient of the Fields Medal—the first woman, and the first Iranian, to receive this award [Carey 14, NODET 14].

One of the authors, Kiumars Sharif, participated in NODET schools as a student and is currently employed as a mathematics teacher by the NODET program. The impetus for this project came about because we observed that students in NODET programs often have a difficult time understanding fractals, infinite series, and related concepts, in part because it can be difficult to provide concrete examples. We took an informal survey of other NODET teachers and found that this seemed to be a common difficulty. However, as paper folders, we've encountered several examples—particularly the recursive "tower" structures pioneered by Shuzo Fujimoto [Fujimoto 10] and Chris Palmer—that have helped us understand these concepts at an intuitive level, so we decided to try and build a group of lessons that might develop this same hands-on understanding in a classroom setting.

It should be noted that while this project was executed in a setting where gifted students were our primary subjects, these activities are by no means limited to those circumstances—we tried to design these curricula in a fairly general manner, so they could be used in other schools as well. We chose to focus on middle school students for the bulk of our project, because we had more experience working with this age group. One of the experimental advantages is that they have not encountered concepts like limits, infinity, or convergent series in their mathematics classes, so we can see more clearly whether our approach is successful.

The NODET extra-curricular mathematics curriculum uses a variety of educational approaches, but we chose to go with a project-based learning model. After some introduction to a topic, students are assigned a few activities by the teacher, and then they choose a larger creative project to pursue on their own, with the guidance of their teacher. This type of structure helps students pick up the fundamentals of a subject, but still gives them room to come to terms with the concepts in their own way. At the end of the class, projects are shown at an exhibition day, alongside projects from all other science subjects taught at the school.

Our pedagogical approach is similar to the Schoolwide Enrichment Model developed by Joseph Renzulli and Sally Reis. In this framework, students are encouraged to identify a topic relevant to their own experience; then, they are prompted to explore the topic

FIGURE 1. Interior of Sheikh Lutfollah Mosque (left). Iranian enamel work (right). (Images courtesy of Ali Bahmani.)

Step	Stairs produced in this iteration	Number of layers of paper
1	1	1
2	2	$1 + 2 = 3$
3	4	$1 + 2 + 4 = 7$
n	$2^{(n-1)}$	$2^0 + 2^1 + 2^2 + \ldots + 2^{(n-1)} = 2^n - 1$

TABLE 1. Layers of paper in the pop-up stairs.

analytically, and the learning process culminates in a project geared toward an audience. For further discussion of this and other pedagogical approaches in NODET schools, see [Ghahremani 13].

During the lessons, we focus on how the folded pieces can be used as an opportunity for abstraction of the set of problems in each activity and to investigate the answers. As we progress through the folded piece, we engage the students by asking them to predict or calculate what will happen in the next step. We have them create and fill in tables of information about the attributes of the construction at each step, and eventually we help them extrapolate their data to the nth step and come up with an algebraic expression that fits the data they've observed.

We had one origami class in a male middle school with 7 students (seventh grade), and two classes in a female high school (ninth and tenth grades), each class with 12 students. There were 20 class sessions of 90 minutes each spread across the school year as an extra-curricular program. While the topics of this paper were the main focus of the class, other origami subjects were also taught. We also had a three-hour workshop on self-similarity and fractals at a male high school for students in grades 9–11. Classes and the workshop were taught by both Ali Bahmani and Kiumars Sharif. In this paper, we have extracted four activities from these classes, which are related to our discussions and ideas about teaching fractals.

3. Activities

3.1. Pop-Up Stairs. The goal of this activity is to engage the students in a model and a lesson that have a balance between theory and hands-on experience. This recursive method for making stairs can open the door for a discussion about recursive algorithms, a topic that we return to in the fourth activity.

As a first activity, a simple and beautiful self-similar structure is used to introduce some concepts in more concrete detail. First, we explain the process for making this pop-up: A piece of A4 paper is folded in half, and then a slit is cut perpendicular to the folded edge, which goes halfway down. The paper to the right side of this slit is reverse-folded inward. Then, this process is repeated on all of the right-hand edges, for several iterations. (See Figure 2.)

After each student has made a model, we pose a series of analytical questions. We start out with simple questions like, "After step 3 of this process, how many layers of paper do we have?" (see Table 1) or "Do you think you can repeat this process? Will we ever run out of paper? If yes, What if we had started with a larger sheet of paper and then generalized to the nth step?" The goal is to help students understand the sequence as a result of a recursive geometric process. Then, we ask the students to prove that the height of each stair during any step will be equal.

In the second half of this activity, students are asked to examine their staircase in profile and to calculate the area represented by its silhouette when viewed from the side.

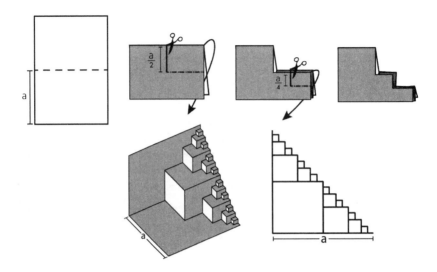

FIGURE 2. Instruction for making a pop-up stairs (top). Isometric and side views of the stairs (bottom). (Diagrams by Andrew Hudson.)

Step	Stairs produced in this iteration	Area of each stair in this iteration
1	1	$\left(\frac{a}{2}\right)^2$
2	2	$\left(\frac{a}{4}\right)^2$
3	4	$\left(\frac{a}{8}\right)^2$
n	$2^{(n-1)}$	$\left(\frac{a}{2^n}\right)^2$

Step	Sum of the areas	Cumulative sum of the areas
1	$\left(\frac{a}{2}\right)^2$	$\left(\frac{a}{2}\right)^2$
2	$2\left(\frac{a}{4}\right)^2$	$\left(\frac{a}{2}\right)^2 + 2\left(\frac{a}{4}\right)^2$
3	$4\left(\frac{a}{8}\right)^2$	$\left(\frac{a}{2}\right)^2 + 2\left(\frac{a}{4}\right)^2 + 4\left(\frac{a}{8}\right)^2$
n	$2^{(n-1)}\left(\frac{a}{2^n}\right)^2$	$\sum_{i=1}^{n} 2^{(i-1)}\left(\frac{a}{2^i}\right)^2$

TABLE 2. Area of the stairs in profile.

They do this as a sum of squares—first calculating the area of the square in each iteration, then counting (or calculating) the number of squares of that size, and then adding these together at each iteration. (See Table 2.)

3.2. Bar Spirals. The Bar Spiral activity is more theoretical in nature. The paper is mostly a visualization tool, and not so much an object to be analyzed. The mathematical modeling here is much more important than the folding concepts.

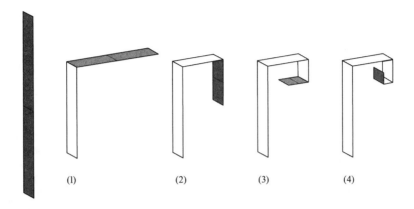

(1)   (2)   (3)   (4)

FIGURE 3. Process of making a Bar Spiral. The active segment in each step is shaded, and the next fold is indicated. (Diagram by Ali Bahmani.)

Step	Length of active segment	Sum of inactive segments
1	$\frac{1}{2}$	$\frac{1}{2}$
2	$\frac{1}{4}$	$\frac{1}{2} + \frac{1}{4}$
3	$\frac{1}{8}$	$\frac{1}{2} + \frac{1}{4} + \frac{1}{8}$
4	$\frac{1}{16}$	$\frac{1}{2} + \frac{1}{4} + \frac{1}{8} + \frac{1}{16}$
n	$\frac{1}{2^n}$	$\frac{1}{2} + \frac{1}{4} + \frac{1}{8} + \frac{1}{16} + \cdots + \frac{1}{2^n}$

TABLE 3. Dimensions of the Bar Spiral When the active segment is folded in half.

In this activity, students explore the effects of a simple recursion operation. Students encounter the concept of infinitesimal quantities, probably for the first time if this activity is done with seventh graders. This activity requires students to be more fluent with algebra than the first one, but it should still be accessible with some guidance from the teacher. Students should be introduced to a method of n-section such as Fujimoto's iterative approximation at the beginning of this lesson; we used the corresponding activity from Thomas Hull's *Project Origami* [Hull 12].

First, we hand students a narrow strip of paper and explain the folding process. We start off with the whole strip being defined as the *active area*: the part of the paper in a given step on which the folding algorithm will be performed. Each step takes the active area of the paper and folds the raw edge over to the end of the active area, unfolding to a 90° angle. This deactivates half of the area, leaving the other half to be used as the active area in the next iteration. The resulting pattern is a rough approximation of a logarithmic spiral. (See Figure 3.)

FIGURE 4. Fourth iteration of SierpinsQube fractal pyramid. (Image courtesy of Ali Bahmani.)

Similar to the first activity, we use the folded form as a platform for an analytical exploration of this structure. We again pose questions to the students and have them construct a table like Table 3.

Then, we ask the students, "Will the strip of paper ever intersect itself during this process?" The answer, of course, is no—in order for this to happen, the active segment has to be longer than the segment deactivated two iterations ago. We ask students to prove that this answer will hold for any given step of the process.

Now we repeat the process again, but with a different parameter: instead of folding $1/2$ of the active segment, we pick a different fraction, such as $1/3$, then go through the same process of constructing a table and asking analytical questions. Finally, we generalize the process to the fraction $1/m$.

For higher grades (ninth and tenth), we then ask, "Is there a ratio and iteration at which the paper becomes tangent to itself?" Students should be able to extrapolate from what they've learned to find the ratio. One can see that the ratio is related to the golden ratio, $1 + \varphi$.

3.3. Fractal Pyramid: SierpinsQube. This activity uses a simple modular cube, SierpinsQube, designed by Kiumars Sharif (Figure 4), which is constructed at different sizes to create the building blocks for a fractal. Instructions for this model can be seen in Figure 5 [Sharif and Bahmani 14]. Because the model is simple, it is suitable even for the more inexperienced folders, and it makes a good team activity. In addition to having more complex calculations, this activity extends the use of spatial visualization. Students should already know how to calculate the volume of a cube.

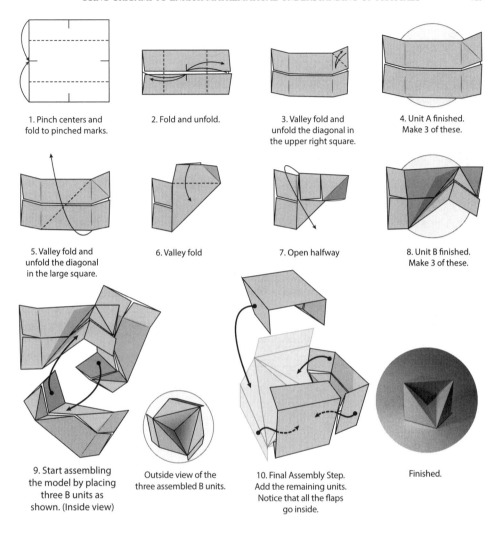

1. Pinch centers and fold to pinched marks.

2. Fold and unfold.

3. Valley fold and unfold the diagonal in the upper right square.

4. Unit A finished. Make 3 of these.

5. Valley fold and unfold the diagonal in the large square.

6. Valley fold

7. Open halfway

8. Unit B finished. Make 3 of these.

9. Start assembling the model by placing three B units as shown. (Inside view)

Outside view of the three assembled B units.

10. Final Assembly Step. Add the remaining units. Notice that all the flaps go inside.

Finished.

FIGURE 5. Instructions for making the SierpinsQube. (Inspired by David Mitchell's Columbus Cube [Mitchell 11]. Model by Kiumars Sharif; diagrams by Ali Bahmani.)

First, we teach them to make a simple cube, using a module designed by Paul Jackson [Jackson 08]. Then, we have them make a cube with papers that are half as long on each side as the ones they used for the original, and we ask them to compare the edge lengths, face areas, and volumes of the two different-sized cubes. After working with the Jackson cube, we teach students to make the Columbus Cube by David Mitchell [Mitchell 11, Zodl 11]. This modular has one corner sunk inward, so that the plane of reflection bisects three edges of the original cube. We construct another cube with half the edge length and ask similar questions about the ratio of various measurements of the cubes. Students should be led to the realization that, for example, the volume will always be 1:8, regardless of what shape is being scaled down.

FIGURE 6. Students exploring Chris K. Palmer's Flower Tower (half-opened; left) and Shuzo Fujimoto's Hydrangea (right). (Models folded by Ali Bahmani. Images courtesy of Ali Bahmani.)

After these concepts are laid out, we move on to making the SierpinsQube. Note that for classes with some extra time, we may take a moment to compare three models and discuss how origami design often starts out as a process of making variations on an existing model. On this, we have the students work together, folding modulars at three different sizes, to build the Sierpinski fractal. After building the third iteration of the fractal, we ask students to calculate how many cubes would be in the fourth iteration by counting how many are added in each existing iteration. From there, we generalize how many cubes will be added in any given iteration, as in Table 3. We follow this up with a similar exploration of the volume of the cubes.

3.4. Showing Origami Examples. We end the instructional part of the unit by showing examples of fractal sequences in origami and other geometric art. This inspires the students while they choose their projects—but also provides an opportunity to reinforce students' ability to visually recognize partial infinite sequences, to demonstrate some different forms that sequences can take, and to show how the concepts of iteration and self-similarity apply to more complex fractals. For our students in Iran, this is also an opportunity to connect these concepts to the rich geometric heritage of the culture around them. Along with photos of origami pieces by Shuzo Fujimoto, Chris K. Palmer, and the authors (Figure 6), we show the students photos of fractal patterns in Islamic art and architecture around Iran (Figure 1). It's possible that our students have seen some of these architectural features before, but likely they were not looking for the geometric structure of the ornamentation, so they will see it from a fresh perspective.

If time allows, and the teacher is sufficiently confident in his/her own folding ability, it would be possible to lead a group of interested students in folding a single-sheet recursive model, or to demonstrate the folding process for students. This adds to the students' conception of these iterative algorithms as potentially very complex processes, and we have found these models in particular to be a memorable and joyful folding experience. During the course of this study, we did not have the time to incorporate this idea; but, we have successfully taught such models to students of this age before.

4. Exhibition Day Projects

After the activities described above, students are given time to choose and pursue a project, with some guidance from their teacher. In the NODET schools, the purpose of this sort of extracurricular class is to give students a chance to consider a unique problem and

FIGURE 7. Exhibition day: A student showing a single-sheet recursive model to the audience (left), and a big recursive modular cube that some students made from business cards. (Images courtesy of Ali Bahmani.)

explore it on their own; this last part is, by design, less structured. Students brainstorm some problems they might like to study, and the teacher guides them to refine one of these ideas into a project, which might realistically be completed by the student.

One of the classes we worked with took a field trip to an area with several old buildings in the Iranian-Islamic architectural style. Students were asked to explore the buildings, asking themselves, "What kinds of symmetry can I find? What sorts of polygons are there on these buildings? Are there any fractals or other patterns? If there are, why do you think these patterns are fractals?" Students were asked to keep these examples in mind for their exhibition day projects.

Many of the projects involved studying or reproducing one-sheet recursive models, such as Chris Palmer's Flower Tower [Shafer and Palmer 12] or some spiral models by Tomoko Fuse [Fuse 12]. Another project looked at what polygons could be found in the cross sections of various solids—in particular, Francesco Mancini's Two Piece Pyramid Puzzle [Mancini 14] drew a lot of attention from other students and parents during exhibition day. (See other examples in Figure 7.)

5. Conclusion

In the seventh-grade classes, Kiumars Sharif was also teaching the primary mathematics course for these students (in addition to the extracurricular mathematics class where we used our lessons). Several of the concepts used in these lessons tied in nicely with the primary mathematics class. In the geometry curriculum, they have a section that relates to the surface area and volume of solids. Also, in algebra, the students work with rational numbers, variables, and exponents.

One origami class was of particular interest: Of the seven students who took part, four had done poorly during their first semester of geometry. But, in the second semester, after the origami class had finished, these four students not only did much better in their geometry class, but also did considerably better in their algebra class compared to the first semester. We see this as further anecdotal evidence of the effect that Christine Edison noted in her presentation at 5OSME: that origami is useful in helping relatively lower-achieving students engage more effectively with the curriculum [Edison 11]. It would be premature to state this as an experimental conclusion at this point, but this use of origami would be an interesting avenue for further research.

When teachers in most mathematics classes we've encountered start to teach subjects like recursive functions, limits, and sequences and series with a discussion on their convergence or divergence, after a quick introduction on the subject, they jump on the techniques used to solve the common problems and examples—without providing a solid background and explanation on why the subject matters. Our approach, however, helps students to view the subject as a challenge and to investigate the solutions with the help of their teacher and other resources. In this case, mathematics serves as a genuine problem-solving tool, not merely something that we require them to memorize for their exams.

In our program, we tried to design sets of activities that help students to form an understanding of sequences and series, which serve as a good opening to discussing fractal-related concepts. We hope that these activities will help teachers pave the way for a more thorough exploration of fractals, in their own class or in a subsequent one.

The program was well-received by students, and this material could be integrated into the main mathematics curriculum. Moving forward, we would like to try our approach with other mathematics topics and grade levels, and we hope that other teachers will find our lessons useful enough to implement them in their own programs.

References

[Carey 14] Bjorn Carey. "Stanford's Maryam Mirzakhani Wins Fields Medal." *Stanford News*, http://news. stanford.edu/news/2014/august/fields-medal-mirzakhani-081214.html, August 12, 2014.

[Edison 11] Christine Edison. "Narratives of Success: Teaching Origami in Low-Income Urban Communities." In *Origami⁵: Fifth International Meeting of Origami Science, Mathematics, and Education*, edited by Patsy Wang-Iverson, Robert J. Lang, and Mark Yim, pp. 165–172. Boca Raton, FL: A K Peters/CRC Press, 2011. MR2866909 (2012h:00044)

[Fujimoto 10] Shuzo Fujimoto. *Origami Ajisaiori: Fujimoto Shuzo Warudo*. Tokyo: Seibundo Shinkosha, 2010.

[Fuse 12] Tomoko Fuse. *Spiral: Origami | Art | Design*. Freising, Germany: Viereck Verlag, 2012.

[Ghahremani 13] Mehdi Ghahremani. "Considering Science Teachers' Conceptions of Critical Thinking Pedagogy in Several of Iran's Special Gifted Schools: A Multi-Phased Study." Master's thesis, University of British Columbia, Okanagan, 2013. (Available at https://circle.ubc.ca/bitstream/handle/2429/45168/ubc_ 2013_fall_ghahremani_mehdi.pdf?sequence=1.)

[Hudson 11] Andrew Hudson. "Polygon Symmetry Systems." In *Origami⁵: Fifth International Meeting of Origami Science, Mathematics, and Education*, edited by Patsy Wang-Iverson, Robert J. Lang, and Mark Yim, pp. 81–88. Boca Raton, FL: A K Peters/CRC Press, 2011. MR2866909 (2012h:00044)

[Hull 12] Thomas Hull. *Project Origami: Activities for Exploring Mathematics*, Second Edition. Boca Raton, FL: A K Peters/CRC Press, 2012, MR2330113 (2008d:00001)

[Jackson 08] Paul Jackson. "How to Make the Jackson Cube." YouTube video, https://www.youtube.com/watch? v=2m_m2ZKEBLI, uploaded April 22, 2008.

[Mancini 14] Francesco Mancini. "Diagrams: Pyramid Puzzle." *The Fold* 21 (2014), article no. 10. (Available at https://origamiusa.org/thefold/article/diagrams-pyramid-puzzle.)

[Mitchell 11] David Mitchell. *Building with Butterflies*, Second Edition. New Delhi: Water Trade Publications, 2011.

[NODET 14] "National Organization for Development of Exceptional Talents." *Wikipedia*, http://en.wikipedia. org/wiki/National_Organization_for_Development_of_Exceptional_Talents, accessed July 2014.

[Palmer 14] Chris K. Palmer. *Shadowfolds*. https://www.shadowfold.com, accessed July 2014.

[Shafer and Palmer 12] Jeremy Shafer. "Flower Tower by Chris K. Palmer (Tutorial)." YouTube video, https:// www.youtube.com/watch?v=0FVH157LdME, uploaded September 15, 2012.

[Sharif and Bahmani 14] Kiumars Sharif (with diagrams by Ali Bahmani). "SierpinsQube." In *26th International Origami Convention Book*, pp. 109–110. Berlin: Origami Deutschland, 2014.

[Zeno 14] Zeno of Elea. *Achilles and the Tortoise Paradox and Dichotomy Paradox.* http://en.wikipedia.org/wiki/ Zeno's_paradoxes, accessed July 2014.

[Zodl 11] Zodl, Evan. "Origami Columbus Tower by David Mitchell (Folding Instructions)." YouTube video, https://www.youtube.com/watch?v=6u-1a1UFj_k, uploaded June 21, 2011.

UNIVERSITY OF TEHRAN, IRAN
E-mail address: alibmn@gmail.com

UNIVERSITY OF TEHRAN, IRAN
E-mail address: qmars.sharif@gmail.com

SOUTHERN ILLINOIS UNIVERSITY, CARBONDALE, IL
E-mail address: andrew.hudson13@gmail.com

Using the Fujimoto Approximation Technique to Teach Chaos Theory to High School Students

Leon Poladian

1. Introduction

The now-standard origami method to fold a strip of paper into equal $n$ths was developed by Shuzo Fujimoto and Masami Nishiwaki [Fujimoto and Nishiwaki 82] and also independently by James Brunton [Brunton 73]. The process can find better and better approximations to the positions of the desired creases by an iterated sequence of folds. Previous work on the so-called *Fujimoto approximation technique* has connected it to binary representations of fractions [Lang 88, Tanton 01, Hull 06] and the orders of elements in modulo arithmetic [Veenstra 09]. In particular, the idea of reading the binary representation of a fraction backward to obtain the necessary sequences of creases to use in the Fujimoto method is explored in detail in [Tanton 01] and [Hull 06].

Iterated sequences also feature prominently in chaos theory. Arithmetic and geometric progressions are generated by *linear* recurrence relations and have simple and highly predictable behaviors. On the other hand, sequences generated by *nonlinear* recurrence relations can exhibit the types of complicated behavior associated with chaos [Devaney 89]. The logistic map, which is a quadratic recurrence, was popularized in the late 1970s as an archetypical example of chaos [May 76].

Folding paper, manipulating simple fractions, and exploring decimal and binary representations are activities accessible to young teenage students. The mathematical relationship between the Fujimoto approximation and chaos theory can be the basis of a deep enrichment activity for slightly older high school mathematics students. The teaching context used as the basis of this paper is an intensive two- to three-hours-per-day, one-week-long activity with gifted and talented senior high school students; but, the same activities might also be adapted for other groups of students over a longer, less-intensive time frame.

Such activities if properly scaffolded can lead students toward many of the deepest results in both number theory and chaos theory. These two topics (and other areas of maths such as geometry and graph theory) provide a wide and varied landscape of accessible examples of varied complexity to explore and allow for students to form, propose, and discuss conjectures. The useful article [Mason 06] presents and analyzes case studies of mathematical enrichment activities that successfully combine modeling, coaching, scaffolding, articulation, reflection, and exploration. These combinations are specifically chosen to help students emulate the way experts approach mathematics and are associated with an educational theory called *cognitive apprenticeship* [Collins et al. 87]. This is a theory of the educational process where a master of some skill teaches that skill to an

©2015 American Mathematical Society

apprentice by one-on-one methods similar to those used traditionally in manual arts and crafts. This teaching approach has been successfully used for several decades at the National Mathematics Summer School in Australia and similar programs in other countries [Poladian and Rylands 13].

Section 3 gives an overview of those aspects of the Fujimoto approximation technique that are relevant to this presentation of how I teach chaos. Likewise, Section 4 gives a very brief overview of the important aspects of chaos theory in the context of sequences generated by iterating simple nonlinear functions, and goes on to discuss the inverse relationship between the Fujimoto and chaotic sequences. Section 5 considers the pedagogical issues and presents some more details on how chaos and the Fujimoto technique are presented to my students and how the students responded. Finally, the conclusion contains some thoughts about variations to the content and what I might try in the future.

2. The Fujimoto Approximation Technique

Imagine a piece of paper (see Figure 1) in which we systematically make vertical creases. At each step we make a new crease by folding (and then immediately unfolding) either the left or the right edge of the paper to the previous crease. If we denote the left edge of the paper with the number 0 and the right edge with the number 1, then if x is the location of the current crease, the next crease is given by one of the two functions,

$$(2.1) \qquad L(x) = \frac{1}{2}x, \qquad R(x) = \frac{1}{2}(x + 1),$$

depending on from which side the paper is folded. Let's assume the initial crease is the left edge of the paper at $x = 0$. Consider, for example, the sequence of four folds shown in Figure 1.

The position of each successive crease corresponds to the value of the following successively nested functions:

$$(2.2a) \qquad R(0) \quad = \quad \frac{1}{2} = 0.1_2,$$

$$(2.2b) \qquad L(R(0)) \quad = \quad \frac{1}{4} = 0.01_2,$$

$$(2.2c) \qquad R(L(R(0))) \quad = \quad \frac{5}{8} = 0.101_2,$$

$$(2.2d) \qquad R(R(L(R(0)))) \quad = \quad \frac{13}{16} = 0.1101_2,$$

where the binary (or base 2) representation of each fraction is also given. Notice that the sequence of L's and R's occurring in the nested functions corresponds precisely to the sequence of 0's and 1's to the right of the dot in the binary representations.

Thus, any *finite* sequence of folds produces creases at positions that are fractions with denominators that are powers of 2; a crease at any such fraction can be obtained with only a finite sequence of folds. The pattern of folds for each fraction can be obtained directly from the binary representation.

Any other real number in the interval $(0, 1)$ can be obtained approximately, and the accuracy of the approximation increases by a factor of 2 with each additional fold. In particular, rational numbers correspond to recurring sequences of folds. For example,

$$\frac{3}{7} = 0.\overline{011}_2$$

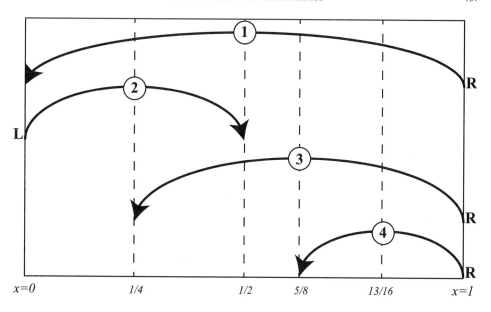

FIGURE 1. Sequence of four folds from the right, left, right, and right edges, which produce, in order, creases at positions $\frac{1}{2}$, $\frac{1}{4}$, $\frac{5}{8}$, and finally $\frac{13}{16}$.

and can be approximated by folds corresponding to the following nested functions:

$$(2.3a) \qquad LRR(0) \; = \; \frac{3}{8} = 0.011_2,$$

$$(2.3b) \qquad (LRR)^2(0) \; = \; \frac{27}{64} = 0.011011_2,$$

$$(2.3c) \qquad (LRR)^3(0) \; = \; \frac{219}{512} = 0.011011011_2,$$

and so on. Some parentheses in the nested functions on the left have been suppressed for notational convenience. The limiting value $\frac{3}{7}$ of this sequence of approximations can be obtained as the solution of the equation

$$(2.4) \qquad LRR(x) = x.$$

The sequence is convergent because the magnitudes of the gradients or slopes of the functions being applied are less than unity: in fact, $L'(x) = R'(x) = \frac{1}{2}$, which means that the error in the approximation decreases by precisely $\frac{1}{2}$ each time a function is applied (in other words, the error in the location of each creases decreases by a half with each new fold).

This is indeed the original practical application of the Fujimoto approximation to folding paper into $n$ths. If $x_{\text{init}} \approx \frac{3}{7}$, say, with a certain error ε, then a fold from the right produces a crease at $R(x_{\text{init}})$, which is, in turn, an approximation to $R(\frac{3}{7}) = \frac{5}{7}$ but the error is now only $\frac{1}{2}\varepsilon$. The next fold produces an approximation to $RR(\frac{3}{7}) = R(\frac{5}{7}) = \frac{6}{7}$ with an error of only $\frac{1}{4}\varepsilon$, and the third fold gives an approximation to $LRR(\frac{3}{7}) = LR(\frac{5}{7}) = L(\frac{6}{7}) = \frac{3}{7}$, which now has an error of only $\frac{1}{8}\varepsilon$. Once the desired accuracy at $\frac{3}{7}$ has been achieved, all the remaining creases at $\frac{p}{7}$ can be obtained with the same or greater accuracy.

3. Chaotic Sequences

3.1. The shift map. Conventional approaches to chaotic sequences start with the shift map

(3.1)
$$S(x) = \begin{cases} 2x, & x < \frac{1}{2}; \\ 2x - 1, & x \geq \frac{1}{2}. \end{cases}$$

The shift map can also be written in the compact notation $S(x) = \{2x\}$ where the $\{\}$ brackets indicate the *fractional part*. The reason for the name will become apparent when numbers are written in binary form (see next section).

Given any initial value in the interval $[0, 1]$, the shift map can be iteratively used to generate a sequence of numbers that remain in this interval. For example, if we start with $\frac{13}{16}$ and iterate, we obtain the sequence

(3.2)
$$\frac{13}{16}, \frac{5}{8}, \frac{1}{4}, \frac{1}{2}, 0, 0, 0, \ldots;$$

on the other hand, if we start with $\frac{3}{7}$ and iterate, we obtain

(3.3)
$$\frac{3}{7}, \frac{6}{7}, \frac{5}{7}, \frac{3}{7}, \frac{6}{7}, \frac{5}{7}, \frac{3}{7}, \frac{6}{7}, \frac{5}{7}, \ldots.$$

Rational numbers with a denominator that is a power of 2 have a finite sequence of positive numbers followed by a trail of zeros, and other rational numbers lead to cyclic sequences; if we were to start with an irrational number, the sequence would neither reach zero nor repeat.

Sequences obtained by iterating with $x_{n+1} = S(x_n)$ exhibit the three defining properties of chaotic sequences [Devaney 89]:

- existence of periodic cycles of all orders,
- sensitivity to initial conditions,
- transitivity.

The first property is demonstrated by the observation that sequences generated by irreducible fractions with a denominator of the form $2^n - 1$ create cycles of length n.

The second property of sensitivity to initial conditions follows because $S'(x) = 2$ almost everywhere (except at the discontinuity at $x = 0$): the slope of $S(x)$ determines the rate at which the spacing between any two very closely spaced initial values will increase with each iteration.

Transitivity means that given any two non-empty subintervals of $[0, 1]$ (no matter how small), there exists a point in one of the subintervals that after iterating a certain number of times will land within the other subinterval.

In addition, the binary representations of irreducible fractions with a denominator of the form $2^n - 1$ are periodic with a cycle of length n. This last property (and indeed all three properties) can more easily be deduced from the binary representation of the numbers and how the shift map $S(x)$ acts on that representation.

3.2. Symbolic representations and binary numbers. Given a sequence generated by $S(x)$, a symbolic representation can be obtained by replacing each value x_n in the sequence with the symbol 0 if $x_n < \frac{1}{2}$ and the symbol 1 if $x_n \geq \frac{1}{2}$ and then simply concatenating the symbols into a string. Thus, the sequence beginning with $\frac{13}{16}$ becomes

(3.4)
$$1, 1, 0, 1, 0, 0, 0, 0, 0, 0, 0, 0, \ldots \equiv 110 1\overline{0}$$

and the sequence beginning with $\frac{3}{7}$ becomes

(3.5) $$0, 1, 1, 0, 1, 1, 0, 1, 1, \ldots \equiv \overline{011}.$$

The overline indicates that the corresponding symbols are then repeated indefinitely.

Note that this symbolic representation corresponds precisely [Lang 88, Devaney 89, Tanton 01, Hull 06] to the binary representation of each fraction (the part to the right of the point). Thus,

(3.6) $$\frac{13}{16} = 0.1101\overline{0}_2 \equiv 0.1101_2$$

and

(3.7) $$\frac{3}{7} = 0.\overline{011}_2.$$

Note the usual convention that a terminating binary number is equivalent to that number followed by an infinite sequence of zeros. Applying $S(x)$ to a value x is equivalent to shifting all the binary digits in the representation of x one place to the left and replacing the bit to the left of the dot by 0. For this reason, $S(x)$ is often called the shift map.

The transitivity property mentioned in the previous section is easily demonstrated using the binary representation. Take any two real numbers in the interval $[0, 1]$ and their corresponding binary approximations, for example,

(3.8) $$\frac{1}{\sqrt{2}} \approx 0.10110101000001001111_2,$$

(3.9) $$\frac{\pi}{4} \approx 0.11001001000011111101_2.$$

Suppose we now take an initial value that corresponds to a concatenation of the binary sequences above:

(3.10) $$x_0 = 0.1011010100000100111111001001000011111101_2.$$

The sequence generated by applying $S(x)$ iteratively to x_0 will start with a value that is an extremely accurate approximation to $\frac{1}{\sqrt{2}}$ (the error is less than 2^{-20}), and after 20 applications the value reached will now be an extremely accurate approximation to $\frac{\pi}{4}$. Thus, one can easily find sequences that start near any point and approach near to any other point. As an aside, this is the underlying mathematical idea behind the way chaos is applied to make large changes in the flight paths of satellites using very little fuel [Ott 02, Chapter 10 and Figure 10.7].

3.3. Inverse relationships. Now $S(L(x)) = S(R(x)) = x$ for $x \in [0, 1)$, and furthermore $L(S(x)) = x$ for $x \in [0, \frac{1}{2})$ and $R(S(x)) = x$ for $x \in [\frac{1}{2}, 1)$. Thus, there exists an inverse relationship between the pair of functions l and R and the non-injective function $S(x)$.

Therefore, given any finite length sequence of values in $[0, 1)$ that satisfies $x_{n+1} = S(x_n)$ and an accompanying sequence of symbols or bits X_n such that $X_n = 0$ if $x_n < \frac{1}{2}$ and $X_n = 1$ if $x_n \geq \frac{1}{2}$, then one can use the symbolic sequence and the final value in the numerical sequence to generate the entire sequence but in revese order by applying $x_n = L(x_{n+1})$ if $X_n = 0$ and $x_n = R(x_{n+1})$ if $X_n = 1$.

Thus, for each initial value the sequence of bits 0 or 1 obtained using the shift map and the symbolic rules above corresponds to the sequence of corresponding creases L or R required by the Fujimoto approximation—but that the order in which the creases should be applied is read from *right-to-left*. Hence, the shift map and the Fujimoto process are working with corresponding sequences but in *opposite* directions.

In chaos theory a symbolic sequence such as 01110111 is obtained *after* computing a sequence using the shift map and is interpreted from *left-to-right*; by contrast, in the Fujimoto approach one is given the sequence of lefts and rights *before* commencing the construction and the folds or functions are applied by interpreting the corresponding sequence from *right-to-left*. This inverse relationship holds on many levels.

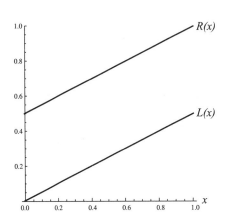 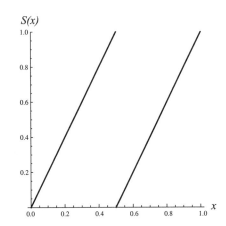

FIGURE 2. The graph on the left shows the two functions $L(x)$ and $R(x)$ used in the Fujimoto technique; the graph on the right shows the function $S(x)$ used in chaos theory.

The Fujimoto technique is a process that *improves* the accuracy of the approximation with each new crease; if we interpret an improvement in accuracy as the revelation of additional bits in a binary expansion of some fraction, then this is a process where information increases. In contrast, generating a sequence with the shift map is a process that moves the bits in the binary representation of the initial value x_0 to the left, and if only an approximation of x_0 is known, then each iteration decreases the amount of information retained about this initial approximation. That these two processes are *inverses* of each other is also revealed by the factors of $\frac{1}{2}$ that appear in $L(x)$ and $R(x)$ and the corresponding factors of 2 that appear in $S(x)$. The inverse relation is obviously manifested when graphs of these functions are compared, as in Figure 2.

Thus, chaos and the Fujimoto technique share those properties that are not associated with a forward or backward direction: the transitivity property and the property that cycles of all possible lengths occur. The dependence of initial states is different: chaos has exponential *sensitivity* to initial conditions (small variations in the initial value increase exponentially) and Fujimoto approximation has the exponential *insensitivity* to initial conditions (small errors in guessing the location of the initial crease decrease exponentially).

4. Pedagogical Issues

I have taught chaos theory to gifted and talented senior high school mathematics students for almost two decades using a particular style of discovery learning. Guided reinvention [Freudenthal 73, Treffers 87, Gravemeijer 94] is the principle that students should experience learning mathematics as a process similar to the process by which mathematics was invented. Hans Freudenthal stated that students should not be considered as passive recipients of ready-made mathematics, but rather that education should guide the students toward using opportunities to reinvent mathematics by doing it themselves [Freudenthal 73].

Guidance is provided by starting with familiar contexts; here, the prior knowledge of decimal representations and whether they terminate, repeat, or neither is used as scaffolding. Students are encouraged to think more deeply about why some fractions result in a terminating decimal expansion and others lead to repeating sequences. The decimal version of the shift map $D(x) = \{10x\}$ is introduced *before* the binary version $S(x) = \{2x\}$. Typical open-ended motivational questions are the following:

- How can we classify numbers based on the long-term behavior of their decimal representation? For example, what might the words *terminating*, *recurring*, and *non-recurring* mean? Which numbers correspond to which types of behavior?
- Can a number have two different decimal representations? If so, why and determine which numbers have non-unique representations? If not, why not?

Some of these questions lead to interesting debates that are presented in tutorials [Poladian and Rylands 13].

In January 2014, I also introduced the Fujimoto approximation as a tactile manifestation of an iterated process. Although the underlying mathematics is virtually identical that of to the shift map, the emotional reaction to folding paper was extremely positive and some students not enthused with the algebraic approach engaged with the open-ended exploratory nature of the paper folding. The motivational questions on the Fujimoto technique begin with straightforward simple cases and gradually become more abstract [Mason 06], as shown below:

- What fraction is represented by the finite sequence *LRR*?
- What sequence represents the fraction $\frac{7}{16}$?
- What fraction is represented by the recurring sequence $\overline{LRR}$?
- What fraction is represented by the empty sequence?
- Can every number between 0 and 1 be obtained by a Fujimoto sequence of folds? If so, explain how to do it. If not, explain which numbers cannot be represented.
- Is there a connection between Fujimoto sequences and the other representations you have already seen? Give a detailed explanation.

Within hours, several students discovered the link between binary expansions and folding paper into $n$ths without any prompting beyond questions like those above.

Another valuable reason to show students the Fujimoto method is that origami is a manifestly *continuous* process (there is no cutting or tearing involved); in contrast, $S(x)$ is a *discontinuous* function and some students erroneously conclude that the unexpected properties of chaotic sequences are caused by discontinuity! To demonstrate that discontinuity is not relevant, in traditional expositions of chaos two other functions are introduced (see left-hand graphs in Figure 3): a continuous piecewise-linear function called the *tent map*,

$$(4.1) \qquad T(x) = \begin{cases} 2x, & x < \frac{1}{2}, \\ 2 - 2x, & x \geq \frac{1}{2}, \end{cases}$$

and a smooth quadratic function called the *logistic map*,

$$(4.2) \qquad Q(x) = 4x(1 - x).$$

The tent map $T(x)$ is also associated with a *continuous* and tactile process: the kneading of dough as done by bakers. The operation involves repeatedly folding a piece of dough in half and then stretching it out to its original size. Using real dough is messy, and unless students are very good with their hands, it is hard to accurately study the action of $T(x)$ using modeling clay such as plasticine; conversely, almost anyone can fold paper accurately.

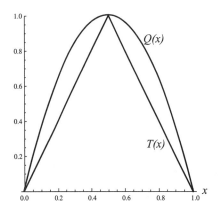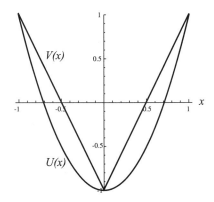

FIGURE 3. Piecewise-linear and quadratic functions that can be used to generate chaotic seeuqnces. The graphs on the left show the traditional functions $T(x)$ and $Q(x)$ used to explain chaos; the graphs on the right show $V(x)$ and $U(x)$, which I use when teaching chaos.

Sequences generated by any of the functions mentioned so far exhibit chaos. Unfortunately, compared to the shift map, the tent map $T(x)$ is a slightly more tedious function to do mental arithmetic with and this small inconvenience is sufficient to disengage even some gifted and talented students. Even worse, a calculator, spreadsheet, or graph paper is usually required to study sequences generated by the quadratic logistic map $Q(x)$; again, this leads either to disengagement or distraction by the device. If students are not free to think while calculating, they are more likely to adopt surface approaches to learning. Some teenagers have become used to immediate gratification and rapid feedback processes, and so even mathematically gifted students often suffer from lack of perseverance or task commitment [Renzulli and Reis 97, pp. 5–14].

For this reason, in my course I have invented and introduced two other functions:

$$(4.3) \qquad\qquad\qquad V(x) = 2|x| - 1$$

and

$$(4.4) \qquad\qquad\qquad U(x) = 2x^2 - 1$$

(see right-hand graphs in Figure 3). Mental arithmetic with $V(x)$ is extremely fast and all the students are able to generate sequences of sufficient complexity to discover interesting cycles without losing enthusiasm. Although a calculator is still needed to explore the behavior of $U(x)$, its structure makes the keystrokes required less error prone and much faster.

Thus, although all these different functions and processes demonstrate the same facts about chaotic sequences, each has its merits and faults, and careful consideration is warranted in designing learning tasks for different types of students.

5. Conclusion

Mathematics students vary enormously in what motivates them and under what situations they will engage with deep learning. Within a group of gifted and talented students, this variation might be even more extreme; students have begun to develop preferred modes of approach: algebraic, verbal, symbolic, graphical, numerical, explorative, deductive, etc. Using origami adds a tactile and extra dimension to the other modes and makes chaos even more fun!

Future activities might look at the Fujimoto technique and provide some specific exercises to explore the transitivity property in more detail. For example, given an existing crease at an unknown location, how can one use L and R folds to discover simple rational approximations (and for the better students, one can ask how the Fujimoto result compares to the approximation obtained from the simple bisection method or to the more powerful number-theoretic approximation using continued fractions). Having explored this, another problem might be as follows: given two creases, how can one use a sequence of fold, starting from one of them, to get an efficient approximation to the other (better than that obtained by starting from scratch)?

Several months after the class had concluded, one student posted on a Facebook group that she had chosen to study Fujimoto approximation as a school project and had independently determined (i.e., without looking for the theory online) the Fujimoto sequences for all odd denominator fractions less than 20 by systematic exploration (rather than using any theoretical construct such as binary representations). Comments to that post, from other students, identified binary representations as relevant to the project. The decisions to engage with a topic again, months after the original classes, and to also discuss this topic with excitement on social media suggest that at least for some students the Fujimoto technique has added a new layer to their experience of chaos.

References

[Brunton 73] James Brunton. "Mathematical Exercises in Paper Folding: I." *Mathematics in School* 2:4 (1973), 25–26.

[Collins et al. 87] Allan Collins, John S. Brown and Susan E. Newman. "Cognitive Apprenticeship: Teaching the Craft of Reading, Writing and Mathematics." Technical Report No. 403, Bolt, Beranek and Newman, Inc., Cambridge, MA, 1987.

[Devaney 89] Robert L. Devaney. *An Introduction to Chaotic Dynamical Systems*. Second Edition. Redwood City, CA: Addison-Wesley, 1989. MR1046376 (91a:58114)

[Freudenthal 73] Hans Freudenthal.. *Mathematics as an Educational Task*. Dordrecht: Reidel, 1973. MR0462822 (57:2795)

[Fujimoto and Nishiwaki 82] Shuzo Fujimoto and Masami Nishiwaki. *Seizo suru origami asobi no shoutai (Invitation to Playing Creatively with Origami, in Japanese)*. Tokyo: Asahi Culture Center, 1982.

[Gravemeijer 94] Koeno Gravemeijer. *Developing Realistic Mathematics Education*. Utrecht: CD Beta Press, 1994.

[Hull 06] Thomas Hull. *Project Origami: Activities for Exploring Mathematics*. Wellesley, MA: A K Peters, 2006. MR2330113 (2008d:00001)

[Lang 88] Robert J. Lang. "Four Problems III." *British Origami* 132 (1988), 7–11.

[Mason 06] John Mason. "What Makes an Example Exemplary: Pedagogical and Didactical Issues in Appreciating Multiplicative Structures." In *Number Theory in Education*, edited by Rina Zazkis and Stephen R. Campbell, pp. 41–68. London: Lawrence Erlbaum Associates, 2006.

[May 76] Robert M. May. "Simple Mathematical Models with Very Complicated Dynamics." *Nature* 261:5560 (1976), 459–467.

[Ott 02] Edward Ott. *Chaos in Dynamical Systems*, Second Edition. Cambridge, MA: Cambridge University Press, 2002. MR1924000 (2004a:37001)

[Poladian and Rylands 13] Leon Poladian and Leanne R. Rylands. "Thinking Deeply of Simple Things: 45 Years of the National Mathematics Summer School." In *Procedings of the 24th Biennial Conference of the Australian Association of Mathematics Teachers, Mathematics: Launching Futures*, edited by Sandra Herbert, Julie Tillyer, and Toby Spencer, pp. 142–148. Adelaide: AAMT Inc., 2013.

[Renzulli and Reis 97] Joseph S. Renzulli and Sally M. Reis. *The Schoolwide Enrichment Model*, Second Edition. Mansfield: Creative Learning Press, 1997. MR1628193 (99e:11068)

[Tanton 01] James Tanton. "A Dozen Questions about the Powers of Two." *Math Horizons* 8 (2001), 5–10.

[Treffers 87] Adrian Treffers. *Three Dimensions: A Model of Goal and Theory Description in Mathematics Instruction—The Wiskobas Project*. Dordrecht: Reidel, 1987.

[Veenstra 09] Tamara B. Veenstra. "A Number Theory Application to the Fujimoto Approximation Technique." In *Origami⁴: Fourth International Meeting of Origami Science, Mathematics, and Education*, edited by Robert J. Lang, pp. 405–415. Wellesley, MA: A K Peters, 2009. MR2590566

SCHOOL OF MATHEMATICS AND STATISTICS, THE UNIVERSITY OF SYDNEY, AUSTRALIA
E-mail address: leon.poladian@sydney.edu.au

Index